THE GERMAN NAVAL MUTINIES

OF WORLD WAR I

The German Naval
Mutinies of World War I

DANIEL HORN

RUTGERS UNIVERSITY PRESS

NEW BRUNSWICK, NEW JERSEY

For Shari

Contents

Preface

Twice during the course of the First World War, in August 1917 and in October-November 1918, the High Seas Fleet of the German navy was convulsed by mutinies of its sailors and stokers. While the first revolt, actually more a wildcat strike than a full-fledged mutiny, was easily suppressed by harsh punishment, the second uprising of the German sailors was much more effective. Unwilling to support what they termed an "admirals' rebellion" against the government by sailing out on an illegal suicide mission against the British fleet, the enlisted men assumed control over their ships. They ousted their officers from their positions of authority, they took over the two major German naval bases, at Kiel and at Wilhelmshaven, and thus launched the November Revolution which destroyed the German Empire.

Since their occurrence these mutinies have been the subject of an acrimonious controversy of considerable political significance. Thus, for instance, as early as October 1917, Vladimir Ilich Lenin, about to launch his Bolshevik Revolution in Russia, found comfort and hope in the uprising of the German sailors. In an article entitled "The Crisis Is Upon Us," he declared that the German naval mutiny signified that the proletariat of that nation and especially the men of its armed services were prepared for the "great crisis" and would stand with the Russian peasants, workers, and soldiers in forming the vanguard of the "approaching World Revolution." Although the German sailors ultimately disproved Lenin's prediction by refusing to become Bolsheviks and failing to join their Russian comrades in a world revolution, Lenin had fired the first round in the debate that was to embroil the Weimar Republic in never-ending conflict.

In the era of the Weimar Republic, rightist historians, officers, and politicians delighted in accusing their opponents on the left of fomenting the naval rebellions by means of revolutionary subversion of the fleet. In an unprecedented display of historical showmanship, the notorious *Dolchstossprozess* of 1925, the well-known Stab-in-the-Back-Trial, the right tried to demonstrate publicly the guilt and complicity of the left, especially that of the Independent Social Democrats (the USPD), for its alleged treason against Germany. One of the central issues, both at the Munich Trial and the somewhat more sedate but much more protracted proceedings of the Reichstag Investigating Committee that inconclusively deliberated over the causes of Germany's collapse, was the cause of the naval mutinies.

Placed on the defensive by the intransigent accusations of the right, the USPD, its parent party, the Majority Social Democratic Party (the SPD), as well as the moderate, democratic parties, tried to ward off the indictment. Therefore these parties and the historians who supported them rejected all of these allegations and ascribed the origins of the naval revolts to the men's inadequate rations, their abysmal living conditions, their ill treatment by the officers, their war-weariness, and their determination to end the senseless slaughter of the war. The only result of these highly emotional debates was a great mass of extremely polemical and inconclusive literature which merely proved that it was impossible to arrive at a calm, objective, and considered historical judgment of these important events in the turbulent political atmosphere of the ill-fated Weimar Republic.

Since the naval archives were virtually closed to researchers of leftist affiliations and since those of the right refused to reveal any incriminatory evidence that might impede the rebuilding of the navy and tarnish the reputation of its officer corps, no impartial study of these mutinies could be made. Possibly because the historians and politicians could not solve the problem of the mutinies, and certainly because the mutinies abounded in drama, pathos, and excitement, they have fascinated the imagination of a number of literary figures. They inspired the German communist dramatist and poet Ernst Toller to write a stirring and impassioned social play, *Draw the Fires*, which was dedicated to the memory of the two enlisted men who were executed for rebellion. At a later date the contemporary German writer Theodor Plivier produced an equally momentous novel based on the mutinies and the conditions in the German navy—*The Kaiser's Coolies.*

Even after World War II, the controversy over the mutinies did not diminish in fervor. In East Germany the new communist government and its historians sought to establish credentials for ruling by claiming the spirited proletarians in the World War I navy as the ancestors of their regime and by accusing the democratic socialists of having betrayed their movement. In West Germany, too, the issue has not been allowed to die. A few years ago Colonel Behrmann of the Defense Ministry, a former military adviser to the SPD, stirred up the controversy anew when he suggested to an audience of naval officers at Flensburg that the two men executed for mutiny in 1917 were martyrs for German freedom and ought therefore to be raised to the status of national heroes. Outraged, the officers rose and left the hall in protest. After fifty years of such charges and protests, it should be obvious that the causes of the mutinies are much too complex to be resolved by repeating old slogans.

During my stay in Germany in 1965, I made a thorough investigation of the documentary material from the former naval archives now located at the Militärgeschichtliches Forschungsamt in Freiburg im Breisgau. In addition, I was also afforded the opportunity to consult the vital but hitherto unused Haussmann Nachlass at the Württembergisches Staatsarchiv in Stuttgart as well as the valuable holdings of the Bundesarchiv in Koblez and the Stadtarchiv at Kiel. Although these archives supply enough evidence to support a staggering indictment of the German naval officer corps and fully bear out the allegations of the left that an "admirals' rebellion" triggered the November 1918 Revolution, they do not completely solve the problem of the mutinies. The underlying causes for the collapse of the German navy must be sought in terms of a broader perspective, one which examines the social and political history of the navy over an extensive period of time and relates it to the general development of German society.

This reveals that the dramatic events of 1917 and 1918 were the outcome of a twenty-year-old social conflict within the navy between the adherents of the old order in Germany—the emergent caste of feudalized naval officers—and the proponents of a new, more democratic and egalitarian system—the enlisted men. By following the evolution of that conflict and its intensification during the first three years of the war, one can learn not only why the enlisted men rebelled against their officers, but also why these officers pursued a course that was bound to result in mutiny and revolution. Accordingly, in this study the events that lead to the first wave of revolutionary unrest in the fleet in 1917 receive proportionately greater attention than the more spectacular course of the October-November 1918 mutinies which are viewed as the culmination of a process that went back as far as 1898.

It goes without saying that I am indebted to many people for this study. Drs. Arenz and Meyerhöfer of the Militärgeschichtliches Forschungsamt were invariably helpful and instructive during my stay in Freiburg. I am particularly grateful to Dr. Jürgen Rohwer of the Bibliothek für Zeitgeschichte in Stuttgart for not only placing at my disposal the vast resources of his library, but also for arranging for me to meet Admirals Günther Horstmann, Wolfgang Kähler, Friedrich Rüge and Herr Rudolf Krohne, all of whom were kind enough to impart to me their impressions of the World War I German navy and its mutinies.

For reading the entire manuscript and his helpful suggestions, I am deeply grateful to Robert A. Kann. For its financial support of this project from the very beginning, I should like to thank the Rutgers University Research Council. For typing and retyping the manuscript, I would like to thank Roberta Weber for her patience and fortitude. For her unfailing patience with the German naval mutinies over a long period of time, I thank my wife.

New Brunswick, New Jersey
November 1968

THE GERMAN NAVAL MUTINIES

OF WORLD WAR I

i

The German Navy in
Peace and War

One of the best-loved institutions in Wilhelmine Germany was the Imperial Navy. The populace showered their affection and adulation upon the *Blauen Jungen*, the bluejackets. This popularity dated back as far as the 1848 Revolution, when the German liberals had founded a navy by means of a public subscription to demonstrate their country's newly found national unity and freedom. Even the failure of that revolution and Germany's conquest by a militaristic and conservative Prussia did not diminish the love of the navy by the middle class and the masses. By way of contrast the army, caste-ridden, conservative, and dominated by the Junker aristocracy, was widely hated and feared.

During World War I, however, a startling change took place. The navy turned out to be a very imposing but quite useless instrument. Its former popularity spent, it became a hotbed of discontent and class conflict that erupted in a mutiny in August 1917 and a revolution in October–November 1918. So far no adequate explanation for this astonishing transformation has been produced. Little is known of the history of the navy and its place in Wilhelmine Germany before and during the war.[1] Yet the social and political conflicts that tore at the fibers of German society as a whole and threatened to disrupt it by revolution played a crucial role in the growth, planning, and personnel practices of the navy. Indeed, the navy formed a microcosm in which the very same tensions that plagued German society in general were played out on a more intensive and ultimately more destructive scale.

One of the major reasons for the popularity of the navy was that its original social structure avoided most of the class divisions that marked the conservative Junker-dominated Prussian army. As a rule naval officers were drawn from young men of middle-class backgrounds who would or could not enter the aristocratic officer corps of the army. Hence the traditional caste prejudice, the snobbery, and militarism of the Prussian army were noticeably absent in the navy.[2] Until 1898, when Germany launched her ambitious program of naval expansion, the navy was still small and compact enough to accommodate a variety of classes, to integrate them, and to create a unique esprit de corps.

At that time the navy was the most cosmopolitan of armed services. Its officers and crews traveled widely and visited the far-flung corners of the globe. Their exposure to a variety of social, political, and intellectual systems fostered increased tolerance and liberalism. Consequently naval discipline was much milder than that of the army; the men were treated with greater respect and leniency, and therefore stood on much closer terms with their superiors.

With the advent of Admiral Alfred von Tirpitz as Secretary of the Navy in 1898 these egalitarian, cosmopolitan, and tolerant attitudes began to vanish. Whereas the old navy consisted largely of cruisers employed in foreign waters, a relatively small but highly effective naval apparatus, Tirpitz persuaded Kaiser Wilhelm II to assemble a fleet of battleships capable of challenging Britain's traditional domination of the seas in a future war. In order to obtain the funds for such a fleet, Tirpitz enlisted the support of not only middle-class liberals and professors but also a number of chauvinistic and militant pressure groups such as the Pan-German League, the Naval League, and the Colonial Society.[3] Assiduously directed by the navy, these groups clamored loudly for big appropriations and the construction of a fleet to rival that of the British. Tirpitz's propaganda campaign was a great success. The German Reichstag never failed to provide the funds for battleships. The consequences of the construction of a fleet of battleships were fateful for the navy. Instead of visiting far-off countries as agents of good will, the new ships of the German navy, especially after 1906, were confined to the North Sea, posed at England's throat as an ever ready dagger.

As Germany's ships grew in size and fighting power with the introduction of the Dreadnought type after 1906, a psychological and sociological transformation took place in the navy. Its rising prestige attracted increasing numbers of officers from the aristocracy and the upper middle class. Gradually the naval officer corps became more socially exclusive and restrictive, placing increasing emphasis on recruiting politically reliable and socially acceptable cadets.

Captain Lothar Persius, who resigned from the navy in 1912 because of his opposition to Tirpitz and who subsequently became one of its most outspoken critics as naval correspondent for the *Berliner Tageblatt*, reports that it always helped to have political connections. In 1883 when he had arrived to take his entrance examination, he had brought with him a letter from the Chief of the Admiralty stating "Bearer [of letter], the prospective naval cadet, L.P., is to be enrolled."[4]

Subsequently it became even more important for prospective candidates to have the proper social, economic, and political background. The 1912 official statement on admission into the officer corps stated that "the imperial navy recruits its officers from all classes of the population whose nobility of thought, whose loyalty and devotion to the Kaiser and the Reich, whose mode of life and social mores approximate the officer's profession." However, the regulations also specified that the candidate would have to be socially prominent enough to gain admission as a subaltern in a local regiment of the army.[5] In addition, the candidates' fathers were expected to meet relatively stringent financial requirements. They were obliged to pledge in writing the "modest" sum of approximately 7,500 marks for their son's support during his years of training and early career.[6] It was further recommended that the candidate spend at least six months at Oxford, Cambridge, or Grenoble to prepare himself for his language examination.[7]

As the ranks of the naval cadet corps came increasingly to be dominated by the prosperous bourgeoisie and, to a lesser extent, by the nobility, it became virtually impossible for an enterprising sailor to rise from the ranks and to obtain a commission.[8] Gradually, traditional differences between the army and navy began to disappear. The major distinction remaining was that the navy never established select or elite ships—it maintained no equivalent of the army's guard regiments—and thereby avoided the army's extreme social differentiation.[9]

Even a glance at one of the crew chronicles or class yearbooks of the German naval academy will demonstrate this transformation. The class of 1912, for instance, enrolled at least 25 noblemen, among whom were a Prince of Siam, a von Bredow, a von Jagow, a von Krosigk, a von Schwerin, a von Treskow, and a von Willamowitz-Moellendorff. The majority of the cadets still came from the bourgeoisie. There were 49 sons of naval and army officers, 12 sons of estate owners, 11 sons of clergymen, 16 sons of professors or academicians, 35 sons of industrialists or merchants, and only two farmers' sons.[10]

On the basis of this evidence, it appears that the nobility was a distinct minority in a naval officer corps dominated by the bourgeoisie. Nevertheless, it would be incorrect to maintain, as does Jonathan Steinberg, that the navy was "neither Prussian nor conservative," or, for that matter, aristocratic.[11] Such a contention ignores the fact that the officer corps lost much, if not indeed most, of its former liberalism as its bourgeois members began to amalgamate with their noble colleagues in a process that can best be termed "the feudalization of the bourgeoisie." The nonnoble officers reacted to the aristocrats in their ranks by trying to ape the airs of the feudal Junker class, by looking down upon their social inferiors, and by cultivating an excessively gruff and somewhat ludicrous military tone.[12] They threw overboard their former liberalism and their approval of social mobility and anxiously closed ranks with the aristocracy to protect themselves against infiltration by "the lower classes." [13] As Drascher puts it, the naval officer corps, although "the special representative of the bourgeoisie in the armed service," quickly took on "the characteristic of aristocratic privilege." [14]

Captain Persius, who once served as a member of the cadet selection committee of the navy, explains how this process worked. Before a candidate was admitted as a cadet, every aspect of his and his family's political, social, and financial record was investigated in detail with the aid of the government and the police. This close scrutiny continued throughout an officer's career. When he contemplated marriage, the same procedure was instituted for his bride and her family. Just as a young man was certain to be denied admission into the navy as an officer if his father ran an open mercantile establishment or a retail store, even if he did not personally work at the counter, so was an officer denied permission to become engaged or to marry if his prospective father-in-law was tainted by a menial occupation. Even "the slightest blemish of honor in the history of the family" was enough to warrant a denial from his commander.[15]

As the naval officer corps cultivated these aristocratic airs and pretensions, it also made a decided effort to suppress and thwart the drive toward advancement of inferior social groups such as engineering officers and warrant officers. Naval engineers were looked down upon as technical personnel. Officers openly maintained that it was only right that "technicians" should occupy an inferior position because they were not "real soldiers." [16]

In order to confine the engineers in a subordinate position, Vice Admiral von Cörper, the inspector of the navy's education department, suggested in 1911 that naval engineers be drawn from families of lower than middle-class background in the future so that they would give up their social pretensions and content themselves with the position "they deserve." The director of the engineering school, to whom this directive was addressed, agreed wholeheartedly. He felt that the time had come to take "energetic steps" to return these officers to their proper place because it had come to his attention that a young engineer and his bride had had the audacity to pay a social call on a naval officer.

In the light of these attitudes it was natural that the navy should try to segregate the engineers socially from the rest of the officers. As late as 1914 they were still denied access to officers' clubs. Even while they were on duty, however, they were kept in their proper place. Not even the highest engineering officer, the *Oberchefsingenieur* (equivalent in rank to a captain), was permitted to issue orders to a mere lieutenant. Young naval officers, however, were frequently placed in command of senior engineers.[17]

Even harsher was the treatment the navy meted out to its long-term noncommissioned officers who rose to the rank of warrant or deck officer. These were men who possessed some special skill. It generally took them twelve to twenty years to achieve this rank. Despite their age, skill, and experience, they were treated with contempt by the regular officers. Often they were not even accorded the courtesy of being addressed with the polite "*Sie.*" They were forbidden any social intercourse with the regular officers. The right to maintain their own meeting rooms or clubs was denied them. During the war, when there was a critical shortage of experienced officers throughout the navy, not a single deck officer among the hundreds capable of handling such a job was promoted into the officer corps. Even the army was more liberal than this. It did not hesitate to promote such men to the rank of acting officer during the war.[18]

Why did the navy refuse to imitate the army in this respect? The answer is not immediately apparent. Opinion in naval circles was divided. While some of the more liberal officers regretted such a policy, others insisted that deck officers could not be promoted because the navy did not have enough experienced petty officers to replace them.[19] Most officers, however, would have agreed with the navy's official spokesman, Vice Admiral Adolf von Trotha. He stated that the deck officers' lack of formal education made it difficult to integrate them into the officer corps and that it was therefore best not to create a second-class or inferior group of officers.[20] Yet on June 16, 1918, Trotha privately admitted that the primary reason for the exclusion of the deck officers was social. They would cut "a comic figure" in the convivial atmosphere of the officers' mess. This would destroy its "spirit of comraderie," and since it would be impossible to dislodge them once the war was over, it would bring about a highly undesirable "revolutionary change in the composition of the officer corps." [21]

In growing more and more exclusive, the naval officer corps demonstrated that it had ceased to be a mere occupational group and that it had developed into a caste. Its members then cultivated a distinct caste spirit, *Kastengeist*, and allowed it to dominate their actions. Feeling that patriotism, honor, and love for the service was their monopoly, they increasingly based their treatment of their subordinates upon compulsion and force. Discipline in the enlisted ranks grew ever more stringent, the navy going so far as to admit that it had abandoned the British disciplinary system in favor of a "truly Prussian one." [22]

Thus the brutality and caste system of the Prussian drill field and barracks life was introduced in a service that had formerly avoided all manifestations of Prussian militarism. By the outbreak of the war, most of the officers had succumbed to the new spirit. Characteristic of the caste mentality that prevailed in the naval officer corps as late as the fall of 1917 is the vehement protest of

the captain of the *König Wilhelm* to the proposed abolition of
flogging for cabin boys. Maintaining strenuously that boys of fifteen could easily tolerate ten lashes, the captain asserted that such
a punishment was ideal because it did not outrage the boys' honor.
In his estimation they possessed very little honor to begin with
and their pride was protected by the fact that floggings were
never conducted publicly but only in the presence of their immediate superiors.[23]

Equally revealing of the new mentality of the officer corps is
the fact that officers openly referred to their subordinates as unpatriotic fellows,[24] and that it took the Kaiser until October 1916
to persuade the navy to stop shackling enlisted men in irons when
they were placed under arrest.[25]

It is clear that the navy under Tirpitz's direction developed a
caste spirit that opened a fateful rift between the officers and enlisted men. The most obvious manifestations of this new spirit
were narrow-mindedness and intolerance. Tirpitz's new naval
officer did not, as has been maintained, develop "familiarity with
world politics, linguistic skill, and a certain amount of diplomatic
ability." [26] On the contrary, almost the exact opposite occurred in
the German fleet.

Tirpitz's battle fleet hardly ever sailed in foreign waters. It was
largely confined to monotonous maneuvers in the North Sea or
the Baltic. Hence only a small number of officers ever visited foreign lands once their cadet voyage was over.[27] Moreover, the con-
centration of the fleet in home waters deprived Germany's naval
commanders of the opportunity to exercise independent commands as in the past.[28] In Tirpitz's new navy they were reduced to
"steamship chauffeurs" who merely sailed in the wake of their
squadron flagship, worried about never-ending inspections, lived
in fear over their promotions, and drove their crews by ceaseless
drill.[29] Thus relegated to the function of technicians, Germany's
naval officers lost their culture and cosmopolitanism. Their boring
routines made them warlike, aggressive, intolerant, and disdainful
of their men. Hence it was only natural that they complete the

transition and develop a caste mentality very much like that of the Prussian army officer. As the British naval attaché to Berlin put it so well, German naval officers "impress one rather as being soldiers at sea than seamen." [30]

The transformation of the German navy after 1898 also affected the enlisted men. Before 1898 the navy had been able to rely on long-term enlistments from the coastal areas and fishing towns. As the fleet multiplied in size this source began to give out, and it became necessary to tap the vast manpower reservoir of the industrial cities. Moreover, the highly sophisticated apparatus and machinery of the new fleet required the services of skilled and educated personnel. To run these modern ships was a complicated job that could no longer be performed by simple and docile fishermen. As a result, the navy had to draft into its enlisted ranks for three-year terms technicians and skilled artisans who came from large cities, who were members of trade unions, who were infected by the bacillus of socialism, and who were trained to think and act in terms of the class struggle.[31]

Nearly fifty percent of the men then serving in the German navy can be classified as technical personnel. The army's ratio was much lower. For every army technician there were eight regular soldiers who generally came from a conservative and easily led peasantry.[32] In order to recruit and retain its technical personnel the navy was obliged to make the service attractive. Naval technicians received higher pay and larger clothing allotments than their army counterparts. Promotions in the enlisted ranks came more rapidly. In the army it generally took twelve years before a man could become a noncommissioned officer; in the navy it could on occasion be done in a year and a half. Even more importantly, naval technicians received better treatment and rations than their comrades in the army. In the navy the purely military training period was much briefer, and they were not required to render the same sort of *Kadavergehorsam* (blind, deathlike obedience) as their army equivalents.[33] These relative advantages, however, did not assuage the navy's enlisted men. On the contrary, such advantages heightened their resentment of the officers and the power they wielded.

The entry of such a group of class-conscious, unionized workers into the navy was bound to result in a clash between them and the officer corps. Even before the war aggravated tensions between the officers and the men, before the onset of hunger, starvation, and all the other privations the war brought in its wake, the navy was threatened by a potentially explosive situation. Two hostile classes extremely conscious of their positions and power confronted each other. The officers, determined to preserve their privileges and to enhance their power, demanded absolute obedience, respect, and discipline, while the men were equally resolved to improve their lot, to raise their status, and to win greater freedom.

This social conflict was by no means confined to the navy. Within the political structure of Germany a similar struggle of even larger proportion was being waged. The lower classes were trying to improve their status, to gain new political and social rights, and were assailing the bastions of the conservative, Junker-dominated German state. The defenders of the established order —the landed aristocracy and the industrialists—like the naval officers, clung tenaciously to their privileges and refused to yield to the clamor of the masses. In both instances, within the empire as within the navy, tensions were mounting. German society and its smaller component, the navy, were both heading toward a crisis. World War I accentuated that crisis and drove it into the open.

The outbreak of the First World War was greeted with shouts of jubilation in the German navy. Here was the opportunity for which it had been waiting and training for so long. For a service untested in battle, the war constituted a chance to establish a reputation and, above all, to defeat the English and wrest from them control of the seas. Now the moment had arrived for the German fleet to justify its enormous expense and the irreparable harm it had caused in forcing England to abandon her traditionally neutrality and to join France and Russia in an alliance.

Almost from the beginning of the war it was evident that Grand Admiral Tirpitz and his naval planners had committed a number of blunders in their buildup of the High Seas Fleet. The basic intention of Tirpitz's renowned "risk theory," the intellectual basis for the construction of that fleet, had been the search for an Anglo-German naval alliance rather than war. Accordingly, the Grand Admiral had always insisted that Germany did not require as large a navy as that of England. According to the theory, the risk of England's losing part of her fleet in any future naval battle with Germany that might involve the loss of her domination of the seas would act as a deterrent and eventually compel her to seek a diplomatic naval accommodation with her German rival.[34] But no such accommodation had materialized. Indeed, Germany's naval pressure and competition had been instrumental in preventing the very rapprochement that Tirpitz and the German Foreign Office desired.

Now that the unexpected had come about, the German navy found to its dismay that it was hopelessly outnumbered by the British navy. At first this did not prevent the optimism of Germany's naval leaders. They calculated that the British would capitalize on numerical superiority and establish a close blockade of the German coast in order to starve Germany into submission by preventing the importation of food and other vital commodities. A close blockade, the German Admiralty felt, would work to Germany's advantage. It would enable her to wear down the British fleet in a series of minor engagements in which Germany, operating close to her home bases on the North Sea and able to choose when and where to engage small enemy contingents, would eventually establish an equilibrium of forces. Once this was achieved, the High Seas Fleet would engage the British Grand Fleet in a major and decisive battle that would decide in Germany's favor the outcome of the war at sea.

This forecast, too, was based on a number of fallacies. Although it was not unreasonable to expect that the commander of the British Grand Fleet, Admiral Jellicoe, would continue the Nelsonian tradition of seeking out the enemy and destroying him in battle, Germany's naval strategists failed to realize that England's worldwide naval commitments demanded that such a risky encounter be avoided. As Winston Churchill, then First Lord of the Admiralty, so aptly phrased it, "Jellicoe was the only man who could lose the war in an afternoon" (if he allowed himself to become involved in an unsuccessful battle with the Germans). Thus instead of confronting the German High Seas Fleet or establishing a close blockade of Germany's coast, the English navy was secretly ordered as early as 1912 to adopt a much safer strategy of maintaining a blockade over the exits of the North Sea.[35]

England had no need to risk her fleet so long as her favorable geographic situation and her naval bases at Rosyth near Edinburgh, Cromarty at Moray Firth, and Scapa Flow in the Orkneys prevented the German fleet from escaping from the North Sea and England slowly succeeded in strangling German seaborne trade.[36]

This was Tirpitz's second great miscalculation. So preoccupied was he in his risk theory and his battle fleet that he failed to realize that neither would be effective unless England cooperated to the extent of allowing emotion and pride to overcome reason. In the words of the noted expert on German military history, Professor Gerhard Ritter, Tirpitz's navy "overestimated its own strength by far" and in typical German militaristic fashion manifested an almost complete lack of understanding of its opponent's views and interests.[37]

These miscalculations and errors were bound to affect Germany's conduct of the war. First of all, Germany's numerical naval inferiority dictated against sailing out into a pitched battle with the British. It was feared that the entire fleet might thus be lost in one engagement and that she would then be deprived of a vital bargaining point at the end of the war. In short, the German fleet was too large "to die with honor, but still too small in order to triumph over the British under all circumstances." [38] This had been realized long before the war by a number of naval strategists, most prominent among whom were Admirals Galster and Heeringen. In 1907 Galster suggested that Tirpitz's "parade ships" could perform no useful function in any future war and recommended the construction of coastal batteries and submarines in their place. When Chancellor Bülow endorsed this recommendation, Tirpitz threatened to resign and the matter was dropped.[39]

In the Imperial German Navy, strategic and technical considerations almost always seemed to take second place to personal and political factors. Thus, for instance, Tirpitz had a personal preference for battleships and communicated it to the Kaiser. Battleships were much more imposing and menacing than cruisers and submarines.[40] Both the Kaiser and his chief naval adviser were extremely concerned with manifesting an illusion of power even if it did not exist in reality. To illustrate this point we have a report of a conversation that Captain Persius had with the Kaiser in 1905. Persius, having recently returned from a voyage to the Far East, reported that the Chinese had not been impressed by his ship because it had only one smokestack. He commented that they would have been far more impressed by a weaker, less well-armed vessel if it only had more smokestacks. To this the Kaiser responded by exclaiming, "No! No, this is the way it is everywhere, not only in China! People want to have sand thrown in their eyes. 'The sound of hammering is part of working,' I keep telling Tirpitz. A tub like that must appear powerful, powerful. That's the main thing." [41]

Accordingly, most prewar German battleships were equipped with multiple smokestacks, thick combat rigging, and many small-caliber guns. Thus was constructed what critics delighted to call a "bluff or parade fleet" composed of ships that looked strong but were actually much less powerful than their English equivalents. It became traditional for Germany to build ships fairly bristling with guns. The British, however, increasingly concentrated on installing a few but powerful pieces of heavy artillery. Consequently German ships went into the war equipped with heavy, medium, and light artillery, none of which was a match for the heavier 38.5 cm. guns of the British.[42] To a layman this may not appear a serious failing. But from a naval point of view this policy turned out to be a blunder of the first order. Throughout the war it gave the British the inestimable advantage of outranging their German opponents, being able to remain out of range while shelling the German ships to pieces.

One of the reasons why the German navy cultivated illusion rather than real power in its construction program was its concern for the passage of its budgets. The Reichstag, which Tirpitz understood to perfection, preferred voting large sums of money for impressive-looking projects. Moreover, battleships were found eminently more suitable for the lavish entertainment of Reichstag deputies than vessels such as submarines.[43]

All these miscalculations and errors mount up to a startling indictment of Tirpitz as a naval planner and administrator. Indeed, the weight of evidence against him is such that one can hardly avoid agreeing with Ritter that Tirpitz's lifework was nothing but a "gruesome error" and "an enormous speculative failure." [44]

During the war the High Seas Fleet was to pay a high price for these errors. Unable because of a numerical inferiority to risk a direct confrontation with the Grand Fleet, the German fleet was condemned to sit and wait until the English made a mistake, placed themselves in an exposed position, or lost patience and attacked on Germany's home ground. If, on the other hand, the British avoided these errors and relied on the effectiveness of their blockade to demoralize Germany into suing for peace, then Germany had little choice but to institute a counterblockade against England with her submarines. Only the submarine could escape the imprisonment of the North Sea and prey upon the vulnerable merchant shipping, upon which the island nation was dependent for her food imports.

This fact should have been recognized long before the war. But Tirpitz was such an accomplished propagandist and politician that hardly anyone questioned his policies. Therefore the construction of a fleet consisting almost exclusively of great battleships went virtually unchallenged.

Germany had perfected the submarine long before the war and led the world in submarine technology. Although merchant raiders have traditionally been the most successful weapon of a weak naval power against a strong power such as England, Germany did not even begin to embark upon a submarine construction program of any significance until 1912. In that year a small special fund was created in the naval budget for the annual construction of six submarines.[45]

Curiously enough, not even the outbreak of the war and the growing realization as it progressed that Germany's High Seas Fleet could not defeat the English sufficed to bring about a drastic change in construction priorities for submarines. When the war started, Germany had only twenty-eight submarines fit for sea duty, but no crash building program was so much as contemplated. As in the past, battleship construction continued to be emphasized. During the first few months of the war, no fewer than four battleships—the *Kronprinz, Markgraf, Grosser Kurfürst*, and *König*—were launched. Despite the fact that a single battleship required as much material and labor in its construction as twenty submarines, the German navy persisted in compounding its peacetime errors. In 1916, more than two years after the outbreak of the war, the navy commissioned four recently built ships —the battleships *Baden* and *Bayern*—and two battle cruisers—the *Derfflinger* and *Lützow*.

Not even the battle of Jutland on May 31–June 1, 1916, could make the navy abandon its preference for battleships. At this, the only major naval engagement of the war that came about by accident, the German navy acquitted itself unexpectedly well. The German ships were outnumbered two to one by the British, who also had a decided superiority in range and firing power. Yet the Germans managed because of their superior training and audacity in the face of danger to sink nearly twice as many English ships as they lost, and they suffered only one third as many casualties. In that sense, Jutland may well be regarded as a victory for the High Seas Fleet of its technical proficiency and the dedication of its crews.

In a realistic sense, however, the outcome of that battle is subject to a great deal of controversy. Many naval historians, some of them German, argue that the Battle of Jutland was not really a German victory; it did not for a single moment jeopardize England's control of the seas. No matter how many ships the Germans sank, these experts contend, the British fleet never lost control of the battle.[46] While the British failed to capitalize fully on their superiority because of overly cautious leadership, an inferior grade of gun powder, and armor plating, it was the Germans who broke off and retreated in order to save the remnants of their numerically smaller fleet. Hence it can be said that the British, by preserving their domination of the seas, in effect won the battle and that Germany, at best, won merely a moral victory.

The most telling argument against German naval planning is that the High Seas Fleet, even at its single moment of glory, could not basically affect the general naval situation. Paradoxically, this argument was advanced by none other than Admiral Reinhard Scheer, the commander of the High Seas Fleet. When he submitted his report of the battle to the Kaiser, Scheer confessed that his fleet could never hope to defeat the British navy and to lift its blockade. In his estimation, only the submarines could win the war.[47]

In the light of this admission, it is incredible that a year later, in May of 1917, two months after embarking upon a massive campaign of unrestricted submarine warfare, German shipyards still had eight ships of the line under construction while a mere forty-seven submarines were saddled with the virtually impossible task of fulfilling the Admiralty's promise that they would succeed in starving England to death in six months.[48]

What were the reasons for this failure to build the only weapon that, according to the navy, was capable of winning the war?

Why did it have to be coerced to accelerate construction by the intervention of sea-power-conscious Reichstag deputies and the civilian government?[49]

While Tirpitz remained Secretary of the Navy, large-scale submarine construction was regarded as "too radical a solution," one that might prove too shattering of the "lifework of Grand Admiral von Tirpitz."[50] But even Tirpitz's departure from office in March 1916 did not alter the navy's position. In the spring of 1917 his successor, Admiral Eduard von Capelle, appearing before a secret committee session of the Reichstag, admonished the navy's critics to pause and reflect, "what would happen to the organization and promotion [ladder] of the navy, if U-boats were to supplant battleships." Moreover, Capelle also expressed concern over the postwar naval budget if too many submarines were built, and he indicated that he had already taken steps to provide for "submarine cemeteries."[51]

In short, Capelle in effect admitted that the balance of the navy's organizational table and the anticipated difficulty of integrating large number of submarine lieutenants and lieutenant-commanders in the postwar navy were more important than winning the war in the stipulated period of six months.[52]

Persius had encountered this same sort of reasoning in 1912 when he was told by the naval authorities that "submarines are commanded by lieutenants and lieutenant-commanders while ships of the line are [commanded] by captains and squadrons of them by admirals. Therefore admirals and senior officers can only be promoted if large warships are built."[53]

Thus the German navy refused to construct and use the only weapon which, if its number had been multiplied twice or three times, might have won the war. Moreover, that decision was not prompted by military misconceptions or errors. It was the inevitable result of a consistent policy that sought to further the interests of a single class at the expense of all other considerations. The German navy had long ago created a system whose purpose it was to protect and advance the status of its officer corps. Military factors were sublimated whenever they came into conflict with this aim.

This misguided policy and Tirpitz's other miscalculations were bound to have severe repercussions during the remainder of the naval war. Because of its numerical inferiority the High Seas Fleet was in effect condemned to prolonged inactivity throughout the war. This inactivity, however, must not be construed to imply that the battle fleet merely spent its time lying at anchor. On the contrary, the fleet had to maintain a constant state of readiness, it was compelled to sail on numerous patrols, it had to act as a screen for active vessels such as U-boats, cruisers, and minesweepers; in short, it had to be kept perpetually busy performing all sorts of tasks for which it had not been built.

Aside from a number of minor engagements with the British such as the Battle of Helgoland and the Battle of Dogger Bank, the German High Seas Fleet saw no real action until the Battle of Jutland in June 1916. This could not help but affect its morale and aggravate the internal social conflicts that had plagued it since before the war.

During the first two years of the war the High Seas Fleet spent much of its time lurking along the German coast. Only at rare intervals did it furtively steal out to cover a sortie or a bombardment of some English town by the cruiser squadron. For the most part the fleet stood by in wait for a battle that was not to materialize.

Soon the effects of such a routine began to make themselves felt. Inactivity, boredom, and monotony became a daily part of life in the High Seas Fleet. Its officers and men came to feel that they were merely wasting their time. Since the other units of the navy—the torpedo boats, submarines, minesweepers, and patrol boats—performed a multiplicity of useful and necessary tasks, the men on the big ships felt all the worse.

At first their discontent focused primarily on the lack of action and on unfavorable comparisons to the army's great victories.

The officers and men found it disconcerting to read inscribed in huge letters along the walls of Wilhelmshaven:

> Lieb' Vaterland, magst ruhig sein,
> Die Flotte schläfft im Hafen ein.[54]
>
> *Dear Fatherland, rest in peace,*
> *The fleet lies sleeping in port.*

More serious, however, were the rumors to the effect that the inactivity of the navy was the fault of Commander of the High Seas Fleet Admiral von Ingenohl, who had an English mistress and was therefore presumed to be reluctant to fight against her country.[55] As continued idleness created mounting disaffection, the navy began to lose its status as the darling of the people and was reduced to the level of a stepchild among the armed services.[56]

This loss of prestige was keenly felt by the naval officer corps. As early as the summer of 1915 the morale of the officers constituted a serious problem for the navy. On July 6, 1915, Admiral Bachmann, Chief of Staff of the Admiralty, expressed concern that the long waiting and lack of action were undermining the energy of the fleet, sowing despair and discontent. He feared that this would ultimately lead to a complete loss of idealism.[57] Another officer, Captain (later Vice Admiral) von Trotha, also sensed this despair. He maintained, however, that the fault did not lie with the navy but with the government. Many officers blamed the government's overly cautious policy for their inability to sail into battle. Accepting this argument without hesitation, Trotha went on to recommend that all power over the navy be concentrated in the hands of a single dynamic leader, namely Grand Admiral von Tirpitz.[58]

Giving vent to this kind of feeling throughout the summer and fall of 1915, a resentful and dissident officer corps made life difficult for the navy. Many officers, despite express orders from their

superiors, sought transfer into the army. Others refused to accept
the Iron Cross and similar decorations. They spread rumors about
their commander, Ingenohl, and blamed him and Chancellor von
Bethmann-Hollweg, the head of the civilian government, for
what they termed the cowardly tactics of the navy.[59] So dangerous and widespread was this movement[60] that at last the Kaiser felt
compelled to intervene personally. On November 7, 1915, Wilhelm II ordered the officers to refrain from their "almost criminal
rumors and denunciations," and to "practice the most far-
reaching self-restraint" lest their conduct undermine the morale
of their subordinates.[61] Never before had the Kaiser addressed his
officers in such sharp terms.

All in all, it would be fair to say that the officers' resentment at
their inactivity and lack of battle contact with the enemy had
produced a serious wave of unrest. This indicated that they could
be relied on to perform their duties only to the extent that the
orders they were expected to execute did not conflict with their
own code of honor and their belief that only a policy of forceful,
direct action could produce a satisfactory solution for Germany's
military and political problems. Their assault upon the civilian
government opened an ever growing rift that would at a later
date have fateful consequences, not only for the navy but for the
entire German Empire. More immediately, however, the officers'
resentful behavior and independent attitude could not help but
affect the morale of the crews.

The enlisted men of the German High Seas Fleet, no less than
their officers, suffered from inactivity. However, theirs was a
different kind of suffering. The officers were chagrinned primarily because they were not winning fame and glory for themselves in battle and were being eclipsed by the army officers. The
enlisted men felt all these things and, in addition, were made to
bear the brunt of their superiors' discontent while at the same
time their lives were made miserable by the lack of even the basic
comforts and amenities of military life.

Seaman Richard Stumpf of the battleship *Helgoland* left a diary that accurately describes the feelings and emotions of the enlisted men. Stumpf and his comrades had been deliriously happy at the outbreak of the war when they faced the exciting prospect of confronting the British fleet in battle.[62] This early enthusiasm was soon dissipated by inactivity and a growing conflict with their officers.

Whenever during the early months of the war the High Seas Fleet sailed out for battle, Stumpf's ship was suffused with happiness and enthusiasm. The men went about their work eagerly and with great hope. No sooner, however, did the fleet turn about without having encountered the enemy than "boundless disappointment" appeared everywhere.[63] At first the men were merely unhappy with their routine. This consisted primarily of the most stultifying and monotonous sort of "positional warfare," which never led to the exhilaration of battle, was incredibly boring, and seldom gave them a real opportunity to relax.[64]

Most of the time the battleships of the German navy stood on a three- or six-hour alert even while they lay in port. This did not permit the men much time for relaxation ashore. They were kept busy, week after week and month after month, at all sorts of non-combat duties like squadron maneuvers, artillery exercises, and target towing.[65]

Only occasionally was this sort of duty relieved by sailing out on patrol, taking on coal, or traversing the Kiel Canal back to the North Sea. Clearly this routine afforded the men very little rest,[66] even less variation, and soon bored them to distraction. As one officer put it so succinctly: "Yet the work was done. Daily. It was not very interesting, but it was [done with] discipline." [67]

Both officers and enlisted men agreed that the monotony of this routine ruined their morale.[68] One sailor, Joachim Ringelnatz, who was soon to become an officer, found the routine so deadening that he seriously considered deserting.[69] In fact, it frequently got so bad that Seaman Stumpf very properly blamed it for creating a "prison psychosis" among the crews.

One can get used to anything, but it is extremely difficult to be kept waiting all the time in the knowledge that our tremendous power is being wasted. The atmosphere is strained and embittered. One can sense it among the officers and the men. Happy songs and joyful games are no longer in evidence. We are virtually at each other's throats. The happy spirit of comraderie [that existed at the beginning of the war] has vanished and has been supplanted by depression. No wonder all of us wish to leave the ship . . .[70]

The officers responded to this situation by inventing a multiplicity of tasks to keep their men busy and to occupy their minds. However, since they themselves were resentful and bored, they fulfilled the letter of their obligation but ignored the spirit. Stumpf describes how one of his superiors handled the men's recreation and physical exercise: "Yesterday one of these gentlemen took his division to town for a walk . . . He made them run through town in double-time and chased them up and down. It was supposed to be a military excursion! Our recreation consists of marching up and down in closed ranks and making us lie in the mud on the parade grounds." [71]

It stood to reason that the officers should emphasize the most easily discernible and most easily conducted activity—military drill. Thus the men were drilled, marched, and barked at in typical Prussian style, but nothing was done to lift their sagging spirits. This excessive carping on discipline and military form never achieved its intended effect. On the contrary, it lowered the men's morale and, in addition, made them detest their officers. According to Stumpf, the crews resented this harassment. It undermined their "love and devotion to the service" and on occasion even incited them to petty acts of sabotage.[72]

The navy's morale problem grew worse with time. As Germany gradually began to expand her submarine force in 1916, noticeable changes began to take place in the personnel of the High Seas Fleet. The expanding submarine fleet required large numbers of young enterprising officers. The surface fleet was therefore turned into a reservoir of manpower.[73] Of course, the most ca-

pable of the officers, usually either Kapitänleutnants or Oberleut-
nants, those who had the best control over their men and had
served with them for a long time, were selected to serve on the U-
boats and other small vessels.[74]

The officers who remained behind on the big ships were either
older men, not suitable for service on the submarines, or extremely young men who had very little experience. Frequently an
experienced and beloved division officer would be replaced by a
young ensign or lieutenant of eighteen or nineteen years who
sought to hide his ignorance and insecurity by maintaining great
strictness and cultivating an air of aloofness.[75]

The older officers who remained quickly became disillusioned
and apathetic. As senior officers, their contact with the enlisted
men was limited. Generally they allowed the junior officers a free
hand with them. They performed their duties listlessly, and at best
supervised their juniors in a haphazard fashion.[76]

Even if the submarines had not drained the High Seas Fleet of
some of its best officers, the rapid wartime expansion of the navy
was bound to affect the quality of the officer corps. Even so
staunch a defender of the navy as Admiral von Trotha concedes
that the tenfold increase in the size of the navy created an officer
problem. Newly commissioned officers no longer received the
traditional three and a half years of training at the naval academy,
and as a result inferior officers were stationed on the large ships.[77]

As naval division officers became increasingly younger and
more inexperienced, the crews grew older, more experienced, and
greatly disillusioned. A dangerous age or generation problem was
arising in the fleet. By the summer of 1917 when the first mutiny
convulsed the navy, most of the enlisted men had already accumulated long years of service in the navy. Of the 1,230–man
crew of the *König Albert*, 17 men had served for six years, 228
for five years, 311 for four years, and 197 for three years.[78] This
could not help but widen the gulf between the men and their
young officers. In addition to age and experience, many of the
new officers lacked the tact, the maturity, and the know-how to

set a good example for their men. Thus they failed to realize that
the men were most sensitive about such things as the equitable
distribution of food, leaves and promotions.[79] Moreover, the
young officers were either unwilling or unable to do anything to
raise the faltering morale of their crews.

They did nothing to make such tedious but very time-
consuming tasks as taking on coal interesting or acceptable. Unlike their counterparts in the British navy who tried to make a
game or a sport out of these strenuous and boring activities, German offices generally stood by listlessly barking orders while the
men grumbled and grew dissatisfied. The English officers converted even coaling and minelaying into a tolerable experience
because they did not hesitate to participate alongside their men.
The German officers, however, felt that such menial tasks would
demean their exalted status and refused to pitch in, thus fostering
resentment and hatred.[80]

After the war German officers cited numerous reasons why the
navy found it impossible to relieve the monotony and boredom of
the crews. They claimed that because of Germany's peculiar geographic situation the fleet was compelled to conduct its maneuvers and firing practice at the bleak and dismal mouths of rivers
and that there was only one location, Altenbruch Roads, that had
facilities for sports. Moreover, Germany's major naval base at
Wilhelmshaven could not be used as a recreational center because
the ships had to be kept on three-hour alerts that did not permit
the crews to go beyond the confines of the city.[81] Yet at Scapa
Flow, an even bleaker and less populated location, the British
navy managed to conduct under similar conditions of preparedness
such sports as football, boxing, racing, and rowing. Moreover,
all large British vessels were equipped with reading and billiard
rooms, and the crews were urged to pursue such varied activities
as painting, theatricals, and movies.[82]

The German navy, however, never made any real effort to care
for the comfort or spiritual life of its men. For example, from the
outbreak of the war until well into the summer of 1915, the en-

listed men in the German fleet had to go without tables, chairs, and other furniture. All these combustible furnishings had been removed in August 1914, and no one bothered to install noncombustible substitutes in their place.[83] Furthermore, it was not until the summer of 1915 that film projectors were placed on board their ships.[84]

Another interesting illustration of the difference between the British navy and that of Germany was the seating rules established for the theater at Flensburg. The entire loge of the Flensburg theater was reserved for the use of officers. The balcony and the orchestra were set aside for officers and midshipmen. The remaining seats were for deck officers and petty officers. Where were the common sailors and stokers to sit? [85]

These one-sided privileges were by no means confined to recreation. For instance, in the interest of secrecy and to prevent leakage of vital intelligence to the enemy, the German navy provided only limited access to shore for its enlisted men. Even married men were not usually permitted to live ashore with their families. Yet the youngest bachelor officers were given complete freedom to go and live ashore. They were allowed to set up apartments for mistresses, among whom, according to Alboldt, there must have been many spies for naval secrets regularly leaked out and became public knowledge. Higher officers, too, were equally lax, making no effort to impose security regulations upon themselves. Often they discussed secret naval dispositions in public.[86]

The enlisted men, much more than their officers, needed a chance to get away from their "iron prisons." [87] The maintenance of their morale demanded that they be given periodic leaves to recuperate nerves worn raw by the stultifying routine on the big ships. However, the German navy had no precise regulations to ensure an equitable distribution of leaves. Although the men were theoretically entitled to three weeks of leave a year,[88] generally leaves were granted only when ships entered dock for repair. Consequently, certain ships, because of faulty construction, sometimes because of accident and more rarely because of damages sustained in battle, spent more time in dock, affording their crews more leave.[89] Also, sailors were usually luckier than the engine room crew. Unlike those of technicians, sailors' services were not needed while the ship was undergoing repairs. Hence sailors usually enjoyed a more liberal leave policy. In addition and engendering much resentment, men who possessed gold currency and who were willing to exchange it, received preference in terms of leaves.[90]

As if this were not enough, the great majority of officers never made the attempt to stimulate their men intellectually or to keep them informed of the state of the war and the role of the navy within the war. This failure in *"Innere Führung,"* internal leadership as it came to be called after World War II, contributed significantly to the discontent of the crews.[91] Instead of capitalizing on the men's yearning for knowledge and information regarding the great issues of the war and making tedious routines more acceptable by explaining their purpose, the officers generally adhered to the peacetime practice of lecturing on such subjects as the Articles of War, military courtesy, discipline, or the working of some weapon.[92] Very frequently the men sailed out on missions totally ignorant of their objective because their officers did not trouble to confide in them.[93] The job of public information officer was generally held in such low esteem that it was assigned to the very youngest and least-experienced officers. These, not knowing what to say, would frequently make an ill-prepared speech based on that day's newspaper or, more often than not, would recite some lecture that the men had heard a hundred times before.[94] On those rare occasions when officers did bestir themselves to lecture about the war, they often attempted to paint the situation in a more optimistic light than was warranted. Consequently, the men saw right through this stratagem and refused to believe anything they were told. Instead they paid credence to the multitude of rumors that abounded in the navy.[95]

Why was the German naval officer corps unable or unwilling to counteract the effects of military inactivity, boredom, and discontent among its crews? Why were no steps taken to remedy this increasingly dangerous situation, and why did the German officers not emulate the British in this respect? The social attitudes and the caste spirit prevailing in the German naval officer corps provide an answer. Unlike the English officers, who possessed an almost instinctive feeling that they had to maintain close contact with their men in order to understand them and keep them under control, the German officers, because of their caste spirit, labored under the misconception that the best way to maintain their authority was to remain as aloof as possible from their subordinates, thus failing to "understand the psychology of their men" and the "special circumstances" of the war.[96] Here was a failure, "a psychological failure," of which virtually all of Germany's naval officers from the Chief of the High Seas Fleet on down to the lowliest ensign were guilty.[97]

The majority of officers were so dominated by their caste spirit (*Kastengeist*) that they lacked the ability to put themselves into their men's shoes. Therefore they showed little understanding for their men's needs and problems. From their first day in the navy they had been trained to regard themselves as infinitely superior to their men. So conscious were they of their exalted status, and the privileges that went with it, that they hardly ever troubled themselves about the mental and physical welfare of their subordinates. Moreover, they were also convinced that their men had been so well trained and conditioned to obey any order without question that it never occurred to them that their authority could ever be rejected. As one embittered former petty officer put it, the officers were so accustomed to blind obedience that not even warnings of impending unrest among the crews could disturb their complacency. On those occasions

they gave a reflective little smile, spoke of loyalty to the oath and of discipline, and, in the event of a "failure to obey," of radical means such as "imprisonment." So convinced was the active naval officer of absolute, blind obedience that he simply could not conceive that this mass [of men] could one day rise up in mutiny.[98]

Actually, there was no real cause to fear a mutiny in the summer of 1916. Conditions in the fleet were not bad enough nor had the spirit of the men declined sufficiently to make this a real possibility. Most of the men were ardent patriots, animated by a sincere love of the navy and the conviction that they were fighting for a good cause. Even those men who were Social Democrats and antimilitarists were still patriotic and eager to defend their country.[99] Their discontent during the first two years of war was largely the product of the ceaseless routine and their officers' callousness. It should by no means be regarded as sufficient cause for a revolution. The basic prerequisites for a real mutiny—deep, abiding dissatisfaction and alienation, a common cause to unite them, and an organization to carry out a rebellion—were still lacking.

True, the men were disappointed in their officers, resentful about their living conditions and their constant harassment, and above all, deeply bored with the role they played in the war. Indeed, in the words of Admiral von Tirpitz, only "men with fish blood" in their veins could have tolerated such a life without experiencing some ill effects.[100] However, the situation was not yet irreparable.

That the navy was still basically healthy in 1916 is amply demonstrated by the men's response to the prospect of going into action or leaving the repressive atmosphere of their ships on furlough. Whenever leaves were granted, there was a sudden and dramatic improvement in the men's morale.[101]

When the High Seas Fleet finally saw some action, the change was more dramatic still. Thus, in June 1916 the Battle of Jutland transported Stumpf into such ecstasy that he prefaced his description of the battle with the inspiring words: "Finally, finally— At last, the momentous event which for twenty-two months has been the object of our longings, emotions and thoughts has arrived. For many years we have hoped, worked and drilled with great fervor for this. I truly don't know how to begin!" [102]

Even the Communists who have long maintained that the proletarian sailors and stokers of the German navy began organizing for revolution as early as 1915 are forced to admit that to them the Battle of Jutland came as a great disappointment. It resulted in "a tremendous change of morale" and wiped out the embryonic revolutionary movement they allege existed among the enlisted men.[103] As Wilhelm Weber, one of the leaders of the 1917 mutiny, describes it, there would have been no mutiny if there had been more such battles, because

> It produced an entirely different spirit and an entirely different relationship between the officers and the men. . . . It never occurred to me that I should not participate. It was quite natural for me to execute the various motions that had been drilled into me and I am convinced, utterly convinced, that even Sachse [the intellectual leader of the 1917 movement] would have done the same.[104]

If it had been possible for the men to get into action occasionally, if leaves had come more regularly, and if some effort had been made to divert their attention from the deadening monotony of life in the fleet, even the officers' irresponsibility and caste spirit could not have undermined their healthy spirit.

ii

The Social and Political
Conflict in the Navy

After the Battle of Jutland the German fleet entered a prolonged, unrelieved, and exhausting period of inactivity. This lasted almost one and a half years, extending from June 1916 to the invasion of the Baltic islands of Dago, Moon, and Ösel in October 1917.[1] During this interval the High Seas Fleet was totally unable to affect the course of the war. Admiral Scheer admitted as much to the Kaiser in his report after the great battle.[2] The impotence of the surface fleet prompted the navy to shift its attention to its submarines. Submarine raids upon British shipping were intensified progressively until the beginning of 1917, when Germany fatefully embarked upon a campaign of unrestricted submarine warfare. The acceleration of U-boat activity relegated the High Seas fleet to the role of an auxiliary weapon. Its main task became the protection of submarines and the minesweepers that cleared channels for them out to the North Sea.[3] The great ships, themselves extremely susceptible to enemy submarine attacks and chance mines, proved inadequate even for this limited task. Admiral Galster insists that they were employed for this purpose principally to create the illusion "that they were not inactive, but that they were rendering a valuable service in the war." [4]

It was during this period of inactivity and monotony that the latent social and political conflict between the officers and enlisted men turned into a festering sore that was to erupt in mutiny during July and August, 1917. The three underlying causes for that mutiny—the increasingly unbearable harassment of the enlisted men by their officers, the outbreak of an acrimonious struggle between the crews and the officers for equitable rations, and a sharp and basic disagreement among them over Germany's domestic and foreign policy—can be traced back to this period of time. Their cumulative impact, however, was deferred until the summer of 1917.

Richard Stumpf, that astute sailor-diarist on board the *Helgoland*, was quick to sense the results of the navy's new strategy upon his shipmates. The men felt that they were wasting their time. They objected to everything, even the most reasonable measures and regulations. "Since we have such limited contact with the actual war," he noted, "we wage a sort of internal war among ourselves on the ship." [5]

There were ample causes for war. The men slaved and engaged in perpetual drill, but the officers sat about idle, cleaning and polishing their fingernails and combing their hair.[6] The difference in living conditions between the officers and the men was emphasized by their close proximity on the ships. The crews saw that their superiors ate better food, went ashore whenever they pleased, had special clubs for their entertainment, and enjoyed a much more liberal leave policy.[7] Since one class was given all the privileges while they were withheld from the other, the traditional social gulf in the German navy grew into a huge rift. In the close quarters of the battleships these inequities piled tension upon tension and created an explosive situation.

The officers' aloofness and unconcern for the mental and physical well-being of their men aided the process of alienation. After the war some of the more moderate officers admitted this. Freiherr von Forstner concedes that ambitious young officers occasionally were harsh toward their men, but quickly adds that this practice was frowned upon.[8] The suffering enlisted men, however, could not regard it so philosophically. Imagine the feeling of Stoker First Class Lürs of the *Prinzregent Luitpold*. Returning two days late from leave to attend his father's funeral, he was accosted by an officer who shouted, "And even if your mother, too, had drowned, you should have returned on time!" [9] This was by no means an isolated case. On the *Friedrich der Grosse* a sailor was denied leave to attend his mother's burial. Yet an entire division was kept up one whole night standing by to man a boat for an officer whose child was sick. When some of the crew members of that ship came back aboard slightly tipsy, they received three days' arrest. But an officer who returned roaring drunk was merely confined to quarters for a day.[10]

A few instances will serve to document the disparity of treatment between the enlisted men and the officers in terms of discipline and punishment. Seaman Calmus of the *Rheinland* was sentenced to four weeks of punitive drill for playing a prank on an officer. While serving his punishment on deck one day, he noticed a number of officers watching him with delight. Losing his temper, he shouted, "You people back aft gorge yourselves and get drunk while our kind has to drill for no reason!" To this the captain replied, "We don't care whether you drop dead or not. The main thing is the battle readiness of the ship. Men are immaterial; we can get as many as we need." For his outburst Calmus was locked up for three months.[11] Officers, however, were treated extremely leniently even for serious infractions. Kapitänleutnant Fünfstück, formerly executive officer on the light cruiser *Hamburg*, openly consorted with "two female persons" with whom an officer "cannot appear in public." Inviting these ladies to his quarters, he plied them with drink. A heated exchange of words ensued during which the unfortunate officer was repeatedly struck on the head with a stick by one of the females. For this Fünfstück received a mere warning.[12] On another occasion, Kapitänleutnant Kossack of the battle cruiser *Derfflinger* was found guilty of repeated sexual molestation of his men. The navy requested that he be dishonorably discharged. The Kaiser, however, regarded this too heavy a punishment and issued a mere warning.[13] On the other hand, Oberleutnant Polenz was severely reprimanded for allegedly harming the reputation of the officer corps by a "dishonorable friendship" with a subordinate and for revealing "intimate secrets" to an enlisted man.[14]

This sort of behavior was widespread. Yet in virtually all cases the officers were treated with great leniency, a fact that may well explain their misconduct throughout the war. At any rate, as late as October 1917 Admiral Bachmann, commander of the Baltic naval station at Kiel, still had cause to complain about the general conduct of his officers. Many of them were drunk upon leaving their officers' club on the Feldstrasse. They made noise on the streets "with loud singing, yelling and barking of naval and engine room orders and by holding footraces." "Women of questionable reputation" frequented the entrance of the club. The outraged citizens, disturbed in their sleep, responded by shouting curses and obscenities. The Admiral concluded that such behavior on the part of his officers was inexcusable and was "responsible for causing irreparable harm to the reputation of the officer corps." [15]

Not only on shore but also on the ships the officers undermined their own authority in this fashion. While their ship was anchored at Zeebrugge the officers of the light cruiser *Nürnberg* brought a number of prostitutes on board for a celebration. The enlisted men were ordered to wait on them and looked on as the girls were stripped and dressed in officers' uniforms. One of these parties became so raucous that the first officer spread some mustard on his naked behind and stuck it out of a porthole. Thereupon his colleagues shouted, "Look at our newest searchlight!" [16]

This incident is extreme. Yet the complaints of the crew, even by the standards of the Oberpräsident of the province of Schleswig-Holstein, "cannot be doubted in their truthfulness." [17] Thus the men in compartments 3, 4, and 5 of the *Nürnberg* were not allowed to run the ventilators in their stiflingly hot sleeping quarters "lest the monotonous humming" disturb the officers on the deck above. The disrespect of the officers for the sensibilities of their men went so far that on one occasion Leutnants Laurents and Köhler threw food at each other in full sight of their hungry crew.[18]

Inactive and bored, the officers manifested an almost incredible lack of restraint in their own behavior but refused to tolerate even the slightest infraction of the rules by the men. Life for the enlisted men became increasingly less tolerable. Very frequently they would deliberately overstay their leaves and go to prison simply to get away from their ships. One man, about to serve a stint in prison for such an offense, confided to Joachim Ringelnatz, "The officers are enjoying life. We do not serve the Fatherland but the officers." For once philosophical about his lot as an enlisted man, Ringelnatz thought, "How can one hold these young officers responsible for accepting what comforts were available during this dreadful time" and for living "after their own fashion and manner of thinking." [19]

Most of the men, however, were unable to muster such tolerance. They could not understand why their officers enjoyed extensive privileges while they were denied the most basic amenities. They might even have tolerated these one-sided privileges if they had been treated fairly and equitably. But even Admiral Scheer, commander of the High Seas Fleet, admits that "gross errors" were frequently made in the treatment of the men, especially in such matters as leaves, petitions, and complaints.[20]

It would be hard to exaggerate the ill will these errors generated. There was one sailor whose wife was due to have a baby on the last day of his leave. Dutifully, he wired for an extension of his leave, but he was turned down. And so the man had to return, leaving behind a dead wife, a dead baby, and a three-year-old child. Another man received three telegrams informing him that his wife was dying. Not until she was already dead was he granted leave to visit her.[21]

What made things worse was the callous response of the officers to the plight of their men. Actuated by caste spirit, the officers regarded their men as inferior beings, without rights and feelings, and treated them accordingly. All of the ships maintained a so-called reserve fund. Each payday the enlisted men each contributed ten pfennigs to aid the needy families of the crew. Thus if there was an illness in the family an enlisted man could apply for aid and would generally receive ten to twenty marks.

During the war the officers and their wives abused that fund in such a fashion that it became a major source for contention and class conflict. On the *König Albert* a petty officer applied for aid on behalf of his sick wife. It so happened that the captain's wife was in charge of the fund. At the fund's expense the exalted lady dispatched a representative from Berlin to travel to Frankfurt to examine the merits of the case. When she looked around and inquired about the wife's health, the lady investigator's eye fell upon a handsome wardrobe standing in the corner. With the words, "Why don't you sell the wardrobe? Then you'll have some money," she stalked out. A similar case took place on the *Prinzregent Luitpold*. A stoker requested help for his wife. An officer's lady paid a visit and stated, "Yes, my dear woman, we cannot help you. If you want some help, why don't you knit stockings for the officers' ladies?" [22]

Deck or warrant officers and petty officers were treated with equal disregard. Practically every officer, even if he served in a staff position, was eventually awarded some medal or other, most commonly the Iron Cross. However, petty officers, many of whom performed great feats of valor, particularly on small vulnerable craft such as submarines and torpedo boats which saw considerable action, were hardly ever considered worthy of such distinction.[23] Nor were they treated with respect by officers far junior to them in service or in age.[24] The older men found this especially galling. They resented seeing young boys coming aboard as raw cadets who soon became ensigns and lieutenants[25] and then proceeded to address older, married men with expressions such as "You camel humps and monkey faces!" or "Go away you pig! You stink, you beast!" [26]

Such ill treatment and lack of respect by their officers caused the men to develop deep and bitter hatred against the entire officer corps and the navy. One future mutineer, Johann Beckers, describes the feelings of his comrades on the *Prinzregent Luitpold*:

> The crew did much cursing, clenched its fists, but did nothing. However, some of us took this ill treatment very much to heart. For my own part, I burned it into my memory and was determined even then to defend myself . . . if an opportunity should ever present itself.[27]

By way of contrast, we have the views of a sailor who did not participate in the 1917 mutiny and who was not a socialist. Richard Stumpf of the battleship *Helgoland* was an ardent Catholic and a devout monarchist. He abhorred socialism, opposed the establishment of a parliamentary system of government in Germany, and classified himself as a "fanatic patriot." [28] Surprisingly enough, this conservative sailor reacted with even greater vehemence to the officers' unjust and arbitrary treatment. In February 1917 he wrote:

> Truly, if I still possessed even a shred of honor, I would have to jump at the scoundrel's throat. There may come a day when I shall lose control over myself. If it were not for my parents and relatives, I would long since have vented my wrath on one of these fellows who has done everything in his power to destroy my ideals, my love of the Fatherland and my sense of justice. The military system has accomplished what no book, no newspaper, and no Socialist could ever have done. I have learned to hate and despise its authority more than anything else in the world. This authority is not based on any

distinctive superiority, but relies solely on the fear of the paragraphs of the naval code of justice. August Bebel, for all your efforts on behalf of the poor, suppressed soldiers, I wish to thank you even in your grave.[29]

That this conservative, Catholic sailor should invoke the name of August Bebel, one of the founders and leaders of German Social Democracy, reveals the revolutionary changes that such ill treatment could engender. Only the most bitter humiliation and discrimination could drive so loyal a man as Stumpf to utter these words. How much more radical then was the effect of these abuses upon the men who had been raised in the socialist, antimilitaristic tradition!

As if these things had not been enough to embitter the men, a cause of even greater potency was added to the deteriorating condition of the German High Seas fleet during the winter of 1916–17 in the form of a great food shortage. The poor weather during the summer of 1916 had produced a meager harvest for Germany. The onset of an unusually cold autumn with freezing temperatures, the prelude of an even severer winter, had blighted the crucial potato harvest. This plus the impossibility of making up the resulting food deficit through extensive imports, because of the ever tightening British blockade, produced the so-called turnip winter of 1916–17, during which the staple item for the German population became the lowly turnip. In the navy this situation resulted in a drastic curtailment of rations. To their previous resentment the enlisted men now added the horrors of hunger and starvation.

If the officers had shared this hunger and privation with the men, common suffering might have improved their relationship and ameliorated the class conflict. But the class-conscious and caste-ridden German naval officer corps refused to avail itself of this opportunity. Instead it aggravated the conflict. Insisting on their privileges and determined to maintain their superiority over the men, the officers allowed a revolutionary situation to arise in the fleet by their stubborn maintenance of unequal rations.

After the war German naval officers tried very hard to persuade the nation that they were not responsible for the mutinies and that they never gave the men cause to rebel. They attempted to show that the food in the navy was adequate even during the catastrophic turnip winter of 1916–17 and that they were no better fed than the men.[30]

Even a cursory glance at the records is enough to disprove this contention. As early as June 20, 1916, Admiral von Krosigk, chief of the Wilhelmshaven naval station, ordered a reduction in potato rations to 1,500 grams (slightly more than 3 pounds) a week per man. He recommended using substitutes such as packaged and dehydrated vegetables.[31] Six months later, when the food shortage was at its worst, von Batocki, the War Food Commissioner, ordered Admiral von Capelle, the Secretary of the Navy, to cut rations once more. Sloughing off any possible argument, Batocki admonished Capelle to forget his peacetime conceptions of the men's food requirements.[32] Nevertheless, on December 21, 1916, the navy's liaison officer with the War Food Office, Kapitän Schramm, objected that rations in the navy had reached the lowest permissible point. No further reduction was possible. In fact, the navy had found that certain categories of enlisted men, especially heavy laborers such as stokers, "had collapsed before their furnaces" and therefore had to be issued extra rations.[33]

Despite admissions of this sort, which must have been circulated in the navy, certain officers contend that the enlisted men ate better than the civilian population of Germany, that they received more food than heavy laborers, and that only during the turnip winter did their diet become somewhat "skimpy and monotonous." [34] Admiral von Trotha carried this line of argument even further by asserting that the men enjoyed an adequate diet in comparison to the civilian population and than they actually often ate better than their officers.[35] He even went to the trouble of publishing statistics to substantiate his point. Comparing the diet of the crew of the *Markgraf* with that of the citizens of the city of Dresden for the week of August 6 to August 12, 1916, von Trotha concluded that the sailors were immeasurably better off.

Markgraf		Dresden	
Meat (fresh and		Meat with bones	125 grams
preserved) . . .	1170 grams		
Bread, cereals and		Bread and cereals	2999.5 grams
rice	4270 grams		
Butter and fat . . .	150 grams	Butter and fat .	62.5 grams
Cheese	70 grams	Cheese	16 grams
Fresh potatoes . . .	1500 grams	Potatoes . . .	1500 grams
Dehydrated potatoes	135 grams		
Peas	300 grams	Peas	62.5 grams
Dehydrated		Turnips . . .	25 grams
vegetables . . .	80 grams		
Fresh white cabbage	1000 grams		
Sauerkraut	250 grams		
Dehydrated fruit . .	200 grams		
Sugar	310 grams	Sugar	187 grams
Marmalade and		Syrup and	
artificial honey . .	575 grams	artificial honey	112.5 grams[36]

Unfortunately, the admiral's figures do not cover the crucial period of the turnip winter of 1916–17. Furthermore, his figures neglect mentioning the existence of a black market. This enabled the more prosperous citizens of the town to acquire extra food by illegal means. But because of their meager salaries, the enlisted men could hardly avail themselves of such food.

More moderate officers, such as Freiherr von Forstner, concede that the men's food "left something to be desired" at this time.[37] The stokers in particular were susceptible to a debilitating insufficiency of food. For their arduous labors in the engine room they were normally provided special rations of fat or sausage. But frequently, this supplementary ration was either not issued or arbitrarily diminished. Hence when they worked in hot weather they often "fell down like flies" from exhaustion and heat prostration.[38] Even men who worked far less strenuously than the stokers were affected by inadequate rations. Ringelnatz complains that he always ate stews with nothing solid to chew. His teeth became brittle. Most of the men were undernourished and reported to sick bay with great regularity.[39] Even Stumpf, whose patriotism ordinarily made him avoid such mundane complaints, had to protest the lack of nutrition in his diet, the poor taste of the food, and its extreme monotony. The men of the High Seas Fleet were most commonly served a concoction called *Drahtverhau* (literally, chopped barbed wire). Stumpf states it was composed of 75 percent water, 10 percent *Oldenburger* (sausage), 3 percent potatoes, 2 percent peas, one percent yellow turnips, one half percent beef, one half percent vinegar, one quarter percent fat, while on top there floated something which defied analysis but the mere sight of which turned one's stomach.[40]

The men's food may be characterized as barely sufficient to sustain normal activity, lacking in bulk and variety, totally unappetizing. But many naval officers insisted that the only difference between their rations and those of the men was the method of preparation. Since the officers' meals were prepared in a separate kitchen in small quantities, they could be cooked with greater care and therefore looked more attractive. The men were convinced, however, that their officers ate much better than they.[41] Their empty stomachs would not have troubled them half so much had they known that they were not alone in their suffering and that their superiors shared their sacrifice. Before the Reichstag Investigating Committee, Willi Weber, one of the leading figures of the 1917 mutiny, summed up the men's feelings on that point by stating, "If our stomachs had been full or if we had seen that everything was the same [for the officers and the men], then it would never have come to disorders. Then no investigating committee would be deliberating about these questions at this time." [42] In short, the crews were not merely discontented because they were hungry, but rather because they were hungry while their officers went around well fed.

Undeniably, there were major differences in rations between the officers and enlisted men. Naval regulations stipulated that each enlisted man was entitled to 1.32 marks worth of food per day. Officers, on the other hand, received 3.65 marks for their mess expenses, of which 2.15 marks was usually spent on food while the rest went for drink, occasional banquets, and other expenses. Nevertheless it is plain that they received nearly twice as much money for food as their men. Even when the men's food allowance was raised to 1.75 marks per day in the fall of 1917, there remained a sizable difference.[43] Moreover, not all of the men's food allowance was actually spent on food. Frequently the cooks were ordered to save 10 percent of this amount. According to Ringelnatz, who made a careful study of food prices, the men could have fared reasonably well had they been given their food allowance in cash. The men never saw their money, however. All they ever got, week after week, was the same unnutritious and unappetizing *Drahtverhau*.[44]

Even more demoralizing for the sailors and stokers was that their officers maintained their own separate kitchens. In fact, on some of the larger ships there were three separate kitchens, one for the men, one for the officers, and one for the deck officers.[45] Even so staunch a defender of the officers corps as Admiral von Trotha concedes that the high morale and lack of revolutionary activity among the men who served on torpedo boats, patrol boats, and trawlers might be attributed to the fact that their officers, in addition to being exposed to the same dangers as the men, shared a common kitchen and ate the same food as the crew.[46]

The existence of separate kitchens in the High Seas Fleet gave rise to many abuses, inequities, and raised a host of suspicions. It stands to reason that the small officers' galleys could prepare more appetizing food than the huge galleys that served thousands of men. The officers also enjoyed a much more varied diet because it was easier to purchase food in small amounts. More importantly, however, the small officers' mess could serve certain kinds of foods that the men hardly ever saw. The classic example of this is eggs. Von Trotha informs us that the cooks on the *Friedrich der Grosse* tried to prepare eggs for a crew of 1,200 men. The men refused to eat the eggs and threw them out. Maybe, the admiral adds, because they were "no longer quite fresh." Nevertheless eggs were a frequent food for the officers. "Yet fried eggs," von Trotha states, "when carried across the deck, had a distinctly provoking effect on the crew and dockyard workers." [47]

The disparity in rations widened the gulf between the officers and the men and brought the class conflict in the navy to its most dangerous phase, the struggle for the full stomach. It was almost inevitable that the hungry men believed that a large part of the food which their officers consumed so conspicuously came from their own rations. On the *Hindenburg*, for example, the crew suspected their officers of having made off with a donation of 2,400 eggs and several hundred pounds of bacon.[48] As late as 1918, after this situation had supposedly been corrected as a result of the August 1917 mutiny, the crew of the *Nürnberg* presented a detailed memorandum accusing the officers of stealing rations. The men maintained that the commander of the ship, Fregattenkapitän Quaet Faslem, had a loaf of bread delivered to his quarters on shore each day. They also alleged that he took from the ship's larder two pounds of sausage, one pound of butter, one pound of sugar, two pounds of ham, a one pound box of sardines, and a five pound can of meat. On the same day, First Officer Lerche stole five pounds of butter, five pounds of bockwurst, one pound of sugar, and ten eggs. Two days later he took five pounds of meat, and on April 28 a cake of an "approximate circumference of 40.60 centimeters." [49]

Many men must have suspected, when they saw food of peacetime proportions and quality carried into the officers' mess that "these good rations . . . could not be quite possible without a diminution of the crew's rations." [50] Regardless of the origins of this food, they had ample opportunity to observe that their officers were not starving and on occasion even squandered and wasted precious food right before their eyes. Johann Beckers reports that on the *Stettin* the officers held many banquets. When they got drunk they would break out with the song "Deutschland, Deutschland über Alles" and throw sandwiches against the wall." [51] Even without such waste, Beckers is convinced that "the smell of roasting [meat] coming from the officers' galley heightened, indeed cultivated, the entire crew's longing for peace." [52]

Joachim Ringelnatz, one of the few enlisted men in the German navy who made the transition to officer, has left a stirring record of his experiences during these times. As an enlisted man he had gone hungry much of the time and had grown to hate his life in the navy. All of this changed when he was promoted. Every two weeks he was given a chance to buy coffee, cheese, sugar, oatmeal, beans, peas, and other "rare commodities" and had enough food left over to send home to his relatives. Even while availing himself of this new prerogative, he felt ashamed before the men who witnessed this privilege and preferential treatment.[53]

It is quite possible that the men would have complained less about their rations if their time could have been kept occupied with useful activity. However, by 1916–17 the commanders, realizing that their crews could not work efficiently on their meager rations, tried to conserve their strength by drastically reducing the amount of time formerly spent on drill and calisthenics.[54] But this new leisure was by no means a blessing because it aggravated the men's boredom. This fed their perpetual hunger and made them spend their days in grumbling and muttering. Seaman Crisper, formerly of the *Friedrich der Grosse*, testified that he felt so hungry most of the time because he was bored. He found, however, that his ravenous hunger disappeared when he was transferred to the naval infantry brigade in Flanders. Even though his rations were no better there, he was kept busy by the fighting. He no longer felt so bored, and consequently his hunger pangs vanished.[55] Still another result of the drastic deterioration of the food situation in the navy was the relaxation of discipline. Time

formerly spent on infantry drill and rifle practice was greatly cur-
tailed throughout the long turnip winter. Most importantly, the
stringent observance of all the rules and regulations was frequently suspended. The officers accustomed themselves to the
men's grumbling and disaffected demeanor and accepted it as normal.

It was almost inevitable that news about abuses, particularly
those concerning the buying and taking of food by officers,
should leak out to the civilian population.[56] On July 23, 1917, Admiral Capelle worriedly wrote Scheer that it was rumored in the
Reichstag that officers "were taking large quantities of food off
the ships to provide for their families and that donations to the
[enlisted men's] canteens were being sold." [57] Surprisingly, the
commander of the High Seas Fleet did not deny the charge, in
effect conceding that it was true. Moreover, in the characteristic
fashion of the officer corps, he also did nothing constructive to
correct the situation. Nonchalantly, Scheer commanded that an
order prohibiting such practices be read to the officers every
three months and warned mildly that "if this improper exploitation" continued he would be forced to forbid altogether the taking of food from the ships.[58] Even after a mutiny had indicated to
what an extent the disparity in rations had alienated and radicalized the enlisted men, Scheer still found it necessary to admonish
his officers in October 1917 that they were to avoid giving the
impression that they ate significantly better than their men.[59]

It is clear that the unequal distribution of rations in 1916–17
constituted a very serious problem which was consistently ignored by the responsible officers. As a result, the navy's belated
denials on that score ring hollow and unconvincing. Let us take
the case of the *Prinzregent Luitpold*. A few days after the 1917
mutiny had broken out on his ship Captain von Hornhardt submitted a report on the food situation. In an attempt to minimize
any differences and inequalities in the matter of food, Hornhardt
insisted that his had been the first ship to institute rationing for

officers. He maintained that meals in the officers' mess were very brief. There had been no banquets since 1916. His officers had not even used up their ration of a 100 liters of beer during the month of July. Much more revealing than this line of protest is the record of the officers' menu for the week of July 30 to August 4, 1917. It indicated that they did not fare badly at all.

For Sunday lunch they had two slices of roast pork, peas and carrots, three potatoes. For dessert they had cherries. At dinner that day they had 50 grams of cold cuts, cucumber salad, and two slices of cheese.

Lunch on Monday consisted of soup with noodles, two slices of boiled beef, beans, and dehydrated potatoes. Currants were the dessert. At supper they had dehydrated vegetables and soft cheese.

On Tuesday they ate barley soup, boiled sausages, puree of peas, and sauerkraut plus three pears for lunch. Two slices of ham, two slices of cheese, and cucumber salad made up their supper.

Wednesday's lunch consisted of soup, two slices of beef, cabbage, dehydrated potatoes, and fruit. For supper they ate three slices of jellied meat and two slices of cheese.

On Thursday they were served pea soup, two slices of tripe, turnips, and dehydrated potatoes. No dessert is listed. In the evening they had eggs with left-over rice and curry sauce and 50 grams of cold cuts.

On Friday lunch consisted of their version of *Drahtverhau*, soup cooked with beef and dehydrated potatoes. There was fruit for dessert. At supper they had one pork cutlet and two slices of cheese.

The last day of the week, Saturday, they were given soup, three slices of meatloaf with white cabbage, and dehydrated potatoes. Dessert consisted of baked plums. Supper was comprised of the usual 50 grams of cold cuts and two slices of cheese. For their daily breakfast the officers were served coffee, 10 grams of butter, and marmalade. On Sundays and Thursdays they received a supplemental ration of a tomato or three slices of sausage and 10 grams of butter.

All in all, the officers' menu was not luxurious. Certainly it did not equal their peacetime diet. But it was more than adequate, despite the overemphasis on dehydrated potatoes. However, there were some compensations. Hornhardt reports that each officer was issued eight bottles of wine that week.[60]

By way of contrast, even by Captain von Hornhardt's description, the men were infinitely worse off. They ate their meal (and it usually was only one meal) consisting of one liter of *Drahtverhau* readily and generally asked for more. Still they complained that they were hungry, especially in the evening, and stated that they did not get enough bread. Even the occasional distribution of soup, sausage, or cheese did not satisfy them.

The cause for the men's hunger becomes apparent when one examines their menu for the week of August 5 to August 11 and compares it with the officers' meals. For some reason Hornhardt did not report the men's menu for the same week as that of the officers, but gave that for the week following the mutiny, from August 5 to August 11. On Sunday the men were issued soup, goulash with macaroni, and fruitcup. In the evening they received coffee.

On Monday they got plums and dumplings. That evening they were given hard-tack soup. On Tuesday morning, when the ship took on coal, they were issued barley groats in the morning. At noon they ate peas and meat, and for their evening meal received some cooked sausage. Wednesday's meal consisted of beans with pork and beer. In the evening the men were given an egg each.

Fresh bone soup with noodles, Königsberger Klops (meat balls), and potatoes constituted their rations for Thursday. On Friday they were again issued plums and dumplings and on Saturday dehydrated vegetables and gelatin.[61]

Even more galling to the men than this glaring disparity in rations was the officers' reaction to their hunger. Blinded by *Kas-*

tengeist, the officers simply could not understand the men's resentment and complaints. Instead of paying attention to their grumbling, the officers disregarded the symptoms of impending unrest and insisted on the retention of their privileges. At the same time they frequently ignored the obligations that went along with these privileges.

Naval regulations stipulated that the captain, the first officer, and the ship's doctor were to conduct a daily *Essenprobe* (food test) of the men's rations.[62] Most of the time the officers did not regard this obligation as serious enough to warrant their attention and allowed their quartermasters and cooks a free hand with the men's food. The actions of Korvettenkapitän Herzbruch, at that time first officer of the *Helgoland*, might serve as an illustration of the officers' attitude. In January 1917 one of the cooks presented Herzbruch with a meal for inspection. Herzbruch responded by shouting, "Go to hell and don't bother me again with this stuff. . . . I don't want my appetite ruined every day!!!" [63]

Officers such as Kapitän Langemak of the *Thüringen*, who discerned the close relationship between food and morale, must have been rare in the navy. His is the only recorded instance of a commander to press formal charges against a subordinate for ignoring the men's food. He castigated his quartermaster by stating, "It has come to my attention that you take insufficient interest in the rations and welfare of the crew and do not provide for sufficient variety [of foods]. This is what is responsible for the low state of morale among the men." [64]

Unfortunately, on most ships the captain was not nearly so perspicacious and watchful. For instance, when the enlisted men of the *Nürnberg* lodged a complaint that they were starving while their officers ate five-course meals, their first officer, Leutnant Beelitz, retorted:

> Today some men stepped forward requesting more bread. There is no more bread. Therefore you will have to go hungry. In case one of you should starve to death, I shall be only too glad to have him buried with full honors. . . .[65]

Such instances were by no means confined to a few ships. On virtually every vessel of the High Seas Fleet such cases occurred with alarming frequency. Thus the captain of the *Moltke* is alleged to have told his men that "the food is still too good. Hardtack and salt water would be good enough." [66] Captain Fuchs of the *Friedrich der Grosse* is said to have told his crew to "eat stones instead of bread," [67] while one of the officers on the *Berlin* exclaimed while stalking through the crew's quarters at meal time, "Here this band of whores is eating once again." [68]

Even when the officers did not openly insult the men, they frequently treated them with almost inhuman unconcern. When the crew of the *Helgoland* complained that the potatoes they were given were inedible because they had frozen and were rotting, the first officer proclaimed, "Men, I demand that you respect your First Officer's time and that you cease complaining about matters which he cannot remedy. If you do not like the potatoes this way —then don't eat them! If anyone complains again, I shall have him locked up!" [69]

It is very difficult to understand how the officers could behave this way. Did they not realize that they were goading the men beyond human endurance and undermining their morale and loyalty? Were they not aware that conditions were very different in other navies and that the American officers had voluntarily given up their own kitchens when their country entered the war? Did they not know that the food in the British navy was much better and that its officers observed strict rationing and ate no better than their subordinates.[70]

The German officers corps was not so blind that it was unaware of this. A few officers even admitted that the maintenance of such inequalities was bad. However, hardly any of them figured these inequalities might eventually contribute to the outbreak of an enlisted men's rebellion in the fleet. One officer belatedly exclaimed, "Who would have thought of it!" [71] Even those who thought of it did very little. Admiral Behncke admits that it would have been "correct" if the officers and the men had eaten the same food,[72] while Admiral Trotha states that the possibility of abolishing separate food allowances and adopting a system of central food purchasing and feeding was considered in 1917 by the naval authorities. It was decided, however, that this would create difficulties for the smaller vessels.[73] It is difficult to believe that the navy could allow such a disastrous deterioration of the men's standard of living to take place simply for the sake of bureaucratic uniformity.

Actually, the real reason is quite simple. The German naval officers, throughout the war, were engaged in a struggle to preserve their status, their special privileges, and to assert and enhance their superiority over their subordinates. Therefore they felt it inconsistent with their honor to lower themselves to the men's level, to yield to their demands, or to heed the dictates of reason. They clung tenaciously to their caste privileges and gambled on the men's fear and sense of obedience to avert trouble.[74] One astute former officer describes why his colleagues behaved the way they did and why they refused to give in on this issue:

> No one will deny that the officers did not know how to die for their country . . . But they did not know how to live for it and and make sacrifices for it. There was so much carousing that I could not bear it. While such festivities were going on I would usually volunteer for duty. They took place in full view of the crew. The consequences were inevitable. Once when I proposed (after the events of 1917) that our mess agree to eat the [same] rations as the men, only one other person agreed. It was the general consensus that this would constitute a cowardly retreat before the crew. This is what I call lack of patriotism and outright stupidity.[75]

Antagonized by starvation rations, ill treatment, and glaring inequalities, the sailors and stokers grew to detest and despise their officers during the long winter of 1916–17. It is unlikely, however, that they would have resorted to a rebellion even under these circumstances if they had not been goaded beyond the limits of their endurance by the politics of the officer corps.

After more than two years of war, the men became increasingly war-weary. Having lost hope of a quick decision on the battlefields, and plagued by all sorts of deprivation, many of them felt that the time had come to end the war by means of a negotiated settlement. This feeling was not shared by the officers. They wanted the fight to continue until Germany won an undisputed victory over her enemies, and they urged their men to hold on. Thus arose a political rift of major proportions that was to play a prominent role in the spring of 1917 in causing the men to band together to resist their superiors.

From the very beginning of the peace debate in Germany, the enlisted men regarded their officers' desire to continue the war as an unscrupulous attempt to perpetuate their privileges and to exploit them. Writing as early as November 1916, Stumpf described his alienation from the officers and their policies:

. . . My hatred for the navy keeps growing. I now realize better than ever before, how stupid we really are to do all the work while those who merely look on get all the pay. We live in an unjust and evil world. Should the opportunity ever arise, I will be only too happy to make it better. Damn the officers! Never again shall they be allowed to drag us into a war! Let them either practice some honorable profession or drop dead! They shall no longer earn a living from our stupidity and grow fat on our money.[76]

Sensing the rising tide of war-weariness, pessimism, and defeatism that swept through not only the enlisted ranks but the entire nation, Germany's military leaders, especially the newly appointed Supreme Command of the Army, consisting of Field-marshal Paul von Hindenburg and First Quartermaster General Erich Ludendorff, became determined to win a quick victory at any cost. The leaders of the German military establishment knew that the war constituted the supreme test not only of the army and navy but also of the political system that enabled them to wield such inordinate power within the state. If they lost the war or merely achieved a return of the former status quo, their power and preeminence would soon vanish. For them the war therefore became a last means of averting the imminent and dreaded advent of a "democratic flood." The Chief of the German General Staff Hindenburg, resented the demand of the lower classes, expressed in the Reichstag by their representatives, that Germany liberalize her political institutions as a reward for their sacrifice and loyalty. He denied that the war had given Germany any reason to make democratic reforms that might upset the traditional order of the state with its "discipline and work." [77]

While Hindenburg merely harbored a strong antidemocratic bias, his ambitious and able assistant General Ludendorff was much more actively engaged in the struggle against democracy. Hiding behind Hindenburg's immense prestige and popularity, he made it his personal mission to thwart the reformers. Ludendorff realized that the almost unlimited power of the officers corps could not be preserved in a democratic state. Consequently, he adhored the very thought of reform and developed an intense hatred for Chancellor von Bethmann-Hollweg. Outraged by Bethmann-Hollweg's vague promises of constitutional reform and his inability to hold the leftist political parties in check, Ludendorff ultimately became convinced that the chancellor would have to be dismissed lest he undermine the very foundations of the German Empire and the army.[78]

The naval officer corps fully shared these views. Grand Admiral von Tirpitz, for example, publicly stated that he was "convinced from the beginning of the war, that a defeat in the war would almost inevitably be followed by revolution." [79] Tirpitz and his colleagues feared that the war was lost if Germany could not succeed in exacting huge territorial and financial compensations from her enemies. Both army and navy officers therefore advocated using the most ruthless weapons to gain the victory needed to preserve their power. Thinking almost exclusively in military and class terms, Germany's military leaders in the fall of 1916 hit upon the idea of ending the war quickly by a campaign of unrestricted submarine warfare against England.

Paradoxically, the staunchest advocate of this policy was the navy. Since the outbreak of the war the number of German submarines had not grown appreciably. For a blockade of the entire coast of Great Britain the German navy had at its disposal a mere 103 U-boats. Only a third of these could be used at any given time.[80] Yet the Admiralty and especially the Chief of the Admiralty Staff, Admiral von Holtzendorff, broadcast a guarantee that England could be brought to her knees within six months.[81] Thus persuaded, Hindenburg and Ludendorff rode rough-shod over the objections of Bethmann-Hollweg's civilian government and in January 1917 convinced the Kaiser to launch on February 1 a most fateful campaign of unrestricted submarine warfare.[82]

Riding high on the crest of their victory in the submarine issue, the military became increasingly political, allying themselves closer than ever before with the conservative ruling classes of the Junkers and industrialists. These two groups enthusiastically supported annexations of enemy territory and tenaciously resisted any domestic reform.[83] In this fashion and by denying the lower classes the reforms they so ardently desired, the Conservatives and their military partners disrupted the political party truce, the *Burgfrieden*, that had been concluded in August of 1914. The Social Democrats (the SPD), the Progressives, and the left wings of the Center and the National Liberals retaliated by raising the demand for the immediate reform of Germany's undemocratic political institutions and the negotiation of a moderate peace. Amidst mounting bitterness, a great political battle broke loose in Germany in the spring of 1917.

Thus began the succession of events which saw the army increasingly embroiled in domestic politics and using its power and prestige for purely political ends. The army formed the vanguard of the opposition to the reform of the inequitous three-class franchise system of Prussia. It opposed with determination the attempt of the reformers to establish ministerial responsibility and parliamentary government. And above all, in July 1917, it fought a bitter battle to prevent the Reichstag majority composed of the

SPD, the Progressives, and the left wings of the Center and National Liberal Party, from passing its Peace Resolution calling for the immediate conclusion of a peace without territorial annexations and indemnities.

Germany's military leaders, both in the army and navy, possessed a number of outstanding qualities. They were well endowed with courage, with tenacity, with technical proficiency; but as politicians and as a ruling group they lacked some essential characteristics. They had never learned the art of judging the popular temperament and of making timely concessions, especially when their own political and social status was at stake.

Generals Hindenburg and Ludendorff proved unable to compromise with the left. For that reason they regarded each of Chancellor von Bethmann-Hollweg's steps in the direction of reform as a sign of weakness and cowardice. When Bethmann succeeded in persuading the Kaiser to issue his April 1917 Easter Message promising his Prussian subjects a liberalization of their franchise, Ludendorff regarded this timely step as a mere "kowtow to the Russian Revolution," and he refused to give it his endorsement. Even more tragically, the Supreme Command construed the Reichstag Peace Resolution of July 1917 as a grave threat to the army. Blaming Bethmann-Hollweg for the passage of the Peace Resolution, the two generals intervened decisively. They presented Wilhelm II with an ultimatum demanding Bethmann's dismissal. Having thus succeeded in ridding themselves of the chancellor, they were instrumental in appointing as his successor the incompetent but safely conservative Georg Michaelis, who became their tool in the fight against the democrats and the supporters of a negotiated peace.

Just as the army lacked understanding for the feelings of the people, so did the navy fail to fathom the psychology of its enlisted men. Though the navy must have been aware that a large percentage of its enlisted men were Social Democrats and that an even larger number came from the working classes, it consistently opposed all proposals for political reform. Instead of placating the men by indicating that they would not block a gradual liberalization, the officers subjected them to venomous harangues against socialism, reform, and the Peace Resolution. Both by word and deed the naval officers thus heaped fuel on the men's discontent. In short, the naval officer was as short-sighted as his counterpart in the army and as stubborn in his refusal to make the sort of concessions that might have gained him the good will of his subordinates.

As a result, the stokers and sailors of the navy came to identify more and more closely with the working classes and to adopt their political program. Just like the workers, many enlisted men were shocked by the way the wealthy classes mocked the hungry poor people by blatant displays of wealth during their winter of starvation. Stumpf, for instance, was scandalized that the stores of Kiel and Wilhelmshaven openly offered for sale expensive delicacies that only the rich could afford but which incited the poor to "class hatred." [84]

Through their close contact with the civilian population of the port towns the sailors and stokers gained considerable sympathy for the plight of the working class. Their feelings of unity with that class were heightened when they were put to work in the naval shipyards at a paltry hourly salary of 10 pfennigs. There they came in touch with the highly skilled and organized workers and could not help but absorb some of their political views.[85] They came to feel that they, too, were "workers rather than soldiers." [86]

In their despair the sailors and stokers increasingly turned to pacifism. Among the literature most in demand by the crew of the *Friedrich der Grosse* were Bertha von Suttner's *Die Waffen nieder* and other pacifist writings.[87] Moreover, the men were realistic enough to understand that the highly publicized submarine campaign was not having its desired effect and would not bring the war to a rapid close. Rejecting the navy's official propaganda, they contemptuously termed it "the swindle of the submarine campaign." [88]

Discouraged, dejected, and extremely war-weary, the sailors and stokers of the High Seas Fleet welcomed the news of the outbreak of the March 1917 Revolution in Russia. Not only did the revolution engender hopes for an early peace, but it also enhanced the possibilities that German domestic reform would now proceed at an accelerated pace. Contrary to the assertions of the communists, the Revolution did not encourage the German sailors to attempt to emulate the Russian peasants and soldiers.[89]

The Russian Revolution had a much subtler effect.[90] It intensified the men's longing for peace and their desire for political reform at home.[91] Thus Ringelnatz exclaimed, "Oh, how I wish the war were finally over! For my part I would not care if we suffered a great defeat if it would only help us to obtain a halfway acceptable peace." [92] More politically aware personalities, such as Stumpf, actually feared a great victory, because it might serve to fortify the regime in Germany, as had the wars of 1813 and 1866 for Prussia.[93] At any rate, it is quite clear that after March 1917 the enlisted men in the navy began to develop interest in Germany's foreign and domestic policies and increasingly supported the program of the Social Democrats. It was this identification and the feeling that the SPD represented the little man that caused the crew of the *Helgoland* to announce support of a program calling for the immediate conclusion of peace, the demobilization of the army and the navy, and the appointment of the Socialist Philipp Scheidemann as chancellor and the radical Spartacist Karl Liebknecht as minister of war.[94]

Some of the more radical men criticized the gradualist and slow approach of the SPD and turned their hopes to a newly founded splinter group of that party, the Independent Social Democratic Party (USPD). Basically, the Independent Socialists did not differ greatly either in aims or methods from the Majority Socialists, the parent party. As their founding congress at Gotha in April 1917 indicated, the Independent Socialists wanted to retain parliamentary methods and emphatically rejected a revolutionary course. Their disagreement with the Majority and the reason for their split with it centered on conflicting attitudes toward the war. While the Majority endorsed the war and supported it by voting credits in the Reichstag, the Independents viewed it as an imperialistic venture not deserving the support of the German proletariat. In domestic affairs the USPD refused to adhere to the *Burgfrieden*. Hence it was in a position to shout louder and more demandingly for reform, both in the Reichstag and in its principal journal, the *Leipziger Volkszeitung*.

It was only natural that some of the more impatient sailors and stokers should prefer to turn to this party and that they should seek information about the true course of the war and politics in the pages of this newspaper. The *Leipziger Volkszeitung*'s strident criticisms of the ruling classes conformed to their own experiences and coincided with their own "hatred and thoughts of revenge against the existing authorities and their most immediate representative, the officers." [95] Actually, it hardly mattered whether or not the men read this paper. Right in the navy, on their own ships, there was provocation enough for them to develop an abiding hatred for their officers and the conservative ruling class of the nation.

The German navy, like the army, pursued grandiose dreams of annexations and assiduously sought to convert the men to support its foreign policy. On May 18, 1917, the Admiralty presented its territorial demands to the government. In the Atlantic the navy wanted to annex a part of the Azores and the African port of Dakar. In the Mediterranean it wanted to obtain possession of the Albanian port of Valona while in the Pacific it demanded New Caledonia and the right to establish stations on a number of French and English islands.[96]

In order to realize these ambitions, the German navy had even before the outbreak of the war formed close bonds with the Pan-German League, the Colonial Society, the Navy League, and a host of similar nationalistic and expansionist organizations. In return for their support the navy encouraged the dissemination of their propaganda and literature among the enlisted ranks and gave official sanction to their conservative political program. "The exaggerated nationalism of the Pan-German press and its support by the officer corps," according to Admiral Galster, "brought great harm to the navy and the German people." [97]

Although it is an established fact that most naval officers endorsed and worked for the highly political Pan-German program, after the war they claimed that they had been entirely apolitical and that they "were unfamiliar with questions of party struggles and domestic politics." [98] As devout nationalists and confirmed conservatives, most officers saw nothing wrong with the demands of the Pan-German League. Admittedly, Admirals Scheer, Hipper, and Trotha were never "politically active personalities" in the usual sense of the term. Yet their nationalism and conservatism prompted them to pursue the most political goals.[99] They took it for granted that the nationalist program of the Pan-Germans was properly patriotic and that their own attempts to indoctrinate the men in its spirit were innocent. For that reason they considered it in the best interest of the navy to attack proposals for reform; they did not wish to be placed at the mercy of an international-minded and possibly socialist legislature. As Trotha put it so ingenuously in his defense of the officer corps,

> We knew that we had nothing to do with politics. . . . Thus we undoubtedly paid too little and amateurish attention to the forces at work among the people . . . We did not know how to deal with these questions as they appeared on the ships. Our eyes had been trained exclusively for the service and our view was directed solely at the war.[100]

With this line of reasoning von Trotha and his fellow officers could well maintain that they were unpolitical, that they never spread Pan-German propaganda, and that they consistently sought to avoid political issues.[101]

All the evidence, however, points to the opposite conclusion. Virtually all the officers who gave lectures were oriented in a Pan-German and annexationist direction. Most often the officer in charge of public information, usually a very young and inexperienced officer, would seize on any convenient piece of literature and read it to the men or lecture to them on it. Since the reading of most officers was largely confined to annexationist, Pan-German newspapers such as the *Deutsche Tageszeitung*, the *Tägliche Rundschau*, the *Deutsche Zeitung*, and the *Kieler Neuesten Nachrichten*,[102] their instruction was bound to contain heavy doses of political propaganda.

These practices were in keeping with the official guidelines for instructing enlisted men. In July 1917 General Ludendorff issued an order for the establishment of *Vaterländischer Unterricht*, patriotic instruction. He insisted in this directive that "Idle talk of peace, just like pessimism, will prolong the war," and maintained that the men must be taught to reject the enemy's attempts to deprive Germany of the fruits of her victories "through peace negotiations."[103] Joachim Ringelnatz, who had recently been promoted and was now an officer, reports that he was under secret orders "to hammer hate into the men" against all of Germany's foes but especially against America.[104]

Emil Alboldt, a former deck officer and a postwar Secretary of the Navy, observes that when the *Vaterländischer Unterricht* was finally instituted officially in the navy in the fall of 1917, it was such a crude and obvious attempt at indoctrination that it was derisively called "four to five o'clock love of the Fatherland," and that it repelled and demoralized even the most loyal enlisted men.[105]

In addition to propagandizing annexations, naval and army officers frequently subjected the Reichstag and particularly reformist deputies who favored a negotiated peace to the most scathing denunciations.[106] One prominent officer, Admiral Hopmann, said of the Reichstag's Peace Resolution that "it was and remains a fateful admission of weakness which the head of the government should have beaten to death with a cudgel when it first made its appearance."[107]

Many naval officers regarded the July 1917 Peace Resolution

and Chancellor von Bethmann-Hollweg's flirtation with its advocates as an act of treason. Making no effort to hide their feelings, they declared that they would welcome Bethmann's dismissal and the assumption of power by a strong man such as Admiral Tirpitz or Fieldmarshal Hindenburg.[108] Also bitterly opposed by the officers were the Reichstag's strivings for political reform and democratic change. A pamphlet entitled "World Democracy" bearing the heading "for official use only," which circulated in the armed forces in 1917, slandered the reformers by asserting that "those who do not stop the democratic and international efforts at the threshhold are working for the enemy, they are not working for true freedom and equality but for the interests of an international band of swindlers." [109]

Occasionally the officers enlisted outside help to aid them in their political indoctrination. The *Helgoland* was frequently visited by Pastor Felten from Bremen who lectured on the virtues of the military, the necessity of annexations, and other related subjects.[110] Even Stumpf could not help becoming disenchanted with this. After all, this was the only viewpoint ever disseminated in the navy.[111] Losing patience in May 1917, he exclaimed, "I am almost convinced that priests are merely officers in civilian dress. And perhaps they have even more to gain from the ignorance of the masses than the officers." [112]

Within a month his ire was again aroused when the captain of the *Helgoland*, on the anniversary of the Battle of Jutland, delivered a speech on the evils of the parliamentary system of government and the socialist menace. He declared:

. . . Our enemies pursue one particular goal, namely, to break the bonds between our Supreme War Lord, and his army and navy. Once the Hohenzollern are expelled, they will impose upon us a parliamentary system of government resembling that of England and France. Then we shall be ruled by merchants, lawyers and journalists just like they. . . . You must oppose all those who want a parliamentary system of government in Germany and must never forget that Germany's greatness stands and falls with the existence of its Imperial dynasty, its army and its young navy. Remember one thing: The Social Democrats of all the nations we are fighting wish to destroy us. They are extremely nationalistic; only our Socialists are internationalists.

The political polarization between the officers and the enlisted men that such speeches engendered is aptly described by Stumpf's response. "If I were an officer," he thought to himself, "I would agree wholeheartedly," but as an "unpropertied proletarian, I would rather be a slave to the English than a German sailor! My ideal is to approach the English-American form of government." [113]

The naval officers' real political attitude is best illustrated by the position they took regarding the Fatherland Party (*Vaterlandspartei*). The evidence in this connection actually deals with the period after the enlisted men's mutiny of August 1917. Until that time, however, neither the government nor the navy took any official interest in political propaganda, principally because it was taken for granted that leftist propaganda was illegal while that of the right had official approval. At any rate, this documentation amply reveals that the officers' protestations of political innocence are completely unjustified.

A rightist, annexationist, semipolitical party—the Fatherland Party, was founded in September 1917 by Grand Admiral von Tirpitz and Wolfgang Kapp, the leader of the notorious 1920 Kapp Putsch against the Weimar Republic. It was the avowed purpose of that party to counteract the Reichstag's Peace Resolution of July 19, 1917, and to prevent the reform of the Prussian franchise and the establishment of a parliamentary system of government in Germany. In virtually every respect its program was identical to that of the Pan-German League except that it refused to call itself a political party.[114]

On August 24, 1917, shortly before the official founding of the Fatherland Party, Admiral von Capelle, the Secretary of the Navy, ordered all naval commanders to put a stop to "the official dissemination of political material, regardless of direction," among the men. Capelle objected to the circulation in the navy of a particularly virulent pamphlet, the so-called Lehmann brochure, that libeled von Bethmann-Hollweg and the entire German government and demanded incredible territorial annexations.[115] Admiral Prince Henry of Prussia, the Kaiser's younger brother who was commander of German naval forces in the Baltic, replied for the navy. Exuding nothing but contempt for civilian rule and political considerations and revealing the navy's curious interpretation of what constituted politics, Henry asserted belligerently,

> As military commander I hold myself solely responsible for the maintenance of good discipline and a loyal monarchical and patriotic spirit in my command. . . . Hence it must remain within my discretion to choose in what fashion I shall influence the thoughts of my subordinates.

Protesting that he had no desire to introduce party politics into the navy, he maintained that he regarded it his obligation to "spread good political literature" and was thus unable to accept "his Excellency's proposals." [116] The prince was not alone in his defiance of the government and the Secretary of the Navy. On September 3, 1917, Admiral Scheer advised Capelle that he too had "very reluctantly" decided not to obey his order.[117] Admiral Bachmann, the commander of the Kiel naval station, also sent in a refusal and stated that Capelle must have meant his order to apply only to "one-sided political party material." Surely he would not object to "good political writings of a general nationalistic nature" from reaching higher staff officers who needed to impart "a healthy instruction" to their subordinates.[118]

Once again Capelle addressed the prince, who by now had become the leader of the naval opposition. In much stronger terms than before, Capelle insisted that the official dissemination of propaganda cease immediately, and he warned of possible repercussions if the Reichstag were informed. Unequivocally stating that this was a question of domestic politics solely subject to his jurisdiction, he threatened to appeal to the Kaiser if he were not obeyed.

The threat was to no avail. Prince Henry refused to budge. Brusquely rejecting the Reichstag's competence in matters of a "purely military nature," he maintained that he would welcome a ruling by the Kaiser. Going still further, he advised Capelle that he saw no reason why his officers should not join the *Vaterlandspartei* because it was not a real political party but a patriotic organization. Nevertheless, he would advise them, for strategic reasons, against doing so. It would create a much better impression if that party recruited its members for the fight against a peace of renunciation among the bourgeoisie rather than in "the military party." Finally, he had no objections if his officers wished to "promote the good cause" by making financial contributions.[119] On September 18 Admiral von Krosigk, the commander of the Wilhelmshaven naval base, informed Capelle that he had urged his officers to personally refrain from joining the new party but that he had encouraged them to give it their financial support by enrolling their wives and paying double dues.[120]

The officers' defiance of orders from a military superior has been called "an outright rebellion on the part of the front-line military" against the control of a responsible minister.[121] This may be a trifle too harsh a judgment. Nevertheless, it indicates to what lengths naval commanders were willing to go to subject their men to their own variety of political indoctrination. In flagrant disregard of official injunctions, they continued to spread Pan-German propaganda in the navy. In fact, it was not until February 1918 that the chief of the Kaiser's naval cabinet, Admiral von Müller, was finally able to put a temporary stop to these activities. On that date he made an example of von Krosigk by issuing an official reprimand and ordering him to stop his deception.[122]

If the naval commanders could so impudently ignore the orders of their superiors, it takes no great imagination to visualize the massive scale of propaganda and indoctrination they must have conducted prior to its prohibition. Yet the very same officers who openly flaunted the Secretary of the Navy, the civilian government, and the Reichstag in this matter showed amazing alacrity in preventing the spread of propaganda by other parties. For instance, the same Admiral Bachmann who had endorsed the dissemination of Pan-German literature in the fleet, on June 4, 1917, issued an angry directive prohibiting enlisted men from attending socialist lectures. It had come to his attention that about fifty members of the armed services, most of them sailors, had attended a lecture by the Majority Socialist Reichstag Deputy Landsberg on the theme, "The Demands of the German People." Irately the admiral reminded his commanders to enforce his Station Order Number 185 of May 5, 1917. This stated that all military personnel were forbidden "any participation in meetings and assemblies —regardless of political orientation—without obtaining special official sanction." [123] By the same token, Admiral von Krosigk of the Wilhelmshaven naval station cautioned his subordinates on June 22, 1917, to keep a careful watch on the activities of the Independent Socialists. In his opinion they were conducting "dangerous agitation" against existing government institutions and were seeking to proselytize the "workers for their cause." In a typical display of naval impartiality, he recommended that strong steps be taken against them at once, but warned his subordinates to avoid giving the appearance that these measures were directed at the party as such.[124]

The navy's insubordination during August and September 1917 transcends the issue of political propaganda. It reveals something much more important and fateful about the officer corps. The officers never hesitated disobeying orders, especially when these orders stemmed from civilians or from the civilian controlled Secretary of the Navy,[125] or when they felt that these commands were not in the best interests of the navy. For these reasons, the officers disobeyed not only Capelle's injunctions against political propaganda, but also his order of June 20, 1917, for the establishment of enlisted men's food complaint committees. Similarly, and even more fatefully, at a later date they refused to abide by the government's decision that the war was irretrievably lost; they insisted on launching a last, desperate attack against the British Grand Fleet to preserve the honor and prestige of the navy. This flagrant sort of disobedience and rebellion against nonmilitary policy decisions was to be a major cause for the rise of a resistance movement among the men in the spring of 1917 and their uprising in October-November 1918, which became the first act of the German Revolution.

The propaganda controversy of 1917 illustrates that the naval officers considered themselves a specially privileged group endowed with rights and prerogatives that could not possibly be granted any other group. Thus while they conducted a vigorous political campaign on the ships, they would not for a minute consider allowing the men the same privilege. Admiral Bachmann's stringent order makes that point very clear. Moreover, when the naval authorities discovered in August 1917 that some of the enlisted men had clandestinely organized a movement supporting the conclusion of an early peace without annexations and indemnities, which was the officially proclaimed policy of the German government, the men were accused of mutiny and subjected to court-martials. For engaging in politics the sailors and stokers were given death sentences and long prison terms. But the officers who pursued a policy diametrically opposed to that of the government were not even brought to trial, were never accused of any crime, and were even allowed to sit as judges over the men. As Wilhelm Dittmann put it so aptly, "The enlisted man had to pay with jail and death sentences for what their officers demanded as their inalienable right." [126]

The officers apparently never gave much thought to the fact that their political activities might have an adverse effect upon the enlisted men. Had they examined the situation rationally, they would have had to conclude that such practice could only undermine their authority and earn them the hatred of the men. The officers, however, lacked the imagination to see it that way. Instead, the men were forced to attend indoctrination sessions which invariably left them with the feeling that their officers were their political enemies.

The more the officers agitated and coerced, the more determined grew the resistence of the men. When the Bachmann Order was posted on the *Friedrich der Grosse*, it was immediately torn down.[127] Albin Köbis of the *Prinzregent Luitpold* summarized the men's reaction very succinctly at his interrogation before the naval lawyers. He maintained that the enlisted men's movement in the navy was of relatively recent origin and could be considered primarily "a counter-action against the Pan-German type of propaganda which had been disseminated with increasing intensity by the officers." [128]

Characteristic of the extreme polarization caused by the officers' political agitation is a jingle popular among the enlisted men at that time, which stated:

> Gleiche Löhnung, gleiches Essen,
> Und der Krieg wär längst vergessen! [129]

> *Equal pay, equal food,*
> *And the war would long have been forgotten!*

The sailors and stokers of the High Seas Fleet were tired of war and their officers' sterile arguments for its continuation. They wanted peace immediately. They had gone hungry and borne ill treatment long enough. Slowly they began to resist their oppressors, taking the first tentative steps to ameliorate their lot and to hasten the coming of peace. The conditions for the first naval mutiny were ripening.

iii

The Origin of the Enlisted
Men's Movement

During the terrible turnip winter of 1916–17 the conflict between
the enlisted men and the officers of the German navy reached a
critical stage. Gnawing hunger, ill treatment, and war-weariness
drove many of the men to the point of desperation, but there was
virtually nothing that they could do to ameliorate their lot.

Most of the men knew from experience that it was futile to
complain to the officers about their plight. They rarely complained, not because they suffered from what one prominent officer called a sense of "false shyness," [1] but because they knew that
the caste-ridden officer corps was unwilling to listen to their
grievances. Thus, for example, the established naval procedure
demanded that the men wait until they were punished before they
could register a protest. Also, complaints concerning mistreatment by a superior could only be lodged at daily morning inspection. Moreover, the petty officers, wise in the ways of the navy,

frequently "instructed" their men not to complain at all. This "hurt enormously" the enlisted men's confidence in the officers and "gave rise to mistrust." [2]

As a result, the men rarely complained. Instead they nursed their grievances and dreamed of resistance. Many of them yearned for the day "when justice would begin to dawn" for them and wishfully toyed with the idea of cutting their officers' throats.[3] But they must have realized that such plans were doomed to fail. They were far too divided among themselves and lacking in unity to overthrow the power and prestige of their superiors. Most of them were long accustomed to render blind, corpslike obedience. Consequently they perpetuated the traditional rivalry between the sailors who worked on deck and the soot-covered stokers of the engine room crew[4] rather than organize large-scale resistance.

Now and again, however, a sailor or stoker would resort to an act of desperation by simply striking out against his officers and the navy. On the *Helgoland* a disgruntled enlisted man removed the safety pin from one of the big guns and cut all the lines amidship.[5] But most frequently the men stole food or remained absent without leave.[6] Sometimes they deliberately disobeyed orders and calmly went off to prison where there was less harassment. Certain officers insist that the men did this knowing that their punishment would be mild and that it was the Kaiser's custom to grant an amnesty every January 27 when his birthday rolled around.[7]

The battleship *Prinzregent Luitpold*, for example, had what was considered an unruly crew. The men were treated with corresponding harshness by their officers. Consequently, the *Prinzregent Luitpold* quickly gained the reputation of being the "convict ship" of the fleet.[8] According to the tables compiled by Kapitänleutnant Herzbruch, the much-feared and despised first officer of that ship, the *Prinzregent* had the following punishment rate in the period December 1, 1916, to March 31, 1917:

MINOR PUNISHMENT

Month	Petty officers	Enlisted men	Total	Strength	Percentage
December	5	17	22	1220	1.8
January	8	28	36	1231	2.9
February	7	37	44	1233	3.6
March	6	25	31	1236	2.5

MAJOR PUNISHMENT

Month	Petty officers	Enlisted men	Total	Strength	Percentage
December	4	32	36	1220	3.0
January	3	20	23	1231	1.9
February	8	19	27	1233	2.1
March	5	26	31	1236	2.5

Thus hardly a month went by without nearly 5 percent of the crew receiving some sort of punishment. Significantly, the most frequent offenses were remaining absent without leave and disobedience of orders. There were 19 cases of men who overstayed their leaves and 24 cases of refusals to obey the orders of some superior.[9]

The same factors that drove certain men to commit all sorts of disciplinary infractions during the fall of 1916 and the spring of 1917[10] served to drive others to begin to band together, to organize, and to plot resistance. Almost invariably the first manifestations of collective resistance on the part of the men centered on the question of food or other rations.[11] Thus when rations were initially reduced on the *Helgoland* in the fall of 1916 and the men were given their first taste of the kind of food that was to become customary throughout the winter, the members of the First Division jointly decided to refuse to accept their food.[12] When, by the same token, the Fleet Command in 1916 ordered a reduction in soap rations and decreed that in the future the men were to use only sand, rags, and a weak soda solution for washing their clothes,[13] this engendered great resentment. Soon soap for personal hygiene was also reduced and set at a monthly ration of 50 grams. The stokers who worked in the grime and coal dust of the engine rooms found this especially irksome. They could no longer keep themselves clean no matter how hard they scrubbed. Nevertheless, the officers made it a point to check their hands for cleanliness at Sunday inspections.[14]

The first case of organized resistance on board the *Friedrich der Grosse* arose from this situation. Willi Sachse informs us that in March 1917 the second stokers' watch decided not to perform its duties until the regular soap ration had been restored. According to Sachse, after some initial hesitation the officers gave in, and this incident thus "constituted the first political success of our organization." The soap question had driven the men to act in concert and had prompted them to work out a plan of action against their officers. It is to be noted, however, that only the stokers—not the sailors—had reacted in this fashion. Therefore the officers found it easy to retaliate. They held an inspection at which the stokers were made to stand naked for three quarters of an hour while being checked over to see, in the words of one officer, that they did not sell their soap to their "whores in Kiel." [15]

These two incidents were the product of an entire winter's organizational activity. By no stretch of the imagination could this be considered significant progress. While it is undeniable that bad rations and ill treatment served to bring the men together against their officers, the limited results that were achieved in this fashion make one wonder how long it would have taken the enlisted men to organize a mutiny. If poor food and bad conditions alone were responsible for the August 1917 rebellion, the process of organization should have been much more rapid. Under those circumstances, the men should have revolted at the height of the turnip winter, when rations were at their worst and not when they were about to improve—in July and August. It is possible to deduce from this slow rate of progress that the question of food and treatment alone did not drive the men to rebel. Therefore it is reasonable to suppose that something else was needed to make them organize rapidly and effectively, and to stage an uprising.

Generally, the men reacted negatively to inadequate rations and abysmal living conditions. A more powerful and positive stimulus was needed, and this could only be provided by the officers. Thus Richard Stumpf kept hoping that the men would unite to fight for their rights. He realized, however, that this would not happen unless the officers carried "their madness to such a point" that the men would finally be forced to abandon their restraint and to stage an uprising.[16]

Blind to the needs of the men and animated primarily by its caste spirit, the naval officer corps inadvertently provided the impetus the discontented crews needed to organize by bringing politics into the fleet and by its arbitrary rule. Since the disruption of the political party truce, the *Burgfrieden*, early in 1917, virtually all the naval officers had actively advocated continuing the war, pursued Pan-German war aims, and resisted the pleading of the lower classes for domestic reform. The one-sided political propaganda campaign they waged in the fleet caused many enlisted men, not only former members of the Social Democratic Party (the SPD), to regard their officers as selfish warmongers who wanted war to keep the proletariat in their place. Hence an embryonic peace movement began to grow rapidly in the enlisted ranks of the navy.

The enlisted men's strong desire for peace plus the officers' opposition to reform served to unite the formerly divided crews. Outward symptoms of the political schism between the enlisted men and the officers appeared as early as January 30, 1917, when the stokers on board the *Oldenburg* scrawled antiwar slogans on the ship's bulletin board. One man wrote, "Down with the war! We want peace!" Machinist Jenssen wrote underneath:

> Was sind die deutschen Soldaten?
> Weisse Sklaven!
> Nieder mit den Aristokraten!
> Hoch die weissen Sklaven!

What are German sailors?
White slaves!
Down with the aristocrats!
Long live the white slaves!

Still another man expressed the feelings of many enlisted men by stating,

> Wir kämpfen nicht für Vaterland,
> Wir kämpfen nicht für Gott;
> Wir kämpfen für das reiche Pack,
> Wir Armen gehen kapott!

> *We do not fight for Fatherland,*
> *We do not fight for God;*
> *We fight for a pack of plutocrats,*
> *While we poor go to ruin!*[17]

Even more revealing were the events that transpired on the *Moltke* and the *Prinzregent Luitpold* shortly thereafter. When the crews of these two ships were asked by their officers to subscribe to a new war loan, they refused. One sailor, Seaman First Class Preuschkat, stepped forward as their spokesman and proclaimed that he saw no reason why they should sign. For this he was degraded in rank, and soon thereafter transferred.[18]

As the officers slowly began to detect these signs of mounting unrest and the coalescence of unity among the men, they attempted to suppress it. In numerous lectures and indoctrination sessions they railed against the Russian Revolution and Karl Liebknecht, the chief of the revolutionary Spartacists.[19] They tried to prevent the men from listening to political lectures by the left, joining leftist political parties, and reading socialist newspapers. This prompted Admiral Bachmann to issue his order at the end of May prohibiting the men from participating in any sort of political activity.[20] The naval authorities worked themselves into a frenzy in the spring of 1917 to root out malcontents and potential organizers. On the *Helgoland* the officers went so far as to offer a reward of 3,000 marks to anyone who would expose "traitors" seeking to spread mistrust and dissention in the ranks.[21]

These attempts, however, failed to achieve their desired goal. The men could not understand why they could not hold political discussions while the officers were privileged to engage in politics at will and to proselytize their cause in official lectures. As the crew of the cruiser *Nürnberg* later put it so succinctly, "The law under which the sailor is placed is trampled underfoot by his superiors." This "arbitrariness of the officers, their disregard for existing regulations and laws . . . have bent the bow to the point of rupture" and created the conditions for mutiny.[22]

Since they were forbidden to engage in politics and in many instances even to read socialist newspapers, the men of the fleet began to resort to secrecy and evasion. An additional factor in uniting the men and driving them into common resistance against their officers was thus created.

The bewilderment of the officers at the rise of resistance among their subordinates must have mounted appreciably after June 20, 1917. On that date Admiral von Capelle, the Secretary of the Navy, handed down an order calling for the establishment of a *Menagekommission*, food complaint committee, on all ships. The *Menagekommission* was to consist of spokesmen for the enlisted men and was empowered to register complaints regarding rations and their distribution.[23] When his order came under fire from the commanders, Capelle explained that the army planned to establish such institutions in each of its units to prevent abuses in rationing. This had compelled him to grant a similar concession for the navy. However, the new food complaints committees would not impair the powers of the ship commanders in the least. They would retain the right to select the committee members. Furthermore, the Naval Construction Division at Wilhelmshaven had set up such committees long ago and had even empowered the men to elect their own spokesmen without engendering any radicalism or insubordination.[24]

Despite the Secretary's anxious efforts to mollify his commanders, they responded to his directive with traditional disquiet and opposition. Between June 20 and August 15, 1917, an acrimonious correspondence shuttled back and forth between Berlin and the naval bases of Kiel and Wilhelmshaven as the commanders refused to obey the orders of their superior.[25] On July 20 the Commander of the High Seas Fleet, Admiral Scheer, replied that he regarded the *Menagekommission* as "an infringement on purely military matters." The Commander of the First Squadron, Admiral Eberhardt Schmidt, asserted that such matters should not be regulated too closely, while Admiral Behncke, his colleague in the Third Squadron, complained that the order had been released "without consulting the Front." [26]

No doubt the admirals feared that the committees might develop into a radical institution and make it appear as though the men's complaints were justified. As Captain Brüninghaus later put it, the officers were afraid that "such an institution, which manifested such a strong resemblance to a sailors' council," could easily be transformed by the men into something political.[27] On September 18 Admiral Schmidt voiced the navy's real position even more pointedly. The commanders had no objection so long as the committees were established "as a favor" that could be rescinded if misused and was accepted by such by the crews. However, he regarded it as "objectionable on military-disciplinary grounds" when such committees were set up on the order of a higher authority and came to be looked upon by the men as an "inalienable and irrevocable right." [28]

If only the officers had reconciled themselves to the inevitable and allowed this grievance machinery to be established, they might have spared themselves a great deal of trouble. Had they yielded gracefully, their concession of the *Menagekommissionen* might have acted the part of an invaluable safety valve by putting a stop to the growing discontent and radicalism in the ranks and by placing their relationship with the men on a much sounder and more amicable footing. On the other hand, their stubborn resistance to the *Menagekommission* served to confirm the men's suspicion that their officers had something to hide and were stealing their food. Ultimately this led the men to organize resistance, to adopt conspiratorial methods, and to become involved in politics. The one great unifying factor that could bring all the men together had been provided by the resistance of the naval commanders.

Even before the enlisted men in the High Seas Fleet began their struggle for the *Menagekommission*, their social and political rift with the officers had resulted in the development of an embryonic resistance movement and the creation of a cadre of leaders. Undoubtedly a number of men in the German navy welcomed the Russian Revolution and identified with the aims of the Bolsheviks and their German equivalent, the Spartacists. Stoker First Class Alfred Rebe of the battlecruiser *Moltke*, for instance, can be described as one of the first Bolsheviks.[29] After the war he became the editor of the *Rote Fahne*, a prominent communist newspaper. However, most of the enlisted men in the fleet did not share Rebe's political training and ideological fanaticism. Even the most radical ones and those who had been deeply involved with the socialist movement prior to the war long remained politically quiescent. Until the spring of 1917 there was no political discussion or agitation in the fleet. It required the full impact of the disastrous winter, the attendant food shortages, and the launching of a Pan-German propaganda campaign before the men bestirred themselves to oppose their officers' policies.[30]

When the enlisted men found that their complaints about inadequate rations were consistently ignored by the officer corps, they lost all confidence in the navy.[31] As a result they began to hold meetings to discover ways to improve their situation. At first these were clandestine affairs conducted in some remote corner of the ship. The structure of the ships was ideal for such secret conversations. On the large battleships and cruisers the officers either could not or would not supervise their men closely at all times. Therefore there were ample opportunities to carry on discussions.[32]

Initially these discussions dealt exclusively with the men's grievances about rations. Almost inevitably, however, the scope of the meetings was enlarged to include topics such as the war, domestic politics, and the question of peace. Since most of the men lacked political education, these discussions frequently deteriorated into rambling and useless debates. However, they quickly discovered that the Independent Socialist *Leipziger Volkszeitung* as well as some of the Majority Socialist organs such as *Vorwärts* provided them with ample material for discussion. At that time most ships had not yet prohibited these papers, and the men could subscribe freely if they could raise the necessary funds. Because their meager salaries made it an economic hardship to subscribe, several men often shared the cost of a subscription.[33]

On the *Friedrich der Grosse* the newspapers generally arrived in the evening. The men would then take them ashore to read and discuss in the taverns of Wilhelmshaven. Willi Sachse's group of comrades from the engine room made it a practice to gather around a table at a tavern by the name of Kummer. This was a favorite hangout for the stokers and a convenient place to discuss the news and the latest developments in the war.[34] There, too, the discussion initially centered around the question of food and the stokers' other grievances, but gradually drifted off to the situation at home and the men's desire for peace.[35]

In this relatively aimless fashion the leadership of the August mutiny was developed. Among the stokers who frequented the Kummer, the most prominent figure was twenty-two-year-old Stoker First Class Willi Sachse. Born and raised in Leipzig, Sachse was a mechanic by trade, had belonged to the Social Democratic Youth Movement before the war, and was extremely well versed in socialist literature.[36] Sachse was by far the most intelligent and politically conscious man among the stokers and was widely respected for that reason. Endowed with an excellent memory, Sachse was able to quote to his comrades the Program of the Socialist Party, from Karl Marx's *Kapital* and the writings of August Bebel, the founder of the German Social Democratic Party.[37]

Reichstag Deputy Dittmann of the Independent Social Democratic Party (the USPD), who had occasion to meet Sachse both during and after the war, characterized him as a "political fanatic with a strong psychopathic bent." [38] Even if Sachse was not actually psychopathic, he certainly enjoyed his reputation among the crew of the *Friedrich der Grosse* and liked, according to his shipmates and fellow mutineer Wilhelm Weber, to talk as though he were acting out a role in a "planned world revolution." [39] Sachse found it easy to impress and overwhelm his comrades, to dominate the meetings at the Kummer, and to give the impression that he was "the brain" of their movement.

One evening in June 1917 as Sachse and his cohorts were holding forth at the Kummer, the group came across an article in the local paper, the *Wilhelmshavener Tageblatt*, that arrested its attention. The article stated that the Secreary of the Navy had recently announced in the Reichstag that he would establish food complaint committees on all the ships. The stokers had never heard of such an institution before save on the *Baden*. Someone suggested that they speak to their first officer about it. At that moment a sailor from *Friedrich der Grosse* whom they hardly knew entered into the conversation.[40]

Max Reichpietsch, who made his entrance into history in this fashion, has puzzled not only his comrades in the navy, the naval authorities, and lawyers who interrogated him and finally sentenced him to death, but also historians. Born to poor working class parents in the Berlin proletarian suburb of Neukölln in 1894, Max Reichpietsch attended Communal School Number 240 until the age of fourteen. Subsequently, he worked for two years in a screw factory and later shifted to carpentry work. On July 16, 1912, he volunteered for a four-year enlistment in the navy. He was an obscure young man, but his record was unblemished. In 1912 his divisional training commander described him as a "good, useful man, not lacking in ability and clean in his habits." [41]

When Deputy Wilhelm Dittmann met him five years later in the Reichstag, Dittmann gained the impression of "a very alert and intelligent young man . . . totally lacking in experience and political education" and possessing "rather naive and muddled ideas in political matters." [42] Another deputy, Hugo Haase, who also met Reichpietsch at about that time called him a "man of lofty ideals." [43]

Despite these qualities, Reichpietsch did not fare well in the navy. Within six months of his enlistment he began to get into trouble with his superiors. On January 24, 1913, he was punished for failing to report to his post on time. Less than a month later he was given a week's arrest for relieving himself on deck. On April 12, 1913, he was convicted of theft on four counts and sentenced by a court martial to twenty-eight days of imprisonment. Graver still were the charges leveled against him in April 1915. On that occasion he was accused, tried, and convicted on a charge of military theft, sentenced to five months of imprisonment at the fortress of Cologne, and was reduced from the status of seaman first class to that of second class. [44]

He was accused of having stolen from his superior, Lieutenant Jordan, a pair of boots and 430 marks. Reichpietsch and his principal witness contended that he had merely borrowed the lieutenant's boots to impress the girls in Wilhelmshaven and that he had never touched any of the money. However, 120 marks had been found in his possession; he had recently bought a watch and a ring and paid off his bar bills. Hence the judges rejected the argument that he had earned this money through the illegal sale of cigarettes. Finally, Reichpietsch gave in, submitted a full confession, and received his sentence. [45]

Reichpietsch was very bitter when he emerged from prison. He particularly resented his demotion to the status of second class seaman. This deprived him of the right to wear a cockade and a band with the name of his ship on his sailor's cap. After participating with credit in the battle of Jutland, Reichpietsch applied for restoration to his former rank. His request was endorsed by his entire division on the *Friedrich der Grosse*. Nevertheless, Lieutenant Jordan refused. Thereupon Reichpietsch informed a friend that he intended to go to Berlin to obtain the help of some Reichstag deputy. He also threatened that he would complain about the food and poor conditions on board the ship. Despite his resentment, however, Reichpietsch's conduct continued to improve. Consequently, in March 1917 he regained his coveted cockade and cap ribbon.[46]

Upon hearing at the Kummer of Admiral von Capelle's order, Reichpietsch became very enthusiastic. He told Sachse and the other stokers that he would obtain the support of the sailors on the *Friedrich der Grosse* and that they would participate in waging a resolute fight to obtain the creation of such a committee. At long last the men had found a cause over which they could unite to begin forming an effective organization against their officers.

This organizing process on the *Friedrich der Grosse* was accelerated when the ship received orders to sail from Wilhelmshaven to Kiel. Since the ship would be placed under the jurisdiction of the Baltic Naval Command of Admiral Bachmann while at Kiel, his order prohibiting any sort of political activity was posted on the bulletin board. The men were outraged at this violation of their rights. They became determined not to tolerate this new injustice. The naval authorities' blindness in the matter of the *Menagekommission* and the blatant partisanship of the Bachmann order goaded the men to proceed from talk to action.

Reichpietsch, having arrived in Kiel, went to see Sachse and reported that he had been successful in obtaining the wholehearted support of the sailors in the struggle for a food complaint committee. Even more importantly Reichpietsch suggested that he might use his impending leave to go to Berlin to speak with some deputies of the Independent Social Democratic Party. He wanted to learn if the Bachmann order was legal and if the men were actually entitled to form a food complaint committee. Sachse and a friend by the name of Franz Müller endorsed Reichpietsch's idea at once. However, since they were not certain whether they liked the Independents better than the Majority Socialists, they urged him to call upon representatives of both socialist parties for help.[47]

When Reichpietsch left for Berlin in June 1917 there was no political or revolutionary organization on board the *Friedrich der Grosse*. The men on that ship were dissatisfied, hungry, and filled with hatred for their officers. They occasionally came together for informal discussions and had gone so far as to agree to bury their past differences in order to present a united front. Finally, goaded to the point of explosion by the arbitrary behavior of their superiors, they had dispatched one of their number to Berlin to inquire what might be done to make their lives more bearable and to obtain the rights which were their due.[48]

There was nothing unusual or illegal about Max Reichpietsch's proposed visit to the Reichstag deputies. This was a traditional recourse of men who could not obtain satisfaction from their superiors. Thus it was common for Catholic sailors to lodge their complaints with their Centrist deputy in the Reichstag.[49] By the same token, in order to obtain faster results, the enlisted men in the fleet tended to complain to the most radical Reichstag deputy available. When the crew of the *Helgoland* were unjustly threatened with a reduction in rations, there was an almost natural tendency for the men to appeal to Karl Liebknecht.[50]

The fact that Reichpietsch was instructed by his comrades to visit both Independent and Majority Socialist deputies is very revealing. It indicates that the men did not distinguish between these two parties and that their movement, if it can be called that, still lacked any sort of concrete political orientation. Most of all in June and July of 1917 the men of the *Friedrich der Grosse* wanted a more adequate diet and the privilege of inspecting their food accounts. These motives plus a personal grudge against the navy prompted Max Reichpietsch to undertake his conversations with the deputies.

Conservative historians in Germany and naval officers have traditionally maintained that the naval mutiny of August 1917 was the result of the political subversion of the fleet by the Independent Social Democrats. In an effort to clear the navy of blame, they have contended that the spirit of dissatisfaction and rebellion among the enlisted men was not caused by any legitimate grievances regarding living conditions but is to be attributed exclusively to the revolutionary propaganda of the extreme left. Thus Captain Brüninghaus, one of the spokesmen for the navy after the war, insists that the few isolated "mistakes" in the handling of the men could not possibly be held responsible for the outbreak of a mutiny. In his opinion these rare abuses were "brilliantly exploited" by certain leaders in the crews to create a "purely political movement" which sought peace at any cost by emulating Russia. Finally, Brüninghaus asserts that the contact with the USPD enabled these leaders to obtain the intellectual direction they needed to foment the mutiny.[51] This thesis found its ablest protagonist in Admiral von Trotha who maintained, "In short, the movement in the navy . . . is not the product of military abuses and errors . . . but of a carefully planned and organized political conspiracy to revolutionize the entire German nation . . ."[52]

This view is still very much alive in Germany. Admiral Bauer in his recent book, *Reichsleitung und U-bootseinsatz, 1914–1918*, holds the USPD responsible for importing mutiny into the fleet.[53] Even more recently, in 1963, the writer of a manual on naval history which is widely used in the present Federal Navy, attributes the 1917 mutiny to the "revolutionary activity" of the Independent Socialists.[54]

All of these writers charge that the chain of events that led to the outbreak of the August mutiny began when Max Reichpietsch established a direct revolutionary connection with the central leadership of the party at its headquarters in Berlin.

For example, Admiral von Trotha postulates, "by means of this connection, Reichpietsch's work received the initial support that enabled him to create a strong organization within the navy, to recruit members in large numbers, and to place the members obtained in this fashion at the service of the aims of the USPD." [55]

Therefore, Reichpietsch's trip acquires crucial significance. Did Reichpietsch's visit with the USPD deputies indeed constitute the beginnings of an organized effort to revolutionize the navy? Did that party actually instruct him to foment rebellion in the navy and to organize a strike for peace? Was the USPD really a revolutionary party that would stop at nothing to obtain its ends and was it willing to risk its entire future on the actions of a simple sailor?

According to all indications, Reichpietsch went to Berlin to visit his parents and to obtain the views of some socialist deputies on the establishment of a *Menagekommission* and the legality of the Bachmann order. He took along the text of that order and a list of complaints drafted by Sachse.[56]

Reichpietsch could hardly have arrived home in a happy frame of mind. He resented his punishments and treatment by the navy. He was also bitter about the general conditions in the fleet. His return home could not possibly have improved his mood. In front of every bakery there were lines of dejected civilians, with shabby clothing, their shoes frequently shod with wood instead of leather. He must have sensed their profound war-weariness. Above all, he must have noted the resigned and depressed look on the people's faces.[57]

Reichpietsch's depression must have taken a turn for the worse when a war widow with whom he was acquainted offered to prostitute herself to him to feed her hungry children. "This offer, born of the desperate need of this woman must have had a terribly painful impact upon Reichpietsch. It might well be that he became determined at that moment to do everything within his power to bring the war to a rapid close." [58]

Shortly after undergoing this disturbing experience, Reichpietsch paid a visit to the central offices of the Independent Social Democratic Party at 21 Schiffbauerdamm, near the Reichstag. He was received by Deputy Wilhelm Dittmann, a short man with a pointed beard and a mercurial temperament. Dittmann was forty-three years old, a former carpenter, currently a prominent news-paperman and a leading member of the Independent Party Direc-tory.[59] At first Dittmann refused to speak to Reichpietsch. He referred him to his colleague, Deputy Vogtherr, who was the party's expert on naval matters. However, when he found out that Vogtherr was not in Berlin, Dittmann gave in. He listened to Reichpietsch's complaints, heard his description of happenings in the fleet, and read the letter which Sachse had sent along. The entire interview lasted less than a half hour. Finally, Dittmann advised the sailor to come back again when Vogtherr was present.

Having finished his meeting with Reichpietsch, Dittmann con-ducted him into the adjoining office. There he introduced him to Frau Luise Zietz, a fiery little woman, a brilliant party organizer, and an important member of the party hierarchy. Reichpietsch repeated his story to Frau Zietz. He told her that the sailors and stokers of the *Friedrich der Grosse* sympathized with USPD and that fifty to sixty copies of the *Leipziger Volkszeitung* came aboard every day. Thereupon the emotional Frau Zietz shouted, "We ought to be ashamed of ourselves before the sailors; they are further advanced than we!"

Later the naval prosecutors were to contend that Frau Zietz had encouraged the sailors to organize a rebellion. Actually, the re-mark was merely Frau Zietz's way of expressing her delight at hearing of the success of the Wilhelmshaven sailors. They had managed to organize a USPD group whereas the party had failed to establish more than a mere foothold in that industrial center.[60]

Within a few days Reichpietsch returned for a second meeting with the USPD. This time he did not go to the party headquarters but to its conference room in the Reichstag building. To his friends on the *Friedrich der Grosse* Reichpietsch later described this meeting as a "sort of party conference." [61] But it was nothing of the kind. First he conferred with Ewald Vogtherr, the USPD secretary. After a few minutes Dittmann strolled in with the chairman of the party, Hugo Haase. This brilliant fifty-four-year-old Jewish lawyer represented the city of Königsberg in the Reichstag and was regarded by friends and opponents alike as scrupulously honest. It is not quite clear whether or not Frau Zietz was present.[62] Apparently the deputies drifted in and out of the conference room whenever they had to appear upon the floor of the Reichstag. Haase reports that his conversation with Reichpietsch could not have lasted more than ten minutes.[63]

Vogtherr reports that Reichpietsch presented no complaints. Instead he tried to impress the deputies with the support the USPD enjoyed in the fleet. He feared, however, that the USPD might be prohibited soon, but promised that the men would continue to support the party regardless of official oppression. Vogtherr responded by stating that the navy was not empowered to suppress any newspapers. He may also have expressed satisfaction that his party had so many supporters in the navy.[64]

Haase's recollections are much hazier. According to him, Reichpietsch made no mention of any organization in the fleet, but did indicate that the men held occasional meetings on shore. The lawyer from Königsberg liked Reichpietsch. Hence he cautioned him to be very careful. Although such meetings were not illegal, he felt that the naval authorities might use them as a pretext for getting the men into trouble.[65]

Dittmann's conversation with Reichpietsch forms the most controversial part of the meeting. When he heard Reichpietsch's description of the discussions that the men conducted on shore, Dittmann intervened and counseled the sailor to be extremely cautious. He advised the men not to place too much faith in the government's proclamation of political neutrality, that the men had better proceed with care or the navy might "place a noose around their necks." In addition, Dittmann told Reichpietsch that he did not expect the sailors to join the USPD. Although membership in the party was not illegal, Dittmann advised that the men did not need to join for financial reasons. The party did not require their "formal membership" but was much more interested in attracting their "spiritual adherence." Therefore, Dittmann continued, "the men should proceed as before" to busy themselves with attracting readers for the USPD press.

In an effort to cheer the young sailor, Dittmann may have told Reichpietsch and his comrades not to despair but to look with confidence in the direction of Stockholm. An International Socialist Peace Congress was shortly to convene there to work out a way to conclude the war. Moreover, if the sailors and stokers insisted on joining the USPD, there was no reason why arrangements could not be made for them to join the party at the local level. Dittmann then provided Reichpietsch with the addresses of various party functionaries, both in Berlin and along the seaboard. Finally, Dittmann and Vogtherr handed Reichpietsch a number of political pamphlets and assured him that he could obtain more from Party Treasurer Herbst.[66] At the latter's office Reichpietsch enrolled himself as a member of the USPD. Herbst, apparently unaware of Dittmann's advice, promised additional literature and handed Reichpietsch thirty applications for party memberships, which he was assured would be free to naval personnel.[67]

This then was the extent of Reichpietsch's direct contact with the Independent Social Democrats. On the basis of these two conversations the naval authorities built their case against Reichpietsch and executed him for inciting to mutiny. Hence it is of crucial importance not only to consider precisely what took place at these meetings, but also to assess their immediate influence and effects.

Superficially speaking, nothing of momentous importance had occurred. Reichpietsch had merely done something that many sailors and soldiers had done when they visited their Reichstag representatives and informed them of the conditions prevailing in their units. There were some essential differences, however, that set these meetings apart from all the rest. First of all, Reichpietsch did not represent simply himself. When he talked with the leaders of the USPD he spoke as the representative of a group of men on the *Friedrich der Grosse.* Thus in a certain sense he acted as their delegate. Moreover, he had been specifically instructed by Sachse to raise a number of points with the deputies. He was to find out if the Bachmann order was legal, and whether the men were entitled to form food complaint committees. Finally, he was also supposed to pass on to the deputies a list of the crew's major grievances and complaints.

Reichpietsch's execution of his mission did not conform entirely with his instructions. He never carried out his comrades' request that he visit a deputy of the Majority Socialist Party, preferably Scheidemann, although he left Dittmann with the impression, after their second meeting, that he was about to seek out Deputy Stücklen of that party.[68] Furthermore, Reichpietsch largely neglected the complaints of the crew. Instead he concentrated on political matters. Thereby he conveyed the erroneous impression that the men were already organized and were merely waiting for the USPD to step in to provide intellectual and tactical leadership.

It would seem, on the basis of the fragmentary evidence available, that Reichpietsch had decided while in Berlin to convert the spontaneous protest organization on *Friedrich der Grosse* into a political movement. This may be why he refrained from raising the question of the food complaint committee and the men's grievances to the foreground of his discussions. This may also be why he exaggerated the strength of the enlisted men's movement and why he made it the most important part of his mission to obtain the deputies' advice on the establishment of a peace movement in the navy.

Despite the post-August 1917 charges of the right that Reichpietsch's meeting with the party leaders was the first step in a concerted campaign to foment rebellion in the fleet, the USPD had not committed any illegal acts. The deputies were entitled to speak with an adherent of their party even if he did come in uniform. They were also permitted by law to provide him with literature and to encourage the readings of their party materials. All of these writings had been passed by the censor. Actually they were Reichstag speeches by Haase and Dittmann, which could be read in most newspapers in Germany. In addition the deputies were justified in informing Reichpietsch that there was no law forbidding the men to join their party and that they considered the Bachmann order illegal. Hence from the strictly legal point of view, the deputies had not transgressed the boundaries of the law.

In a different sense, however, they had assumed a grave responsibility in their talks with the sailor. Knowing that Reichpietsch was "totally lacking in experience and political education," they had treated him as if he were a seasoned political organizer about to embark on a routine, harmless assignment. The deputies should have known that any sailor or stoker who defied the navy's ban on attendance at political rallies and the reading of political party tracts would wind up in serious difficulties. Surely they also knew that the authorities would suppress any illicit movement and recruiting drive in the ranks. This would explain why Dittmann and Haase repeatedly cautioned Reichpietsch to exercise great care. Thus the deputies must have realized that they were exposing Reichpietsch and his comrades on the *Friedrich der Grosse* to grave peril.

From a moral point of view, the USPD leaders might have made it very clear to Reichpietsch that it was highly dangerous for the men to defy the navy's illegal ban by organizing resistance. They might have advised him that they did not wish the sailors to assume the risks of underground organization. If the USPD had behaved like most other parties, it would probably have told him that his complaints had been noted and would be taken up with the proper authorities. Possibly the deputies might have promised that they would present the matter before the Reichstag and that the men were to wait to see what could be achieved in this fashion.

The USPD, however, was not like the other parties in the Reichstag. It had broken away from its parent Social Democratic

Party in March 1916 and had begun to lead an independent political existence only since April 1917. At its founding congress at
Gotha it had organized itself as a loose oppositional political fed-
eration of disparate groups. Moreover, the USPD was still engaged in a relentless struggle with the Majority Socialist Party.
Everywhere in Germany it was engaged in a conflict for adherents and influence among the working classes. But the USPD discovered to its dismay that the Majority Socialists would stop at
nothing to deprive it of its hard-won gains. In an acrimonious
struggle the Independents managed to acquire control of the
Vorwärts, the leading socialist newspaper in Germany, by gaining direction of its editorial board. Thereupon the Majority party
allied with the government, stepped in, and once again took
charge of the paper.[69]

The Independents were convinced that only a policy of utmost
opposition to the government and its annexationist foreign policy
could bring peace to Germany. Also, they were thoroughly disillusioned about the Reichstag's ability to compel the government
to pursue a sane foreign and domestic policy. They looked upon
the Reichstag's struggle for power as mere shadowboxing, which
could not possibly dislodge the conservatives and the annexation-
ists from their position of power.

For these reasons the USPD wanted to exploit the war-
weariness, the despair, and the sinking morale of the German people in June and July 1917, to bring the war to a close, and to
reform Germany's political institutions. However, the USPD had
not yet decided what methods it would use. The extreme left
wing of the party, the Spartacists and the Gruppe International,
favored a revolutionary course and the staging of an uprising.
The right wing, which included the former revisionists and the
parliamentary socialists, while not entirely disavowing such a
course, still hoped to achieve its aims by peaceful means if the
proletarian masses of Germany could be persuaded to flock into
their party in significant numbers.[70] These elements within the
USPD hoped that the growing strength of their party would al-

low them to discredit the progovernment Majority Socialists at the International Socialist Peace Congress at Stockholm.

Wilhelm Dittmann was certainly no revolutionary. As soon as he was confronted with the specter of communism in 1919 he rejoined the Majority Socialist Party. Yet he welcomed the opportunity presented by Max Reichpietsch. Through Reichpietsch and his comrades in the navy, the USPD could steal a march on the Majority Socialists, who refused to recruit members in the armed services. At the same time, gaining the support of the sailors constituted a form of insurance in the event the reactionaries and militarists in Germany forced the USPD to stage a revolutionary uprising. These calculations could hardly have been altogether absent from Dittmann's thinking when he indirectly encouraged Reichpietsch to recruit members for his party, to spread its propaganda by means of the *Leipziger Volkszeitung* and other political tracts, and to win over new adherents for the cause of a non-annexationist peace.

The USPD's and Dittmann's behavior toward Reichpietsch depicts how very slim the margin separating legal from revolutionary tactics was for that party. It would undoubtedly be wrong to characterize the USPD as a revolutionary party.[71] However, one cannot ignore the influence exerted by that party's powerful left wing and the intransigent opposition to all reform and a negotiated peace by Germany's ruling class. Such a combination was enough to compel even moderates like Dittmann and Haase to occasionally flirt with the idea of revolution in the event all parliamentary and legal pressures proved useless. The USPD's attitude is therefore best described as equivocal and uncertain. In the final analysis, its choice of tactics would depend upon external circumstances.

The German naval authorities and conservative historians have never troubled themselves with such nuances. With characteristic forcefulness they have traditionally contended that Dittmann actually plotted a mutiny which was to be the prelude of a nationwide revolution. If we assume momentarily that they are correct in this appraisal, it is extremely unlikely that Dittmann would have been foolhardy enough to select the first discontented sailor he met and to build an elaborate and highly dangerous plot around him. Such an argument does not do justice to Dittmann's intelligence and political shrewdness. If Dittmann and his colleagues had indeed wanted to organize a mutiny, they certainly would not have had to resort to Reichpietsch. They could surely have found someone, possibly some officer or at least a petty officer, who was more highly placed, more reliable, better trained and educated, to implement this scheme than a common sailor whom they had only seen twice.[72]

While it would be unreasonable to attribute such stupidity to Dittmann, it is not at all far-fetched to describe him as a clever opportunist. As such, he saw in Reichpietsch a wonderful chance to gain the support of the sailors and stokers. By encouraging Reichpietsch to propagandize the aims of the USPD among the enlisted men in the navy, the USPD had much to gain and little to lose. Reichpietsch could bring new members into the party and expand its influence in the navy. Moreover, the cost to the party was very low. All Reichpietsch wanted was a few pamphlets and speeches. Furthermore, if it should ever come to a revolution, the USPD would then be in the position to control a force of armed men to fight against the police and the army. On the other hand, if things went wrong, Dittmann and the USPD could easily repudiate Reichpietsch and his comrades. They could then maintain, as they did a few months later, that they had never encouraged the men to join the party or to work for it, that the men had done so on their own volition. In short, the most reasonable interpretation of Dittmann's indirect encouragement of Reichpietsch is that it was dictated by political opportunism and expediency.[73]

Greatly impressed by the attention that had been accorded him by the Reichstag deputies and vaguely assured that the USPD would support the strivings of the enlisted men by supplying them with literature and intellectual support in their struggle for peace and against their officers, Reichpietsch returned to his ship.

Before his trip to Berlin he had been considered a rather timid man, "extremely reticent and cautious";[74] after his return on June 21, he exuded confidence. His comrade Beckers found that he was "extremely proud" to have consorted with the deputies in Berlin.[75] Sachse describes him as "secretive, acting self-important and filled with fanatic enthusiasm for the USPD." He behaved as though he had become one of the "initiated and an agent for the USPD to the men." [76] Apparently his contact with the deputies had gone to Reichpietsch's head. He acted as though he were "heart and soul" their man,[77] and he could no longer restrain himself. When one of his closest personal friends, Seaman Geisteuer, warned him about his radical talk, Reichpietsch exclaimed, "Nothing can happen to me. I have the deputies behind me!" [78]

Bit by bit, Reichpietsch told his comrades what had happened in Berlin. Each time, however, his tale became more fanciful. With each retelling his mission rose in importance. Soon he spoke of an interview with Frau Zietz and Dittmann that lasted from one to two hours; that he had been instructed "to carry on and spread the movement" in the navy, that the men should formally join the USPD and that they should look with confidence in the direction of Stockholm." [79]

Although it is uncertain whether Dittmann ever uttered these words,[80] after he had been back on the ship for awhile Reichpietsch announced that he had been instructed to build a movement in the navy so that the men would support the USPD's peace policy by refusing to obey orders and waging a general strike if the Stockholm Peace Congress should fail.[81] Moreover, Reichpietsch also decided that the movement which sprang up around him on the *Friedrich der Grosse* and from there spread to the other ships should try to establish its strength and support for the USPD by drawing up lists of names of men who wished to join the party. This would enable the deputies to produce proof at Stockholm that the navy stood behind them.

One may surmise from this drastic transformation of Reichpietsch's character that a variety of personal reasons, possibly his bitter hatred for the navy, his insecurity about his status as a former convict, and the singular attention shown him by the deputies, prompted him to greatly exaggerate his visits in the Reichstag in order to enhance his standing in the eyes of his comrades in the navy. At any rate, he never gave a complete report of his real activities in Berlin, but shrouded himself in mystery by hinting that he knew much more than he was willing to tell. Periodically he would release a bit of information "in order to cheer up his comrades" and to make them dependent upon him.[82]

In this fashion Reichpietsch managed within relatively short time to stimulate the growth of a semipolitical movement among the enlisted men. Laboring under the misapprehension that they possessed the active support of a major political party in the Reichstag, Reichpietsch's misguided followers sought to bring about a rapid improvement of conditions in the navy by recruiting members for the USPD and preparing for a general strike which would end the war.

Reichpietsch's efforts to organize a political movement among the enlisted men was to contribute significantly to a mutinous spirit in the navy. It is unlikely, however, that his amateurish propaganda and organizational activities would have born fruit if it had not been for the men's abysmal living conditions, their complete mistrust of the officer corps, and their determination to take steps to ameliorate their lot. In fact, it is very likely that the men would have organized their resistance even without Reichpietsch and his politically oriented colleagues on the *Friedrich der Grosse*. By June 1917 the enlisted men of the German navy had become determined to obtain their food complaint committees and were prepared to resort to drastic means to attain their goal.

iv

The August 1917 Mutiny:
Strike or Naval Rebellion?

It was a wet rainy morning on August 2, 1917, as Korvettenkapitän Herzbruch began making his rounds on the *Prinzregent Luitpold* as she lay anchored at Wilhelmshaven. A strange sight greeted the officer's eyes as he paced through the crew's quarters. The ship was virtually deserted. Between 6:30 and 7:30 that morning about 600 men—sailors, stokers, stewards, and radio operators from all the ship's divisions—had streamed over the gangplank to the dock. Only slightly more than 100 men had stayed behind. Herzbruch responded by despatching a patrol of three officers and ten petty officers to bring the missing men back.

However, they were nowhere in sight. They had set off earlier in the streaming rain toward the little town of Rüstersiel. Before their departure, Stoker Albin Köbis had addressed them on the dock. "Comrades of the Third Watch! We are walking out in order to protest . . . [the impending imprisonment of our fellow-stokers]. In order to avoid creating a dangerous situation, we shall stay away no more than three hours." As they tramped off toward the White Swan Tavern the men were in a holiday mood, happy to leave their ship behind.

Their exuberance persisted after they had arrived at their destination. Someone played a tune on the piano, and a number of them began to dance. Once again Stoker Köbis stepped forward. Striking a discordant note amidst the general levity, he bellowed to the men that they "had broken loose too soon." The real blow against the navy would come in two or three weeks. Then they would have with them 850 men from the *Friedrich der Grosse*, 400 men from the *König Albert*, 350 men from the *Westfalen*, and the entire crew of the *Pillau*. In conclusion, he shouted, "We are the true patriots! Down with the war! We no longer want to fight this war!" [1]

At this point—it was about 10 o'clock—the constable of Rüstersiel appeared at the tavern with five or six of his men. He demanded that the sailors and stokers break up their meeting and allow themselves to be marched back to their ship under guard. The *Prinzregent Luitpold* crew refused to obey. Nevertheless, soon thereafter they assembled in orderly fashion outside the tavern. Then they marched off toward Wilhelmshaven. Despite the torrential rain, they sang lusty reservist songs. Every once in a while the constable attempted to gain control over the procession by posting his men on its flanks. Each time, however, the column ground to a halt. The men would not proceed until the guards were withdrawn.

Marching along in this fashion, they had reached the paved highway leading into town, when an officer, Kapitänleutnant von Weyers,[2] came toward them on a bicycle. The men were marching in the middle of the roadway. Maintaining their pace, they compelled him to veer into the deep puddles along the sides of the road. Suddenly the officer turned, sped to the head of the column and shouted, "Halt! Stand still!"

No one obeyed. Thereupon he issued the command again. All at once the men stopped. He demanded that they allow them-

selves to be led back to the ship, but again they refused. Threatening that they would therefore be marched back as prisoners, he
turned his bicycle around and sped off in the direction of the
shore patrol at the naval infantry barracks.

Sobered and frightened by the threats, the sailors and stokers
resumed their march home, trotting in double-time. Avoiding the
barracks by taking a side street, they raced toward their ship.
Along the way they ran into several patrols from other ships.
These, however, simply stood to one side and made no move as
the *Prinzregent* crew, singing all the while, filed onto the dock.

Köbis and Johann Beckers, the other leader of the march, now
realized that things had gone awry. Beckers, in particular, knew
that if the men did not obtain their captain's promise for an amnesty before coming aboard, they would be punished severely.
He attempted therefore to stop them at the dockyard gate. However, there was no halting them as they pushed past him and
boarded the ship.

On the *Prinzregent Luitpold* a flag officer, Admiral von Mauve,
scoldingly demanded an explanation. The members of the *Menagekommission* stepped out of rank and explained that they had
staged their walkout to protest the unfair prison sentences of their
comrades. Listening attentively, the admiral heard them out,
turned to Captain von Hornhardt and with surprise in his voice
demanded to know why he had not been informed of the crew's
unrest and the punitive measures that had precipitated the strike.
According to Beckers, the admiral then demanded "the immediate
dropping of charges against the men." Quieted by von Mauve's
actions, and grateful for the understanding he had shown, the
crew returned to work.

No sooner had the men dispersed than the ship was placed on a
state of alert. No one was permitted to go ashore; the gaurd at the
gangplank was reinforced. At six P.M. the ship was ordered to run
out. Beckers realized at this point that the walkout had backfired.
Quickly conferring with Köbis, he managed to smuggle a
scrawled note to Sachse on the *Friedrich der Grosse* that stated,

"Ship sailing out, apparently under state of siege. If no news in three days, strike!" Thereupon the leaders of the crew were placed under arrest. The movement on the *Prinzregent Luitpold* collapsed.[3]

These events constitute the overt manifestation of the August 1917 naval mutiny, a mutiny which the navy squashed by ultimately handing down for the entire fleet ten death sentences, two of which were actually carried out, and a series of lesser sentences that came to a total of over 360 years of imprisonment.[4] Was the German navy correct in judging these events and the happenings that preceded them as a mutiny, and a politically inspired mutiny at that? Or should these events be construed as a merely "professional strike," a wildcat walkout on the part of desperate sailors and stokers who could no longer bear the arbitrary rule and ill-treatment they suffered at the hands of their officers?

Historical opinion has differed widely on this subject. It would be futile to recount all the emotional and predictable charges and countercharges voiced by the politicians, officers, and historians who were intimately involved with the events. A much more fruitful way of evaluating the problem—one never before attempted precisely because of this emotionalism—is provided by a dispassionate analysis of the enlisted men's movement in the interval between Reichpietsch's visit to Berlin and the walkout on August 2.

When Reichpietsch went on leave in June 1917 the enlisted men's movement was still in its infancy. The sailors and stokers of the German navy were most concerned with their living conditions and showed little knowledge and even less interest in politics and party struggles. The majority of them, however, coming as they did from the working class, had a very highly developed— one might even say an almost inbred—trade-union consciousness. From birth they had been brought up to think along class lines and to wage the proletariat's battle against employers and industrialists. In typical worker fashion they knew how to strike for their rights and the protection of their interests. When their dreadful living conditions failed to improve during the spring of 1917 and their diet continued to hover near the starvation level, a great tide of war-weariness swept over them. Their officers' one-sided propaganda campaign against reform and in favor of territorial annexations, their refusal to grant food complaint committees, and their prohibition of socialist newspapers and meetings prompted the men to begin to think of organizing.

In their developing struggle with their superiors it was only natural that the sailors and stokers should revert to their working-class upbringing and training. After all, they were hardly ever in combat against the enemy and were usually employed more like workers than sailors.[5] Hence when their demands for better food and grievance machinery were thwarted, they gradually fell back on such time-tested means of the trade-union struggle as organizing, collective bargaining, the strike, and the walkout. However, it required time to develop an effective organization. At the beginning of the summer the movement had barely gotten started, and the men's resistance still took the form of isolated instances of obstruction.

The major exception was the *Prinzregent Luitpold*. The crew of that ship had been fed a steady diet of turnips, dehydrated vegetables, and *Drahtverhau* for a long time. The men had reached the point of desperation. On June 6, 1917, the ship's cooks served a particularly nauseating meal. Although the men had not yet organized, the stokers refused to pick up their food both at lunch time and at supper. Thereupon the first officer of the ship, Korvettenkapitän Herzbruch, assembled the men on deck. Berating them, he stated that they must have "gone crazy to refuse their food" and labeled their action as "incorrect and unpatriotic."

The stokers refused to be swayed. They answered that they would gladly eat whatever food was given them if the officers would do the same. It had come to their attention, however, that the officers' mess still served "cutlets the size of a saucer." Since the men remained adamant and Herzbruch could not persuade them to eat their regular meal, he gave in and promised them an issue of bread and bacon and a better supper.[6]

On the surface it appeared that the brief hunger strike on the *Prinzregent Luitpold* had merely resulted in a temporary and partial victory for the crew. But rations did not improve. When the stokers demanded an explanation they were peremptorily turned down by their officers.[7] The crew was still divided by rivalry between the stokers and sailors, and the officers were therefore able to exploit this division by returning to their former complacency and ignoring the demands of their subordinates.

Actually, however, it would be hard to exaggerate the importance of June 6. On that day the engine room crew of the *Prinzregent Luitpold* had inadvertently stumbled upon a most potent weapon—the strike. Without any prior organization, the men had struck and thus managed, even if only temporarily, to impose their will upon their officers. Moreover, and this is most significant, they had done this before the publication of the order for setting up a *Menagekommission* and prior to the establishment of connections with any political party.[8] Thus some of the enlisted men of that ship for the first time seized the initiative, developed a spirit of solidarity, and forged the weapon by which they could force their officers to pay attention to them and negotiate. This first hunger strike was to become the model for a number of similar conflicts on other ships and was to play a dominant role in determining the strategy and the nature of the enlisted men's resistance movement.

Out of the turmoil of the first strike two leaders arose from the crew of the *Prinzregent Luitpold*. They were Stokers Johann Beckers and Albin Köbis. Under their leadership the crew decided shortly after June 6 to establish an organization to make future protests more effective. It was agreed to establish a *Soldatenbund*, a sailors' council, to plan and coordinate any future strikes and to see to it that none of the men picked up any unpalatable food. Beckers, as the elected spokesman of the crew, was to be in charge of all demonstrations.

Whenever he received word from the men who worked in the ship's galley that the food was unsatisfactory, he was empowered to issue a strike call. Delegates (*Vertrauensmänner*) were elected by each of the ship's watches and divisions. They were to maintain close contact with Beckers so that any decision to strike would receive the unanimous support of the entire crew. With representatives in each of the watches and a central leadership at the top, the *Soldatenbund* of the *Prinzregent Luitpold* was organized and run along the military lines of the ship. This made it an ideal protest organization.

Astutely aware that such an organization could not be confined to one ship if it was to produce effective remedies, the crew decided that the leadership of the *Soldatenbund* should be divided into two jobs. There was to be an "outside leader" charged with the task of developing similar organizations and spreading propaganda on the other ships of the fleet. This job was also conferred on Beckers. The task of building up the internal organization on board the *Prinzregent Luitpold* was given to Köbis.[9]

Not long after the strike Beckers and Köbis established contact with the movement on the *Friedrich der Grosse* and its two leaders, Reichpietsch and Sachse. The exact date of this meeting is not known. But in all probability it occurred after Reichpietsch's return from Berlin, and therefore must have taken place after June 21.[10] There is a remote possibility that the leaders already knew one another. More likely, however, the news of Reichpietsch's and Sachse's activities had circulated in the fleet and had thus come to the attention of the two *Prinzregent* leaders. Unfortunately the substance of this conversation is unknown. It may be that the men merely compared notes on conditions on their respective ships and discussed ways of improving them. It is also possible that Beckers and Köbis first heard about the order establishing food complaint committees at this meeting and planned the means by which such a grievance machinery could be instituted on their ship.[11]

Thus the first contact was established between the two ships in the High Seas Fleet that were to contend for leadership of the enlisted men's movement and each of which would try to impress its own particular flavor upon the fleetwide organization they hoped to develop.

Conditions on the *Friedrich der Grosse* had produced a countermovement among the enlisted men and the rise of a leadership consisting of Max Reichpietsch and Willi Sachse. The Bachmann order of May 5 and June 4, 1917 had first been published on the flagship of the fleet; its crew had been the first to find out about the Capelle order for *Menagekommissions*. That vessel had also been the first to establish political relations with the USPD through Reichpietsch. Hence, from the beginning on the *Friedrich der Grosse*, the movement took a political turn.

Political considerations on the *Prinzregent Luitpold* were far less pronounced. The Bachmann order had never been posted.[12] Its crew knew nothing about a *Menagekommission*. On the other hand, on board that ship living conditions were far worse. On this, the "convict ship" of the fleet, a large number of men were disciplinary cases, the entire crew had a bad reputation, and therefore the officers were much harsher and stricter. The first officer, Herzbruch, was renowned for being a martinet who insisted on maintaining tight discipline and was passionately detested by the men. They hated him not only for his harshness but also for sending his orderly into the surrounding countryside to buy hams and other rare delicacies to send home to his wife.[13]

Because of all this, the discontent of *Prinzregent's* crew centered around much more concrete complaints such as living conditions, rations, and ill-treatment. From the very beginning, the movement on the *Prinzregent Luitpold* therefore lacked the political orientation of the *Friedrich der Grosse*. Consequently, it was natural that the *Prinzregent Luitpold* should develop a different kind of leadership.

The principal leader of the enlisted men's movement on the *Prinzregent Luitpold* was Stoker First Class Johann Beckers, a twenty-five-year-old former miner and something of an anarchist.

He possessed at least a rudimentary education, for he was a devout adherent of Max Stirner. Stirner, a noted nineteenth-century exponent of "individualistic" anarchism had preached self-assertive and ruthless class warfare in his famous book, *The Ego and His Own.* Before the war Beckers had belonged to the Free Socialist youth movement. After 1918 he found employment as a clerk in a rental library in Aachen.[14]

Beckers was intensely interested in philosophy, "worshiped Nietzsche," and had somehow come to the conclusion that all wars were morally wrong. Hence he supported the SPD and its stand in favor of a peace without annexations and indemnities. Since his entry into the navy in 1912 he had received three disciplinary punishments. From all accounts, Beckers was clever and intelligent, a good speaker, but somewhat impatient and impulsive.[15]

Closely associated with him as a leader of the resistance movement on board the *Prinzregent Luitpold* was Stoker Albin Köbis. Köbis was also twenty-five years old and came from the working-class district of Pankow-Niederbarnim in Berlin. By profession he was a machinist.[16] Bored and dissatisfied by the humdrum existence of his life, Köbis had spent three and a half years as a stoker on German, Danish, and Norwegian merchantmen prior to his enlistment in the navy in 1912.[17] Like Beckers, he was an anarchist, but was much more direct and forceful in his approach. He had never been actively involved in politics, had studied socialism for two years before losing interest, and was now much preoccupied with philosophy.[18] Köbis' disciplinary record of ten punishments in five years indicates that he was impetuous, found it hard to control himself, and therefore had frequent trouble with his superiors.

The organization which Beckers and Köbis directed on the *Prinzregent Luitpold* reflected their personalities and the conditions prevailing on their ship. Therefore it was much more typical of the sentiment of the majority of the enlisted men in the German navy than the relatively sophisticated and politically conscious movement of Sachse and Reichpietsch on the *Friedrich der*

Grosse. Unlike that ship, which soon after the latter's return from Berlin was to develop an organization whose principal goals were to recruit members for the USPD, to found a party organization in the fleet and in Wilhelmshaven, and to ultimately stage a general strike for peace, the *Soldatenbund* of the *Prinzregent Luitpold* was largely concerned with more immediate abuses and the improvement of the crew's standard of living.

Beckers, in particular, always construed the purpose of the sailors' council to be "primarily the correction of abuses and the common defense of the men." In his estimation, this organization "had nothing at all to do with political matters." In fact, even his efforts to spread the movement to the other ships of the fleet was predicated on that principle. Thus he was able to win adherents for the sailors' cause on the *Westfalen* and *Rheinland* but not on the *Nassau*, where "the food must have been excellent." On ships where discontent was rife Beckers would simply relate the story of the *Prinzregent*'s successful hunger strike and would ask the men to join the movement. Politics were hardly ever mentioned.[19]

News of the *Prinzregent Luitpold*'s hunger strike spread through the fleet. Soon virtually all the men were informed of it. Thus they learned that it was possible to strike with impunity and that all that was required to obtain better rations was unity and organization. Consequently, the *Prinzregent Luitpold* became the model for all the other ships that aspired to improved conditions and sought a way to strike back at their officers. The movement on the convict ship threatened to overshadow the *Friedrich der Grosse*'s bid for leadership in the fleet.

It is significant therefore that even before Reichpietsch had time to indoctrinate his shipmates on the *Friedrich der Grosse*, the crew should stage a very similar strike. During the night of July 4–5, the *Friedrich der Grosse* had conducted artillery practice in the Baltic. In the course of this strenuous labor the crew, ravenous with hunger, had consumed its bread rations for the next day. As a result, on July 5, five hundred crew members resolutely demanded more bread. The officer of the watch was astonished and tried to mollify the men by offering them some coffee. Turning down this compromise, the crew thereupon refused to carry on their duties.

The situation on the *Friedrich der Grosse* became tense when the officers began to arm. It appeared as though fighting might break out. The men, however, stolidly retained their composure and stubbornly ignored all orders to return to work. At the last moment the officers lost their nerve, gave in, and promised to have a meal of groat soup prepared.[20]

The hunger strike of the *Friedrich der Grosse* was a complete success. The men's resistance had once again been effective. They had refused to yield even to the threat of force. Five hundred of them, nearly half the crew, had managed to defeat their officers, proving that so long as they maintained solidarity and a united front they could make their will prevail. Of still greater importance in connection with the *Friedrich der Grosse*'s hunger strike was the fact that the captain, anxious to prevent future confrontations such as this and to prevent a potential uprising, weakened and surrendered completely. He granted the men the right to establish a *Menagekommission* to which they could elect representatives to act as their spokesmen.

This victory plus the unexpected bonus of a food complaint committee that came with it catapulted the organizers of the strike to sudden fame. Reichpietsch, Weber, and Sachse were elected to serve on the *Menagekommission* and were charged with registering all the crew's complaints, not only those dealing with rations, with the ship's authorities.[21] Overnight their tiny clandestine movement was transformed into the unofficial leadership of the crew of a great battleship. The malcontents on the *Friedrich der Grosse* thus found themselves in control of the first real grievance committee in the fleet, the model and envy of all other ships.

Communist historians have long claimed that this strike and its results were the product of the organizational activities of socialistically oriented enlisted men like Reichpietsch and Sachse.[22] The facts, however, hardly justify this claim. It is extremely unlikely that a small number of men, no matter how inspired and dedicated they might have been, could have succeeded in organizing the crew for such a drastic step if the conditions had not been ripe for it. It must be remembered that Reichpietsch's conversion was of very recent origin and that he had returned to the ship less than two weeks before the strike. Moreover, Sachse's part in planning and organizing the strike is highly conjectural. The intellectual leader of the movement on board the *Friedrich der Grosse* had also been on leave and may not even have been back at the time of the strike.[23] Therefore it seems much more likely that the men of the *Friedrich der Grosse*, long disaffected with their life and their treatment and aware of what had transpired on the *Prinzregent Luitpold*, staged a spontaneous strike for more food. It was only natural when their strike resulted in the establishment of a *Menagekommission* that they should elect as their leaders personalities who were well known on the ship and who had some political experience. However, politics could not have played an important role in the strike. It is significant in this connection that the men never raised a demand for a grievance committee and that they seemed startled when the captain granted this concession.

As the sole ship of the fleet to have obtained a *Menagekommission*, the *Friedrich der Grosse* was now in a position to challenge the leadership of the *Prinzregent Luitpold*. Quickly the leaders on the flagship divided their functions to take advantage of their opportunity. Reichpietsch appointed himself as the "inside leader." Sachse was placed in charge of "external affairs," while Wilhelm Weber, a sailor from the casemate deck with a record of eleven disciplinary punishments and one court martial—but who was an excellent speaker—was entrusted with the task of recruitment and propaganda.[24]

Anxius to emulate the achievements of the *Friedrich der Grosse* and obtain a *Menagekommission* of their own, the crews of the other ships in the High Seas Fleet after July 5 came to its leaders for advice and instructions. In this fashion the movement on the *Friedrich der Grosse* and its leaders gained considerable influence in the fleet. The *Prinzregent Luitpold,* the only other center of an enlisted men's movement, was therefore temporarily surpassed by the *Friedrich der Grosse.* However, the *Prinzregent* did not lag too far behind. A few days later the crew of that ship staged a coaling strike that enabled it to obtain its own *Menagekommission.*

The major reason for the strike was the crew's resentment of exploitation by the officers. Prior to refueling one day, the men of the *Prinzregent Luitpold* discovered that their officers had placed bets with their colleagues on other ships that the *Prinzregent* would be the first to finish coaling. Irked by their superiors' disregard for their sensibilities, during the night the crew cut a number of cables and ropes on the coaling tackle and someone scrawled on one of the gun turrets, "Get Herzbruch off our ship and we'll beat the record!" [25]

The next day when the coaling began, the men deliberately slowed down their work to make the officers lose their bet. When some of the men on one of the cranes worked faster than the others, they were treated as strikebreakers and were given a trouncing by their comrades. Then the crew sent a delegation to Herzbruch with a newspaper article on the establishment of *Menagekommissions* and demanded that the *Prinzregent Luitpold's* crew be provided with such a committee.

Herzbruch responded by calling all hands on deck and shouting, "You have gone beserk again! What do you want? You have nothing to demand!" Thereupon several men, including Beckers, stepped forward, reiterated their demand for a food complaint committee, and requested permission to hold elections to select their representatives. At first Herzbruch rejected this out of hand. When, however, the men stood firm, he yielded slightly and stated that he would nominate some men for these positions. But the crew turned down his offer. Finally, he conceded defeat and promised to allow the crew complete freedom in the election of its representatives. He even granted the men permission to hold election meetings on shore because there was not enough room on the ship for mass meetings.

Thus the *Prinzregent*, too, obtained a food complaint committee and won a complete victory over the officers. The crew elected Beckers and Köbis as its representatives on the committee and instructed them not to confine their complaints to food. When they brought up other issues, the officers initially objected but gradually gave in.[26]

The *Friedrich der Grosse*'s and *Prinzregent Luitpold*'s triumph over the matter of the *Menagekommission* at the beginning of July lent great impetus to the enlisted men's resistance movement. Encouraged by the success of these ships, the other crews in the High Seas Fleet began to clamor for similar concessions. In almost every instance they were successful.[27] For example, after the *Helgoland* was granted a complaint committee, the crew went on strike and refused to unload several tons of spoiled flour. Only when the officers strapped on arms and drilled the men did they finally give in. Nevertheless, they went unpunished. This was indeed a startling change. Previously such an act would inevitably have resulted in court-martials and the brig. Now that the men possessed their complaint committee, or "Workers' and Sailors' Council," they could do as they pleased. In fact, Stumpf discovered that his shipmates on the *Helgoland* became so confident when they obtained their *Menagekommission* and their rations improved so remarkably that they almost felt that "the events in Russia [the Russian Revolution] were about to be repeated" in the navy.[28]

Even more indicative of the growing confidence and resolution of the enlisted men to no longer tolerate their former treatment are the events that transpired on the *Prinzregent Luitpold* and on the *Pillau*. On July 19 the crew of *Prinzregent* was presented with a meal consisting of a soup "that was swarming with worms." Although the ship's doctor had passed it as edible, the *Soldatenbund* immediately went into action. Declaring that the men could not eat the soup, it demanded that the doctor subject it to another test. When this was done, he proclaimed that the soup was indeed inedible and stated that he must have been deceived by the cooks.

The galley was thereupon ordered to produce another soup. Within a half hour the cooks produced a "painfully thin" soup for the 1,200 man crew of the *Prinzregent Luitpold*. Once again the committee, calculating that it was impossible to prepare a proper meal in such a short time, ordered the crew to refuse the new soup. It demanded that the men be issued instead some bread "three centimeters thick" with sausage and that a proper meal be prepared for their dinner. As on the other occasions, the second hunger strike on the *Prinzregent* was a success. The men had won another victory and, even more importantly, had seen that their council was capable of rendering the officers impotent.[29]

More dramatic still was the incident that took place on board the *Pillau* on July 20, 1917. Long restive over a variety of abuses and inequities in the matter of leaves, the crew of that cruiser staged a walkout when the leaves that had been promised by the first officer failed to materialize when the ship went into dock for repairs. Without offering any explanation, the first officer had simply canceled all leaves. This enraged the crew to such an extent that 137 men decided to take matters into their own hands and to stage a protest by leaving the ship. They spent the afternoon in a local tavern and returned at five o'clock. Immediately upon their return, however, they set to work and made up the time they had missed by working until 7:45. What was amazing about this incident was not only the audacious behavior of the men, but even more so, the response of the officers. In punishment for their walkout strike, the men were made to serve a mere three hours of punishment exercise.[30]

The inaction of the naval officer corps in the face of the open defiance displayed by the crews in all of these incidents, strikes, and walkouts could not help but convey to the men the impression that the weapons of the trade-union struggle could be used with impunity in the navy so long as they organized, acted in unison, and pursued their goal with determination. This is the only possible explanation for the outbreak of a wave of incidents that bore such a striking similarity to prewar industrial conflicts. Greatly encouraged by the success of this new tactic, the enlisted men's movement was bound to precipitate a grave crisis in the navy.

The mildness of the officers' response to the blatant insubordination of the sailors and stokers is a very puzzling phenomenon. One would have expected that the officers would charge the men who defied them in strikes and walkouts with insubordination and mutiny. Indeed, this is precisely what they did less than a month later on August 2 when the crew of the *Prinzregent Luitpold* staged its famous walkout. During July, however, the officers did little. In a few instances they did impose some mild penalties such as punishment tours, but most often they did not even bother to impose any penalties.

Several reasons for this are possible. It may be that the officers felt that their subordinates were justified in taking these steps and therefore hesitated imposing upon them the draconian measures which a charge of mutiny would inevitably have entailed.[31] It may also be that the officers, too, were discouraged, war-weary, and had lost hope in the navy. Hence they were past caring what the men did so long as their own position was not endangered. The German naval officer corps, however, had never been noted for a strong sense of social justice and had in the past always rigidly insisted upon maintaining its full rights and prerogatives. In the light of the *Kastengeist* that animated most of its members, this is not a very likely response.

It is much more reasonable to suppose that the officers were ashamed to admit their loss of control and their lack of discipline to the higher authorities. It may be that they felt guilty about their own behavior and the various abuses they had allowed to develop and hence feared being charged with negligence and incompetence. Also some of the officers may have realized, albeit somewhat belatedly, that they had in this fashion violated Paragraph LVIII, Article 10 of the Code of Military Justice. This declared that "All those [officers] who neglect their responsibility in the feeding of their subordinates . . . shall be placed under sentence of death for treason." [32]

Since they formed such a closed caste, preserving a "tight unity" and deliberately isolating themselves from the rest of society, it may well be that the officers were reluctant to disrupt their unity and cohesion by preferring charges against their subordinates that might ultimately reflect badly on them and result in a purge of their corps. On another and even more vital occasion the German officer corps reacted precisely in this manner. During October and November 1918, at the time of the outbreak of the actual revolution in the navy, the naval officers responded with equal indecision. In many instances they failed to report that an armed revolt had broken out among their men. Drascher, the sociologist of the German navy, attributes this behavior to the existence of a "misdirected sense of comradeship" in the officer corps. This caused the officers to shrink "from reporting anyone" and created an "understandable shyness" among them about referring such matters to higher authorities because they hoped that "they could quietly [unter der Hand] cope with these difficulties by themselves." [33]

That this was the probable reason for the officers' failure to report these incidents is indicated by the navy's response to a letter written by Seaman Conrad Lotter on July 23, 1917. Lotter, a Catholic sailor serving on the cruiser Bremse, had addressed a letter of complaint about the situation in the navy to Domkapitular Leicht of Cologne. The prelate, in turn, had forwarded it to Deputy Doctor Pfleger, the Center Party's expert on naval affairs in the Reichstag. In his letter the sailor asserted that "severe mutinies that came within an inch of actually overthrowing the officers had recently broken out on some of the ships." He was disturbed that the officers did not punish the implicated men. At the same time, however, Lotter expressed the opinion that the unrest in the fleet was caused by the "bad example set by the officers, insufficient rations, illegal treatment and unfulfilled promises of leaves." [34]

Lotter feared that the situation had deteriorated to such an extent that the officers had lost all authority over their men, the crew of the *Thüringen* having gone so far as spraying a water hose into the officers' mess that soaked all the officers and ruined their meal.

In his letter the Catholic sailor also stated that it was rumored that some of the enlisted men had held meetings with deputies of the Independent Social Democratic party in Berlin. Fearing that this deplorable state of affairs would create a scandal that might discredit the navy, Lotter recommended a parliamentary investigation which would provide full immunity from prosecution for the enlisted men.

Although Deputy Pfleger on July 28 passed on Lotter's letter and endorsed the sailor's demand for an early investigation, the navy tried its best to absolve itself of all guilt. It instituted a half-hearted inquiry. Admiral Hebbinghaus, the Chief of the General Administration Department of the navy, was dispatched to Kiel for a single week to look into the matter. From the beginning, Hebbinghaus indicated that he was more concerned with maintaining good relations with the officer corps than unearthing embarrassing information. On August 4 he wrote back to Berlin that he was proceeding very cautiously so as to avoid the suspicion that he "came as a Grand Inquisitor." He found it convenient to deal almost exclusively with Captain von Trotha, Admiral Scheer's Chief of Staff, and soon came to feel that his mission would not cause "any disruption of a very excellent relationship with him." [35]

It comes as no great surprise, therefore, that in his report of August 7, Admiral Hebbinghaus should maintain that he had not been able to discover any legitimate abuses in the navy. Without having interviewed a single enlisted man, the admiral asserted that all he had found was a single instance in which an officer had called an enlisted man a "*Schweinehund*," and that the officer had been severely punished for this offense.[36]

Surely a more objective investigation, one which included some testimony by enlisted men and was not conducted as this one in the immediate aftermath of the *Prinzregent Luitpold* walkout, the "August mutiny," would not have exonerated the naval officer corps so easily. Even if such an investigation had studiously sought to avoid casting any aspersions on the past behavior of the officer corps, it simply could not skip over the fact that there had been strikes, walkouts, and refusals to obey orders in the fleet and that the officers had never troubled to report them.

Admiral Hebbinghaus, however, was not the only officer who disregarded the "mutinies" of June and July 1917. Kapitän Hornhardt, the commander of the *Prinzregent Luitpold*, in his official report regarding the events on his ship on August 2, also saw fit to make light of previous unrest among his crew. He neglected to mention the coal strike and attributed all difficulties with his men to the problem of preparing new foods, such as dehydrated vegetables and turnips, which "certain bad elements" had exploited to sow dissension.[37]

This defensiveness and fear on the part of the officer corps to admit its loss of control over the men contributed significantly to the radicalization of the crews. The enlisted men must have sensed that their superiors had lost their self-confidence. Since their audacious acts went unpunished, they must have come to feel that they could attain all their desires through organization and concerted action.

It was at this point that semipolitical discussions and planning began to exert a growing influence within the enlisted men's movement and threatened to transform what had started as a simple reaction to abuses within the fleet into a politically oriented peace movement. Max Reichpietsch's visit with the Independent Social Democrats in Berlin may well be regarded as the first political act of the enlisted men. Upon his return to the fleet, Reichpietsch, for a variety of reasons both personal and political, began to agitate among his shipmates for the establishment of an affiliation with the USPD. He was in an excellent position to influence his comrades in this direction. After all, he enjoyed the distinction of having spoken and conferred with the deputies. They had welcomed him and had after a fashion entrusted him with the task of recruiting members for their party in the fleet. When Reichpietsch became the head of the *Menagekommission* on the *Friedrich der Grosse,* his sphere of influence was extended throughout the fleet as various ships sent delegates to inquire of him how they could obtain such committees.

Initially Reichpietsch remained closed-mouthed about his political contacts, merely reiterating in general terms that the men were allowed to join the USPD, that recruitment of members was permissible, and that he had been instructed to look with confidence toward Stockholm, where an international Socialist Congress would shortly convene to work out a way to end the war. Realizing that most of the enlisted men were not ready to join the Independent Social Democrats for purely political reasons, Reichpietsch exploited their war-weariness and desire for peace to aid his recruiting activities. As Philipp Scheidemann wrote, the Stockholm Peace conference "engendered an enormous measure of hope" throughout Germany and "hovered like a new star of Bethlehem . . . leading to the Prince of Peace." [38]

Reichpietsch therefore broached the idea that it would be useful to the USPD if the enlisted men demonstrated their support of peace by compiling lists of signatures in support of the Stockholm Congress. It is possible that the sailor had read a party directive stating that the USPD would welcome a numerical count of its adherents in Germany so that it might gain greater representation at the Stockholm Conference than the Majority Socialists. It may also be that he had somehow overheard a statement by one of the deputies, in the course of his conversations in Berlin, that the USPD possessed a larger following than its rival party and that this fact ought to be documented prior to the Conference.[39] A more likely explanation, however, would be that the idea for such lists was Reichpietsch's personal invention, a device by which he hoped to gain adherents and enhance his importance in the movement.[40]

Evidently Reichpietsch had correctly gauged the will of the men. The lists quickly became very popular. They filled the men's need to express their sentiment against the war. In fact, one might even go so far as to state that the drawing up of what became known as "the Stockholm lists" and the rapid growth of USPD membership in the navy was the natural reaction of men who had had their fill of war and who regarded the Reichstag's fight to pass a Peace Resolution in favor of ending the war as an authoritative repudiation of their officers' annexationism and conservatism.

In the tense political atmosphere that prevailed in Germany during the month of July 1917 it was virtually inevitable that the men should become increasingly concerned with political questions. In that month events of major political importance followed each other in bewildering succession. Stimulated by the steady rise of war-weariness, despair, and defeatism that manifested itself in the population, the moderate parties in the Reichstag—the Majority Social Democrats, the Progressives, the Center, and the National Liberals—at last overcame their differences, combined forces in an interparty committee (the *Interfraktionelle Ausschuss*), and agreed to impose upon the government a twofold program: a war-aims declaration in favor of a negotiated peace without territorial annexations and a domestic program that called for the immediate commencement of reform of Prussia's antiquated franchise system and the establishment of a parliamentary system of government for the Reich.

During the July 1917 crisis precipitated by these demands the new Reichstag majority, which enjoyed mass support among the population, won a number of notable victories. It managed to impose upon Chancellor von Bethmann-Hollweg its much-publicized Peace Resolution; it obtained a promise that franchise reform would begin at once and, most significantly, participated in forcing his dismissal from office.[41] It also played a crucial role in prevailing upon his successor as chancellor, Georg Michaelis, to adopt the Peace Resolution as the German government's official peace policy. Thus on July 19, 1917, when Michaelis publicly accepted the Peace Resolution as the basis for Germany's new foreign policy, it was widely felt by the population as well as by the enlisted men of the navy that the war would now be brought to a rapid conclusion and that the conservative and annexationist forces had been routed.[42]

Reichpietsch, under these circumstances, had plainly struck the one chord that could animate many of the enlisted men to proclaim their support of the USPD. This was not because they endorsed that party's entire political program but rather because to them that party represented the strongest and most outspoken force working for peace in Germany.[43] Hence their support of Reichpietsch and the USPD was largely nonpolitical in nature, merely representing their ardent desire for peace and their adherence to the ideals of the Peace Resolution.[44] This becomes evident as soon as one glances at the text of the most famous of the "Stockholm lists," the one drawn up by the crew of the *König Albert*, which bore the signatures of four hundred men. This document stated:

We, whose names and personal descriptions are attached, herewith join the Independent Social Democratic Party of Germany and declare ourselves to be in agreement with its policies. At the same time, we hereby declare that we endorse a peace without annexations and indemnities and desire an early conclusion of the war. We hope that the Socialist Conference at Stockholm will be crowned with success, that a peace on the principle of the right of self-determination for all peoples will be concluded and that it will put a halt to the murder of peoples and the brethren of the international proletariat. We extend our best wishes for success to the Stockholm Conference and hope that the work of the Independent Social Democratic Party of Germany will be met with success.[45]

This document may well be regarded as a "peace declaration" rather than a political manifesto. In fact, this is precisely what is indicated by the way the men's signatures were collected. The leaders of the crew went through the ship and said to the individual men, "Aren't you in favor of a peace of understanding? Then sign your name." In this fashion they succeeded in attracting many followers who did not support the USPD but rather the SPD and even managed to obtain the support of totally unpolitical men who barely read the statement.[46]

The Independent Socialist leaders knew nothing of these lists. If they had known of them, they would certainly never have given them their sanction for they served no useful purpose to their party. They were not needed for the Stockholm Conference because the International was well aware that the German proletariat wanted peace. Nor could they be presented to the German government because it would have been senseless to inform it that large numbers of enlisted men in the navy supported a peace without annexations. Moreover, there was always the danger that if the lists fell into the hands of the naval authorities they could be used as "proscription lists" to arrest the signers.[47] Hence it can be surmised that the idea for the lists and the recruitment drive for signatures was largely the product of the imagination of Max Reichpietsch.

It has been estimated that during July and August 1917 approximately five thousand sailors and stokers in the German High Seas Fleet pledged their allegiance to the Independent Social Democrats in this fashion. At least two such lists are known to have reached the party. One was sent to Deputy Henke, the USPD's representative in Bremen and the other one made its way to the office of the *Leipziger Volkszeitung*.[48] Despite this astonishing success and the rapid spread of the movement throughout the High Seas Fleet, the Independents' control and influence upon the enlisted men remained extremely limited, indeed largely negligible. This paradoxical state of affairs was not changed in the least by the additional contacts made with the party by a number of sailors and stokers.

Reichpietsch's correspondence with Frau Zietz, for instance, which the naval prosecutors were to label as incontrovertible evidence of the USPD's implication in the naval revolt, merely indicates that the sailor wanted to obtain more literature from the party and that he sent a few sporadic and vague reports of his progress and recruitment. Even the fact that he and some of the other enlisted men used false addresses, intermediaries, and other ruses to circumvent naval censorship does not prove that they were engaging in treasonable political activities.[49] Rather it indicates that they did not want to have their movement uncovered and broken up by the authorities.[50]

An even better argument for rejecting the thesis that the USPD inspired the sailors to rebel is provided by Willi Sachse's visit to Berlin. Shortly after Reichpietsch's return to the fleet it was Sachse's turn to go on leave. Somehow or other, despite his contentions to the contrary, Sachse must have suspected that Reichpietsch had not been completely truthful in his description of his conversations with the deputies. Therefore Sachse used his leave to visit some relatives in Berlin and also to discuss the situation in the navy with Dittmann.

On or about July 2 Sachse made an appearance at the Reichstag building. Dressed in uniform, he asked to speak with Deputy Dittmann and was conducted into the antechamber of Room 12. A little while later Dittmann rushed in. He was in a great hurry because he was scheduled to address the Reichstag. Sachse introduced himself and declared himself to be the author of the letter of complaint that Reichpietsch had presented. Dittmann seemed to remember it and greeted the stoker from the *Friedrich der Grosse* in a friendly manner.

Sachse first inquired if the enlisted men were entitled to form food complaint committees and described the conditions on board the ships. Dittmann appeared to be very distracted. When Sachse tried to hand him a number of applications for party membership, the deputy refused to take them and instructed him to drop them off at his office. Sachse next requested that Dittmann send the men more literature. Dittmann stated that he would be glad to oblige but that the party could not afford to provide it free of charge and advised that the men would have to pay for it.

Sachse was very disappointed in Dittmann and the perfunctory nature of the meeting. The deputy did not even bother to inquire about the progress of the enlisted men's movement and did not seem to take much of an interest in it. He made no mention of politics. Only as he was about to rush off to his meeting did he tell Sachse to carry on, but simultaneously he warned Sachse to exercise great caution. The entire conversation apparently did not last more than five or ten minutes.[51]

The haphazard manner in which Dittmann received Sachse and his cavalier treatment of him should suffice to show that the Independent deputy was not very concerned with the sailors, that he did not want to commit himself to them, and that he was anxious not to tie himself too closely to them. If Dittmann had indeed been bent on instigating an uprising in the navy, he would hardly have held even such a brief meeting in public with a uniformed sailor. If he had really been engaged in planning a rebellion he would certainly have instructed Sachse to return some other time at a less conspicuous place.

At approximately the same time that Sachse had his disappointing confrontation with Dittmann, Stoker Albin Köbis of the *Prinzregent Luitpold* was also visiting Berlin. Informing only his closest colleague Beckers of what he was about to do, Köbis traveled to the capital to consult with a number of figures in the Independent Social Democratic party. It is known that he spoke with a number of people at the home of a certain Dr. Haase (not Hugo Haase, the chairman of the party). The most prominent person at this meeting was Deputy Adolf Hoffmann. Köbis reported on the dismal living conditions in the fleet and asked for advice. Instead, however, he received a warning that the men were under no circumstances to resort to violence and strikes, but should simply forward all their complaints to the USPD. He was further cautioned that any ill-considered action could only harm the men's cause and was advised that "the fruit would have to ripen slowly." [52]

Such a weak, half-hearted, and compromising response from an allegedly revolutionary party was certainly not promising. Neither Sachse nor Köbis was happy. Actually, one might well say that the USPD was a great disappointment to all the enlisted men who came in contact with it save for Reichpietsch. Only Reichpietsch felt convinced that the Independents had a program and a plan for the enlisted men in the navy. As time passed his recollections of his conversations with the deputies dimmed considerably, and he gradually began to add a number of new points.

Originally Reichpietsch had merely contended that he had been instructed "to look toward Stockholm with confidence." [53] Nevertheless, the communist East German historian Bernhard maintains that within one day of his return from Berlin Reichpietsch broached the idea that the men prepare themselves to stage a general strike upon the orders of the USPD in case the Stockholm Peace Conference should fail. [54]

In the light of Sachse's testimony, which is all that exists by way of support, Reichpietsch approached the idea of staging a strike in the fleet much more gradually. It took nearly a month before he actually came out with it. Even then it was met with considerable skepticism on the part of Weber and Sachse. They felt that such a tactic was not in keeping with the traditional methods of social democracy. [55]

The idea of striking and resorting to violence seemed so strange to Sachse and Weber that they refused to believe that the Independent deputies could ever sanction such a thing. Whenever they voiced such doubts, however, Reichpietsch would become mysterious and say, "The use of violence is permissible. The USPD sanctions it. I heard this expressly stated in Berlin." Still Sachse remained suspicious. On July 14 he arranged a meeting for

Reichpietsch with Wilhelm Sens, the USPD's party secretary in Kiel, to clarify the issue. Unequivocally Sens told Reichpietsch that his party did not permit sailors to strike. Enraged, Reichpietsch, according to Sachse, replied sharply, "On the contrary," his agreement with the deputies in Berlin specifically called for "a general strike in the fleet to force the conclusion of peace." When Sens remained unconvinced, Reichpietsch continued with mounting excitement, "A strike by troops to force a peace is permissible; the Berlin deputies have personally told me that!" [56]

Since Reichpietsch's talk of a general strike and violence was to play such a prominent role in radicalizing the enlisted men's movement, his claims must be examined with great care. If the deputies indeed issued such orders to him, they bear a grave responsibility for having led the men astray and for instigating them to revolt. If, on the other hand, no instructions of this sort were ever issued, then the blame for organizing a potentially revolutionary movement in the navy must fall upon Max Riechpietsch.

That the latter alternative is correct is borne out by the testimony that Reichpietsch gave to his naval interrogators on August 10, 1917. This testimony is of such great importance that it must be spelled out in detail because it indicates better than any other piece of evidence the full extent in which Reichpietsch was groping in the dark and how he allowed his imagination to distort the tactics and strategy of the Independent Socialists. Reichpietsch on that occasion stated:

Without any further reservations I admit that I was familiar with the views of the party on the possibility of enforcing the decisions of the Stockholm Conference by means of strikes and refusals to obey orders. I further admit that I and my fellow-accused had come out in support of such a violent implementation. As individuals, however, we were not clear how this was to be done. We stood by for instructions from the party. In our view these were bound to arrive. Instructions of this sort were not specifically [*mit offenen Worten*] mentioned in my conversations with Dittmann. . . . On the other hand, however, I am convinced that Deputy Dittmann's and Frau

Zietz's request that we expand the movement for the USPD as widely
as possible in the fleet, or as he put it, that we should see to it that
the movement was spread throughout the ships, could only have had
one purpose, that of implementing and supporting the party's peace
ideas by means of strikes if necessary. . . .[57]

Reichpietsch's confession clarifies a number of vital issues.
First, it appears that neither Dittmann nor Frau Zietz had said
anything to him about strikes or violence. They had merely
hinted that it would be a good idea if he would recruit a large
following for their party in the navy. Secondly, nothing had been
said by them about any further instructions or orders from the
USPD. Reichpietsch admitted as much when he asserted that
nothing of this sort was expressly stated and when he inadvertently confessed that the plan to strike in support of a resolution
emanating from Stockholm was merely his interpretation of their
vague statements. Clearly, Reichpietsch's unsophisticated and untutored mind had completely misinterpreted Dittmann's and Frau
Zietz's statements and had distorted them into an imaginary set of
instructions to organize the enlisted men to strike and to refuse to
obey the orders of their officers.

It is highly unlikely that Reichpietsch would have invented
such a story for his interrogators. It would have been much more
natural for him to do what all the rest of the accused enlisted men
did when they tried to shift the blame for their actions upon the
shoulders of the deputies in order to lighten their own sentences.
Under the circumstances Reichpietsch should have exaggerated
the encouragement he had received from the USPD and tried to
place upon it as much blame as possible for inciting him to organize a rebellion. Yet he did not do this. Perhaps it was because he
thought that the deputies would be called upon to testify at his
trial and hence feared that they would repudiate his fabrications.
Therefore, although he may have exaggerated the intent of their
statements to some extent, he could not invent any specific evidence to show that they had openly instigated him to revolt. The
fact that Reichpietsch did not implicate the USPD politicians sug-

gests that they had never advocated that he use violence, that they knew nothing of his planned strike, and that they bear no direct legal responsibility for the August mutiny.

Despite the fact that Reichpietsch had invented the plan for a strike in the fleet by himself, the USPD does not emerge without its share of blame. The Independent deputies should have known that an uneducated, politically untrained sailor such as Max Reichpietsch could not be trusted to recruit for their party, that he could well misunderstand his mandate, and that his excessive zeal could easily lead him to commit all sorts of rash acts. They should also have realized that the letters and propaganda material they later sent him would arouse within him the false hope that they would support all of his actions regardless of their consequences. In that sense, the USPD bears considerable moral responsibility for its lack of caution and for its opportunism.

To a certain extent, however, the blame goes even further. The party leaders had not only encouraged Reichpietsch to build up an organization on their behalf in the fleet when they talked to him in Berlin, but had gone further than that when they recommended that he contact their local representatives in Kiel and Wilhelmshaven for aid. However, they never supplied these local agents with specific instructions on how to deal with the sailors, leaving this crucial matter exclusively to the discretion of unsophisticated and relatively inexperienced personnel. This may well be regarded as a poor attempt to slough off their responsibility on subsidiary figures and to conceal their involvement in case things went awry in the fleet.

In this manner Reichpietsch and Sachse were put in touch with Wilhelm Sens, the USPD's organizer in Kiel. Sens proved himself grossly inept and inexperienced in his dealings with the enlisted men. Not only did he provide them with all the party membership cards they wanted, but he also complied with Reichpietsch's request that they be cut down in size for easier concealment. On July 14 he addressed a group of 150 men from the *Friedrich der Grosse* at the Meilenstein Tavern in Kiel [58] and, for some reason, did nothing to inform his superiors that Reichpietsch was under the impression that he had been instructed to organize a strike in the fleet. Emil Büdeler, the USPD's only member in Wilhelmshaven, a simple shipyard clerk, also allowed himself to be exploited by the enlisted men, who made him an illicit post office for mailing their letters and receiving packages of party propaganda.[59]

Despite their opportunism and irresponsibility, it would be a mistake to accuse the USPD leaders of willfully fomenting a mutiny in the fleet. All of their actions point to the opposite conclusion. They were far too cautious to steer such a potentially disastrous course. Thus they were willing at best to give Reichpietsch and his comrades vague promises of support while at the same time they protected themselves by foisting responsibility upon their local representatives.

Yet it was precisely these protective devices and ruses that were to embroil the USPD in such great difficulty. The Independents' studied vagueness and weakly worded warnings could not stop a man like Reichpietsch once he had made up his mind that organization and action was all the men needed to impose their will upon the navy. On the contrary, the ambiguity was the very thing that enabled Reichpietsch to embroider and enlarge his descriptions of his political contact and finally allowed him to come to the erroneous conclusion that the party wanted him to organize a political strike.

Although Reichpietsch made much capital out of his contact with the deputies and was able to attract a considerable following among the enlisted men of the High Seas Fleet who endorsed the collection of lists for the Stockholm Conference and vaguely discussed plans for a general strike, the actual influence of the USPD in the navy remained surprisingly small. No more than 7 or 8 percent of the enlisted men were ever involved in the resistance movement.[60] Moreover, most of the men who joined were not attracted for political reasons. Their primary reasons for joining were that they wanted to obtain food complaint committees, they wanted better living conditions and an end to the war.

Significantly enough, Reichpietsch and Sachse were clever enough to understand this and to adapt their recruitment techniques accordingly. Whenever they tried to recruit new members they started out by talking about food and the desirability of forming a *Menagekommission*, raising the political issue only at the end of their meetings.

Even at political meetings the subject of food always preceded any political discussion. Thus Herr and Frau Mrosewski, the owners of the Tivoli Tavern, testified to the police that the men who met in their establishment always introduced themselves as members of a *Menagekommission* and confined their talk to food while they were being served.[61] This kind of circumspection made it possible for men to belong to the movement without knowing anything of its political aims. This is exactly what happened to Seaman Bieber of the *Helgoland*. An intensely patriotic sailor who was a member of the ultraconservative Fatherland Party, Bieber had been elected to the *Menagekommission* of his ship. In that capacity he met with a number of the major ringleaders. Only when he was arrested and placed on trial did he discover to his great dismay that he was alleged to have belonged to a political movement.[62]

Seaman Schneider of the *Friedrich der Grosse*, a close friend of Reichpietsch, had a similar experience. He asserted, "I attended two or three meetings and hereby state that nothing of a political nature was raised at these meetings. The talk revolved around economic conditions and nothing else." [63] Even Wilhelm Weber, one of the leaders of the movement, feels that the political aspect of the movement was exaggerated out of proportion by Sachse's testimony and the findings of the court-martial. As far as he was concerned the movement's primary purpose was "to found a sailors' council that stemmed from the *Menagekommission* and which was intended to remove the abuses which we suffered by uniting the men. Only gradually did Sachse and Reichpietsch bring forth their actual political goals." [64] Weber testified further that he was frequently approached by crew members of other vessels for advice regarding organizing a *Menagekommission*. He would then ask these people to join the movement whose "aim I described as the improvement of rations and a better way of enforcing the wishes of the *Menagekommission*. . . ." [65]

All this makes it difficult to characterize the movement that grew up on the ships of the High Seas Fleet as political. Undeniably there was a small core of politically oriented leaders such as Reichpietsch and Sachse, but most of the men who joined it and many of those who functioned as its leaders had no concrete political ideas and did not regard themselves as followers of the Independent Socialists. This is especially true of the movement that arose on board the *Prinzeregent Luitpold*.

Beckers and Köbis, the leaders of the enlisted men on that ship, were anarchists who shied away from any political affiliation or movement.[66] Nevertheless, they exploited the men's dissatisfactions to create an indigenous protest movement on the *Prinzregent Luitpold* that bore little more than a superficial resemblance to the much more politically conscious organization developed by Reichpietsch and Sachse on the *Friedrich der Grosse*. The distinction between the political and nonpolitical elements in the enlisted men's movement is nowhere spelled out more clearly than in the struggle for leadership that these two ships waged against each other.

Johann Beckers, who led the famous walkout of the *Prinzregent Luitpold* crew on August 2, describes the acrimonious conflict that developed between him and Reichpietsch in July over the question of a constitution. Beckers had drafted a constitution to unite the amorphous mass of men in the fleet into one coherent organization and presented his draft for adoption at a meeting that took place at the Kieler-Gaarden Tavern. Article IV of Beckers' constitution asserted as the principal goal of the movement the correction of a variety of abuses in the navy and the formulation of a peace proclamation by the men. In order to attain this end Beckers maintained that the men should proceed on their own without waiting for any future resolutions that the

USPD might bring forward in the Reichstag. He felt that the sailors and stokers had no need to follow the orders of that party and wanted them to retain their freedom of action. Reichpietsch at once made vociferous objections. He strongly advocated retaining the connection with the Independent deputies in Berlin and refused to approve Beckers' proposal.[67]

From the very beginning Beckers had been reluctant to accept directions from the *Friedrich der Grosse*. He disliked the political orientation of its leaders and did not want to subordinate the organization on his ship to his rivals. Perhaps he also suspected that Reichpietsch had not told the truth about his political connections in Berlin. His shipmate Köbis had returned from the capital with an entirely different set of impressions of the USPD. He had been instructed to avoid any sort of violence while Reichpietsch kept talking about strikes, revolutions, and the forceful enforcement of the decisions of the Stockholm Conference. As Beckers put it, "I had a certain feeling which I could not prove—that there was no actual connection with Berlin . . ." Consequently, Beckers was unwilling to concede the role of leadership to the *Friedrich der Grosse*. At most he was willing to regard the organization on the *Friedrich der Grosse* as a convenient center or "statistical bureau" for the collection of complaints regarding abuses in the Fleet. When it came to organizing protests or a rebellion, Beckers demurred. As an anarchist he insisted that the "men on our ship were strong enough to defend their own cause."[68]

For all of his singlmindedness and fanaticism, it is unlikely that Reichpietsch could have succeeded in overcoming these centrifugal tendencies and internal divisions with his disjointed ramblings. What was needed to unite the fleet was a cogent, rational appeal to the working-class consciousness and solidarity of the men. Largely by accident, precisely such an appeal was made to a small audience of enlisted men on July 20 at the Deutsches Haus in Wilhelmshaven. Alfred Herre, a former editor of the Independent Socialist *Leipziger Volkszeitung* who had recently been drafted into the II Torpedo Division of Wilhelmshaven, appeared upon the scene and addressed the men.

Herre's speech has been the subject of considerable conjecture and has formed the basis for many accusations of treason. Admiral von Trotha, for instance, insists that Herre's speech exerted a "very special influence on the development of a treasonable organization among the men." [69] Another expert, Dr. Volkmann, maintains that "from this day on there was no longer any doubt regarding the great political influence among the ringleaders of the movement." [70] However, no reliable account of Herre's speech has ever been found. Hence it is impossible to know exactly what he said.

Insofar as one can rely on the very fragmentary evidence that is available, Herre discussed the origins of the war, said something about granting war credits, and spoke at greater length on the subject of a peace without annexations. He also expressed the opinion that the April 1917 strike of the workers of Leipzig for more bread and domestic reforms had ended too soon and hinted that a general strike might soon break out in Germany. In the event that this should come about, he appealed to the men not to participate in its suppression and advised them to ignore the Kaiser's injunction that his soldiers must be prepared to fire on their own relatives upon his orders. [71]

Although Herre clearly stated that the enlisted men were not permitted to become paying members of the USPD and that they were not allowed to collect money for the party, for some unexplained reason—perhaps his inexperience with the navy—he did sanction compiling signatures for the Stockholm lists. However, he made it plain that he was unequivocally opposed to violence. To Weber of the *Friedrich der Grosse* he said, "Avoid any sort of violence! No one will support you. Not even the USPD can or will support you!" [72]

There was actually nothing revolutionary in Herre's speech. But apparently it did contain ambiguities and contradictions that made it possible for it to be interpreted as much more radical than he intended. On the one hand Herre told the enlisted men to stay away from politics. But on the other, he lent his support to Reichpietsch's campaign for signatures. Moreover, he had added a new element to the debates of the enlisted men by his suggestion that the sailors refuse to fire upon their working-class comrades if they were called out to suppress a general strike. All in all, Herre had said nothing that the men had not heard or considered previously.

Why then did his relatively innocuous talk have such a radical and revolutionary impact upon the men? The best explanation is that his speech constituted on a much larger scale a repetition of Reichpietsch's experience with the deputies. Herre's audience was impressed and overawed by his high status just as Reichpietsch had been. Like him, they heard only what they wanted to hear. And just as Reichpietsch had misinterpreted and distorted what he was told because he lacked political experience and sophistication, so their untutored ears converted the jargon of a very ordinary Socialist speech into an incitement to action.

Willi Sachse, who was perhaps the only person in the audience who possessed the requisite training and political experience, must have sensed this. Several months later he stated, "Taken as a whole, Herre's speech contained so many slogans and strong expressions that men who had no theoretical training in socialism could well walk away with it, as they apparently did, in a mood to strike and do violence. Until the time of my arrest Herre's speech formed the major topic of discussion among my comrades and was regarded in a certain sense as an authoritative approval of our program."[73]

Their public declaration to the contrary, the naval authorities must have realized that Herre had not said anything that was flagrantly illegal and revolutionary. Therefore, although they branded him as "the intellectual founder" of the revolutionary movement in the navy, they did not proceed to arrest him until March 3, 1918, almost a year after his speech. Moreover, even then he was merely accused of having delivered a "questionable speech" (*eine bendenkliche Rede*). Final corroboration that Herre's position was legally unassailable came three weeks later, on March 22, 1918, when the North Sea Naval Station at Wilhelmshaven reported that he was about to be released from the service because of mental depression and physical exhaustion and that no court action would be initiated against him for lack of evidence.[74]

The fact that Herre had been misunderstood and misinterpreted by the men does nothing to minimize the profound impact he had upon the resistance movement in the navy. Beckers reports that within a few days four hundred of his shipmates on the *Prinzregent Luitpold* signed up as members of the USPD and that rumors began to circulate that a demonstration "against the war and for peace" would be staged in Wilhelmshaven "within a few months." [75] This is confirmed by Sachse, who states that shortly after Herre's speech the men began to hold regular political meetings at the Tivoli. There they discussed ways in which they could play a trump (*auftrumpfen*) on behalf of the Independent Socialists and their peace program by supporting the Reichstag's July 19 Peace Resolution.[76]

Reichpietsch, in particular, was so impressed by Herre's erudition that he tried to emulate him. In a speech given at the Tivoli shortly after July 20, Reichpietsch demonstrated how badly he had misunderstood the journalist from the *Leipziger Volkszeitung*. To an audience of approximately forty men Reichpietsch proclaimed:

> The class of sailors and stokers stands to lose a great deal if the war is prolonged. Therefore force shall have to be used to bring it to a close. The sailors must unite. Once they are united they must proceed, if necessary with violence, against their officers. It is extremely urgent that the peace movement in the navy be expanded to provide the support needed by our deputies in Stockholm. If the deputies should return without having achieved anything in Stockholm and

turn to the sailors with the call, 'Rise up! Break your chains! Follow the example of Russia!' then everyone will have to know what to do.[77]

This mistaken reaction demonstrates how sadly lacking in political understanding the enlisted men's movement was. Despite increasing numbers of contacts with the outside world, its principal leaders still operated in a political vacuum built on illusion. Moreover, even when the movement thus reached an illusory stage of political development, its rank and file members continued to remain unpolitical and still focused their primary attention on much more immediate matters like food. Whether they liked it or not, the leaders had to adjust themselves to this fact. Thus Oberheizer Fischer of the *Pillau* reports that Reichpietsch's and Sachse's meetings at the Tivoli would always start out with a discussion of ways to improve rations while the question of Stockholm and a sailors' strike was deferred until the end.[78] Moreover, Beckers, one of the ranking leaders of the movement, advocated consistently that such meetings should not deal with political questions at all and should be confined to questions dealing with the *Menagekommissions*. Whenever Reichpietsch was absent from one of the Tivoli meetings Beckers succeeded in making this view prevail. Thus at the meeting of July 30, the discussion centered exclusively on this matter and when someone raised the demand that the men purchase subscriptions to "opposition papers" the motion was brusquely defeated.[79]

The existence of this state of affairs renders largely senseless the claim of the communists that the enlisted men wanted much more than a mere improvement in rations and that they were actually working to create a revolution along the lines of the Russian one.[80] This holds true as well for Sachse's wild, belated, and completely unsubstantiated contention that he and the movement were never dependent upon the USPD and that he had made much more effective and useful contacts with truly revolutionary groups such as the Spartacists and the Gruppe International in Bremen.[81]

Even the much more moderate assertion of contemporary East German communist authors that the men were radicalized by contacts with revolutionary shipyard workers who provided them with information on how to establish revolutionary organizations on board their ships and put them in touch with various leftist groups cannot be substantiated.[82] There were few if any revolutionary dockworkers in Wilhelmshaven. Even the Independent Socialists had not yet succeeded in building up any organization in that city while the situation in Kiel was only slightly better.[83]

At best one might say that the enlisted men's movement in the navy was beginning to become politicized by July 1917, that it had established vague contacts with the USPD in Berlin and some of its local personnel, and that it received its half-hearted and ill-organized aid and advice. By no stretch of the imagination, however, can it be regarded as a revolutionary political movement. It had arisen too spontaneously, it lacked clear and cohesive leadership, it had neither reliable contacts with the USPD nor its support, and, most importantly, the great majority of its members were still not politically oriented enough to form a true revolutionary movement. In short, although politics had begun to creep in at an accelerated pace and although something resembling a central directory had been established on board the *Friedrich der Grosse* and the *Prinzregent Luitpold,* the power of the movement and its mass support still stemmed from the poor conditions in the fleet, the men's alienation from their officers, their resurgent trade-union consciousness, and their intense desire for peace.[84]

It is extremely significant from the point of view of refuting the accusations of the right as well as the exaggerated claims of the left that none of the political discussions, none of the agitation, and none of the contacts with the Independent Socialists had anything to do with the actual outbreak of the so-called August 1917 mutiny on the *Prinzregent Luitpold.*

The crew of that ship was completely disaffected. The stokers, especially, were extremely resentful of their mistreatment by their engine room officer, Engineer Hoffmann. On July 31, after being on watch the whole day, the men of the Third Stokers' Division were informed by an order posted on the bulletin board by Hoffmann that the next day's recreational period consisting of a movie had been canceled and that they were to turn out for infantry drill. The stokers were very disappointed. They had looked forward to the film showing for an entire week. It was the only thing that "distracted them," and it stood in the "forefront of their interests."

At approximately 11:30 that night Oberheizer Kohler, who was not a member of the *Soldatenbund*, informed Beckers of the bad news. "This cannot happen! We are scheduled to have movies! We shall not tolerate this!" Beckers exploded. In a tone of disbelief and with a challenge in his voice, Kohler retorted, "Then show us what your people can do."

Impulsively the leader of the *Prinzregent Luitpold*'s *Soldatenbund* accepted the challenge. Beckers ordered the Third Division not to turn out for the drill in the morning and to register their protest by absenting themselves from the ship for several hours. On the morning of August 1, when the Third Division was piped to duty, all the men had been informed. Forty-seven of them left the ship and walked off. Only the petty officers and thirteen enlisted men of the division remained behind. The protestors lounged around on a nearby dyke most of the morning but returned to the ship on their own volition at approximately eleven o'clock.

When they came ambling back, the ship had been alerted. The men were ordered to line up. The officers walked up and down before them identifying those whom they considered the ringleaders. In this haphazard fashion, eleven men were selected for punishment. It was harsh, unreasonable, and badly administered. They were to be placed under arrest for fourteen to twenty-one days and degraded in rank. Since all of the cells in the ship's brig as well as those of the naval jail in town were filled, however, their punishment had to be postponed.

Resenting the arbitrary selection of scapegoats, the men objected and demanded that Captain von Hornhardt either punish them all or, in order to maintain fairness, that every second man among them should be selected to serve the sentence. When the captain flatly refused this suggestion, word spread through all the ship's divisions that the crew would "not tolerate that and would protest against it." Someone recommended staging a "sympathy" strike on behalf of the Third Division. Although most of the men were acquainted with this term, the majority did not know what it actually meant. Nevertheless, the overwhelming sentiment on board the *Prinzregent Luitpold* was that something be done to protest the captain's decision. Time and again, Beckers was approached by angry sailors and stokers who demanded that he convene a meeting to organize such a strike.

With some reluctance Beckers agreed. Possibly he already regretted his impulsiveness and realized that things were getting out of hand. Therefore, although he acquiesced to the meeting, he declared that delegates from the other ships in the fleet would also have to be invited. In case things did not work out as planned with the sympathy strike, he did not want *Prinzregent Luitpold* to stand alone.

Later that evening of August 1, the men came together in an empty railroad car on the dock. The *Friedrich der Grosse, Kaiser, Kaiserin,* and *Pillau* had dispatched delegates. It was decided that on the following day, on August 2, the entire crew of the *Prinzregent Luitpold* would demonstrate its solidarity with the Third Division by staging a walkout strike.

At no point in this chain of events were politics, peace, or the Independent Socialists ever discussed or mentioned. The irate men simply could no longer bear their officers' arbitrariness and thus decided to protest in the only way they knew—by means of walkouts and strikes. They promptly forgot all their previous political discussions and plans and reacted more like trade-union members whose comrades had been unjustly treated by an employer than like sailors or stokers. Since they lacked any sort of legal training, they had no clear conception that their actions could be regarded as constituting a mutiny. At Albin Köbis' suggestion they decided that if they did not exceed the ship's three-hour state of readiness and returned before that time, nothing serious could happen to them.[85]

Such an optimistic view was not unjustified. After all, there had been a whole series of strikes in the fleet in June and July, the most recent one having taken place on the *Pillau*. None of these had resulted in a charge of mutiny. In fact, most of them had simply been shrugged off as innocent pranks by the naval authorities. Judging from their own experience, the sailors and stokers of the *Prinzregent Luitpold* expected that their sympathy strike could at the very worst bring about the kind of retaliation that had been meted out to the Third Division the day before and against which they were currently planning to demonstrate. Moreover, they had received assurances of support from the other ships and hence felt that they would not stand alone.

Only this can explain their euphoria and lightheartedness on the morning of August 2 as they deserted their ship, struck out for Rüstersiel, and confronted Korvettenkapitän Herzbruch with a great surprise. In their own minds they were not mutinying. They had no political motives. Many of them were unaware or thought nothing of the fact that some of their leaders were in contact with the Independent Socialists. They were merely repeating on a somewhat larger and more spectacular scale what had been done with impunity and with great success on a number of vessels of the High Seas Fleet—striking for their rights and expressing their resurgent working class solidarity and consciousness. Not even when their officers, the police, and the shore patrol were sent after them and their ship was placed under siege did most of them realize that their strike had misfired and that they now faced the grave charge of mutiny and political conspiracy.

My analysis of the development of the enlisted men's movement clearly indicates that there was little substance to these charges. Indeed, the *Prinzregent* walkout constitutes the best proof that the movement was grossly lacking in political inspiration and leadership. No political leadership, least of all an astute and cautious leadership like that of the USPD, would have tolerated a strike over such a trivial issue. Even if it had, it would most certainly have attempted to coordinate it with simultaneous strikes on the other ships of the fleet, or if such a tactic proved impossible to carry out, to at least prevent implicating more men by halting all isolated instances of resistance. However, there was no sign of such coordination or planning. On the contrary, the *Prinzregent* strikers and their comrades on the *Friedrich der Grosse* were arrested without resistance while two weeks later, on August 16, the crew of the *Westfalen*, apparently, oblivious to all that had transpired, staged a totally unrelated wildcat coaling strike.[86]

If the USPD had really been behind the strike, the strikers would surely have made political demands and shouted socialist slogans. Yet the *Prinzregent* mutineers did none of these things, revealing that although they had rediscovered their trade-union consciousness and had developed an affinity for the program of the USPD, they possessed neither sufficient time nor talent to build an effective organization capable of pursuing long-range plans.

Therefore their actions in the eyes of Emil Alboldt, chairman of the Deck Officers' League and Secretary of the Navy under the Weimar Republic, represent nothing more than a prank or joke, a *Dummerjungenstreich*,[87] of the sort that was occasionally practiced in the peacetime navy. According to Alboldt, something of a similar nature had occurred on the old *Oldenburg* in the 1880's when a discontented crew had hoisted a red flag to protest the abuses perpetrated by the first officer, Prince Henry of Prussia.[88] Astonishingly enough in the light of their subsequent reactions, the naval officers initially endorsed this explanation and were visibly shocked when they were informed of the severe sentences that were handed down by the courtmartial.[89]

While it is true that comedy was not altogether lacking in the

Prinzregent Luitpold strike and in the secretive discussions that preceded it and many men regarded it as a mere lark, the dominant mood was one of desperation and tragedy rather than comedy. Hence it would be incorrect to simply dismiss it as a harmless joke.

The *Prinzregent Luitpold* strike was much more serious than that. Although in itself it merely constituted a primitive kind of "professional strike," [90] it was part of a larger movement which under the misguided direction of men like Reichpietsch might have enveloped the entire High Seas Fleet in a general strike or mutiny within a matter of months. But it would be a great mistake and a flagrant violation of historical truth to adopt the navy's position by labeling the events on the *Prinzregent Luitpold* a political mutiny inspired by the agitation of the Independent Social Democrats.

The first tentative steps in the creation of such a myth were taken on August 4 when Captain von Hornhardt submitted his report to his superiors. Instead of interpreting the actions of his crew as the product of long-standing disaffection, mistreatment, war-weariness, and thoughtless impulsiveness, Hornhardt imported a political construction to the affair when he wrote accusingly,

> The events of August 1 and 2, and the discovery of [certain] documents [on board the ship] point to widespread agitation and recruitment by the Independent Social Democratic Party which has undermined the patriotic spirit and military bearing of the crew. Unfortunately, this agitation is aided all too greatly by unavoidable contact with shipyard workers. Moreover, it must also be noted that this agitation is facilitated by the extensive abuse of the right to subscribe to Social Democratic newspapers.[91]

These one-sided accusations quickly found favor with the naval interrogators who were placed in charge of the case. Within a short time they had convinced themselves that the enlisted men had no legitimate complaints, that their healthy spirit could only have been subverted by political propaganda and that a political mutiny of major proportions had been uncovered in the High Seas Fleet.

Closing their minds to any alternate explanation, the naval authorities failed not only to pay heed to the pleas of innocence of the enlisted men but to any evidence that contradicted or weakened this convenient thesis. Thus they ignored Beckers and Köbis when they denied that their actions had been politically inspired but were primarily the "expression of local disaffection" and the product of discriminatory treatment.[92] With equal obstinacy they disregarded all counteraccusations directed against the officer corps as they anxiously sought to protect the navy by shifting its blame on the shoulders of the enlisted men and the USPD. The Stab-in-the-Back Legend was about to be born.

v

Naval Justice: Fair Trial
or Judicial Murder?

An unsuspecting crew stood assembled on the deck of *Prinz-regent Luitpold* as the battleship dropped anchor at Schillig Roads off Wilhelmshaven on August 3. All of a sudden eighteen men who had played a prominent role in the walkout of August 2 were pulled out of rank. An order rang out: "All prisoners, step toward port side!" Only then did the sailors and stokers notice that a machine gun had been trained on them and that a tender was pulling alongside. Thereupon the prisoners were unceremoniously hustled on board the tender, which sped off toward shore.

On their way the prisoners still retained their confidence and optimism. To avoid contradicting each other in the interrogation that was sure to follow, they agreed to place all blame for the walkout on Beckers and Köbis. They hoped that they would be returned to their ship as soon as they had been questioned.[1]

Their optimism was not wholly unjustified. After all, they had not been punished for their hunger strikes, and they knew that the crew of the *Pillau* had been treated with leniency after it had staged a similar walkout. They still entertained the hope that their walkout would be regarded as nothing more than a prank.

Admiral Reinhard Scheer's report the following day seemed to substantiate that hope. The Chief of the High Seas Fleet did not take the *Prinzregent* strike too seriously. Scheer's report of August 5 spoke in a similar vein.[2] As late as August 6, he was still willing to regard the walkout as the outcome of a number of abuses that needed correcting. Therefore he advised all the ships in his command to maintain tight discipline and attempt to establish better relations between their officers and men by treating the men better, distributing leaves more equitably, and enhancing the authority of the petty officers. Only toward the end did he strike a cautionary note when he recommended that the commanders see to it that the *Menagekommissions* on their ships not be allowed to interfere with necessary routines.[3]

On August 9, however, Scheer performed a complete turnabout. At that time he declared "without a doubt there is a connection between the movement [of the enlisted men] and the Independent Social Democratic Party." [4] What was responsible for this sudden reversal in attitude? What aroused the admiral's suspicions to such an extent that he now referred to the men's activities as a "movement"—moreover, a movement with undoubted connections with the USPD, the uprooting of which would require the utmost severity on the part of the navy?

It may well be that Scheer was influenced to some extent by the reports supplied by the various units under his command. For instance, on August 5 the commander of the Fourth Squadron wrote that it had come to his attention that some of his enlisted men had held a meeting in Wilhelmshaven on July 27. Allegedly this meeting had been addressed by an Independent Social Democratic deputy who had urged his audience to contribute money for the Socialist Conference in Stockholm by sending contributions to the official journal of the USPD, the *Leipziger Volkszeitung*.[5] Similarly, the commander of the Naval Forces in the

Baltic on August 7 stated that he had unearthed a movement among his men that "apparently emanated from an anarchistic central headquarters on shore" which pursued revolutionary aims inimical to authority and sought to organize the crews to gain ascendancy over their officers.[6]

Much more disturbing, and hence the probable cause for Scheer's change of mind, were the results of the interrogations conducted among the crews of the *Prinzregent Luitpold* and the *Friedrich der Grosse* by the navy's judicial personnel. It was they and the unorthodox interrogations they conducted, the trial that they dominated, and the sentences they obtained from complaisant court-martial panels that catapulted the case into a major mutiny that ultimately resulted in a host of long prison terms and the execution of two enlisted men.

On August 6 the legal counsel of the Fourth Squadron, *Marinekriegsrat* Doctor Dobring, began to interrogate the men who had participated in the walkout. Turning first to Johann Beckers he set the tone of all the interrogations that were to follow when he introduced Beckers as "one of the death candidates." Throughout a lengthy conversation Dobring kept reiterating to Beckers, "Tell the truth [or] I shall at once demand execution by firing squad. You need not count on mercy." The liberal use of terms such as "hangman," "execution," and "death sentence" so intimidated the usually well-composed Beckers that he was soon ready to sign almost anything placed before him.[7]

Nevertheless, Beckers did not reveal much. He admitted that he sympathized with the aims of the USPD, that he had recruited members for it, and that he had attended several meetings on shore at which politics had been discussed but which centered mainly on organizing *Menagekommissions*. At the same time Beckers strenuously denied that the *Prinzregent Luitpold* strike had anything to do with politics or the USPD. He was also cautious enough not to implicate his comrades.[8]

Two days later, on August 8, Dobring met with much more

success when he applied his interviewing techniques on Willi Sachse. When Sachse entered the interrogation room he saw on the table a revolver and a drawing of a gallows. Dobring told him to take his choice between the two. Thus the interrogator subjected Sachse to "incredible terror and pressure," [9] which was compounded by the fact that Sachse knew that his comrades had been treated the same way.[10]

From the moment that Sachse heard Dobring's questions regarding anarchists and radical socialists, Sachse must have sensed that sooner or later one of his comrades would break down and reveal the enlisted men's connection with the USPD. Doubtlessly concluding that he would be treated much more leniently if he told Dobring all he wanted to hear, Sachse figured it would be best for him to act cooperative and to make a rueful confession. This would not only enable him to ingratiate himself with the authorities but would simultaneously provide him with an extremely valuable argument in his defense—that he had been led astray by the USPD deputies and their propaganda.

Throughout his life Sachse was a practiced opportunist who consistently cared more for his personal fate than for any movement. This is demonstrated not only by his cooperative behavior at his interrogation and court-martial, but by the contempt he later showed for the navy's interrogators and judges who had spared his life, his entry into the Communist Party after his release from prison, his flirtation with the Nazis when they came into power, and his final, fateful switch into the anti-Hitler resistance that led to his death in 1944.

It was this opportunism combined with the fear engendered by Dobring's threats that caused Sachse on August 8 to render the confession that altered the entire nature of the case and thus enabled Admiral Scheer to assert the following day that a revolutionary organization directed by the USPD had been uncovered in the fleet.

Sachse played his rueful role to perfection when he told Dobring that his comrades had decided to stage an anarchistic strike for peace and that they had built up an organization for this purpose under the guise of establishing a *Menagekommission*. In an effort to mitigate his guilt, however, Sachse also invented the story that he had made up his mind to leave that movement just prior to his arrest when it came to his attention that there was a plan afoot to blow up the *Friedrich der Grosse*.[11]

The correctness of Sachse's assumptions were borne out by Dobring's delight. Until Sachse confessed, Dobring had not known that the enlisted men had established contact with the Independent Socialist deputies in Berlin. Therefore he could hardly believe his ears when the stoker began unraveling his tale. Dobring repeatedly admonished Sachse to tell the truth. But when Sachse persisted and protested that he was indeed telling the truth, Dobring had his testimony recorded in the interrogation transcript.[12]

Immensely pleased by this unexpected find, Dobring took an immediate liking for the young stoker. As Dobring later put it, Sachse recognized what he had done and knew that he could not hope to deceive the authorities. With considerable empathy, Dobring therefore projected that Sachse must have figured, "Nothing can help me any longer. Now the truth must come out. I shall be best off if I tell all that happened." Growing more and more congenial during "the most comfortable interrogation" he had ever conducted,[13] Dobring came to feel "that basically Sachse was a decent person who had been misled by special circumstances and who now genuinely regretted his transgression."[14]

Encouraged by Dobring's reaction, Sachse on August 9 supplied more details. He described Reichpietsch's conversations with the deputies in Berlin, listed the dates of various meetings, listed the major speakers at them, and named the enlisted men's leaders on the individual ships. He also reported that at the time of their arrest Beckers and Köbis had sent him a note requesting that he call a strike if he did not hear from them in three days.

Then Sachse revealed what was to be a crucial point in the case built by Dobring—the existence of an "organization" in the fleet with a "headquarters" on the *Friedrich der Grosse* that supported and worked for the USPD. It was this information that enabled Dobring to manufacture the claim that there was a well-organized enlisted men's movement in the navy that pursued the following revolutionary four-point program:

1. Entire fleet to join the USPD if possible and to place itself at its political disposal.
2. To obtain materials for the political purposes of the USPD.
3. Exchange of USPD propaganda for dissemination in the fleet.
4. Forcing [the conclusion] of an early peace without annexations and indemnities by means of the violent implementation of the USPD's program.[15]

The way that Dobring manufactured his case against the enlisted men and the USPD is illustrated by the wording of that program. Despite his efforts at cooperation with Dobring, it is not likely that Sachse actually expressed himself in such precise, numbered terms and that he described such a clearly defined headquarters. At any rate, after the war Sachse denied that he had ever put things that way and charged that it was all Dobring's "fabrication." [16] This is unsubstantiated by the transcript of the interrogation. When Sachse spoke of "the headquarters of the entire organization," he had qualified his statement by adding "if one can call it that." [17] Moreover, Dobring later admitted to the Reichstag Investigating Committee that he was the one who had numbered the four points of the program. Nevertheless, he still insisted that he had neither added nor subtracted a single word.[18]

Upon closer scrutiny, however, it was revealed to what an extent Dobring had enlarged upon and exaggerated Sachse's original testimony to obtain the convictions he wanted and to implicate the Independent Socialists. Point 4 of the alleged revolutionary program in Sachse's interrogation had read: "Forcing [the conclusion] of an early peace without annexations and indemnities by means of the violent implementation of the USPD's program." By August 21 Dobring had expanded that point to read: "Forcing [the conclusion] of an early peace without annexations and indemnities by means of laying down arms, a general strike, and refusal to obey the orders of superiors for the suppression of a strike movement in the navy or among the population." Thus exposed, Dobring reluctantly conceded that he had pieced together the very damaging four-point program on the basis of what he considered a consensus of all the enlisted men's testimony.[19]

Having gotten the idea from Sachse that there existed a movement in the fleet that had established a tenuous link with the Independent Socialists, Dobring became determined to prove by means of the most unorthodox methods that a politically inspired mutinous movement had been at work in the navy. Through the judicious use of Sachse, who became a willing stool pigeon, and by a variety of threats Dobring within a few days accumulated evidence to create a political case against the men and the USPD.

Stenographer Steinmeier reveals how this process worked. The interrogation of Max Reichpietsch on August 10 proved that he was a much more recalcitrant witness than Sachse. He was, in Steinmeier's words, "a close-mouthed, lying and reluctant witness" and was therefore treated "somewhat more harshly than a contrite prisoner like Sachse who confessed." [20] Knowing just "how far he could go," Dobring subjected Reichpietsch to a very rigorous questioning, not mincing words as to what Reichpietsch might expect if he did not cooperate. By producing Sachse at strategic intervals, Dobring broke down Reichpietsch's resistance and at last got him on August 13 to confess the full details of his conversations with the Independent Socialists in Berlin.[21]

Why was Sachse so cooperative while Reichpietsch was not? Surely Sachse was not the only prisoner who realized that he could make things easier for himself by confessing. In at least two other cases enlisted men did just that. One was Seaman Calmus of the *Rheinland*, who invented a fantastic "movie novel confession" in the hope of evading the firing squad,[22] and the other, Seaman Brauener, made a clumsy attempt to obtain a pardon by shifting all blame to the deputies.[23]

In all three cases the men had had very little personal contact with the politicians and hence regarded the deputies as convenient scapegoats upon whom they could unburden their guilt. Reichpietsch, who knew the most about the deputies, however, kept silent until Sachse was brought in. There are two possible reasons for his silence. First, Reichpietsch had had enough personal experience with naval court-martials to know that they were not inclined to show mercy under any circumstance and therefore figured that it was best to keep his mouth shut. Moreover, Reichpietsch knew better than anyone else that the deputies were not guilty and that it would be foolish to implicate them because they could easily repudiate his testimony. Only after Sachse had already revealed the secret and there was nothing more to lose did Reichpietsch begin to cooperate with Dobring.

Having gotten that far with Sachse and Reichpietsch, Dr. Dobring found it relatively easy to coerce the other prisoners to corroborate the existence of a well-organized movement in the fleet with a headquarters on the *Friedrich der Grosse* controlled by the USPD in Berlin.

At first Beckers had staunchly resisted Dobring and his threats of the gallows. However, when he discovered that his comrade Sachse had not only failed to protect him but had actually testified against him by revealing his note of August 2 calling for a general strike in the fleet, he grew so disconsolate on August 16 and 17 that he too confessed everything he had done.[24] Köbis reacted similarly. On August 18 he stated that he had "thus far kept quiet out of consideration for his comrades," but since they had all appeared at his interrogation and implicated him, he was now "willing to acknowledge his full guilt, in organizing the enlisted men's revolt."[25]

Dobring and his fellow interrogators, Loesch and Breil, could hardly have succeeded in breaking the spirit of their prisoners if it had not been for threats, unorthodox suggestion of testimony, and other coercive measures. The constant threats of death so depressed Beckers and Köbis that they planned to commit suicide, by means of a glass splinter the former carried in their clothes, because they "did not want to suffer death on orders." [26]

Weber, too, describes how Dobring worked. Throughout Weber's interrogation Dobring kept referring to an "organization" with a "central headquarters" on the *Friedrich der Grosse*, but Weber was so naive that he never bothered to obtain a definition of these terms. Whenever he tried to object and stated that the enlisted men's movement had arisen because of poor food and bad living conditions, Dobring somehow managed to give his words a political connotation. Dobring "excelled at suggesting testimony" by the simple expedient of stating repeatedly, "If you admit this, it is true—then you may expect mercy. Otherwise your life is over and done with." [27]

Such treatment of prisoners was not at all unusual in the German navy during the summer and fall of 1917. An abundance of evidence relating to a number of subsidiary cases of alleged mutiny on the other ships in the fleet indicates that the enlisted men of the *Prinzregent Luitpold* and *Friedrich der Grosse* were accorded the navy's standard treatment during their interrogatory hearings. Thus, for instance, Seaman Linke of the *Helgoland*, who was innocent of all political leanings, was accidentally drawn into an investigation for mutiny simply because he was a member of the *Menagekommission* on his ship. Actually he was so patriotic that although he was ultimately sentenced to ten years in prison, he joined the Navy League after the war. Of his interrogation by naval counselor Dr. Loesch, Linke declared: "My inexperience was grist to his mill. He dictated the transcript to his stenographer (with whom he was evidently on very close terms), the stenographer wrote, and I was made to sign. I did not care, however, because I hoped that everything would be cleared up at my trial. But our entire case was over in half an hour. I don't recall being asked more than a couple of questions." [28]

In many instances the navy's efforts to obtain desired confessions from the men exceeded the use of mere psychological pressure. Dr. Schroeder, one of the lawyers involved in the *Ziethen* case, reports that the commandant of the Wilhelmshaven naval station ordered that all the men who were to be arrested for signing a USPD list be apprehended shortly before their midday meal so that they would miss being fed and, thus weakened by hunger, would become more amenable to confession.[29]

Still another witness to the methods of the naval authorities is Stoker First Class Alfred Rebe of the *Moltke*. Rebe, a devout Marxist, was arrested early in October 1917 for having spoken out in support of the enlisted men's movement on board the *Prinzregent Luitpold* and for shouting, "Down with the war! Down with militarism!" He was accused of attempting to foment rebellion, although his primary motive was the situation on his ship that provided the men nothing to eat but "turnips, dehydrated vegetables and once again dried turnips."

Yet no hint of the food situation is to be found in the confession that Dobring extracted from him. At his trial Rebe gave the reasons for this strange omission. In a tightly reasoned and impassioned memorandum addressed to the court-martial, he revealed that he had not slept for two days when he was interrogated on October 6. Despite his great fatigue and high state of nervousness, he was grilled by Dobring, who informed him "whether you are shot or sent to jail lies in my hands." Depressed to the point that he "was prepared to sign his own death warrant if it had been demanded," Rebe submitted, not a confession, "but whatever words were placed in my mouth." Nevertheless, he still retained enough presence of mind to complain that his statement regarding rations had been left out of the transcript, but he could not overcome his interrogator's refusal to include it.[30]

In his vain appeal for justice, Rebe reiterated that his sole aim had been the improvement of rations, but as a realist he knew that he would not be believed. Hence he concluded dramatically, now "I take up my cross and bear it to Golgotha as did Jesus of Nazareth, the redeemer of mankind." [31]

For all of his dramatism and his political experience, Rebe was no match for Dobring when he was tried on October 19. Undoubtedly resentful over Rebe's complaints, an irate Dobring told the court that he "was extremely sorry that he had treated this man as decently as he had," and he managed largely without proper "factual or legal evidence" to obtain a conviction. Dobring's disregard for all legal forms shocked even the sensibilities of Admiral Capelle. Writing to the Commander of the High Seas Fleet, Capelle ordered "that he make it clear to *Marinegerichtsrat* Dobring that I cannot condone such conduct." [32]

Despite their subsequent denials, it thus becomes clear that the naval interrogators used considerable coercion upon the defendants.[33] Indeed, one witness before the Reichstag Investigating Committee, Stenographer Steinmeier, while insisting that he had no knowledge of any coercion, inadvertently let slip that, "due to the pressure of work and the lack of personnel," interrogations occasionally had to be conducted in what he euphemistically called "the later hours of the evening." [34] It therefore stands to reason that the prisoners, browbeaten, filled with terror, and politically naive, readily adopted the parlance of the interrogators and used the fateful terms placed in their mouths.[35]

In this fashion the interrogators managed to create the false and alarming impression that a well-organized political movement with far-reaching connections in Berlin had been on the verge of crippling the fleet and imposing an ignominious peace upon Germany. All the talk of organizations, headquarters, and sailors's councils, however, could not mask the fact that the plot that was thus concocted by the authorities had no substance in reality and was largely a "*Möchtegern*," a figment of the desires and imaginations of the interrogators.[36]

Illustrative of the lengths to which Dr. Dobring and his fellow interrogators were willing to go in order to obtain the evidence that would convict men like Reichpietsch and Köbis is their "investigation" of the infamous *Westfalen* case.

During the month of July the battleship *Westfalen* had been alongside the *Friedrich der Grosse* in dock, as a result of which a resistance movement began to develop on the *Westfalen* under the leadership of Seaman Paul Brügge. When Brügge, who was the "soul of the movement," was arrested on August 12 for inciting to rebellion, the men fell back to agitating for improved conditions.[37] Four days later, on August 16, the crew were unexpectedly ordered to load coal, but did not receive their customary supplementary coaling rations. Thereupon the Fourth Division proclaimed a strike and left the ship in protest. However, when the first officer ordered the men to return, they complied at once. Nevertheless, on the next day eight men were arrested. Originally the crew wanted to retaliate immediately by going out on strike again. But the captain called in one of their leaders, Seaman Hans Haase, and promised to reconsider his position if the crew did not resort to drastic means. Haase managed to quiet the men although he could not prevent them from drafting a letter demanding the release of the prisoners. Although it was never posted, the discovery of this letter, exuding nothing but misguided and by now hopelessly belated working class solidarity, prompted the navy to issue four death sentences and a large number of long prison terms. The letter read as follows:

To the Captain of H.M.S. *Westfalen*:
   As a result of recent events on board H.M.S. *Westfalen*, a number of decent and industrious men have suddenly been arrested although in our view they are completely blameless. Hence we specifically demand to know
   1. Why are they being detained?
   2. How long are they to be detained?
   3. What will happen to these men who were rashly and without cause deprived of their freedom?
It will depend upon your exact answer to these questions what countermeasures we shall have to take in order to protect ourselves and our comrades from such attacks. We request a reply in the form of a proclamation within 24 hours. [Signed by]
   Men, who have not been bought by English gold, but who are always ready to serve a just cause and to make their wills prevail.
   In the event that our demands shall not be met, we hereby give

notice that we are strong enough to make our will prevail, if necessary, by means of force. We therefore urge you to respond to our
demands lest we be compelled to resort to violence.
[signed]
H.M.S. *Westfalen*, August 1917[38]

Dr. Loesch, the naval counselor who obtained these death sentences and convictions, blazed a new trail in the annals of German
naval justice by employing spies and agents provocateurs to break
the case. His efforts were greeted with success, but by the time he
had finished his investigation neither he nor his superiors could
any longer separate truth from fiction.

Some time prior to his actual assignment to the *Westfalen* case,
Loesch had made the acquaintance of a strange enlisted man who
served on that ship. This person, Seaman Adams, had suddenly
decided to turn himself in for allegedly having murdered a man in
Baja Granda, Argentina, in 1914. While an investigation by the
navy against him was still pending, probably early in August 1917,
an anonymous note arrived, stating that Adams was one of the
"principal agitators of the revolutionary movement" on the
Westfalen and in the fleet. When this accusation was examined
and compared with samples of Adams' handwriting, it turned out
that none other than he himself had written the note. Having
been exposed, Adams admitted that he had turned himself in simply
because he wanted to get away from his ship.

These actions made it evident that Adams was either "hysterical or a psychopath." The authorities doubted that he was "men-
tally competent" and ordered that he be placed under hospital
observation. However, this did not in the least deter Dr. Loesch
from calling on Adams to ferret out any possible mutinous movement on the *Westfalen*. He instructed Adams to return from the
hospital to his ship to spy on his crew mates and to submit periodic reports about their activities to him and Lieutenants Beyer
and Engel, his immediate superiors.[39]

Reveling in his role as an official spy, Adams soon exceeded his
instructions and developed into an agent provocateur. His reports

to Loesch and the naval authorities conveyed the impression that the *Westfalen* was rife with revolutionary activity and that the men were preparing to stage a bloody uprising against their officers. Yet, according Haase, these "mental fabrications" of the "deranged" Adams were given credence by the navy and were instrumental in convicting a number of the *Westfalen* crew.[40]

Still more revealing of Loesch's tactics of first manufacturing and then breaking the case with the aid of Adams' mendacious reports is the testimony of another defendant, Seaman First Class Johann Siegfried, who stated at his court-martial on November 3 that it was Adams who had first suggested staging a sympathy strike to release the men imprisoned after the coaling strike. Another sailor, Fritz by name, insisted at the same time that Adams was directly responsible for raising the specter of violence on the *Westfalen* that frightened the authorities. He said it was Adams who had proposed that the men toss grenades into the officers' mess.[41]

All this evidence makes it clear that Loesch's agent had played a crucial role in transforming a relatively passive enlisted men's movement into a potentially violent one that led the navy to institute its punitive action against the crew. Loesch's handling of the *Westfalen* case has been called a "classic example of dishonorable and criminal provocation."[42] This term is more than justified when it becomes clear that Loesch employed a number of other spies and agents provocateurs on board that ship,[43] who together with Adams managed to impart a false but very frightening political flavor to the entire case.

After Adams had engineered the arrest of the former leaders, he managed to have himself elected as a delegate and a leader on the *Westfalen*.[44] Working very closely with Loesch and his own officers, Adams then succeeded in goading his comrades into making radical statements at a series of conspiratorial meetings he set up with the approval of the authorities. In order to accumulate damaging evidence against the men, he was also allowed to deposit a radical proclamation at a printer's for publication. On still another occasion, on September 2, he was granted permission by his superiors and the chief of the criminal police in Kiel to hold a political meeting at a tavern on Waisenhofstrasse so that the men could be arrested for illegal assembly and conspiracy. Only when Adams requested additional authorization to instigate his comrades to resist arrest and to try to escape did the police finally exercise some restraint.[45]

The distorted information that was obtained in this manner made it virtually impossible for the command of the High Seas Fleet to understand the true nature of the enlisted men's movement and to treat it accordingly. Most certainly it prompted Admiral Scheer to adopt disproportionately harsh measures. Referring to the events on the *Westfalen* on October 7, 1917, he informed his captains that the enlisted men on that ship pursued their subversive goals with "almost fanatical determination," that the arrest of their leaders did not deter them, and that despite the closest possible surveillance they still persisted in holding illicit meetings.[46] Admiral Bachmann, the commander of the Kiel naval station, too, was deceived by Loesch's information. On September 11, he urged Secretary Capelle to demand that the government "intervene with great severity against the leaders of the movement." [47] Under these circumstances it was virtually inevitable that the naval court-martial would issue death sentences to four men, Haase, Hiller, Siegfried, and Brügge. Three other men were sentenced to fifteen years in jail, one man to twelve years and three others to ten. Only one of the accused, Wölk by name, was acquitted.[48] On November 19, however, Scheer commuted the death sentences, but took care to inform his commanders that he had acted, not out of compassion, but because the *Westfalen* mutineers had conducted their treasonable activities prior to the sentencing of the main ringleaders on the *Friedrich der Grosse* and *Prinzregent Luitpold*.[49]

However revealing and interesting they might be, the pretrial investigations and interrogations of judicial counselors Dobring and Loesch were a mere prelude to a greater miscarriage of justice that was perpetrated upon the enlisted men accused of mutiny during their trial by court-martial.

From the outset it was evident that the court-martial that tried Reichpietsch, Sachse, Weber, Köbis, and Beckers was so preoccupied with white-washing the navy and shifting the blame to the enlisted men and their alleged subverters in the USPD that its investigation was reduced to the level of a formality. At no point did the trial do more than present the evidence and testimony that had been brought out in the pretrial interrogations. Sachse reports that the entire trial lasted all of two days and that no attempt was made to examine the abuses in the fleet that had played such a prominent part in triggering the dissatisfactions of the crews. At one point when Sachse tried to raise the question of the officers' misconduct or "*Schweinereien*," one of the officers on the board went into a fit of hysteria and threatened to run Sachse through with his sword.[50] Beckers later charged that his attorney kept sitting through Prosecutor Dobring's speeches with a smile on his face and had to be called to order when Dobring asked for the death sentence.[51]

Very few details of the trial are known, nor is there much likelihood that its full story will ever be told. The records of the court-martial of the principal defendants have vanished without trace.[52] However, available records of similar proceedings can shed considerable light on the way navy court-martials functioned and the ease with which they handed down convictions. For instance, Handgrödiger, Mathies, Claasen, et. al., of the *Prinzregent Luitpold*, arraigned for participating in the walkout on their ship, found themselves confronted with a court-martial board on which sat Drs. Dobring and Loesch, while another interrogator, judicial counselor Breil, acted as the prosecutor. The sentences were harsh. One man, Spanderer, who was reputed to be a specially dangerous ringleader, was sentenced to death; all but one of the rest received jail sentences of twelve years.[53]

The conduct of the *Westfalen* court-martial is even more revealing of German naval justice. Twenty-four hours before the men were scheduled to go on trial, the navy approached Dr. Brunnemann, a lawyer, with the request that he undertake their defense. Within a day Brunnemann responded by asking for a postponement to read the interrogation transcript and a fifty-page long arraignment. When the navy failed to grant him the requested time, he turned down the case and suggested that it be given to another lawyer "who found it easier to acquaint himself with the evidence." Thereupon a similar offer, with even less time, was made to a Lieutenant Schroeder, with the same result. At the last moment, the navy obtained the services of Counselor Buddenberg, an extreme nationalist, to defend the men.[54]

It should come as no great surprise that when the *Westfalen* trial opened, the judicial chairman of the court-martial board turned out to be Dr. Dobring while Dr. Loesch was the prosecutor. One of the defendants, Paul Brügge, immediately antagonized the prosecutor by refusing to accept his pretrial interrogation as valid evidence against him. He complained that Loesch had confused him, "that his head had been completely turned," and that words had been put into his mouth. This caused Loesch to rise up in anger and to threaten, "If you think that this represents a clever defense, you are damned mistaken." Then he asserted, "The only thing we want of you is a full confession. That is the only thing that might possibly help you." [55]

Poor Brügge could not even rely on his own lawyer for support and protection. At one point Buddenberg intervened on behalf of the prosecution and helped to catch his client in a logical inconsistency. No doubt sensing that this might weaken the defendant, Loesch jumped in and exclaimed, "Brügge, don't be so despicably weak-kneed and at least tell us the truth as before [in the interrogation]. I can tell you right now, and your lawyer will confirm it, so far all those who told the truth here have been lucky while those who lied fared very badly." [56]

This kind of behavior was by no means confined to the *Westfalen* case. It was characteristic of legal practice in the navy throughout the rest of the war. At the beginning of 1918, Wireless Operator Franz Schlegel of the *Ziethen* was tried for mutiny before a court-martial that acted almost in the identical manner. The naval prosecutor, *Marinehilfsgerichtsrat* Dr. Frauen, like his colleagues Dobring and Loesch, did not want to hear "clichés about food." [57] Nor, for that matter, was Schlegel's attorney an improvement over Brunnemann. Defense Attorney Pattow, a reserve officer who had been ordered to take the case, made it clear to the court that he refused to associate himself with the views and actions of his client, but was defending Schlegel only because he deemed it his "damned duty and responsibility." [58]

By piecing together information from the interrogation records, the court-martial proceedings of subsidiary cases, and bits of news that eventually leaked out about the main trial, one can see that the sentences meted out to Reichpietsch, Köbis, Sachse, Beckers, and Weber were the results of similar tactics and illegal procedures, the only difference being that in their cases the men were convicted because of their political inclinations.

It was clear from the start that the basic issue in the case against the ringleaders was their alleged political connection and participation in an Independent Socialist plot to overthrow the navy and the German government. Parodoxically enough, none of the implicated deputies and political leaders of that party, such as Dittmann, Haase, Vogtherr, or Frau Zietz, was ever called upon to testify. According to the views later expressed by the prominent jurist, Dr. Ludwig Herz, this omission was "totally incomprehensible" from a legal point of view and undermined the validity of the entire case, for it meant that the naval court-martial accepted the involvement of the USPD as an established fact solely on the basis of the hearsay testimony of witnesses who were twice removed from the actual events.

To all intents and purposes, the navy's whole case rested on Willi Sachse's dramatic confession. Even Dobring concedes that he was totally unaware of the political factor in the case until Sachse obligingly confessed what Reichpietsch had told him of his dealings with the USPD in Berlin. Although any law school in Germany taught that such testimony could never be used to reveal what had transpired between Reichpietsch and the politicians, the court-martial accepted Sachse's version as proof of the USPD's complicity.[59] Moreover, the navy's lawyers never really examined their key witnesses' reliability and credibility. Dobring was so delighted with Sachse's cooperation that he looked the other way whenever Sachse's actions jeopardized his credibility. Any prosecutor with the least concern for justice would have been extremely wary of a witness like Sachse, who while in jail tried to smuggle out a letter stating that he had fooled all the officials and convinced them to grant him a pardon, on the ground that he had been "led astray" by the deputies, by telling them what they wanted to hear, by putting on a penitential air, and by simulating a sudden interest in religion.[60]

By no stretch of the imagination could Sachse be regarded as a reliable witness.[61] After the war when he became a prominent communist, Sachse wrote an article in the *Neue Zeitung*, the Bavarian organ of that party, in which he refuted all he had said in the past. In 1925 he averred that he had deliberately implicated the USPD in order to steer the navy's investigators away from the track of the protocommunist Gruppe International and the Bremen left radicals, who were really responsible for the growth of the enlisted men's movement.[62] When one strips away all of Sachse's obvious lies, it becomes evident that he and the men who corroborated his testimony in regard to the USPD were bent upon reducing their sentences by the perfectly understandable and commonplace expedient of shifting the blame for their actions upon someone else. Any fair court of law would have taken this motivation into consideration and either disregarded or used this kind of testimony with utmost caution. The naval court-martial, however, consistently ignored this basic principle of legal practice.

Even more damaging to the legal validity of the final verdicts is the fact that the court-martial also permitted what lawyers term a *saltus in demonstrando,* the fallacious use of evidence. The principal argument of the prosecution at the trial was that the enlisted men had decided after Reichpietsch's consultations in Berlin to implement the USPD's stand on the Stockholm Conference's peace resolution by means of a naval strike and that they were equally determined not to obey orders to shoot at civilian demonstrators in the event hunger strikes broke out among the population. The prosecution argued that although the men were not certain how such strikes would come about, they stood ready to act as soon as they got the word from Berlin.

The inherent speciousness of this line of reasoning apparently escaped the court for it failed to realize that under the circumstances the actual outbreak of a naval strike was dependent on a multiplicity of conditions, many of which would never have been fulfilled. From the standpoint of logic, the court's reasoning apparently ran somewhat as follows: If a Stockholm Conference did take place, if it decided to issue a resolution for a peace without annexations and indemnities, if the German government then rejected that resolution, then the enlisted men in the fleet would, if so instructed by the USPD in Berlin, go out on strike and refuse to fire upon workers. Significantly lacking in this argument is the all-important element—namely, proof that the program of the USPD included the use of violence as part of its tactics. This is the *saltus in demonstrando* to which Dr. Herz refers.[63]

Up to a point, it is quite understandable how the officers who sat on the court-martial board could commit such an error. In their eyes any party that was not nationalistic and conservative was tainted with treason. Many officers barely tolerated the reformist Majority Socialists in spite of their enormous contribution to the German war effort. Increasingly swept up by Pan-Germanism and the spirit of the nascent Fatherland Party, they became determined, especially after July 1917, to rout the liberal and socialist forces in Germany in order to ensure a continuation of the war until a glorious peace could be won. Hence they looked upon the USPD's stringent criticism of the government and its refusal to vote war credits as revolutionary. Without overly troubling themselves in this matter, most officers were prepared by their upbringing, political prejudices, and *Kastengeist* to regard the USPD as capable of committing any kind of treason.

This was certainly true of Dr. Dobring, who openly admitted that he was entirely apolitical and knew nothing of party programs. Yet this "political illiterate," [64] as Dittmann once called him, did not hesitate for a moment to base his case on the alleged program of that party.[65]

One might forgive the navy this error if it could be shown that it was committed out of ignorance and naiveté. But this was hardly the case. On August 16, 1917, the Admiralty's chief legal counsel, Dr. Felisch, reported that the Reich deputy prosecutor, Freiherr von Eberg und Rockenstein, had advised him that the navy "was entirely misinformed in regard to the aims of that party," that "many of the things attributed to Deputy Dittmann and Frau Zietz could not have come from them," and that such "vague generalities" would never suffice to prove their complicity.

In another report written that same day, Felisch added a more urgent warning when he stated that he had been informed by the same legal authority that the navy lacked evidence to implicate the USPD in the mutiny and would therefore have to base its case "on different and much deeper grounds than its party program." [66] Both the court and the navy, however, refused to act on this advice.

Persisting in seeking convictions on the basis of the men's alleged political activities, the naval counsellors also ignored their legal obligation to interview the deputies who might have increased or mitigated the defendants' guilt. This was hardly surprising from a prosecutor like Dr. Loesch, who exclaimed at the trial: "Every investigation is harmed irreparably by the need to inform the accused of the charges against him, so that he realizes what it is all about." [67] Dobring's attitude, while not quite as outspoken, was essentially the same in this respect. Stubbornly clinging to an erroneous interpretation of Article 168 of the Military Code of Justice, he insisted as late as 1925 that he was under no obligation to call in civilian witnesses because that article stipulated that an investigation should not be expanded unnecessarily.[68]

Dobring's stand on this point was in direct conflict with accepted legal practice. The noted authority Stenglein, in 1901, had recorded the opinion that a military investigation was charged with responsibility for collecting exhaustive proof both for and against the defendant for presentation before a court-martial.[69] Moreover, established legal practice went even further in its attempts to safeguard the rights of the accused. Article 159 of the Military Code of Justice provided the following regulation:

> The judicial officer or court-martial counselor who is charged with the investigation must in his examination of the evidence bring forth not only those facts that can be used against the accused, but also any evidence that can be used in his favor in the preparation of his defense.[70]

Although it was within the jurisdiction of the court-martial that tried Reichpietsch and his comrades to rectify the mistakes and omissions of the pretrial investigation, it never bestirred itself to do this probably because, in the words of Judicial Counselor Dr. Schroeder, its conception of justice did not include "reasonable consideration" and "social feeling." [71] It confined itself to declaring that it recognized the fact that the defendants had been misled by the deputies and that their presence would hence not be required as mitigation.

Admiral von Capelle, the Secretary of the Navy, probably realized that a miscarriage of justice was about to be perpetrated, but he apparently lacked the strength to assert himself against an officer corps that held him in contempt. As he put it on November 25, 1917, in a draft reply to a charge from the left that the navy had committed judicial murder, "The decision whether or not a hearing [of the deputies] was to take place lay exclusively with the court and I, as head of the navy's justice administration, was obliged not to influence the court in any way." [72] Hence he refrained from interfering even when the court made the men's political connection the chief factor in their conviction.

This was particularly true of the Reichpietsch case. Two days after he had been sentenced to death, Reichpietsch wrote to Dr. Dobring,

> When my sentence was read, I was informed that I had held back information about my visits with Dittmann and the deputies at the Reichstag. If this criticism was at all significant in causing my conviction, I should like to call upon Deputies Haase, Dittmann, Vogterr and Frau Zietz to act as witnesses that I have correctly depicted what [actually] transpired.[73]

As naive as he was, the unfortunate sailor had managed to detect the major loophole in the navy's case and had pointed out the hypocrisy of the court's promise of mitigation.[74] What Reichpietsch could not know, however, was that the navy had kept the deputies out of the case because it feared that they would destroy its case, subject it to wide and unwelcome publicity, and prevent the passage of the death sentences that the navy felt that it needed to maintain discipline in the fleet.

After going through only the pretense of conducting an impartial trial, the court-martial imposed the death sentence upon the five principal defendants for having violated Paragraph 89 and Paragraph 90, Article 6 of the Code of Military Justice. Paragraph 89 defined as treason the giving of aid to a foreign power or the hindering of Germany's war effort. However, the court did not have proof that the men had actually undermined the nation's war effort. There was no hint of any collusion with a foreign power. Hence the court was forced to fall back on Paragraph 90. This defined as treason any "incitement to rebellion" (*Erregung eines Aufstandes*). But it also included a harsher penalty for "completion of treasonable incitement to rebellion" (*Vollendung der kriegsverrätischen Aufstandserregung*). In its interpretation of Paragraph 90, Article 6, the court declared:

> The court views as completion of treasonable incitement to rebellion not only an actual mutiny (*Losschlagen*) and the use of violence, but as also [being present] in the formation of certain specified organizations having treasonable aims that could upon a signal from its leaders strike out at any moment.[75]

This decision, too, was very disputable in terms of legality. In the opinion of many German jurists, including Dr. Felisch, the head of the navy's judicial section, completion of incitement to rebellion necessitated proof of an actual rebellion, or at the very least, some manifestation of violence. On August 16 Felisch maintained that a completed uprising cannot be a latent state, but must be an act that makes its appearance in reality by means of the outbreak of an open rebellion. Thus he felt that the court was within its rights to condemn the men for "attempting to mutiny," which mandated a harsh punishment but not the death penalty.[76]

Another legal authority, Major Brande, who attended the court-martial proceedings on behalf of the Admiralty, concurred with these views and exposed the absurdity of the court's ruling when he wrote,

> An organization cannot be an end in itself. It can only pursue certain goals. Thus one may organize for the cultivation of choral singing, for the attainment of better working conditions and for the staging of a rebellion. Nevertheless, this does not make the organization choral singing, higher wages or rebellion. By the same token, neither is organizing a rebellion the same as staging a real rebellion. All the talk that one will under certain stipulated conditions rebel and all discussion of how this goal can best be achieved, still does not signify a rebellion *per se*, but merely constitutes the preparation for the actual start and outbreak of disorders. Consequently, in the case of Sachse, Reichpietsch *et al.*, one cannot say that the incitement to rebellion has already been completed.[77]

All these legal objections, however, did not deter the court-martial from sentencing the five ringleaders to death. It was virtually a foregone conclusion that a board of officers who lived in the belief that only "draconian measures could prevent infringements against military discipline" would condemn these men. In the past this harsh tradition had made it almost mandatory that court-martial sentences be tempered by pardons.[78]

In this case, too, an attempt was made to lighten the sentences. *Oberkriegsgerichtsrat* De Bary, Admiral Scheer's legal counselor, advised the commander of the High Seas Fleet that he considered the court's interpretation of Paragraph 90, Article 6, "legally vulnerable" and that he "objected to confirming the verdict as it stood." Clearly hinting that a compromise was in order, De Bary indicated that Scheer could avoid having to reverse the court's verdict if he mitigated the sentences and "substituted life imprisonment or long-term jail sentences for the death penalty." [79]

Responsibility for the fate of the condemned men thus rested squarely with Admiral Reinhard Scheer. Originally appointed in 1916 to head the High Seas Fleet because he was regarded as a "man of action" by the naval officer corps, Scheer was a strong and stern leader. He had what Germans call a *"kompromisslose Natur,"* a personality incapable of compromise.

Scheer's general thinking was direct, to the point, and completely uncomplicated by self-doubts. Much of his success as a military leader, particularly at the Battle of Jutland, was based on the fact that he reacted quickly, that he possessed great will power and iron nerves. These very same traits, however, also comprised his greatest weakness. His great self-confidence led Scheer to the mistaken belief that he could master every situation on his own. This resulted in a tendency "for independent behavior and action of his own responsibility," while at the same time, he largely lacked any sense for the "understanding of political considerations." [80]

Scheer deemed it impossible that his officers were in any way responsible for the mutinous behavior of the crews. He was therefore convinced that the unrest of the fleet could only have been caused by the intrusion of politics and the agitation of the USPD. Concerned as he was with the maintenance of the fighting effectiveness of his fleet, he prejudged the entire case as early as August 14 when he voiced his determination to uphold discipline by means of "a few death sentences" and the proscription of the USPD. For these reasons Scheer pushed all inconvenient legal considerations aside and on September 3 signed the death sentences of Reichpietsch and Köbis while commuting those of the three other men. Later describing the situation that had prompted his decision, Scheer wrote in his memoirs:

> Order was restored in the fleet. The court martial had handed down five death sentences and a number of long prison sentences for military rebellion. The right of approval resided with the Commander of the Fleet.
>
> I could have denied myself [that right] and left the decision up to the Supreme War Lord [the Kaiser]. This would have resulted in the following: The Reich Military Tribunal would have been asked to make a recommendation which the Kaiser would in all probability have accepted as the basis for his decision.
>
> However, why should I have placed the responsibility upon the Kaiser when the right of approval lay within my jurisdiction? What was needed was action.
>
> Against the two principal ringleaders I allowed the death sentence to be carried out because I deemed it absolutely necessary for the maintenance of discipline to demonstrate the enormity of their crime to the crews in order to warn them against any future attempts to lead them to violate their oath of loyalty. The less guilty criminals were pardoned to prison terms.[81]

There were a number of errors in Scheer's decision. First of all, he stated that there was a distinction between the kinds of guilt of the condemned men that enabled him to commute the death sentences of three of them. But the court had not drawn any such demarcation line when it had imposed the death penalty on all five of the prisoners. Hence Scheer acted arbitrarily.

Actually he issued pardons to those who appeared properly contrite and who had pleased the interrogators. Sachse, who was almost an artist at this sort of thing and who had broken the case by rendering his confession, was therefore first on the list for a pardon. Weber was encouraged by the navy to ask for a pardon.[82] The fact that he was a member of the Majority Social Democratic Party, was opposed to violence, and claimed that he planned to leave the movement with Sachse also operated in his favor.[83] Beckers, too, by citing his anarchism and opposition to organizations, came up with a plausible explanation that led to the commuting of his sentence. Reichpietsch and Köbis, however, had not been cooperative enough to merit such consideration. Köbis' plea for mercy lacked contrition; he had failed to cooperate fully and had come out with some very radical statements.[84] Reichpietsch was even more vulnerable. It was he who had introduced politics into the fleet and started the enlisted men's movement. He had shown himself to be an uncooperative witness and had confessed only under duress. Moreover, his appeal to the court for clemency, instead of being contrite, posed a challenge to the navy because he demanded to know why the deputies had not been summoned to appear on his behalf.[85]

Of much greater significance than this arbitrary selection was Scheer's deliberate act of preventing the last legal recourse of the condemned men. Although well aware that Paragraph 418 of the Code of Military Justice stipulated that death sentences could only be carried out in the event the Kaiser chose not to show clemency, Scheer preferred to act on his own responsibility and thus deprived the two condemned men of their full legal protection of final appeal.[86]

In the final analysis, Scheer's decision to execute these two men was based on his feeling that "the maintenance of discipline" [87] required some sacrificial victims to discourage his crews from developing a mutinous spirit and consorting with political parties critical of the navy and the government.

By subordinating justice to expediency and *raison d'état*, by prostituting the laws for the sake of discipline and politics, by acting upon the theory of *inter arma silent leges* (in war the laws remain silent), Admiral Scheer and the German navy committed a crime—a crime of such dimensions that it can only be described as "an inexplicable miscarriage of justice" [88] or a "judicial murder."

As a cautious jurist, Dr. Ludwig Herz, the author of the first of these phrases, deliberately avoids using the harsher and more pejorative term. Yet his phrase, a "miscarriage of justice" committed for the sake of discipline and politics, in effect constitutes a charge of judicial murder although it may not fully satisfy all the legal prerequisites of the term proposed by Deputy Dittmann. But the distinctions between the two, if any, are so minute, while the evidence of the navy's intentions is so clear-cut, that one may reasonably conclude that in the case of Max Reichpietsch and Albin Köbis the navy perpetrated a legal murder.

One need not be a lawyer to surmise from the nature of the interrogations, the mockery of a trial that excluded key witnesses, and the refusal to entertain the possibility of an Imperial pardon, that the navy deliberately sacrificed these two men. This is amply borne out by a pathetic epilogue: Max Reichpietsch's farewell letter to his parents and last-minute appeal for clemency. On August 30, 1917, Reichpietsch wrote:

My beloved parents:
   I would have written to let you know about my situation long ago, but wanted to wait until my sentence was pronounced. Now the day has arrived, but it turned out worse than I had anticipated. It is a sentence of death.
   Whether or not it will be carried out or if the Kaiser in his mercy will prevent it, now lies in the hands of God. I no longer have any hope and have closed my life. Who would have thought when we parted in June that we would never see each other again.
   Now, my dear parents, I wish to beg you to please forgive me my

last transgression so that I may peacefully enter that other world where we will one day meet again. I also wish to thank you for all the good things you have done for me. . . .

Please let me know the name and address of the minister or apostle of your congregation. . . . Please forgive me for not writing longer, but my heart is so sad that I find it impossible to continue.

It is very sad as a young man in the bloom of life with a heart full of hope and desire to have to die so soon. To die because of the harsh sentence of a judge.

Greet Willi and Gertrud for me. Embracing and kissing you for the last time,

Your son, Max

There is still one thing that you can do for me. Through a lawyer or an apostle you may lodge an appeal for mercy with the Kaiser in whose hands my life rests at this moment and whose hand will exercise mercy on my behalf.[89]

Although his life hung in the balance, for some reason Reichpietsch's letter was not read by naval counselor Breil, who was in charge of censorship, until September 3. Evidently the navy treated this last, desperate appeal as an ordinary letter that had to wait its turn to be censored. Breil claims that he usually read over a hundred letters a day and that he therefore came upon Reichpietsch's only an hour before he was scheduled to depart from Wilhelmshaven for Cologne to witness the executions that were to take place on the morning of September 5.

Breil discussed the situation with Admiral Meurer, the commander of the Fourth Squadron, who decided that it was no longer possible for the letter to reach its destination before the execution. Therefore its despatch could only "cause trouble." As Meurer later put it in an attempt to justify his decision, "In view of the total situation, above all, out of consideration for the maintenance of absolutely indispensable secrecy for official reasons, the transmission of the letter to the parents could come under consideration only after the execution of the sentence and simultaneously with the notification of death."[90] Nowhere in this bureaucratic jargon will one find a sensible explanation of why no attempt was made to notify Admiral Scheer or to request a stay of execution. It may well be that the naval authorities were so intent upon setting an appropriate example for the crews that they saw to it that there was no time for an appeal.

A glance at the sequence of events should serve to document this point. The court-martial handed down the death sentences on August 26, but Admiral Scheer did not confirm them until a week later, on September 3. Thus Reichpietsch wrote his appeal four days before his sentence was officially confirmed. None of the other four prisoners who were also condemned to death acted in this fashion. Perhaps they did not believe that Scheer would allow them to die, or perhaps they did not know that they were entitled to appeal until their sentences were confirmed. Suffice it to say that none of them made a plea for clemency.

By signing the death sentences of Reichpietsch and Köbis on September 3 and setting the date of their execution on September 5, Scheer saw to it that the normal channels of appeal were closed to the two condemned men. They had barely two days to apply for a pardon to the Kaiser. But by that time, according to Admiral von Capelle, it was already too late. Without offering any explanation he maintains that by September 3 no appeal could have reached the Kaiser in time to stop the executions.[91] Hence Scheer's haste in setting the date of execution effectively deprived Köbis of his right to appeal, while Breil was responsible for seeing to it that Reichpietsch, who had acted independently and in ample time, lost his last chance for life.

Thus at 7:03 in the morning of September 5, 1917, at the Wahn Firing Range near Cologne the two martyrs of naval justice, Max Reichpietsch and Albin Köbis, were shot to death from a distance of five paces by a twenty-man firing squad.[92]

Reichpietsch's macabre story, however, was still not completed. When he left for Cologne, Counselor Breil forgot to take Reichpietsch's letter with him. Even after he returned from the execution, he showed no great haste. It was not until September 10 that he sent Reichpietsch's last letter to Pastor Ehrmann to forward to the dead man's parents.

In an effort to defend the navy against the charges which this kind of behavior was bound to produce, the Secretary of the Navy was quite willing to acknowledge that a mistake had been made in the Reichpietsch case and was fully prepared to sacrifice Breil for his "inexcusable delay." [93] But Breil was simply an inefficient cog in the naval machine that had seen to it that neither justice nor clemency were given to its two victims, thus making a mockery of Capelle's solemn vow that "all guarantees for the impartial administration of justice had been fulfilled." [94]

vi

From Mutiny to Revolution:
The Last Year of War

The discovery of a mutinous movement in the High Seas Fleet must have dealt a stunning blow to the self-esteem of the German naval officer corps. After three years of inactivity and playing an inconsequential role in the war, the sudden realization that its personnel practices had failed and that its professional competence was in jeopardy was more than the pride of most officers could bear. Therefore they sought to sublimate their own inadequacies and sense of guilt by blaming the unrest among the enlisted men upon external agitation. For that reason the news that the Independent Social Democrats were implicated in the mutiny was greeted by the officers as an opportunity to exonerate themselves and regain the respect of the public.

No sacrifice being too great for the preservation of their honor and professional reputation, they decided to blame the mutinies on the USPD deputies. A diversionary maneuver of this sort, however, was bound to have important repercussions. It demanded, first of all, that the guilt of the deputies be demonstrated by means of a public trial. This necessitated finding enough evidence to indict them as well as obtaining from the Reichstag a waiver of their parliamentary immunity. Since it was unlikely that this would easily be forthcoming, the navy also had to be prepared to enter politics, to exert political pressure and, if necessary, to create a major political crisis. Equally important, by refusing to acknowledge any responsibility for the mutiny, the navy deprived itself of the one hope of restoring the confidence and loyalty of its enlisted men—by initiating long overdue reforms. By embarking upon a political witch-hunt instead of facing reality, the navy condemned itself not only to a great political defeat but also to the perpetuation of the conditions that had already produced one mutiny and that would within a year give rise to another.

Happy to have found a convenient scapegoat in the USPD and determined to exploit it to the fullest, Admiral Scheer as early as August 14, 1917, embarked upon a campaign that would lead to disaster. On that date he wrote to Admiral von Capelle urging the Secretary of the Navy to immediately initiate a "political prosecution" of the USPD in order to get at "the roots of the evil" in the navy.[1] Four days later, on the occasion of a visit by the Kaiser and Capelle to Wilhelmshaven, Scheer reiterated his stand in even stronger terms. Describing the mutiny in terms of a "socialist plot," which would necessitate a "few death sentences," he demanded strong action against the implicated deputies. Admiral von Capelle, whose job it was to organize the prosecution, did not ingratiate himself with the irate Scheer when he informed him that the deputies enjoyed parliamentary immunity and simply could not be tried for treason.[2]

Scheer, however, showed little understanding for such technical considerations. As far as he was concerned, the government bore a considerable share of the responsibility for the unrest among his crews because it had allowed the socialist deputies to travel to Stockholm. This in his view had undermined the men's faith in their officers.[3] Hence he felt it only just that the civilian authorities—and they in his estimation included von Capelle—should intervene in the case in order to "protect the fleet against the penetration of political influences." He made it clear that he could not accept responsibility for the conduct of the fleet if this was not done.[4]

Scheer was by no means alone in proposing such drastic solutions. On September 4 Admiral Eberhardt Schmidt, the commander of the Fourth Squadron of the High Seas Fleet, also wrote to Capelle. In his forthright military manner he demanded "the destruction of the USPD headquarters in Berlin" and indicated that Scheer seconded his request.[5] Not even Capelle's own staff was immune to these proposals. Admiral Hebbinghaus stated that he too favored an investigation of the USPD because the people in that party "have shown themselves to be traitors and scoundrels." Hence he urged "no more prevarication, but strong action!" [6]

The navy's cries did not fall on deaf ears. Its demands for the prosecution of the USPD coincided with the wishes of Chancellor Michaelis. A nonentity prior to his appointment to the chancellorship in July 1917 on the insistence of the Supreme Command of the Army, Michaelis had managed within a month to make himself a mortal enemy of the Reichstag majority by his underhanded opposition to its peace resolution and his lackadaisical approach to the problem of internal reform. Increasingly subject to scathing criticism from the Reichstag majority and especially the USPD, Michaelis had no option but to rely increasingly upon the military to help break the power of the Reichstag. He had already begun to consider the idea of dissolving the Reichstag and dispensing with what little parliamentary supervision he had been forced to accept.[7] His plan to divide the Reichstag and to diminish its power found an eager ally in the navy.

As early as August 9 Admiral von Capelle had made the first attempt to split the parties of the Reichstag and to saddle the USPD with a charge of treason. On that date the Secretary of the Navy called upon Friedrich Ebert, the leader of the Majority Socialists, and tried to obtain his support for prosecuting some USPD deputies. After listening to the story of the mutiny and the USPD's alleged role in it, Ebert refused to give such a plan his sanction. Stating that he felt that the Independents "were not so stupid to do such a thing" and that they would never engage in "out and out treason," he suggested that the matter be discussed before a select Reichstag committee. This would ensure that all parties, including the USPD, would reject any "attempt to stage a *putsch*." [8]

Driven by their ambitions and fears, the chancellor and the Secretary of the Navy were not to be deterred. On August 14, in violation of the parliamentary immunity of the deputies and of the party, they authorized a search of the USPD central offices. The police rifled through files and correspondence without unearthing any evidence of complicity in the mutiny.[9] On September 2 the offices of the *Leipziger Volkszeitung* were searched with equally disappointing results.[10] It was discovered that a mere sixty-five enlisted men at the Wilhelmshaven naval base subscribed to that paper.[11]

In the meantime, on August 21, Michaelis had convened a special meeting to map out strategy against the USPD. Capelle was the first to speak. Taking it for granted that the Independent Social Democrats were guilty, he demanded that "all permissible measures" be taken to protect the fleet from the subversion of revolutionary ideas. With mounting emotion, he recommended that no cost was too high to prevent the USPD from undermining discipline in the fleet. However, the hapless Capelle could not produce any evidence that concretely implicated any of the deputies. When this was pointed out by State Prosecutor Richter, a noticeable pall fell upon the meeting. The legal counselor maintained that his reading of the evidence indicated that it was not the deputies who had fomented unrest among the crews but the men themselves. Cautioning the assembly that the deputies could only be convicted with the aid of Reichpietsch and Sachse, he warned against executing these two men.

Neither Michaelis nor Capelle seemed in a mood for such somber predictions. The chancellor expressed regret that no judicial
proof against the deputies had yet come to light, insisted that they
were "morally responsible," and promised that the minute he obtained such proof he would close the Reichstag. If this could not
be done at once, he asserted, "then we will wait until fall." Disregarding Richter's advice and indicating their contempt for judicial proof, both Michaelis and Capelle insisted that the death sentences of the condemned enlisted men be carried out at once.[12]

Three days later at a meeting held at the Admiralty, the navy
revealed some of its motives and plans. Although State Prosecutor
Richter reiterated his opinion that he lacked evidence to prose-
cute the deputies and that it was vital that the only witnesses
against them be kept alive, and although Privy Counselor Felisch
of the Admiralty endorsed this view, as the meeting went on it
became increasingly clear that the navy did not really want a trial
so much as a political victory. As Felisch phrased it, "If the chancellor is as strong as I hope he is, I would advise him to proceed
against the deputies even if their acquittal can be expected in advance. The political gain of rendering the USPD harmless is in
my view far greater than the damage that would be caused by an
acquittal." More directly concerned with the navy, Admiral von
Capelle articulated the same feeling in even bolder terms when he
asserted that never again would there be such a good opportunity
"to proceed against the revolutionary party." Revealing that he
wished to proscribe the USPD without becoming involved in
lengthy and embarrassing explanations over the real causes of the
mutiny, he recommended that the matter not be brought before
the Reichstag. He was afraid that "complaints about trouble with
rations and slaps in the face" would make Reichstag deliberations
"inconclusive." [13]

That the Reichstag could not simply be bypassed because the
navy wished it was demonstrated on August 25 when Michaelis,
still hoping that he could marshal the moderate parties against the
Independents, convened a meeting with some of the important

leaders of the Reichstag. In a session that lasted nearly three hours Michaelis and Capelle unsuccessfully tried to persuade the politicians of the USPD's guilt in order to obtain their acquiescence to a waiver of parliamentary immunity. Instead the deputies turned the tables by insisting on concrete proof and urging the navy not to execute its prisoners and, in the words of Friedrich von Payer, to "allow compassion to prevail." Finally, a disappointed Michaelis was compelled to agree not to proceed against the USPD until such time as more conclusive evidence of its guilt was made available. In return the party leaders consented to keep the news of a mutiny a secret.[14]

The defeat of August 25 placed Capelle in a precarious position. Widely detested by the naval officer corps for being weak-kneed (*schlapp*) and lacking in forcefulness, Capelle could not sit by idly while the alleged instigators of the mutiny remained unpunished. He knew all too well that there were many officers like Captain von Waldeyer-Hartz, who charged that "in the summer of 1917 conditions were such that the navy could have defeated the rebellious and misguided crews in the fleet in a manner that precluded any repetition. . . . However, we were reluctant to use the proper means. Instead of tearing out the infection root and branch, we contented ourselves with a solution that all too plainly bore the marks of a retreat before the revolutionary forces." [15] Even more ominously, his inability to produce the result desired by the navy gradually alienated the Kaiser to the point that he petulantly canceled an audience with Capelle.[16] Thus forced to adopt a stronger stand, Capelle informed Michaelis on September 8 that he was prepared "to intervene on behalf of the fleet with his own person and, if necessary, to create a cabinet crisis" by resigning;[17] at the same time he tried to assuage the angry officer corps and his arch enemy in the navy, Prince Henry of Prussia, by proclaiming that he was merely waiting for proof before proceeding against the deputies.[18]

While he barely managed to hold off his fellow officers in this fashion, the unsuspecting naval secretary was confronted with an even graver threat when, on October 6, the Reichstag began a discussion of Pan-German propaganda in Germany's armed services.[19] Astounded by the Reichstag's audacity in raising such a delicate subject and conscious of its guilt in permitting such propaganda to be waged, the Michaelis government fared badly. Michaelis deliberately absented himself from the debate and allowed his ministers to bear the brunt of the attack with the result that two of them, War Minister von Stein and Vice Chancellor Helfferich, were booed off the rostrum by the angry deputies.[20] Even when the chancellor finally made an appearance before the Reichstag's Main Committee on October 8 and tried to conciliate the politicians, their open disapproval of his policies did not augur well for the future of his administration. Worse than that was the prospect of Admiral von Capelle, for Deputy Dittmann of the Independent Social Democratic Party had arisen and precipitated a crisis when he demanded to know why the navy had executed some of his party's supporters in the fleet.[21]

Both Capelle and Michaelis must have realized that they would be ruined when Dittmann posed this question before the public forum of the Reichstag and they were unable to supply a proper answer. This was especially true of Capelle, who had been advised on October 3 by Dr. Felisch that he was not to let out "even a word" in the Reichstag about the legality of the two executions in the navy because there was no hope that he could emerge victoriously.[22] Thus deprived of ammunition in his defense of the death sentences and unable to substantiate the navy's accusations of treason against the deputies, Capelle must have known that barring a miracle he faced certain disaster on October 9, when the full Reichstag reconvened.

Miracles, however, are seldom produced to order. Nevertheless Capelle must have felt that he had one on his hands on the morning of October 9 as the government reeled under the impact of Dittmann's questions: "Is it true that the navy has handed down sentences amounting to nearly two hundred years of imprisonment to sailors for their alleged adherence to socialist ideas and their recruitment for the Independent Socialist Party? And is it further true that for the same reason some sailors have been sentenced to death and executed?" [23] Capelle had just received a telegram from *Marinehilfsgerichtsrat* Doctor Loesch in Wilhelmshaven stating: "Have unearthed a possible case of treason against the person of His Majesty [the Kaiser]. According to the confession of [Seaman] Calmus, the culprits are Reichstag Deputies Dittmann and Ledebour [working] in conjunction with uniformed German officers and apparently [some] English and French officers." [24]

The story of Paul Calmus and the way he influenced this parliamentary crisis forms one of the most fascinating tales of World War I. But it is more than a mere tale because of what it reveals about the nature of naval justice and the workings of the German naval mentality during World War I.

Early in October 1917 the court of the First Squadron began to consider the case of Calmus, Hannemann, Hillmer, *et al.*, crew members of the *Rheinland*, against whom charges of mutiny had been preferred. By then such investigations had become routine for the navy. Yet this one was to overshadow all the others in importance save for the Reichpietsch and Sachse case. What made this case unique was the personality and testimony of Seaman Paul Calmus, who by his wits managed to elude the firing squad and received instead a mere fifteen-year sentence in jail.

Upon his arrest Calmus realized that he faced almost certain death. He had a bad disciplinary record. Even worse, he had paid a visit to Frau Zietz in Berlin and had corresponded with her regarding propagandistic literature. All this came out at his pretrial interrogation. Calmus felt himself "betrayed," "a cooked goose." [25] Seeking a way to save his life, he may have hit upon the idea of emulating Willi Sachse and submitting a confession of such great interest to the naval authorities that they would be compelled to keep him alive, at least temporarily. [26]

On October 8 Calmus startled Dr. Loesch much as Sachse had Dr. Dobring when he stated that he wished to submit a full confession. He asserted that at the beginning of August the crew of the *Rheinland*, increasingly mistrustful of Reichpietsch's wild claims of USPD support, had collected forty marks and sent Calmus to Berlin to obtain a correct assessment of the situation. When he arrived in Berlin on August 2, Calmus at once made for the USPD offices on the Schiffbauerdamm, only to find them closed. While he stood there a man with a full beard and a fat cigar walked up and addressed him as follows: "Good morning, Herr Calmus. Do you know Dittmann?" Fearing that the stranger was a detective, Calmus denied knowing Dittmann and stated that he had come here merely to say good-bye to one of the girls who worked in the building. The bearded figure smiled, looked him straight in the eye, and asked if he had not really come to make inquiries about the enlisted men's organization in the fleet. Then handing the sailor a card imprinted with "Dittmann, Reichstag Deputy," he instructed Calmus to return at three that afternoon.

Coming back that afternoon, Calmus saw Frau Zietz and obtained her promise that she would supply the fleet with agitational literature. On his way out of the building, Calmus found "Dittmann" waiting for him on the steps. Another man who identified himself as Deputy Ledebour was also present. Walking a short distance, the three men boarded a waiting hack, rode for about twenty minutes, and then changed to a streetcar. When they finally came to a remote section of the city, they dismounted and entered an inconspicuous-looking house.

Becoming more and more dramatic as he continued, Calmus told Loesch that "Dittmann" and Ledebour had taken him upstairs, where they had introduced him to a group of men consisting of one civilian, three army officers, two acting lieutenants, and two noncommissioned officers whose halting accents hinted at their foreign origin. The senior officer present, a major with a monocle in his eye, then turned to Calmus. Stating that he had been informed that Calmus was reliable and could be trusted, he pulled out a dagger and made the sailor swear never to reveal anything that transpired at this meeting. Thereupon he handed

Calmus a Browning pistol for his "personal protection" and began rifling through a briefcase filled with Russian, French, British, and Italian documents bearing official seals. Going straight to the point, the major asked Calmus to recruit members for the USPD in the navy by collecting signatures of membership. In return for such lists he promised to pay 5,000 marks and showed Calmus a leather bag containing that amount in coins.

Stunned by this proposition, Calmus watched as "Dittmann" removed the documents on the table and presented an even more fantastic scheme. In minute detail, "Dittmann" unfolded a plan to assassinate the Kaiser on his next visit to the fleet by means of an "infernal machine." This was to be set off by either Calmus or a confederate whom he was instructed to recruit. In compensation for murdering Wilhelm II he was offered an initial sum of 10,000 marks and ten times that amount upon the successful completion of the assassination. In addition, he was promised that his escape across the border would be arranged.

As "Dittmann" spelled out the details of this plot, Calmus was seized with mounting excitement and terror. The sailor jumped up, drew the pistol he had been given, and told the conspirators to raise their hands. Next he ordered that the documents for the Kaiser's assassination be burned. Slowly he groped his way to the door. Before leaving the apartment, Calmus told the men that he would keep his promise of secrecy but threatened that if they continued to plot the assassination he would go directly to the authorities, even if this meant his own death.

After an encounter with a young woman named Sissy, who tried to detain him in a tavern, and almost bumping into the major with the monocle at the railroad station, Calmus made his way back to Wilhelmshaven, where he was shortly thereafter arrested for his previous agitational activities on the *Rheinland*.[27]

Incredible as it may seem, Calmus' "movie novel confession" was believed by the naval authorities. Stenographer Geier, who took down Calmus' testimony in the pretrial interrogation, states that he was convinced that the sailor was telling the truth. Whenever Geier left out a minor point, Calmus would remind him of it and insist that it be included in the transcript. Moreover, Geier was also impressed by the fact that Calmus had spent the previous night with a local clergyman and thus seemed properly penitent.[28]

Another person involved with the case, Court Stenographer Klima, who recorded the official court-martial proceedings, was persuaded that "here was a man who greatly rued his transgression and wanted to relieve his conscience." Klima also informs us that the interrogator, Dr. Loesch, shared these feelings. Loesch felt that Calmus "had broken down completely," and began to sympathize with him. And although Loesch did not believe all that Calmus had told about the deputies, he was sufficiently impressed by Calmus' insistence and detailed accuracy to report his confession to the authorities in Berlin.[29]

Naval Counselor Loesch, the person most responsible for propagating Calmus' hoax upon the Secretary of the Navy, testified after the war that he was astounded when Calmus came to him on October 8 and made this confession. Although Loesch "regarded it with a great deal of skepticism," he had it taken down word for word and then made up his mind that Calmus' revelations about his contacts with foreign agents warranted notifying Loesch's superiors in Berlin.[30]

It is hard to believe that a trained legal official could be taken in by what Dr. Zweigert of the prosecutor's office was to label so "fictional and incredible [a story] that it cannot merit further consideration." [31] Even more incredible is the fact that Loesch could believe this fantastic tale without bothering to find even rudimentary corroborating evidence. All it would have taken was a telephone call to the Foreign Office to prove that Dittmann could not possibly have met with Calmus because Dittmann had left to attend the Socialist Conference in Stockholm on July 30 and had not returned until August 7.[32]

The only explanation for Loesch's gullibility is that he was trying so hard to implicate the USPD and to produce the evidence that his superiors wanted that he was ready to give credence to anything that confirmed his prejudices. Similarly, the naval court-martial that sentenced Calmus to fifteen years in prison on October 10 stated, in justification of its extraordinarily mild sentence, that his "confession and obvious effort to be penitent" made it unnecessary to delve deeper into the truth and credibility of his statements." [33] So long as the navy obtained the ammunition it needed to slough off its guilt upon the hapless sailors and the USPD, it cared little whether truth or justice was served.

This was all too obvious when on the morning of October 9 Captain Brüninghaus received Loesch's telegram in the Reichstag. Doubtlessly elated by the good news it conveyed, Brüninghaus immediately presented it to Admiral von Capelle, who instructed him to pass it on to Michaelis.[34] The embattled chancellor had originally intended merely to repeat the platitudes he had given the Main Committee the previous day, but the severity of Dittmann's attack calling for his dismissal [35] plus the arrival of the news of Calmus' confession must have changed Michaelis' mind.

Dittmann had made public grave and irrefutable charges against the navy, Michaelis had lost his standing with the Reichstag, and if Michaelis did not register a proper reply that pleased his military supporters, he would have to resign. For that reason the chancellor saw a welcome opportunity in Loesch's telegram. Quickly conferring with Capelle, he gave up his hopelessly inadequate plan and decided to launch a counterattack against the USPD and to unleash the impatient Secretary of the Navy.[36]

Only the knowledge and hope that the long-awaited evidence against the USPD had at last materialized could have prompted Michaelis to violate his agreement with the Reichstag leaders to keep the mutiny a secret. No matter how great a bungler he may have been, it is unreasonable to suppose that he would have made the error of incurring the ire of the Reichstag if he had not been confident that at last he possessed the evidence he needed to attack the USPD, break the Reichstag majority, and possibly dispense with the Reichstag altogether by closing it. Overcome by the false euphoria generated by Loesch's telegram and acting on the spur of the moment, Michaelis and Capelle lunged into their ill-considered attack upon the USPD.[37]

Immediately after Dittmann had finished, Michaelis took the floor. Addressing himself to the main subject under consideration, the official dissemination of Pan-German propaganda in Germany's armed services, he stated that it was his policy to mete out equal and objective treatment to all political parties. But, he continued, this applied only to patriotic and loyal parties that did not endanger the security of the Empire. For him the USPD stood on the other side of that line.[38] Michaelis' attack upon the USPD was really an ill-concealed attempt to place that party outside of the confines of the law. In his brief reply to Dittmann, Michaelis had taken the first step which, if successful, would have resulted in the passage of a new "anti-Socialist law" which would deny the Independents the right to legal existence as a political party.

The next speaker was Admiral von Capelle, whose task it was to deliver the main blow against the USPD by leveling charges of treason to justify such measures. In very specific terms the admiral asserted that he had written proof (*es steht aktenmässig fest*) that the main architect of the mutiny that had recently convulsed the fleet, Seaman Reichpietsch, had presented his plans to deputies Dittmann, Haase, and Vogtherr and had received their "full support" in organizing a rebellion.[39]

Astonished by Capelle's violation of his agreement, the Reichstag was thrown into an uproar. The Majority Socialist Eduard David refused to sanction exceptional laws against any party and accused the chancellor of attempting to stage a coup d'état;[40] the three accused Independents put up a staunch defense by protesting their innocence and challenging the government to prove its charges.[41] The representatives of the bourgeois parties—the Center, the National Liberals, and the Progressives—incensed at Michaelis' and Capelle's breach of confidence submitted angry denunciations calling upon the government to produce its evidence, if it had any, so that the Independents could be put on trial.[42] Culminating what was rapidly taking on all the characteristics of an irretrievable disaster was Friedrich Ebert's demand for a no-confidence resolution.[43]

Michaelis and Capelle had suffered a staggering blow and knew it. Although Michaelis quickly tried to beat a retreat by explaining that he had not intended to propose the passage of exceptional legislation and by defending the legality of the navy's death sentences,[44] nothing could help him now. His "unfortunate improvisation," as Helfferich called it,[45] had backfired. Nothing he could do, not even the attempt to sacrifice Capelle for what he apologetically called an "administrative error" (*ein Fehler der Regie*),[46] could keep him in office long. So great was the public outcry that on November 1 Michaelis was replaced by Georg von Hertling, an ancient Bavarian Centrist politician who showed greater willingness to cooperate with the Reichstag and who was too astute to commit such gross errors of judgment.

Within the intervening time Michaelis and Capelle tried in vain to recoup their position by making feverish efforts to capitalize on the Calmus confession and by finding evidence against Dittmann and Ledebour. Indicating how much faith the authorities placed in the Loesch dispatch is a letter from Admiral von Capelle to Michaelis on October 16, stating his belief that the sailor's confession ought to provide grounds for a trial. He asserted, "At least the testimony of Stoker Calmus reveals certain people in this circle [of USPD deputies] to whom he was sent. The universally awaited 'signal from Berlin' [calling for the outbreak of a mutiny in the fleet] can find no other explanation." [47] As late as October 21 the Kaiser was still confident that he could retain Michaelis and Capelle in office because recently discovered contacts—in all probability those mentioned by Calmus—between the Independent Socialists and the enlisted men might justify instituting a trial against the deputies.[48]

When this new evidence proved ephemeral, the Kaiser had to sacrifice Michaelis, but he stubbornly insisted that he would not sanction the dismissal of a military adviser like Capelle under civilian pressure. Confirming once more that his fall from power was occasioned by the failure of the Calmus confession to provide grounds for a trial, Michaelis on November 2 wrote that it was unfortunate that no real evidence against the deputies had come to light.[49]

Even with Michaelis gone, the navy refused to give up hope. On November 24, almost a month after his dismissal, Dr. Dobring informed Capelle that he was convinced that Dittmann, Haase, Vogtherr, and possibly Ledebour had encouraged the mutinous men in the fleet.[50] Grasping at straws and still determined somehow to pass the blame for the mutiny onto the USPD, the government in November tried to indict Frau Zietz, who did not enjoy parliamentary immunity. But a proceeding conducted before a court at Cöpenick was so inconclusive that in April 1918 the state prosecutor decided to abandon the case for lack of evidence.[51]

All in all, Calmus' grand hoax and the October 9 episode which it had occasioned brought irreparable harm to Germany and the navy. Reacting to the wide publicity given the mutiny by the Reichstag debate on that day, the English picked up the scent of unrest in the fleet. On October 11 the *Manchester Guardian* gleefully reported: "Without a doubt this mutiny is the most serious political event in Germany since the outbreak of the war and, indeed, since 1848. According to the admission of Capelle, the revolutionary movement wanted to overthrow the dynasty and the present political system in order to convert Germany into a democratic republic. The movement wanted to force the conclusion of peace." At about the same time, the British radio broadcaster at Carnavon so magnified these events that he spoke of a major mutiny and the internal destruction of the German fleet.[52]

From a domestic point of view, the consequences of this publicity were equally devastating. Within a short period of time, the extreme left both in and out of Germany managed to make popular martyrs out of Reichpietsch and Köbis. Soon all sorts of songs and proclamations were circulated to commemorate their memory and to foment a revolutionary spirit among the sailors and working classes.[53]

The naval officer corps, having failed to proscribe the USPD, reacted by loosening a campaign of vituperation against the government. Everywhere in its ranks there was talk that the government had left the navy "in the lurch" by allowing the Reichstag and the socialists to take away its "damned right" to take whatever steps it considered necessary to combat the mutinous spirit of its crews.[54] As Captain Waldeyer-Hartz put it, October 9 was the first time that the victorious fleet of the Battle of Jutland "retreated before the banner of insurrection!"[55] Thus was created the myth that the navy could have coped with its troubles if it had not been for the cowardly government that refused to protect it from leftist subversion.[56]

Although Admiral Hebbinghaus at a meeting held in the War Ministry on November 17, 1917, freely admitted that he did not think that the USPD had wanted a mutiny in the fleet, that the entire case had been exaggerated, and that the more one searched the evidence the less conclusive it became, von Trotha never tired of blaming the government for not breaking the alleged tie between the USPD and the sailors.[57] Given the vehemence with which these ideas were expressed and the continuing influence of the admirals in post-World War I Germany, it comes as no great surprise that this myth persists to the present day. As recently as 1962 Kapitänleutnant Förste wrote that it was incomprehensible to him that the government and the Reichstag could not find the strength to take "drastic steps against the enemies of the state" by outlawing the USPD and that he could still insist that Admiral Scheer was in this respect much more far-sighted than the contemporary politicians.[58]

Since the naval authorities assiduously avoided acknowledging the real causes of the unrest among the enlisted men, it was virtually inevitable that they should fail to take the proper steps to regain the trust and loyalty of their men. By their insistence that the sole cause of the mutiny was political propaganda, they adopted a whole series of worthless palliatives and never came to grips with the real problem. At the same time, however, the officers were paralyzed with fear that they would soon be confronted by a renewed and even more potent enlisted men's revolt. Preferring to believe the myth that they had created rather than the harsh realities of the truth, the naval officer corps succumbed to a strange ambivalence, the effects of which can best be discerned by studying the actions of Admiral Scheer and his commanders.

Right after the *Prinzregent Luitpold* walkout, attempts at critical self-analysis had not been totally absent in the navy. Admiral Meurer of the Fourth Squadron had on August 15 maintained that a partial cause of the mutiny was the men's lack of political understanding. Hence he decreed that his senior officers try to influence the men to perform their duty toward the Kaiser and the Reich by means of frank discussions of social and political questions.[59] Going even further, a week later he commanded that petty officers try to cultivate a closer relationship with their men and keep them under closer surveillance by taking meals with them. On August 30 Admiral Hipper extended this order to the entire Reconnaissance Group.[60]

No sooner, however, had the myth of USPD complicity begun to take root than all these healthy signs of objectivity began to dwindle. In a report that revealed nothing so much as a complete lack of understanding for reality, Captain von Hornhardt of the *Prinzregent Luitpold* stated on September 26: "The morale of the crew has been completely restored by the punishment [of the ringleaders] and lectures by officers. The alacrity with which it performs its duties and its military bearing indicate such an improvement that one may say that discipline has been restored to its former level." [61] Exuding an even greater degree of self-deception and wishful thinking was the report from Captain Lefert of the *Friedrich der Grosse*, who wrote on September 28: "Lectures have brought things to such a point that the majority of men will no longer allow themselves to be deceived or misled. I believe that I am not being overly optimistic when I say that the crew has gladly regained its confidence in its superiors. I personally feel myself at ease among the men. This may stem from the fact that they allow me to gauge their real mood." [62]

Mistaking the effects of repression for loyalty was a common occurrence in the German navy in the fall of 1917. Thus Admiral Souchon, commanding the Fourth Squadron, could write on September 30 that most of the men had returned to their senses because of the severe court-martial sentences and the steps taken by their officers. Captain Lefert of the *Friedrich der Grosse* reiterated that all the trouble had been caused "by a small number of bad elements" and that the crews could be kept on the proper road so long as these agitators were removed. To this Souchon added that the "transfer of the infectious element" would restore complete control in his squadron.[63] Reflecting the unwarranted optimism of his commanders, Scheer on October 6 informed the Kaiser that the effectiveness of the High Seas Fleet had been restored and "that all units under my command are now thoroughly under the control of their commanders." [64]

The practice of self-delusion combined with an unwillingness to recognize the real causes of the unrest is illustrated to perfection by Scheer's top-secret order, GG. 6025 B.I., of October 7, 1917. This order, really a lengthy memorandum on the mutiny, provides some vital insights into the mentality of Admiral Scheer and the officer corps.

Although Scheer expressed a willingness to undertake certain reforms, his refusal to acknowledge the guilt of his officers severely limited the opportunities for change. While admitting that "many gross errors" had been committed in the matter of leaves, petitions, and complaints by enlisted men, Scheer insisted that these errors were important primarily because they had given "the ill-intentioned elements a welcome weapon for agitation." Similarly, he conceded that differences in rations had played an important role in alienating the men, but he once again asserted that this had been exaggerated out of all proportion by vicious rumors. Therefore he ordered that "every utterance of this sort must be tracked down without fail until it is either proven true or until the rumor mongerer can be brought to account." However, he avoided prescribing a genuine remedy by mildly urging his officers to refrain from maintaining "a substantially different" diet from their men. Instead of punishing officers who had violated this injunction, Scheer cautiously recommended that they mend their ways, but he neglected to put teeth into his injunction by failing to specify what punishment, if any, he would mete out to violators.

On the whole, Scheer's October 7 order was negative in tone, stressing repression rather than reform. Thus the section on the USPD and its alleged revolutionary influence upon the men was given disproportionate emphasis. Perpetuating the myth of a USPD conspiracy, Scheer declared that the execution and imprisonment of the ringleaders would not suffice to uproot the movement in the fleet. Ingenuously he ordered his officers to watch out for the following signs of continuing revolutionary activity by the USPD: enlisted men's correspondence that began with the letter U, had an S in the middle, and ended with a P; men keeping their left hand in their pocket on even days of the week and the right hand on odd numbered days; the possession of metal plates with the code number of their ships; and the use of recognition signals such as "may one play cards here?" [65]

Relying principally on the death sentences he had handed down and the increased surveillance of his officers to bring the enlisted men back to order, Scheer and his commanders failed to understand that they had merely produced a superficial and temporary peace.[66] The harsh court-martial sentences may have intimidated some men, but they also enraged a number of others to such an extent that they would do anything in revenge. As Stumpf saw it, the executions and long jail sentences had the following effect:

"Half of the men are apathetic, a quarter of them regard this as an outrage and feel sorry for the poor devils, while fewer than another quarter are ready to act and seek revenge." [67]

True, the enlisted men's movement collapsed when its leaders were arrested. Without direction, the rest of the men lacked the ability to rebuild it under the close scrutiny of their superiors. But they became more sullen and resentful than ever before. From the very beginning of the postmutiny era, the men indicated that they were merely yielding to superior force and would never again trust their officers. When the Kaiser visited the fleet in August many of the sailors refused to shout their traditional greeting of "Hurrah" and shouted "Hunger" instead.[68]

Even when their hunger was satisfied by a remarkable improvement in rations at the beginning of September[69] and they ate better than in peace time,[70] the enlisted men's resentment did not abate. The sailors and stokers could not forgive the navy for its injustice and the judicial murders it had committed. As that perceptive sailor on the *Helgoland*, Richard Stumpf, phrased it, "Our trust in the courts, our respect for our officers, and our love for the Fatherland were blighted." [71]

No doubt sensing this sullenness and resentment, the naval officer corps responded with fear, mistrust, and suspicion, refused to institute reforms, and contented itself with passing a variety of useless and occasionally harmful stopgap measures. Even Scheer was clever enough to recognize that he had not done enough to restore the loyalty of the men. In a previously undiscovered letter, Scheer confessed to Admiral von Trotha on January 3, 1919, that he had been responsible for the failure to stop the growth of the "revolutionary movement" in the fleet because he had not done enough "to undermine the agitation" by having the officers "set a good example, by lectures and the introduction of timely reforms." [72] Although Scheer never managed to overcome his feeling that the fleet had been ruined by a revolutionary movement, for a time, at least, he was honest enough with himself to recog-

nize that his postmutiny policy, by neglecting sorely needed reforms and failing to curb the irresponsibility of the officer corps,
had never come close to restoring the confidence and loyalty of
the crews.

Prevented by pride, *Kastengeist*, and sheer stubbornness from
changing its mode of behavior, the German naval officer corps
headed toward its doom when it opted for repression instead of
reform. Deluding itself into believing that most of its men were
loyal and had been misled by troublemakers, the officer corps
sought to solve its problem by trying after August 1917 to transfer these men off their ships to various shore installations. Exact
figures for this practice are not available, but it was widely used in
the navy. In this fashion large numbers of men were palmed off
on the Kiel and Wilhelmshaven naval stations while an even larger
number were sent to serve with the Naval Infantry Brigade in
Flanders.[73]

Demonstrating the complete uselessness of this method is the
example of Wilhelmshaven. On August 16 the North Sea naval
station indicated its willingness to accept 150 to 180 politically
unreliable men from the fleet, but only on the condition that their
"discipline was good" (*Bedingung ist gute Führung*).[74] The
process by which the men were selected was extremely haphazard. On August 22 the *Kaiser* put out a list of names of men to be
transferred ashore "because it is highly probable that they have
bad political views and because their influence upon their comrades represents a danger to the ship."

Revealing how bureaucratic, formalistic, and futile the entire
project was are the descriptions of the men by their officers.
There was Seaman General, a man of "thoroughly bad thoughts"
who set a bad example and tended "to agitate his comrades and
make them discontented." Seaman Domagal was judged "lacking
in thought" and a "bad example," while Stoker Balszum was accused of having "a poor patriotic attitude," making "derogatory
remarks," and "criticizing the measures of his superiors." [75] These

stereotyped descriptions suggest that the officers were merely getting rid of men against whom they bore a grudge rather than carefully winnowing political leaders.

Moreover, such indiscriminate mass purges could not go on indefinitely. Within a month of the inception of this policy, the Wilhelmshaven naval station was beginning to be filled and refused to accept any more bad men.[76] On November 19, 1917, Admiral Scheer, realizing that abuses had crept into the selection process, was compelled to issue orders that he would no longer sanction the transfer of men whose conduct books merely bore the entry "bad political attitude," but would have to demand that in the future only those who failed to maintain "military discipline," who were of "undoubted dishonorable character" and gave evidence that they were about to undermine the discipline of the crews would be considered for transfer.[77]

Finally, early in December the entire transfer process ground to a halt as the commandant of the Wilhelmshaven base, Admiral von Krosigk, indignantly refused to continue playing the role of the navy's garbage dump. Stating that "the effort to strengthen and maintain morale on the ships must not lead to the collection of all the worst elements in the fleet in the shore units and especially in the main naval base of Wilhelmshaven," he warned that he could not find employment for them or officers to supervise them. Therefore he feared that they would "continue to remain in most intimate contact with the crews of the fleet." [78] Von Krosigk was correct. The navy's reckless desire to weed out unreliable elements had overburdened all shore installations. In November 1918 it was precisely this element that rose up against the naval authority and made Kiel and Wilhelmshaven the main centers of rebellion.

Having exhausted the transfer method, the navy adopted alternative policies with equally bad effect. Filled with fear that a real revolutionary movement had infiltrated its enlisted ranks, the navy desperately sought to uncover overt signs of revolutionary organization and thereby antagonized even its staunchest supporters. In a panic over the discovery of agitational pamphlets in dockyard latrines, all commands were alerted on November 7 to keep their men under closest surveillance in the hope of ferreting out the revolutionary organization. At first it was thought that an infallible sign of membership in such an organization was wearing a red thread in the enlisted men's uniform collar.[79] Although Scheer admitted that he lacked conclusive proof that this was true, he commanded that no more red thread be used and threatend that all men who violated his order be punished for disobedience.[80]

Even before his order was published, individual commanders had already taken the situation in hand by punishing innocent men. Two sailors on the *Kaiserin* were disciplined for "being out of uniform" because they wore "the Socialist sign" in their collars, while at least one unfortunate man on the *Hagen* was transferred to *Kaiserin* on October 13 for committing a similar offense.[81] Yet as early as October 8 the *Prinzregent Luitpold* had reported that twenty of its crew members with "unblemished attitudes" had been discovered wearing red thread. They had explained that they used it because they had much red thread and could find no other use for it.[82]

Such manifestations of panic enhanced tensions in the fleet and facilitated the spread of rumors. In the fall of 1917 it was whispered that an uprising had broken out in Wilhelmshaven and that a number of men had been shot. Also it was said that the rebellious crew on the *Seydlitz* had drowned its captain by throwing him overboard while the commander of another large vessel, either the *Markgraf* or *König*, had also been heaved over the side but had been saved. Still another rumor had it that the *Derfflinger*, extensively damaged by sabotage, was undergoing repairs in Hamburg. Realizing that these rumors could be very demoralizing, Admiral Scheer on October 22 blithely decreed that they cease forthwith.[83]

Equally bad for the morale of the enlisted men were the navy's clumsy attempts to indoctrinate its crews. In an effort to deny the men access to the ideas of the USPD, all pamphlets, newspapers, and meetings connected with that party were prohibited on October 23. Fifteen newspapers were thus placed on the forbidden list.[84] While the officers were given a free hand to lecture to the men as they pleased and to subject them to a constant stream of Pan-German propaganda,[85] the navy kept issuing admonitions that attendance of party meetings and rallies was prohibited.[86] Nevertheless, in Kiel at least, the *Vaterlandspartei* was allowed free reign because the commandant of the naval station held that this group was not really a political party.[87]

All other dissident groups were harassed unmercifully. This was true even of the members of the sect of Seventh Day Adventists, who, it was alleged, encouraged the men to desert and advised them not to sign up for war loans. Accordingly, preachers of that faith were denied travel and speaking permits and were kept under close scrutiny.[88] The same treatment was accorded the USPD when it tried to organize meetings for the townspeople of Kiel. When the noted socialist revisionist Eduard Bernstein was scheduled to address a group of his party followers in Kiel on December 17, 1917, the naval police closed the meeting because Bernstein was considered a dangerous "agitator." [89] The Wilhelmshaven naval station behaved similarly in the period from February to June 1918. It allowed five meetings of the *Vaterlandspartei*, one for the National Liberals, one for the Progressives, one for the Majority Socialists, 18 trade union meetings, and 192 nonpolitical meetings. But the Independent Social Democrats were never issued a permit, while one meeting by Seventh Day Adventists was closed down as soon as it opened.[90]

The effects of these prohibitions are not quite clear. According to Ringelnatz they merely called the men's attention to the forbidden newspapers and added to their resentment.[91] There are indications that these prohibitions, mainly directed against the USPD, merely replaced the propaganda of the party by the much more virulent one of the left radicals and Spartacists. For instance, on March 3, 1918, one pamphlet discovered in the latrine of the

Imperial Shipyard at Kiel called upon the sailors to emulate their "brothers in Russia" and concluded by declaring "Down with Imperialism! Make war on war! Long live peace!" [92] As late as March 27, 1918, Admiral von Trotha was still concerned about the fairly wide dissemination of this type of propaganda in the fleet and recommended that it might help if the nightly blackout of Kiel which facilitated the distribution of such material were lifted.[93]

As a consequence of its unwillingness to institute effective reforms, the navy lived in constant dread of the outbreak of an insurrection among its crews. Report after report issued by individual commands belied the official optimism that morale in the fleet had returned to normalcy.[94] On December 31, 1917, the High Seas Fleet admitted that the morale of the enlisted men was slumping, that disaffection and boredom were rampant, and that discipline had slackened considerably.[95]

So frightened was the navy that it believed the most absurd reports. In mid-February 1918 a report that a Dane had been apprehended while in the process of inciting enlisted men to blow up their ships[96] was taken at face value. Even more indicative of the panic and fear that engulfed the officer corps and the paralysis it engendered is a report by the chief of staff of the Kiel naval station dated April 16, 1918. Admiral Küsel, the author of this report, revealed that agitators were once again at work in the docks and shipyards at Kiel and that it was feared that they might infect the fleet. One agitator in particular, Karl Artelt of the First Dock Division, seemed highly dangerous. At a socialist meeting held at the trade union building in Kiel on April 12, which was attended by no fewer than twenty-five to thirty petty officers in uniform, Artelt had made an inflammatory speech calling for union with the USPD. Hence Küsel demanded unequivocally that "every commander, every officer, must recognize the responsibility he bears in this matter. People like that must be punished and immediately transferred from Kiel to the front." [97] Despite these grave warnings, however, Artelt remained in Kiel, apparently undisturbed by the commander of the First Dock Division or by Küsel.

Yet there is ample evidence that punitive measures became the order of the day in the navy. On a single ship for which we have figures, the *Nürnberg*, the first officer handed down 230 days of imprisonment, 18 days of mild arrest, 152 hours of punitive exercise, and 50 hours of punitive watches in the period from November 1917 to April 1918.[98] In 1918 the slightest incident that hinted at a repetition of the previous year's strikes was treated as though it were a major mutiny. For instance, when it was discovered that the crew of the *Friedrich der Grosse* had tossed some rotten eggs overboard, the navy instituted a full-scale investigation. Although it was shown that the "eggs did not smell too bad," the naval authorities could not understand how "the green looks of the eggs" could have revolted the men into discarding them in such blatant fashion.[99]

Equally exaggerated was the navy's response to a hunger strike on the workship *Bosnia* in February 1918. Disgusted with receiving white cabbage for two days in succession, the crew of that ship had simply refused to pick up its food. Once again an investigation was launched, and Counselor Breil was placed in charge. Although it was obvious from the outset that there were no political motives behind the hunger strike, Admiral Souchon in whose command the *Bosnia* resided, punished all the mess leaders.[100]

The one thing that might have halted the inexorable drift toward another rebellion, namely, the immediate remedy of abuses, was never attempted. In fact, one may safely say that abuses were allowed to flourish without impediment in the navy, contributing in no small measure to its ultimate collapse. As one young sailor, who served on a torpedo boat on which conditions were admittedly far better than on the big ships, described it, the German navy continued to be "ruled by absolutism somewhat tempered by inefficiency and sloppiness (*Schlamperei*)." [101]

The officers' *Kastengeist* remained undiminished in the last year of the Imperial Navy, and the enlisted men's alienation continued to grow. In 1918 the navy still treated its engineering officers as an inferior caste, forbade them social intercourse with regular officers, and persisted in barring "the doors to their aspirations." Even greater disregard was shown the deck officers. When it became necessary to admit them into the officers' club in Kiel, the chairman of that club, Captain Mysing, submitted an official objection. He complained that the whole arrangement was unsatisfactory because it had been observed that some of the deck officers "did not depart from the club immediately after their meal," but stayed on in the building. Indeed, a few of them had been audacious enough to sit on the veranda listening to band concerts.[102]

Despised as a group, individual deck officers were also frequently subjected to harassment by regular officers. One such example is the case of Deck Officer Kamerowski, an older man. A young naval officer, Lieutenant Schmidt, on one occasion addressed him as follows: "You must have gone totally insane, you cur! Get out of here, you scoundrel!" When the older man stalked off in anger, court-martial proceedings were initiated against him.[103]

Still more significantly, the situation of enlisted men, rather than improving, continued to deteriorate. By the spring of 1918 their rations were cut drastically; hunger and deprivation once more stalked their ranks. Despite repeated injunctions on the part of higher authorities like Admiral Küsel that "we officers have an obligation to scrupulously observe all regulations concerning rations and to avoid any action that might arouse even suspicion of taking improper advantages," [104] the officer corps manifested as blatant disregard of the enlisted men's sensibilities in this crucial area as in the past. A graphic illustration of this occurred at submarine school in Kiel at the end of October 1918, a few days before the outbreak of the mutiny that was to destroy the navy. One of the cooks in that unit brought Oberleutnant Seeburg a breakfast consisting of a pot of hot chocolate, a number of slices of bread with a fairly sizable pat of butter, and a plate of sliced ham. The lieutenant looked at his meal, called for the cook and exclaimed: "If you ever again serve me such fat ham, I shall have you locked up!" At that the crew of the school almost mutinied.[105]

Cases of arbitrary treatment on the part of officers abounded. Thus, for no apparent reason, the Kiel naval station command issued orders forbidding enlisted men the use of the main entrance of the railroad station. The naval command in Cuxhaven established special patrols whose sole function it was to see to it that officers were saluted properly and that enlisted men stepped off the sidewalk whenever they passed an officer.[106]

On individual ships of the High Seas Fleet conditions were no better. For instance, on the *Regensburg* in June 1918 whenever the officers decided to visit the bordellos of Kiel, the crew was invariably summoned to row them into town and wait for their return. One night the officers left the men shivering all night in their boat until, by morning, the men instituted a house-to-house search for them. Later they submitted a complaint and were promised by Admiral von Capelle that the officers would be punished. Yet only one officer was confined to quarters for several days while the rest got off unscathed.[107]

Even so ardent an advocate of German naval power as Deputy Struve was compelled by these many abuses to exclaim in disgust, "Why will the officers not realize where this must lead? . . . It is high time in the interest of the navy that some changes—indeed, sweeping changes—are made as soon as possible." [108]

It was indeed time for a change in the navy, for that organization by its handling of the 1917 mutiny and its unregenerate conduct since that time had made itself so detested by its enlisted personnel that a real mutiny was in the offing. After more than four years of war and constant exposure to mistreatment by their officers, the sailors and stokers of the German navy were ready to resort to any means to remedy their plight. No socialist, no Spartacist propaganda or subversion was required to bring them to that conclusion.[109] Their life in the navy had taught them better than any socialist pamphlet could that their superiors were nothing more than "better paid and better fed masters" [110] whose absolute power they could no longer stomach.

vii

Admirals' Rebellion or Sailors' Mutiny?

Rushing to meet its imminent destiny in November 1918, the Imperial Navy was increasingly dominated by the series of military and political developments that shaped the history of Germany.

In July 1918 General Ludendorff's mammoth spring offensive on the Western Front, which was expected to win the war, came to a halt before the gates of Paris. By the beginning of August the tide had begun to turn against Germany, and on August 8 came the debacle of the Allied breakthrough at Amiens. Having gambled on a total victory, Ludendorff had thrown in the last of his military reserves during the offensive. He had no choice therefore but to inform a startled Kaiser and government on August 14 that the war was lost. A mere two weeks later this man whose fateful influence and power had driven Germany to the brink of the abyss took an even more humiliating step, in an attempt to avert a total military collapse, by demanding an immediate armistice and a complete democratization of the country's political life.

Obediently following orders in this "revolution from above," Chancellor Hertling resigned his office to make way for a reformist government headed by the liberal Prince Max of Baden. The prince introduced his new government and reform proposals to the Reichstag on October 5. By October 26, all his measures having been passed, the German Empire was transformed into a democratic, parliamentary monarchy.

The ease with which this profound transition was accomplished must not be allowed to conceal the fateful rift caused by the loss of the war and the demise of the semiabsolute state. The ruling classes of German society—the land-owning aristocracy, the industrialists, and most importantly from our point of view the officer corps of the navy and of the army—were convulsed with shock and grief. Under the impact of these precipitous changes, the self-confidence and arrogance of the officers turned into fear, despair, and humiliation. Bitter anger and resentment at their military and political defeat alternated with a mood of total despondency and near paralysis. But among the lower classes—the workers, sailors, and soldiers—the end of the war and the onset of popular government was met with an overwhelming feeling of relief. During the last tragic weeks of the war as an agonized Germany sought an armistice, these diametrically opposite responses were to precipitate a mutiny that caused the final collapse of the Imperial Navy.

The causes of that mutiny have long been debated, but until the post-World War II opening of the naval archives it was impossible to determine with any degree of authority whether responsibility for this momentous event ought to be ascribed to the enlisted men who rebelled against their officers or to the officers for their alleged rebellion against the government.[1] Documentary evidence now available, however, provides conclusive proof that an admirals' rebellion was responsible for the collapse of the German navy.[2]

The German navy died when the upper echelons of the caste-ridden, irresponsible officer corps, unable to reconcile themselves to Germany's inglorious military defeat in the war, the advent of parliamentary government, and the end of their power and prestige, rebelled against the government of Prince Max von Baden. This rebellion took the form of an attempt on the part of the admirals to order the High Seas Fleet out on a desperate and heroic but completely hopeless and illegal suicide mission against the British. Justifiably outraged by the admirals' rebellion and the decision to sacrifice their lives on the eve of the armistice, the enlisted men sabotaged the suicide mission by their refusal to sail out. When the naval authorities then branded them traitors and threatened harsh reprisals, the enlisted men rose up in a full-fledged military rebellion that swept away the power of a moribund and half-paralyzed officer corps.

Admiral Reinhard Scheer bears a large measure of responsibility for all that transpired in the navy after August 1918. On August 11, 1918, he was appointed Chief of the Admiralty Staff, replacing Admiral von Holtzendorff. As the hero of the Battle of Jutland and an outspoken advocate of an activist policy for the navy, Scheer possessed the complete confidence of the officer corps, which hoped that he would pursue an aggressive form of warfare that would permit it to gain some fame and glory before the fighting ended.

Quickly justifying this trust, Scheer insisted that the powers of his office be expanded and that he be invested with the right to coordinate and plan all future naval policy—in short, that he be endowed with the powers of Chief of Naval Command, *Chef der Seekriegsleitung*.[3] It is unlikely that Scheer, who had in the past shown no flair or understanding for politics, would have fought so strenuously over this issue if it had not been for the advice of his close friend and adviser, Captain Magnus von Levetzow,[4] whom he appointed as his Chief of Staff. Almost from the day that he assumed office, Scheer played the role of a passive Hindenburg to Levetzow's dynamic and domineering Ludendorff.[5]

With this kind of leadership, the navy soon fell prey to the most narrow-minded, reactionary, and irresponsible policies of Levetzow and his close ally in the High Seas Fleet, Admiral von Trotha. Trotha had recently assumed the job of Chief of Staff to the new Commander of the High Seas Fleet, Admiral Franz Hipper. It was catastrophic for the German navy that it acquired this kind of leadership at such a time. Both Levetzow and Trotha were noted for their marked antipathy toward democracy, parliamentary government, and the idea of a negotiated peace. Levetzow, the more radical of the two, regarded the discredited Ludendorff as "the greatest man" produced by the war,[6] while at the same time he had an absolute abhorrence for all those who stood opposed to militarism.

Characteristic of his attitude is a letter he wrote to Hermann Göring stating that he always considered the naval critic, Captain Lothar Persius, "one of the greatest scoundrels and traitors to the Fatherland." [7] To his intimate political colleague, the Pan-German leader Heinrich Class, Levetzow declared that he considered Prince Max a "donkey" and a "traitor," that the socialists were a horde of "red rascals," and that if "we do not put an end to parliamentary government, everything will be over for Germany." [8]

Appearing before the Dolchstross Tribunal in Munich in October 1925, Levetzow, who was one of the principal engineers of this infamous trial—the purpose of which was to discredit and destroy the democratic and socialistic parties of the Weimar Republic[9]—publicly manifested his contempt for the government and politicians. He did a great deal of shouting and refused to testify on any of the political issues of the naval mutinies. In typical militaristic fashion, he proclaimed "I am and remain a soldier. Regarding political happenings and events that do not concern my job, I shall not give any information." [10]

Von Trotha shared many of Levetzow's prejudices, but he was much less out-spoken about them. Nevertheless, he, too, deplored Germany's transition to a parliamentary form of government. He felt that the agitation for peace and the "advance in Germany's political life by fifty years" that occurred in the fall of 1918 were bound to result in the "overboiling of the nation's nerves and brain," and feared that they would undermine the authority of the officers.[11]

These views, shared by a large majority of the officers, saw to it that the navy was several steps behind even the most rabid reactionaries and conservatives when it came to making timely and necessary concessions. Thus, even after the Conservative Party had given up its opposition to domestic reform and capitulated to the temper of new times, the navy persisted in its determination to resist Germany's inexorable march toward democracy and peace. It was therefore inevitable that the new naval leadership would clash head-on with the desires of its own enlisted men, those of the overwhelming majority of the German people, and, most immediately, those of the new government.

An additional source of friction, which in a sense symbolized and reflected the navy's growing isolation in German society, was Admiral Scheer's ambition to make a name for himself and to satisfy his officers' craving for action by embarking on an ambitious but belated crash program of submarine construction. No sooner was he in power than he pushed through a plan, the so-called Scheer Program, to build thirty-six new submarines a month.[12] Although the war was practically over, and the enemy's convoy system had largely rendered Germany's submarine campaign ineffective,[13] Scheer stubbornly insisted on defying reality,[14] principally because he could not reconcile himself to commanding an idle and useless fleet.

Scheer persisted in this defiance even when it became known on October 14 that President Wilson of the United States, in his Peace Note, had demanded a complete cessation of submarine attacks upon passenger vessels in return for an armistice. Scheer belligerently told the government that "the navy does not need an armistice" and declared that he would give up submarine warfare only if it would guarantee the army the cease-fire it needed and if it were understood that the navy would regain complete operational freedom for the High Seas Fleet.[15]

By no means having conceded defeat, Scheer continued to cause great difficulty for Prince Max when, on October 20, he aligned himself with Ludendorff and refused to give up his submarine campaign. Only when the Prince made a constitutional issue out of the matter by threatening to resign, and thus obtained the Kaiser's support, did Scheer grudgingly acquiesce.[16]

As always, Scheer's obstructionism and reluctant retreat before the dictates of reason were prompted not so much by military considerations as by the question of preserving the honor and prestige of the navy. He could not tolerate the thought that the navy should give up the fight even before the army, because he wanted to spare his officers this humiliation and blow to their prestige.

The major reason why Scheer eventually gave in with much better grace than Ludendorff, who was compelled to resign over this issue,[17] is that he had already begun to consider an alternative plan to save the navy's face.[18] Ever since Germany's defeat had become a certainty, a number of influential naval officers had busied themselves with working out plans to avert the dreadful disaster of the fleet lying uselessly in port when the fighting ended, and winding up, as Ludendorff had predicted, "paying the bill" by being handed over to the British.[19]

On October 5, 1918, Captain Michaelis, the Director of the General Navy Department, by all indications a moderate and dispassionate officer, proposed to Admiral Levetzow that the High Seas Fleet be thrown into battle against the English in order to preserve its future in the postwar world. Greatly depressed by the prospect of "unacceptable conditions of peace," Michaelis wanted to revive the sagging morale of the German people by means of a "visible military success." Such a success, in his estimation, could only be brought about at this stage by a great victory of the entire German navy over the British fleet. Weighing the possible outcome of such a venture, Michaelis declared, "I am completely convinced that it would be a clear gamble [*ein glatter Hazard*], but when there is no other alternative, such a gamble may be justified."

Obviously sincere in his attempt to obtain a better peace for Germany, Michaelis recommended that the thought of preserving the fleet be thrown overboard since "the possession or non-possession of a fleet could no longer make any difference." He suggested therefore that if the entire surface fleet plus the submarines confronted the British in battle, the chances of success might not be "altogether slight." At any rate, he concluded, "if we should obtain a peace of surrender [*ein Unterwerfungsfrieden*], the submarine will be outlawed as a weapon against merchant shipping and our great fleet will be ruined for at least a number of decades, partly because it will be considered useless and partly because we shall be totally unable, from a financial point of view, to build a new fleet." [20]

Grappling with the same problem but animated by entirely different and much less altruistic motives, Admiral von Trotha, the Chief of Staff of the High Seas Fleet, on October 8 submitted a very similar plan to the *Seekriegsleitung* bearing the endorsement of Admiral Hipper. Von Trotha recommended that the German Fleet sail into a final battle if the British invaded the German Bight, if submarine warfare were abandoned completely, if it were to Germany's advantage to cease submarine warfare and administer a "severe blow to England's seapower," or, finally, if the High Seas Fleet were threatened by a "humiliating end." [21]

Clearly demonstrating that he was not really interested in the problem of submarine warfare, the body of Trotha's memorandum deals almost exclusively with the High Seas Fleet. Spelling out what would within three weeks become the dominant idea of the German naval officer corps, Trotha insisted that the highest goal for the fleet was a "final battle." This battle, however, was not to be waged so much for the benefit of the beleaguered German nation as for the future of the German navy. "From an honorable battle of our fleet, even if it should prove to be battle which will bring about its death . . . ," Trotha predicted, "a new future German fleet will arise; a fleet that is shackled by a humiliating peace, shall have no future."

Demonstrating conclusively that Trotha's decision to seek battle was basically animated by his strong desire to preserve the honor of the officer corps and fleet is a covering letter he sent to Levetzow along with his memorandum. In this Trotha dropped his constraint and pleaded, "It goes without saying that we live in dread fear of the thought that our fleet could shamefully allow itself to be destroyed from inside without having engaged in battle. An engagement, even if it means dying in honor, is still worthwhile because it would inflict a severe wound on England. . . . You must feel this as much as we do. Nevertheless, I implore you, do not permit the power of our fleet to be bargained away or allow it to die in disgrace."

No sooner had he articulated the idea of a final engagement or, as it soon came to be termed, a last *Flottenvorstoss*, than Trotha began to translate it into reality, thus eclipsing Michaelis' plan. With Hipper's consent the Chief of Staff of the High Seas Fleet, along with three other officers, began on October 10 to work out the details of an operational order.[22] That Trotha's recommendation had fallen upon receptive ears is indicated by Levetzow's reply on October 11. Stating that he would never allow the fleet to be subjected to a peace "that would bring with it harm or ruination," Levetzow endorsed his friend's plan, but postponed its implementation until the suspension of the submarine campaign.[23]

As soon as it appeared that the navy could not stand up to the government's pressure for the cessation of submarine warfare, Levetzow shifted his ground and enthusiastically adopted Trotha's plan. In a hitherto undiscovered letter of great importance the Chief of Staff of the *Seekriegsleitung* admitted he was responsible for approving Trotha's planned mission against England. During a sleepless night on the train from Cologne to Berlin on October 15–16, he had given up hope in the submarine cam-

paign and had therefore drafted a memorandum advocating a
Flottenvorstoss that received Scheer's immediate approval.

Writing of the reasons that had prompted this momentous decision, Levetzow revealed that considerations of honor were of
paramount importance in launching what was rapidly becoming a
suicide mission for the navy. "Even if the fleet had been destroyed," he reminisced to Trotha, "our proud, old Imperial Fleet
with its officers and men would now be lying in immortal fame at
the bottom of the sea instead of having been preserved in order to
cover itself in cowardly fashion with disgrace, the humiliation of
revolution, and delivery [to England] for internment." [24]

Scheer did not need much prompting from his chief of staff to
sanction this mission. He had already decided on October 15 in
his guidelines for future naval policy that "the fleet must be engaged in battle," even though it was not expected to "decisively
alter the course of events" because, as he put it, "it is a question of
honor and of the existence [*eine Ehren und Existenzfrage*] for
the navy to have done its utmost." [25]

One may conclude from the alacrity with which Trotha's plan
was adopted that the highest echelons of the navy had decided
that the future of the German naval officer corps and of the fleet
was in such great jeopardy, if it continued to be inactive and useless, that any gamble, even if it meant the sinking of the entire
fleet, was justified. Actually there was no political or military
necessity for such a drastic step. But during World War I the
German navy was not primarily concerned with military or political necessities. As in the past, its principal motivating force continued to be an exaggerated regard for the pride and prestige of an
officer corps that had never fulfilled its ambitious expectations and
was now threatened with the shameful prospect of ending the war
in disgrace.

Having already opted for the *Flottenvorstoss*, Scheer was able
to beat a relatively well-organized retreat from his original position on the submarine issue. Thus, when on October 15 the government demanded that the navy stop its U-boat attacks upon

passenger ships, Scheer, evidently taking Michaelis' advice, insisted on suspending all submarine activity directed against enemy merchant shipping.²⁶

While he retreated step by step from his stand on the submarine campaign, Scheer gradually prepared the ground for the projected *Flottenvorstoss*. Realizing full well that neither the Kaiser nor Prince Max would allow him to gamble away the fleet, Scheer cautiously kept them ignorant of his real design by resorting to all sorts of subterfuge. On the morning of October 18, for instance, he hinted in very vague terms to the Kaiser that he would not allow his fleet to remain idle. Without mentioning the plan to attack, he stated, "In the event we are forced to give up submarine warfare without in return obtaining a cease-fire, the fleet shall again become available for other tasks." ²⁷

On October 20, when the Kaiser and the government finally reached the decision to override Scheer and Ludendorff by suspending attacks against passenger ships, Scheer proceeded one step further along the path of deception and dishonesty, if not indeed outright mutiny. On that occasion, when Prince Max "implored the admiral most urgently that the navy would have to accept the inevitable since any incident that might disrupt the peace negotiations was to be avoided at all cost," Scheer replied with assurances of "the fullest loyalty of the navy which would be demonstrated by the recall of all submarines." But Scheer immediately violated his pledge when, in preparation for the *Flottenvorstoss*, he slyly declared that "the High Seas Fleet by being relieved of the tasks of [covering] submarine warfare had now regained its operational freedom." ²⁸

After the war the navy invented all sorts of excuses for Scheer's underhanded and unethical behavior. Writing to Colonel Niemann on June 18, 1927, Admiral von Levetzow reported that Scheer had not informed the Kaiser of his specific plan on October 18 because it had not yet achieved final and concrete form and was therefore subject to all the vagaries and uncertainties of naval warfare. As far as the chancellor was concerned, Levetzow asserted, Prince Max had been informed but had evidently not understood what Scheer meant by the phrase, ". . . the fleet . . . has regained its operational freedom." However, this was only natural because the prince "did not even understand his own job," and it was "actually none of his business." Levetzow felt that Scheer had told Prince Max more than enough because every bit of military information given him "was immediately released to the whole world [*sofort urbi et orbi preisgegeben wurde*]." [29]

Scheer, too, tried to justify his deception of Prince Max by claiming that he had informed the chancellor of his plans, even if only indirectly. It was therefore Max's obligation, if he did not want a naval attack to take place, to specifically order Scheer to desist from carrying out the *Flottenvorstoss*.[30] The absurdity of the argument that the chancellor should have asked Scheer to cancel an attack of which he had absolutely no knowledge need not detain us here.

The real reason behind Scheer's refusal to carry out his obligation to the government was his fear that the projected attack would be called off.[31] The Chief of the Admiralty knew intuitively that neither the chancellor, nor for that matter Wilhelm II, would for a moment sanction the gambling away of the lives of 80,000 sailors and stokers and disrupting the armistice negotiations.[32] In an effort to forestall action by the politicians, Scheer deliberately kept them in the dark while the unauthorized plan for the suicide mission was quickly developed into its final form.[33]

Spurred on by a consuming desire to save face and to present the government with an irreversible *fait accompli*, the naval command realized that it would have to act with great speed and resort to unorthodox methods in order to implement its plan. Within a week after Scheer had endorsed the *Flottenvorstoss* in principle, on October 22, Admiral von Levetzow arrived in Wilhelmshaven bearing for Admiral Hipper the following order: "High Seas Fleet shall attack and engage in battle the English Fleet." Indicative of the navy's furtiveness and consciousness of

its guilt is the fact that Levetzow did not present this all-
important command in customary written form, but gave it
verbally.[34]

Equally revealing of the sense of desperation that animated the
naval command was von Trotha's reminder that nothing be allowed to delay the *Flottenvorstoss* because the country "was
rushing toward an armistice at full speed." Conclusive proof that
they were bent on executing an illegal suicide mission was the fact
that Levetzow and Trotha, at a later meeting that same day, discussed in all seriousness, albeit inconclusively, whether or not the
Kaiser should ship out with the fleet for the "final battle." Moreover, Levetzow unequivocally admitted that Scheer was acting
entirely on his own responsibility and had not informed anyone
of the battle order because he deemed it "a matter of necessity
that the fleet be engaged in a fight to the finish." [35]

In its headlong rush to meet a bloody but glorious fate at the
hands of the English, the German navy on October 26 passed up
its last chance to subordinate itself to the will of the Kaiser and
the Reichstag. On that day Scheer and Levetzow had an audience
with Wilhelm II. He informed them that he had just dismissed
Ludendorff and had approved the constitutional changes demanded by the Reichstag—subordinating all military authority to
the civilian government. According to the notes made by
Levetzow, Wilhelm II declared "military authorities were not to
deal in political matters" and that the Reichstag's legislation "subordinating the military authorities to the civilian authorities had
his approval." [36]

This constituted a very clear injunction that the chancellor,
Prince Max von Baden, was now in charge of major military decisions and that the navy would have to obtain his permission before embarking on any major enterprise. Scheer, however, deliberately ignored this new state of affairs. As he later declared in his
memoirs, "I did not regard it necessary to obtain a repetition of
the Kaiser's approval since I had already secured his basic agree-

ment on October 18. In addition, I feared that this could cause further delay and was [thus] prepared to act on my own responsibility." [37]

By acting on his own responsibility and persisting in keeping his plans secret, Scheer defied the Kaiser, bypassed the responsible chancellor, violated the constitution, and thus committed an act that can only be described as mutiny or rebellion.

Trying very hard to eradicate this charge, Scheer in 1926 resorted to outright sophistry when he wrote, "I specifically reiterate that I did not recognize the chancellor's competence over operative measures and for that reason did not seek his approval." According to Scheer's sudden legalistic frame of mind, the Kaiser's injunction of October 26 was not binding upon the navy. In his view Article 53 of the revised constitution did not apply to matters of command. In his opinion that article, stating "the . . . transfer, promotion and resignation of the officials and officers of the navy shall take place with the consent of the Chancellor of the Reich," might have given Prince Max control over personnel matters, but it by no means conferred upon him the right to intervene in operational questions which still resided completely with the Kaiser.[38]

Scheer's retrospective constitutional hair-splitting relies exclusively upon a strict interpretation of the mere letter of the new law, but completely ignores its spirit. Certainly the constitutional modifications of October 28 did not mean to confine the chancellor's supervision to the appointment of promotion of naval officers. This was merely the Reichstag's traditional, parliamentary way of expressing its wish that the military be made responsible to the civilian branch of government. This was also what the Kaiser had in mind when he made it a special point to inform his admirals of the recent change. Moreover, as though it needed further clarification, the government's and the Kaiser's note to President Wilson on October 27 indicated in undisputable terms that Germany's "military rulers" and "monarchical autocrats" had been deprived of their former power, which now rested in the hands of the representatives of the German people.[39]

As Hans Delbrück, Germany's most renowned military historian, put it, the Kaiser's statement on October 26 had "expressly placed the military leadership under the civilian government." Therefore it was incumbent upon the navy to obtain "a direct, and not merely indirect authorization from the chancellor for an act of such political and diplomatic importance." [40] However, even if these constitutional changes had never taken place, and even if the Kaiser had never made these remarks, Scheer was still obliged to seek Wilhelm II's approval.

Throughout the war Wilhelm II had shown grave concern for the gradual erosion of his power of command by the military.[41] For that reason he had issued an order on May 31, 1917, declaring that the navy had his permission to engage only in operations that would ensure "that the Commander of the High Seas Fleet would be able to disengage at the proper time in order to make certain the avoidance of a battle against superior forces under an unfavorable tactical-strategic condition." Prophetically concluding his order, the Kaiser had added a sentence that could only have been composed with a situation such as this in mind which stated, "Such a final engagement in battle on the part of my fleet remains dependent upon my own orders according to the overall situation of the war." [42]

It hardly mattered therefore whether or not Scheer recognized the recent constitutional changes. Even if he did not and still thought himself bound exclusively to the Kaiser, it was his obligation to inform his royal superior of his projected *Flottenvorstoss* in precise terms and to obtain his direct approval. Moreover, it may also be argued that a highly political act, such as a last-minute attack upon England, necessitated obtaining the prior consent of the government regardless of any specific constitutional provisions.[43]

The *Seekriegsleitung*'s conscious decision to bypass all higher authority and to act on its own responsibility can therefore have only one meaning: the admirals had become convinced that the future of the navy and of the officer corps demanded a final heroic battle and that nothing, not even the death of the fleet or the probable disruption of the armistice negotiations, could be allowed to interfere with that goal. Consequently, their plan and the attempt to implement it on October 29, 1918, constitute a clear-cut case of rebellion.[44]

The navy's long and determined effort to conceal the true nature of its plans provides additional proof of its guilt. No sooner had the *Flottenvorstoss* been aborted by the resistance of the enlisted men than the navy began its process of myth-making. On November 3 Levetzow visited a distraught Admiral Hipper and Trotha in Wilhelmshaven and with them concocted what in all probability was the first great lie about the causes of the 1918 naval mutiny.[45] Completely reversing the causality of events and concealing the true cause for the enlisted men's revolt, Levetzow instructed his two colleagues to say that the navy had acted purely defensively. Planning to avert a threatened attack by the British Fleet in the German Bight, it had decided to send out its submarines. Since these could only stay out at sea for a limited period of time, it planned that the High Seas Fleet should sail out in the direction of Hoofden. This would lure the British out to sea, where they would be destroyed by waiting submarines. However, the outbreak of disorders in the fleet had prompted cancellation of this innocuous plan.[46]

With unprecedented effrontery the navy sought to cover up its tracks in this fashion and even had the audacity to enlist the aid of the government in dispelling the "legend of a suicide mission." On November 4 the new Secretary of the Navy, Ritter von Mann, who had recently replaced the ailing and discredited Capelle, enjoined the government in panic-stricken tones to help the navy quell the mutiny that had broken out in its ranks by releasing "an explanatory statement" denying that the "officers planned to destroy the fleet so as to avoid handing it over to the enemy."[47]

Conveying the impression that the mission against which the men had rebelled "had been an ordinary exercise, the same sort that had frequently been employed in recent times to keep the crews busy," [48] Mann persuaded the government to issue such a declaration through the editorial offices of the SPD journal, the *Vorwärts*. Bearing the signatures of Prince Max, Philipp Scheidemann, and the Secretary of the Navy, this document stated:

> According to reports we have heard it is evident that the current excitement in the fleet has been caused by stupid rumors. These claim that the officers of the navy disagreed with the peace policy of the government and were therefore planning a *coup* that would lead to the useless death of the ships' crews. The officers of the navy are obedient to the government. The accusations against them are unfounded. No one is planning to uselessly gamble away the lives of fellow-citizens and fathers of families.[49]

By once again transferring its guilt upon the men and by having the government condemn their action, the navy expanded the scope of the original enlisted men's rebellion. It made it impossible for the men to return to their duties without the risk of sharing the fate of Reichpietsch and Köbis. Thus the navy played a significant role in transforming the enlisted men's mutiny into a major rebellion that quickly spread over the entire seaboard.

Having resorted to deception and lies, the navy could not stop. On November 16, 1918, Admiral von Trotha visited the offices of the *Vorwärts* again and told its staff that the navy had acted purely defensively in its abortive *Flottenvorstoss*, that it had never sought a battle with the British, and was merely intent on severing the enemy's lines of communication.[50]

For years after the war the navy kept insisting on this point and claiming that the *Flottenvorstoss* had merely aimed at relieving the army's right flank in Belgium. It did not hesitate to trot out the venerable General von Kuhl to support the assertion that it had intended to prevent a British invasion of Holland through Flanders.[51]

The Dolchstoss Trial changed all that, however. At last pressured to admit that the real motive behind the *Flottenvorstoss* had been a final battle with the English,[52] the officers were at first greatly embarrassed and confused. Herr Nottweg, something of an expert on naval matters, gave up the idea of writing a book on the naval mutinies because he "could not promise that it would be of use to the naval officer corps" and because he feared that an investigation "would at the very least not exonerate" it, especially so because of the "catastrophical" confusion of various explanations of the *Flottenvorstoss*.[53] Having been exposed, the officers recovered quickly and turned their argument around by stating that their *Flottenvorstoss* was bound to have resulted in a great German victory. Now they declared that a German naval attack on the Flemish coast and the mouth of the Thames could not have failed to flush the British fleet from its northern bases whereupon it would have been subjected to ferocious submarine attacks that would have weakened it to such an extent that it would have easily fallen prey to the main body of the High Seas Fleet.[54]

Deliberately blinding themselves to the fact that their *Flotten-vorstoss* had been a "decision for heroic suicide," [55] the officers in their appraisals consistently ignored several vital factors that could not have helped but to affect the outcome of their plan. They totally discounted the fact that the British possessed a two-to-one superiority in fighting ships, that they were under no compulsion to fight, and that usefulness of German submarines in a battle against armored warships was uncertain at best.[56] It is unlikely that the German navy could have emerged from such an encounter with anything less than staggering losses if indeed it would have emerged at all, given the determination of its commanders not to retreat.[57]

In the light of the navy's irrational behavior in the planning and concealment of the *Flottenvorstoss*, it was to be expected that it would also not behave with great rationality in its execution. Driven by the desire to retain its prestige and maintain its code of honor even at the cost of sacrificing the fleet, the naval officer corps never really bothered to investigate the morale of the crews and the battle-readiness of the High Seas Fleet. In their eagerness to have their final battle, the naval officers disregarded the all too obvious danger signals and unthinkingly plunged ahead with their plan.

That the battle-readiness of the fleet had deteriorated drastically since the fall of 1917 was widely recognized by the navy. Thus, for instance, Admiral von Trotha complained to Levetzow on August 22 that the shake-up of commands that had accompanied the creation of the new *Seekriegsleitung* was having a very deleterious effect on the fleet. "The unrest in all the leading echelons," he wrote, "and the insecurity among the commanders will persist for a while longer. At present the situation is worst on the light cruisers for which we are having great difficulty finding commanders." As late as October 8, the date on which he submitted his memorandum advocating the *Flottenvorstoss*, the Chief of Staff of the High Seas Fleet had still not solved his personnel problems. On that date he once again addressed Levetzow and pleaded, "Please return [Admiral] Meurer to us soon! We need at least a few personalities [in the fleet]. Lately we have been compelled to give up a tremendous number of them. We shall be unable to handle the problem of the crews with mediocre and bad material." [58]

The rapid change-over in officers was clearly undermining not only the fighting effectiveness of the ships but was also creating considerable unrest among the crews. It had been estimated that between August and October 1918, 48.4 percent of the captains and 45.4 percent of the first officers of the squadrons that would bear the brunt of any projected battle had been transferred from their commands. Worse than that was the fact that a number of ships simultaneously lost both their commanders and first officers. These were the *Bayern, Von der Tann, Königsberg*, and *Brummer*. [59]

As if prospect of going into battle with mediocre, bad, or inexperienced officers was not enough to jeopardize the success of the *Flottenvorstoss*, danger signals of even greater importance warned against carrying out the plan. Reports on the enlisted men's attitude cast grave doubts on the reliability of the crews. As early as April 22, 1918, it was feared in the navy that enlisted men would seek to demonstrate their solidarity with the workers on May Day.[60] On July 29 the Wilhelmshaven naval station submitted a report stating that it was likely that strikes might break out in six or eight weeks and that the USPD was again subverting the men to its peace propaganda.[61]

Instead of improving, the situation became progressively worse as Germany's military position began to crumble, and it looked as though the war would soon be lost. On September 21 warnings were received that a metal workers' strike on behalf of peace was scheduled for the beginning of October, and it was feared that it would spread to the navy.[62] Even more disquieting was the report by a Berlin informant that the enlisted men in Kiel, Wilhelmshaven, and Friedrichsort would leave their ships in protest on October 12 or October 18 if the war was not over by then.[63]

Actually, the Fleet Command did not need all these outside reports to tell it of its morale problems. There were plenty of signs right on the ships. Indicating that he was well aware that the men were restless to the point of rebellion, that his petty and deck officers had become unreliable and were inciting the men, who went around humming ditties such as *"Wir kämpfen nicht um Deutschlands Ehre, wir kämpfen nur für Millionaire,"* [64] is a report by Admiral Hipper dated October 10. However, apparently he did not know how to draw the proper conclusions from his information. Neither did the command of the First Squadron, which responded to this report by issuing orders to all its officers to combat the defeatism in the ranks and boost the men's morale by pointing out to them "the consequences of a bad peace." [65]

Having decided to embark on its final mission, the navy simply could not bring itself to face reality by canceling the enterprise. Thus on October 18 Hipper once again warned his commanders that a revolution might break out in the fleet any moment. Foreign agents were at work bribing the men to mutiny when they confronted the British Fleet at sea. A plan to render the crews incapable of action by plying their food with sedatives had also come to light.[66] However, Hipper did nothing to dissuade his impatient Chief of Staff from attempting to execute the mission that he had planned.

Incredible as it may seem, on October 15 when Admiral von Levetzow asked Trotha if, from a material and personnel point of view, the fleet was ready to embark upon the *Flottenvorstoss*, the latter simply dismissed the question with a flat affirmative and presented the operational plan for the attack that he had worked out.[67] The only explanation for this complete misrepresentation of the true state of affairs is that Trotha no longer cared about the fighting effectiveness of a fleet that was scheduled merely to "go down with honor" in the "death ride" that had been planned for it. He was prepared to accept any risk to save the honor of the navy and to preserve its future.

Confirming the correctness of this explanation and refuting the possible objection that he had merely committed a great error in judgment, is von Trotha's own testimony. In an apologia for the *Flottenvorstoss*, he declared, "I accept the judgment of having shown a frightful lack of understanding for the situation. But I could not reconcile it with my conscience and concept of duty if I had not done everything until the last moment before arms were downed to relieve the heavily beleaguered Western Front and to deal the enemy a blow that might possibly have deprived him of his dominion of the seas." [68] This indicates that he really understood the situation, but was prepared to accept the risk of mutiny, not for the sake of the Western Front or for control of the seas, but for a navy and an officer corps that could not survive the shame of sitting out the last disastrous days of the war inactive and useless in port.

This determination, which was shared by many officers, made it easy for the navy to disregard all the portents of doom. Undeterred by any considerations of safety and elementary security, the officer corps behaved as though nothing mattered any longer save its own concept of honor. On October 22 Admiral von Levetzow arrived in Wilhelmshaven and told a fairly large group of staff officers of the navy's negotiations with the government and of their outcome. Although the text of his speech is not available, Levetzow's penchant for verbal heroics and his boundless contempt of the government must have made it very clear to his audience what the purpose of the coming mission was.[69] At any rate, within a few days the rumor had spread as far as Cuxhaven that the fleet was about to steam out for a "great battle." [70]

Despondent over Germany's military defeat on the Western Front and the collapse of their political world, the officers of the fleet enthusiastically acclaimed the suicidal plan. Consequently, it did not take long before the rumor of an imminent *Flottenvorstoss* took hold and spread to every naval installation. Even before the High Seas Fleet received orders to assemble at Wilhelmshaven for the impending attack, it was widely known that something unusual was afoot. The men could not help sensing from the intemperate talk of their officers that they rejected the government of Prince Max and what they considered as a cowardly foreign and domestic policy.

Deputy Struve, an astute observer of the navy, found that between October 18 and 20 commanders of various vessels pursued "policies in direct opposition to the government in that they quite openly criticize the government's recent acts and attempt to influence their crews in this sense through deck and petty officers." Even more startlingly, Struve discovered that it was rumored "that the officers will not obey orders in the future, but want to sail their ships out to sea for a final attack in force [*einen letzten Gewaltvorstoss*]." It had come to his attention that Captain von Schlick, "one of the biggest autocrats in the navy," had told his crew that the members of the new government were "idiots" and then subjected their measures "to the most incredible criticism." [71]

Once again and for the last time, the great social and political rift that divided the officers and enlisted men opened up into a fateful chasm. Resenting the inglorious defeat of Germany, the humiliation that attended the request for an armistice, and the loss of power and prestige that the establishment of a democratic order would bring in its wake, the officers refused to accommodate themselves to the new situation. Consequently, they desperately sought to avert the fate that awaited them by their almost universal endorsement of a suicide mission. On the other hand, the proletarian sailors and stokers could not possibly be expected to accept their officers' feudal ideal that death was preferable to disgrace. When the military power that had held the German Empire together since its inception was defeated and discredited, their faith in it as well as their fear of its coercive power vanished.[72] Animated by their desire for peace, they became determined not to continue the war for what President Wilson called their "military rulers and monarchical autocrats." [73]

Driven by the reckless desire for a final battle to justify their existence, the naval officers, in the closing days of October 1918, displayed complete indifference to the sensibilities of their men and grossly misjudged their political temperament. Thus, for instance, Fregattenkapitän Hintzmann agreed that Germany's request for an armistice must have had "a certain effect" on the crews. But he conjectured that they shared their officers' feeling to "keep a stiff upper lip" [*die Ohren erst doppelt steif halten*] and were therefore depressed by the government's cowardly retreat before the demands of the Allies.[74] This kind of thinking blinded the officers to the dreadful misery prevailing in Germany's cities, where the populace, living without coal for fuel, without adequate clothing, and with empty stomachs, fell an easy prey to the dreadful flu epidemic that raged through Europe. This same sort of insensitivity also made it impossible for them to fathom the war-weariness and defeatism that spread with incredible speed through the enlisted ranks as sailors and shipyard workers from the evacuated ports in Flanders returned to Germany filled with rumors of military collapse, chaos, and treason.[75] Consequently they could not understand that some of the younger men were beginning to turn to Bolshevism for solace, while the older men,[76] family men with children who were generally over forty years old and comprised an increasing percentage of naval personnel, numbly looked forward to nothing but the end of the war and the chance to go home.[77]

As if this were not enough, the navy compounded its psychological error by maintaining absolute official silence about the impending *Flottenvorstoss*. Arguing that this secrecy was justified by the necessity of maintaining tight security to preserve the element of surprise,[78] the navy refused to confide its plans to enlisted men while the officers, who had found out about it unofficially, were afforded liberty to boast about their glorious mission.

When, as was inevitable, the men found out about what was being planned for them and reacted by refusing to weigh anchor, the navy absurdly charged the government with having leaked the news.[79] Subsequently, it has also been alleged that the communists had placed one of their men in the *Seekriegsleitung*, in the person of Admiral Scheer's lackey, and thus spread the news to various underground groups on the ships and in port.[80] However, it is fairly evident that the officers saw to it that there was no need to resort to a conspiracy theory.[81]

As early as October 27, when the various squadrons and units of the High Seas Fleet began to get under way to the assembly area at Schillig Roads off Wilhelmshaven, an air of intense nervousness and excitement pervaded the fleet. In the Fourth Battle Squadron the men were upset at having their stay in Kiel interrupted so precipitously.[82] The crews immediately sensed that something more than an ordinary exercise was in the offing. Even ships in dock for repairs, such as the *Pillau* and *Königsberg*, were under orders to sail out.[83] Since it was highly unusual for the entire fleet to congregate at Wilhelmshaven, the sailors realized that they were about to sail on a very unusual mission.[84]

Everywhere it was rumored that the fleet was about to meet the British in battle. No official word, however, was forthcoming.

Plagued as they were by resentment and war-weariness, it was not likely that the men would have been overjoyed at this prospect. Chances are that if they had received a plausible official explanation, they might still have mustered sufficient patriotism to sail out on a mission intended to relieve the Western Front and to obtain a better armistice.[85] Instead, however, they heard only whispered rumors from the officers' messes that the fleet was about to go on a death ride, a suicide mission.

All of the men who were later interrogated on this point agreed that they heard this news from their officers.[86] The crew of the *Thüringen*, for instance, unanimously declared that it found out that the projected mission was a death ride when their officers held a drinking bout in their mess on October 29. According to Seaman Scheidemann, one particularly garrulous officer, Kapitän-leutnant Rudloff, told his fellow officers, "We shall fire our last 2,000 rounds at the English and then go down with honor. Better an honorable death than a life of shame." [87] Obermatrose King of the same ship asserted that he thus found out that "the officers wanted to fight a battle at sea. The Kaiser and Ludendorff had abdicated. The officers wanted to overthrow the present government and to attack without its consent. . . ." [88] Still another rumor had it that the Kaiser had embarked on the *Baden* because he had been disgraced and wanted to seek his death with the fleet.[89]

Similar manifestations of irresponsibility occurred on virtually all the ships. On the *Markgraf* it was rumored that the officers were about to defy the government and disrupt the armistice negotiations because they realized that they would be "penniless" when the war was over.[90] The same story was repeated on the *Derfflinger*, where it was reported that the officers had taken their private possessions ashore and one of them had written a letter stating, "We shall not subject ourselves to this disgrace; we would rather die like heroes." [91]

Reacting with horror and outrage, the enlisted men rushed to the defense of the government by refusing to make ready for sea.[92] On October 27, when the time came to sail, forty-five stokers on the light cruiser *Strassburg* hid on the dock. After they were rounded up and brought back on board, they told the captain that they did not wish to cooperate with his plan to fight the British.[93] Similarly, the crew of the battlecruiser *Moltke*, perturbed by the signs of an impending battle, disobeyed orders to make ready for sea. On the *Derfflinger*, *Von der Tann*, and *Seydlitz*, the men resorted to passive resistance and refused to board their ships when they were ordered to join the fleet at Schillig Roads.[94]

On October 28 the signs of trouble began to multiply. The crew of the light cruiser *Regensburg* would not clear for sailing in Cuxhaven. Even more fatefully, that afternoon the disorders spread to the Third Battle Squadron anchored off Wilhelmshaven. On the *König* agitators circulated among the crew urging the men not to sail further than Helgoland, to extinguish the fires in the boilers, and to do everything within their power to prevent a sortie against England. The captain had to assemble the entire crew on deck and arrest three men before he regained control. On the *Kronprinz Wilhelm* the crew also became mutinous and charged its officers with plotting to disrupt the armistice negotiations by sailing on a mission from which the ship would never return.[95]

On October 29 the movement spread to the *Markgraf*, where again the crew objected to sailing on "a suicide mission," refused to weigh anchor, and barricaded the gangplanks. A similar incident took place on the *Bayern*.[96]

Determined to carry out his *Flottenvorstoss* regardless of any consequences, and blinding himself to the open opposition of his crews, Admiral Hipper, at a meeting held at eight o'clock in the evening of October 29, decided to proceed as if nothing had happened. He told his commanders that the disturbances were caused "by inappropriate speeches of commanders in the Third Squadron who have lately placed too much stress on the impending peace and too little on the necessity of continuing the fight." [97]

Within two hours, however, Hipper was compelled to cancel his sailing orders. Admiral Kraft, the Commander of the Third Squadron, returned to the flagship, reporting that it was impossible for him to get under way. On the *König* and especially on the *Kronprinz Wilhelm*, the situation had deteriorated to such an extent that the men would permit the squadron to sail no farther than Helgoland. Moreover, there was nothing that Kraft and his officers could do, not even assuring the men that they were merely being asked to participate in a fleet exercise, that would persuade them to sail against the British. When the chief of the reconnaissance squadron concurred with Kraft's appraisal, Hipper reluctantly agreed that the mission could no longer be carried out as planned and would therefore have to be modified. In any event, a thick, impenetrable fog that had descended over Wilhelmshaven forced Hipper to call for a postponement.[98]

Seemingly still determined to carry out at least a part of the *Flottenvorstoss*, Hipper tried to mollify his unruly crews by releasing a communique on October 30. Asserting that the fleet was scheduled to sail out on a purely defensive mission, Hipper proclaimed all those who opposed it were cowards who sought to disrupt the unity of the government and the navy by spreading false rumors on behest of the enemy.[99]

Hipper's belligerent appeal had little impact upon the crews. At another hastily convened squadron commanders' meeting on the afternoon of October 30, the Chief of the High Seas Fleet began to realize that he had lost control over his men. Torn between the conflicting advice of his squadron commanders, he began to vacillate and act with fateful indecision. Undoubtedly impressed by the forceful opinion of Captain Heinrichs, the commander of the torpedo boat flotilla, that he should force the men to sail out because the navy could not allow them "to impose their unauthorized will," Hipper had to balance the cautious views of Admiral Kraft and the chief of the reconnaissance group, who maintained that such a course would invite an open rebellion. As a result, he decided to abandon a large part of the mission, but stubbornly insisted that the submarines were to proceed as ordered and should be covered by the First Squadron. Although he recognized that he had to give up the original plan for the *Flottenvorstoss* because "if the men continued to disobey, it would become necessary to take drastic steps that could lead to a catastrophe of major proportions," [100] his officer's pride could not bear the thought of a complete retreat.

Actually, Hipper had chosen the worst possible course. Once he had abandoned the original plan for the *Flottenvorstoss*, his sailing orders for the First Squadron and the submarines lost all justification. While a mission by the entire fleet might have preserved the honor of the navy by endowing it with the glory of heroic death, the submarines and a single squadron could achieve neither that goal nor any logical military objective. Thus, in the final analysis, Hipper's decision was motivated by nothing more than the instinctual pride and *Kastengeist* of an officer corps that did not know the meaning of timely retreat.

By refusing to heed his own injunction, the Chief of the High Seas Fleet unleashed a regular rebellion in the First Squadron during the night of October 30. When the *Thüringen* was ordered to sail, the men sullenly told their officers that they would not be fooled by the navy's plan to sail into battle squadron by squadron. Storming into the fore battery, a number of rebellious sailors extinguished the lights and cut the anchor cables. The stokers in the engine room refused to feed coal into the furnaces, thus making it impossible to sail. On the *Helgoland*, the *Thüringen*'s sister ship in the First Squadron, the same thing took place as her crew, too, extinguished the lights, sabotaged the search lights, and broke into a munition chamber containing rifles.[101] Only with great difficulty did the officers finally reestablish order on these two ships, but they failed to persuade the men to sail.

Once again the determined resistance of the men forced Hipper to cancel his sailing orders, and once again the Chief of the High Seas Fleet stubbornly remained unwilling to abandon his plan. He acceded to Admiral Kraft's demand that the Third Squadron be detached to the Baltic and Kiel so that the men could see that "we are meeting them half-way in a humane fashion." [102] He insisted, however, with mounting vehemence, that the First Squadron be made to sail, by force if necessary, the next morning.[103]

Admiral Hipper's inconsistency and his vacillation between these two extremes was to have fateful results for the navy as well as for the two squadrons. By releasing the mutinous Third Squadron to Kiel, Hipper foisted his troubles upon an unprepared command at the Baltic naval station and thus spread the rebellion, while his attempts to coerce the First Squadron created the first martyrs of an impending general revolt.

When at noon on October 31 the *Thüringen* was ordered to sail, the officers stood ready and armed; preparations had been made to use naval infantry troops to arrest all those men who resisted.[104] Nevertheless, the crew responded once more by barricading itself in the forward battery and preventing the anchor from being raised. Thereupon the officers and deck officers occupied all the exits while a tender carrying 250 naval infantrymen, two torpedo boats, the *V78* and *S65*, and a submarine drew near.[105] When the captain ordered the men to surrender by coming up on deck one by one, they defiantly demanded that he come down and negotiate with them. Thereupon the torpedo boats and the submarine drew closer and menacingly directed their guns at the *Thüringen*. At that moment, the *Helgoland* tried to come to the aid of her sister ship by turning her 15 cm. cannon against the hostile flotilla. A pitched battle seemed inevitable. At the last minute, however, the *Helgoland* backed down and lowered her guns.

Turning once more to the *Thüringen*, the torpedo boats' threat took effect as the mutineers on board that vessel lost courage and surrendered. This having been accomplished, the infantrymen climbed aboard and arrested 151 sailors and 56 stokers, who, as they were being led away to prison in Wilhelmshaven, sang patriotic songs.[106]

Although this forceful action and the subsequent arrest of a large number of men on the *Thüringen, Helgoland, Markgraf,* and *Grosser Kurfürst* temporarily restored order in the First Squadron, the mutiny could no longer be staved off. When some of the *Ostfriesland*'s stokers were ordered to supplement the depleted crew of the *Thüringen*, thirty of them balked and made it impossible to move the ship.[107] Moreover, the enlisted men's resistance had by this time spread far beyond the First Squadron. During the night of October 30, disorders had broken out in the Fourth Squadron on the *Friedrich der Grosse*, *König Albert*, and *Kaiserin*. On the *Friedrich der Grosse* the crew had turned a deaf ear to all commands to sail and had refused to load coal. By November 1, it succeeded in negotiating a pact with the squadron commander to go back to work in return for an amnesty.[108]

Everywhere the officers were in full retreat, panic-stricken and incapable of coherent action. Johannes Spiess, the commander of the U-boat that compelled the *Thüringen*'s surrender, writes that the incredible confusion in the fleet made it impossible for him to find the commander of the High Seas Fleet. He finally received his orders from Admiral von Trotha, who was already so uncertain and lacking in confidence that he refused to hand him a written order and told him to act on his own responsibility.[109]

Admiral Hipper provides an excellent example of the moral collapse of the naval officer corps in October-November 1918. Hipper, the former chief of the cruiser squadron, had always been noted for his energy and decisiveness. At the Battle of Jutland in 1916 he had with reckless daring driven his cruisers right into the center of the British fleet, thus earning Germany's highest decoration, the *Pour le Mérite*. In this crisis, however, his former self-confidence and energy deserted him. He vacillated much and no longer possessed the determination to bring his rebellious crews back to order.

His tragic hesitation at the moment of greatest danger is apparent in his inept handling of the men and his total misjudgment of the situation. Although by November 1 it was obvious that the men were out of control, Hipper informed Scheer at the *Seekriegsleitung* that he saw no reason why the situation should be viewed pessimistically. Aghast at this calm amidst the disaster that was overtaking the fleet, the *Seekriegsleitung* curtly replied, "We cannot concur with this view. It has been established that a military operation has been ruined by the illegal will of [certain] elements within the crews." Insisting that Hipper take energetic steps to reassert himself, Scheer gave him a free hand to draw officers from the submarines and all naval schools.[110] But the commander of the High Seas Fleet seemed paralyzed. All he could do was to further disperse the fleet, sending the First Squadron to the Elbe, the Third to Kiel, and the Fourth to Wilhelmshaven.[111]

By November 2 it became clear that Hipper had abdicated and was merely concerned to shift his responsibility to someone else's shoulders. In a letter to the *Seekriegsleitung* that day, he claimed that the movement in the fleet was a Bolshevik conspiracy that had "already spread very far." Trying desperately to exonerate himself and the navy, he suggested that the government be informed that the movement was largely directed against it. This would oblige it to release a proclamation admonishing the men that "the success of its peace policy demands absolute discipline and that all orders and measures emanating from commanders were in accordance with the wishes and at the behest of the government." Abdicating his responsibility even further, he recommended an immediate purge of all unreliable elements in the fleet, the decommissioning of certain ships, and a far-reaching change in officers.[112]

On November 3 the progressive deterioration of the navy under the impact of the enlisted men's rebellion became even more pronounced as Hipper informed Levetzow that he "was treading on a volcano" and that the slightest incident could have "incalculable consequences." Admiral von Trotha, his chief of staff, displayed similar symptoms. Trying to shift the blame for the growing rebellion upon the commanders of the First Squadron and of the Reconnaissance Group, he claimed that they had shown themselves incapable of performing their jobs and that their irresponsibility and indecisiveness "had left the Fleet Command in the

lurch." However, when Levetzow later that same day interviewed Commodore Michelsen, the commander of the submarine
fleet, he was told that it was the Fleet Command that had invariably "taken the wrong course" by its "policy of yielding."
Michelsen therefore recommended "a radical change in personnel" that would see to it that "everyone who had failed would
have to go."

Not at all reluctant to snipe at each other, the naval commanders lacked any positive ideas about suppressing the revolt. Hipper
seemed overwhelmed by the problem of dealing with five hundred prisoners. Attempting to palm them off on the army, he suggested that troops stationed in Finland and the Ukraine, fighting
against the Bolsheviks, be dispatched to Wilhelmshaven to take
the prisoners in hand because the garrison was not reliable
enough.

At a later meeting with Admiral von Krosigk, the commandant
of the Wilhelmshaven naval base, Levetzow did not find much
cause for optimism in what was rapidly developing into a debacle
for the navy. Krosigk complained that he only had 200 reliable
men and 15 machine guns at his disposal, and demanded the transfer of 1,000 army troops to relieve him of responsibility for the
naval prisoners. Indicative of the collapse of confidence on the
part of the officer corps and the resignation with which it treated
its greatest crisis, is the fact that at this crucial moment von
Krosigk had the temerity to raise the question of his retirement
with Levetzow.[113]

With incredible speed the enlisted men's resistance to the
navy's *Flottenvorstoss* had toppled the proud officer corps from
the pinnacle of its power to the lowest depths of despair. Overwhelmed by the unexpected resistance of the crews, the officer
corps experienced a "sudden, shattering collapse." [114] A large part
of that collapse, however, stemmed from the officers' knowledge
that they had rebelled against the government and could therefore
not count on its support and protection. Fearful lest they be exposed and completely discredited before the nation, they overre-

acted to the mild-mannered passive resistance of their crews by raising the specter of a Bolshevik revolution and by a complete loss of nerve.

When the leadership of the High Seas Fleet experienced its loss of nerve and "failed at the decisive moment" to issue appropriate orders, the entire officer corps, trained only to obey orders from above, began to flounder in chaos and uncertainty. Consequently, it suffered "an internal Jena" which, like the defeat of the Prussian army at the hands of Napoleon in 1806, rendered it incapable of offering resistance and caused it to capitulate.[115] As Levetzow so aptly summed up the whole situation, "If the Fleet Command had not collapsed completely, the mutiny would never have been fatal . . ." By losing his bearings, "giving in to the mutiny step by step," and then "to top it all off, despatching a squadron to Kiel!" Hipper committed a grave error.[116] But what turned it into a disaster was his attempt to force his will upon the First Squadron. The bewildered officer corps no longer knew what was expected of it, and resigned itself to its fate.

Hoping against hope that its allegations of a Bolshevik conspiracy would mobilize the government against the men, the command of the High Seas Fleet after November 3 tried to pass itself off as the loyal agent of the government. On November 4 Hipper unconvincingly proclaimed, "The fleet receives its orders from the government and carries them out. . . . There exists no conflict between the naval officers and the government. They are in complete agreement with the government and act as its executive agents." [117]

Neither lies of a Bolshevik insurrection, hiding behind the government, nor belated protestations of loyalty could now help the navy. Each of its actions since October 27 had made it increasingly impossible for the men to subject themselves to its authority again. The bond of fear, the blind, corpse-like obedience which the navy had fostered among its crews, was shattered beyond repair by the admirals' rebellion—the attempted *Flottenvorstoss*—and its ineptitude in dealing with the men's righteous counterinsurgency. The Imperial Navy was experiencing its final death throes; the men of the Third Squadron would see to it that it died at its appointed time in Kiel.

The navy was long successful in concealing the real causes for its demise. By putting forth the massive smokescreen that it had been betrayed and destroyed by a Bolshevik conspiracy and the fearful, cowardly, and "un-German" conduct of its enlisted men, who lacked the courage to face the enemy,[118] the navy managed to avoid complete disgrace in the eyes of the German people. Now, however, this myth has been shattered. The German navy met its fate when its officer corps, unable to reconcile itself to the idea of peace, parliamentary government, and democracy, made up its mind to stake its future on one last gambler's throw by defying the government and meeting a suicidal but glorious death in battle. When the sailors and stokers of the High Seas Fleet got wind of this plan, they rose up against their rebellious officers, prevented the fleet from sailing to its probable doom, and thereby saved the armistice. Stricken by fear and pangs of guilt, the navy committed blunder after blunder which served to drive the men further along the road of rebellion.

At no point in this entire sequence of events did party politics play a meaningful role in the actions of the enlisted men. Admittedly they detested their officers' Pan-Germanism, their *Kastengeist*, and lack of human understanding. True, they deeply resented the fate of the 1917 martyrs on the *Friedrich der Grosse* and *Prinzregent Luitpold*. Without a doubt, they were animated by an overwhelming desire for peace and identified to an increasing extent with the Socialists. But they never consciously planned a mutiny. Instead they rose up spontaneously when the officers' rebellion against the government threatened to sacrifice their lives needlessly and ruin the impending peace.

Indicative of the motives that prompted the sailors' actions is the statement of an anonymous enlisted man belonging to the Third Squadron. Speaking to Admiral von Mann in Berlin as a

delegate of his squadron on November 7, the sailor declared:
". . . The entire Third Squadron acclaimed the new direction
[of government]. From the new government we expected the
peace for which we all desperately longed. We sailors have grown
very tired of the long war; we want peace. Unfortunately, the
officers did not share this feeling. . . . A *putsch* was imminent.
We saw that from the various steps taken by the fleet. Fearing
that a *putsch* was about to take place, when the fleet was ordered
to sail out, the crews refused to obey orders . . ." [119]

The most convincing refutation of the navy's case is to be
found in the demands of the mutinous sailors during the course of
their rebellion. Not a trace of bolshevism appears. For example,
when Kapitänleutant Fikentscher asked the men who had barricaded themselves against their officers on the *Thüringen* what it
was they wanted, they replied that they wanted Matthias Erz-
berger, the prominent Centrist Reichstag deputy, to come and
negotiate with them.[120] On another occasion, the men of that same
ship destroyed a portrait of Admiral Scheer and inserted in its
empty frame a newspaper photograph of Philipp Scheidemann, the
Majority Socialist leader who had recently become secretary of
state in the new Prince Max von Baden administration.[121]

On the whole, the demands of the rebellious sailors were extremely modest. On November 7, when their mutiny was already
triumphant in Kiel and Wilhelmshaven, and the authority of the
navy was shattered beyond redemption, the delegates of the
Third Squadron presented their demands to Secretary of the
Navy Ritter von Mann in the form of a seven-point program.
That program constitutes the most convincing evidence that the
men lacked any real political orientation and that their views, according to Conrad Haussmann, the government's representative,
"were free of all ambiguity and political influences."

Of Admiral Ritter von Mann the sailors demanded:

1. Reduction of the punitive powers of the First Officer.
2. Since the trust of the crews in their officers has vanished com-

pletely, for the immediate future a representative of the crews shall be attached to the Admiral so that the crews can feel that things are being handled correctly . . .

3. The men must be granted the right of assembly to speak their minds.
4. All newspapers are to be made available.
5. Equal rations for enlisted men and officers.
6. Freedom not to salute [officers] when off duty.
7. For infractions not concerning matters of honor, no imprisonment but money fines.[122]

In the ensuing debate with the Secretary of the Navy, the enlisted men seemed as anxious as he to ward off my intrusion of bolshevism in the fleet. One of their delegates quietly asserted, "I think that we can honestly take pride in having kept revolution out of the Third Squadron." They readily agreed that their supervisory committee not be called a Sailors' Council because it "smacked of Russian bolshevism" and deferred to his wish that it be named a Delegates' Council instead.[123]

The survival of the navy's myth until the present time owes much to the rise of an incongruous alliance of communist revolutionaries with the reactionary officers. In a vain effort to associate Germany with the "great October Revolution in Russia," German communist historians have maintained over the years that the enlisted men's rebellion was instigated by class-conscious sailors who were in contact with revolutionary Spartacists and left radicals, that the men's refusal to participate in the *Flottenvorstoss* stemmed directly from the propaganda of these groups and proved that the men were consciously imitating the Bolshevik Revolution in Russia. Unable to produce any evidence to substantiate this thesis, they have been placed in the paradoxical position of having to use the navy's myth and its wild charges to refute the historically authentic arguments of the liberals and socialists.[124] After having exhausted this tactic, the communists are compelled to admit reluctantly that the enlisted men's political training was not sufficiently well developed to represent pure bolshevism, but that their efforts aided its cause by preventing "the destruction of the German fleet and the certain death of 80,000 sailors as a last gigantic sacrifice of the insatiable demands of an insane imperialistic war." [125]

Certainly the prevention of that sacrifice was the central aim of the mutiny, but that does not make it a Bolshevik or even a proto-Bolshevik mutiny. Rather it was a mutiny of men who were tired of the war and their lives in the navy and were determined not to become sacrificial lambs to their officers' outworn concept of honor. It was the admirals' rebellion against the government that caused the mass disobedience of the sailors and stokers.[126] The general uprising that was soon to follow was the direct result of the navy's lies and ineptitude.

viii

The Collapse of the Navy

Smarting with humiliation over the disintegration of his fleet, Admiral Scheer plaintively concludes his memoirs, "Upon the hoisting of the red flag the history of the Imperial Navy came to an end." [1] By implying that the hoisting of the flag of revolution automatically ended the existence of the navy and was the product of a well-organized, treasonable Bolshevik or Independent Socialist conspiracy, Scheer avoids discussing what may well be the most interesting and revealing chapter in the history of the German navy.

No doubt influenced by the widespread charges from the right as well as the left that his officers were "responsible for the revolution," that they had "failed abysmally," and "had saddled" the German nation "with this great misery," [2] Scheer, like most of his fellow officers, sought to conceal the details of the naval collapse.

This understandable reluctance to discuss the final phases of the history of the Imperial Navy has for fifty years obscured the real nature of that collapse by substituting rumor and innuendo for facts. What the navy so effectively hid was the simple fact that its own officers through their bungling, incompetence, and abdication of responsibility were to blame for the navy's inglorious end and that there was virtually no Bolshevik influence in the rebellion that overthrew them and spread revolution over Germany.

If the naval officer corps had simply bided its time after the *Flottenvorstoss* had been aborted by the enlisted men, it might have survived the war. Its reputation might have been tarnished, but in all probability it could have escaped being swept away by revolution. Ill trained to cope with rebellion, the German naval officer corps plunged into a debacle from which it was never to recover. Decadent because of *Kastengeist* and morose over the series of misfortunes that had befallen them, the officers inflicted upon themselves their own death blow when, embarking upon a stubbornly short-sighted course of repression, they met with such determined resistance from the enlisted men that their authority and power, like a house of cards, collapsed in a heap at the first breath of a rebellious breeze.

When the Third Squadron of the High Seas Fleet steamed from Wilhelmshaven to Kiel on October 31, 1918, revolution was already imminent. The commander of that squadron, Admiral Kraft, had already made a shambles of the submarine construction division of the navy by refusing to build the requisite number of submarines requested by the Secretary of the Navy, and now his incompetence was about to bring a mutiny and a revolution to Kiel.

Originally Kraft had requested the transfer of his squadron to Kiel in order to show his recalcitrant crews that the navy was not totally devoid of compassion and was capable of compromising with its men. While a rest in the quiet, beautiful, natural surroundings of the Baltic port was indeed a better cure for what ailed the men than Hipper's uncompromising stance with the First Squadron, Admiral Kraft was too much of a German naval officer to neglect availing himself of the traditional weapons of that caste—coercion and reprisals. No sooner had his ships entered the Kaiser Wilhelm Canal than his compassion vanished and the tyrant within him asserted itself. Reneging on his earlier promise of an amnesty, he overrode the crews' objections and began to question individual men for their role in sabotaging the *Flottenvorstoss*. When his squadron had safely dropped anchor at Holtenau near Kiel, he sounded the alarm and while the crews stood at battle stations forty-seven men were placed under arrest. These were despatched to Fort Herwarth while two hundred others were selected for transfer to a penal battalion on shore.[3]

Kraft next insisted on taking his sullen and resentful crews into Kiel despite the objections of Admiral Wilhelm Souchon, the new commander or governor of the Baltic naval station. Although he had just arrived at his post, Souchon had enough sense to realize that the port, already rife with unrest, could not accommodate an additional infusion of rebellious sailors. But Souchon—the hero of the German Mediterranean Squadron who had saved the *Göben* and *Breslau* from falling into the hands of the British at the outbreak of the war by taking them to neutral Constantinople and who was so highly regarded that he had recently been considered for appointment as Secretary of the Navy[4]—could not make his views prevail in the ensuing dispute with an irate and insistent Kraft.[5]

Totally lacking in defensive measures, Kiel lay at the mercy of the rebellious sailors and stokers of the Third Squadron who, from the moment they landed in the city, were determined not to allow their recently arrested comrades to be martyred. Fortified by the knowledge that their united resistance had prevented the projected *Flottenvorstoss*, they were resolved to liberate the prisoners regardless of consequences. At a meeting on November 1 at the Trade Union Hall attended by 250 men from the Third Squadron, it was decided to form a committee to negotiate the prisoners' immediate release. At the same time it was agreed to convene another meeting for the following day in the event that these demands were not met.[6]

Aware of what had transpired at the meeting, Souchon embarked upon a disastrous course when he undertook to support Admiral Kraft's policy of repression. Instead of meeting the enlisted men halfway and negotiating with them, in the words of the socialist *Schleswig-Holsteinische Volkszeitung* he adopted the view that "only brute force could maintain order." [7] He therefore sought to check the "infection" being spread by the Third Squadron by forbidding the meeting arranged for November 2. As a precautionary measure, he sealed off all enlisted men's barracks, while naval infantry troops and special contingents made up of officers, mates, and cadets patrolled the streets.

At the appointed time on November 2 approximately six hundred sailors assembled before the Trade Union Hall. Finding the building closed, they milled about outside, but refused to disperse and return to their ships. Gradually they drifted toward the parade ground behind the building and in the Waldwiese, a large meadow located there, began conducting their meeting.

Quickly rising to a position of leadership within the crowd was Karl Artelt, a young stoker from the First Torpedo Division in Kiel with a "voice like a lion" [8] and the fiery, flashing eyes and the pugnacious chin of a revolutionary.[9] A devout Social Democrat and a former machinist at the Germania Shipyards in Kiel, Artelt had been a troublemaker in the navy since the day of his induction. In June 1917 he was sentenced to six months in prison for making "agitational speeches" at workers' meetings. After his release he was sent to serve on the Flanders Front but managed to return to Germany by feigning insanity. After spending some time in an asylum he was transferred from unit to unit until he wound up in Kiel.[10] Although the navy had recognized his revolutionary propensities and Admiral Küsel, the Chief of Staff of the Kiel Command, had singled him out for shipment to the front, Artelt, through some oversight or bureaucratic mistake on the part of the naval authorities,[11] had managed to remain in Kiel.

Now Artelt shouted that the men were not to disperse and retreat. Instead, they should reconvene the next day at the Wald-

238 ⚓ The Collapse of the Navy

wiese, persist in their demand for the liberation of the prisoners, and seek the support of the shipyard workers. Thereupon five other speakers urged continuing resistance, advocated refusing to obey orders, the use of force against officers who deserved to be "clubbed to death," and the immediate cessation of the war.[12]

Clearly Souchon's stratagem had backfired and had driven the men to assume a much more radical position than they had originally held. Moreover, his threat of armed force also led the local garrison and workers into supporting the sailors, thus creating the conditions for a general insurrection against naval authority.

The first signs of this trend manifested themselves in the First Company of the Sea Battalion. When that unit was issued live ammunition to disperse the crowd, the men without uttering a word refused to obey their officers' order to load and secure, marching off in small groups to their barracks. The Second Company of the same battalion was then pressed into service, but it, too, refused to obey. Equally ominous was the fact that the Independent Socialists that night arrayed themselves on the side of the sailors by printing a manifesto addressed to the workers and garrison of Kiel that proclaimed: "Comrades, do not fire upon your brothers! Workers, stage mass demonstrations; do not leave the sailors in the lurch!" [13]

Although it was general knowledge that on November 3 an even bigger protest demonstration was to be staged, the Kiel naval command lacked a concrete plan to deal with these growing signs of unrest. Too proud to admit defeat before the battle with the enlisted men had begun, Souchon informed the *Seekriegsleitung* that he did not need any help, insisting that "all measures for the maintenance of discipline . . . must be left exclusively in the hands of the Governor." All that he requested from Berlin was that a prominent Social Democratic deputy be sent to Kiel to dissuade the men from staging a rebellion.[14]

On the morning of November 3, Souchon and his chief of staff, Admiral Küsel, continued their display of glacial calm in the face of a potentially explosive situation. Küsel sought to avert the enlisted men's demonstration scheduled for that evening by sounding a general alarm. This he hoped would compel the men to return to their stations where they would receive a "thorough talking-to" by their commanders, who would thus "persuade them to desist from their senseless plans." Rejecting the advice of Admirals Hahn and Langemak that mere speeches would never succeed in quieting the men and that it was necessary to undertake defensive preparations for the major military installations of Kiel, Küsel was commendably moderate but unrealistic in the light of what had already transpired when he kept reiterating that "the entire affair would have to be resolved in peace and quiet; injudicious use of force would lead it [the enlisted men's movement] into a completely wrong channel. There is no reason at all for hasty action." Souchon, overriding the objections of the majority of the officers at that meeting, accepted his chief of staff's overoptimistic advice,[15] and hoped that the sound of the alarm would avert the impending trouble.

Having failed to map out a comprehensive plan, Souchon left it to his officers to fend for themselves with the men. Thus, for instance, Captain Heine exposed the Second Company of the Sea Battalion to an angry tirade in which he demanded that the men be prepared to fire upon their comrades without hesitation. Nevertheless, when they were handed live ammunition and were told to conduct some sixty to seventy crew members of the *Markgraf* to prison, they demurred and were placed under arrest.[16] Still an attempt was made to remove the mutinous *Markgraf* crew from Kiel by ordering the ship to sail. But this order could not be supported by armed force. As a result, most of the sailors and stokers on board that vessel deserted their ship and joined the growing crowd of demonstrators on shore.[17]

Receiving no orders or directives from their superiors, many naval officers displayed an alarming lack of responsibility by choosing this critical juncture to grant their men liberty in town. Fregattenkapitän Waldeyer-Hartz gave a large part of the *Schlesien* crew liberty while Korvettenkapitän Weddigen, commanding the cruiser *Strassburg*, set an entire watch free although he was well aware that trouble was brewing in Kiel. Equally guilty was the First Dock Division, which released the majority of its companies from duty although they constituted the first line of defense in Kiel.[18]

As a direct result of this thoughtlessness and lack of direction, large numbers of men, among them the *Markgraf* crew, were milling about town in an effort to liberate the prisoners of the Third Squadron when the alarm sounded at 4 P.M. Defiantly ignoring this signal, the crowd proceeded to organize its demonstration. Hundreds of other men who knew nothing of the planned protest march found out about it in this fashion. Within a short time a parade consisting of nearly three thousand men was slowly wending its way toward the Waldwiese.[19]

In an hour-long mass meeting that reflected confusion and uncertainty rather than careful organization and planning, the emotions of the men were aroused to a fever pitch. But rising mass hysteria and not the fumbling rhetorical attempts of the leaders accounted for this frenzy. Starting the meeting was an uninspiring historical account of the enlisted men's movement by Karl Artelt, followed by another man who described the 1917 naval mutiny by reading an article from the *Leipziger Volkszeitung*. Next came the chairman of the Kiel Trade Union Council, Majority Socialist Garbe, who asked for a postponement of the demonstration to give the workers a chance to muster their support. Clamoring for action, the mob shouted that proposal down. Finally, when a representative of the USPD and of the shipyard workers proclaimed his solidarity with the sailors, the entire assembly, cheering wildly, started off.

To the tune of "The Internationale" the massive crowd left the Waldwiese at 7 P.M., heading for a nearby prison where it promptly released the inmates. Next it pressed forward in the direction of the large naval prison on the Feldstrasse. By way of the Sophienblatt, the main railroad station, and the Holstenstrasse, passing the Marktplatz and proceeding along the Dänische Strasse and the Brunswicker Strasse, the mob rolled on, disarming a patrol along the way and swelling in numbers as it emptied tavern after tavern.[20]

As it was about to turn from the Brunswicker Strasse into the Karlstrasse, the swollen crowd found its way barred by a patrol in front of the Hoffnung Tavern. Evidently determined not to yield to the weight of numbers and allow itself to be disarmed, the patrol, consisting of forty-eight mates and officer candidates and commanded by a Lieutenant Steinhäuser, stood its ground. Steinhäuser shouted an order for the mob to stop. When this produced no results, he ordered his men to fire a volley into the air. Finally, as the throng of sailors and workers continued to press forward menacingly, he gave the order to fire for effect. In seconds the ground was littered with dead and wounded.

Quickly overcoming its surprise and spurred on with rage, the crowd retaliated by letting loose a hail of stones interspersed with a few rifle shots. Among the first to be struck down with a severe head wound was Lieutenant Steinhäuser. A general melee was avoided only because of the arrival upon the scene of trucks from the Kiel fire department and a number of heavily armed patrols. When the smoke and confusion cleared, it was discovered that eight men had been killed and thirty-nine wounded. The naval rebellion in Kiel had claimed its first grisly victims.[21]

As the mob swiftly dispersed after this bloody encounter, a superficial air of peace and tranquility returned to Kiel. Souchon, no doubt impressed by the apparent effects of this almost Napoleonic whiff of grapeshot, was deceived in thinking that he had regained control over the sailors. Earlier that evening, in a moment of panic, he had sent out a plea for troops to the Ninth Reserve Army Command in Altona.[22] Upon the return of quiet he not only withdrew that request, but also recalled many of his own patrols, disarming them and scattering his forces all over the city.[23]

Souchon, however, had badly misjudged the temper of his sailors. Filled with "a terrible bitterness and the utmost determination to insure the success of their movement so that the martyrs would not have fallen in vain," thousands of enlisted men decided that they would now have to wage a fight to the finish with the navy.[24] The crew of the *Grosser Kurfürst*, for example, responded to the bloodbath on the Karlstrasse by overpowering its officers on the morning of November 4 and marching to the scene of the disaster to swear an oath of vengeance.[25]

Even before he was overwhelmed by the outraged enlisted men, Admiral Souchon realized the mistake he had made. In a report to the *Seekriegsleitung* undoubtedly written during the late hours of the night of November 3–4, the governor stated pessimistically: "For the moment order has been restored. Am confidently hoping to remain in control of the situation. [However,] expect strike at Germania Shipyards on November 4. Events indicate necessity of relieving Kiel.[26]

Souchon's worst premonitions became reality that same morning as with startling suddenness both the garrison and ships rose up against the navy's authority. In the First Torpedo Division, the commander of that unit, Captain Bartels, impervious to the feelings of his men, chose that particular time to deliver a speech in which he declared, "Soldiers are not to meddle in politics! Soldiers will obey, soldiers must obey and soldiers do obey." Thus provided with a perfect opportunity, the leading agitator against the navy in Kiel, Karl Artelt, vaulted upon a table and countered by demanding the immediate establishment of a sailors' council. When the officers tried to silence him by dragging him off the table, they were "mercilessly disarmed by the fists of the sailors," who then stormed into the armory, appropriated rifles, and proceeded to elect their council with Artelt as its chairman.[27] Indicating that this action was widely endorsed in the ranks was the fact that when troops from the First Dock Division were called in to suppress the disorder, they meekly allowed themselves to be disarmed.[28]

In the rapidly expanding rebellion the ships in the harbor proved of little use to the authorities. On the contrary, not only did their crews supply the Kiel garrison with the majority of its "agitators and trouble-makers," but they also seized control of their ships and threatened to bombard any vessel that made a move against the rebels on shore.[29]

When the entire First Torpedo Division, large parts of the Dock Division, and the usually reliable Submarine Division, "the best personnel in Kiel," turned against the officers and announced that they would not raise a hand to defend the prisons against their comrades,[30] Souchon and his staff became aware that they had unleashed a disaster.

New and inexperienced at the job he had held for a mere four days, Souchon hardly knew how to respond. The speed with which the victory at the Karlstrasse the night before had changed into a grim defeat confronted him with an insoluble dilemma. It would have been easiest for him to do what was expected of a national hero and to wage a ruthless battle against his rebellious men regardless of any consequences and costs. On the other hand, since not a single unit in Kiel any longer obeyed his orders and he was left with only officers and cadets to conduct this fight, Souchon knew that such action would be suicidal. As if he needed confirmation of the hopelessness of his position, he received despairing news from the town commandant at 1:45, "The mutiny among the troops continues to spread. Our means for the military suppression of the military are exhausted; we no longer possess any reliable troops. . . ." Consequently, at 2:20 P.M., Souchon announced to the garrison: "In order to prevent bloodshed the governor is prepared to entertain the wishes of the troops. The troops are to be asked at once the reasons for their behavior. Their wishes are to be submitted to me immediately." [31]

By taking the only reasonable course open to him, Souchon made himself the object of scorn of the entire right in Germany. After the war he was arbitrarily condemned for cowardice, incompetence, and lack of willpower[32] by groups that were all too eager to find scapegoats but that never bothered to appraise his position realistically.

So far Souchon had only received one company of reinforcements from Altona, and although three others—a total of six hundred men—were expected, the Ninth Army Command that had despatched them refused to guarantee their loyalty and flatly announced that it could not provide any additional troops.[33] With no support among the civilian population in Kiel and the workers openly sympathizing with the rebels in their fight "against detested militarism and its exponents" in the officer corps, Souchon knew that he would be faced by a general strike by both the Independent and Majority Socialists that day which could only worsen his situation.[34]

When he undertook his negotiations with the enlisted men, the governor hardly expected that he had taken the first step toward a complete capitulation. According to his chief of staff, he hoped that he could thereby win over the more reasonable elements among the men and gain time until reinforcements in the form of additional army troops or governmental representatives arrived.[35]

Although he had committed a number of errors of judgment since coming to Kiel, it was hardly Souchon's fault that his command was so ill prepared to cope with a rebellion.[36] Nor, for that matter, can he be held responsible for the growing determination of the enlisted men to protect themselves against the lies and threats of the naval regime that on November 4 persuaded the government to issue a proclamation condemning their uprising against the *Flottenvorstoss*.[37] Most importantly, however, Souchon cannot be blamed for refusing to wage a hopeless battle against insurmountable odds with the demoralized officers under his command.

One of the most startling surprises and least-known aspects of the naval rebellion of 1918 is the internal collapse of the naval officer corps. Long accustomed to having their orders obeyed unquestioningly and trained to take it for granted that the enlisted men respected their caste, most naval officers were unprepared to cope with their greatest crisis. The moment that their men refused to click heels and stand rigidly at attention before them, their arrogant self-confidence and authority deserted them and they were overcome by indecisiveness and near paralysis. In the face of the first real challenge to their authority by their subordinates, most officers proved themselves either incapable or unwilling to risk their lives for what was clearly becoming a lost cause.[38]

This assertion is amply borne out by the astonishingly low casualty figures in the officer corps during the course of the rebellion. Aside from Lieutenant Steinhäuser, who fell in the act of halting the Kiel demonstrations of November 3, only three other officers risked their lives to preserve the honor of the navy. These were Captain Weniger, the commander of the *König*, and two of his staff members, Korvettenkapitän Heinemann and Lieutenant Zenker. In a vain effort to prevent the hoisting of the red flag on their ship on November 5, all three were riddled with bullets as, with revolver in hand, they sought to keep their crew away from the flagstaff.[39] Only one other officer died in the course of the 1918 rebellion. He was the town commandant of Kiel, who died on November 6 while attempting to escape arrest by a sailors' patrol.[40]

Dubious about his officers' capacity to fight and the army's promises of additional reinforcements,[41] Souchon took the only sensible course by summoning the enlisted men under his command to present their demands to him. If, however, he expected the men to behave with moderation and to feel themselves honored by this concession, Souchon was badly mistaken. Even the preliminary negotiations revealed that the men regarded themselves the real victors in their confrontation with the navy, were determined never again to place themselves under its power, and were beginning to insist upon a variety of governmental changes that had been in the forefront of working-class demands since the breach of the *Burgfrieden* in 1917.

One may obtain a good idea of the desires of the enlisted men and the course upon which they were headed by examining the demands of the First Torpedo Division. When Captain Bartels performed a complete about-face by requesting that the newly formed Sailors' Council of his unit present its demands, the revolutionary assembly drafted a proposal that perfectly reflected the pragmatic, unsophisticated, non-Bolshevik, and non-socialistic nature of their movement. It demanded:

1. The abdication of the Hohenzollern dynasty.
2. The abolition of the state of siege in Germany.
3. The liberation of all prisoners in the Third Squadron.
4. The liberation of all prisoners from the 1917 mutiny.
5. The freeing of all political prisoners.
6. The introduction of free, equal and universal franchise for both men and women.
7. The immediate conclusion of a peace without annexations and indemnities on the basis of the right of self-determination of all peoples.

Astonished by these far-reaching demands, Bartels could only reply, "Yes, Gentlemen, but these are all political demands," demands that he was not empowered to negotiate with them.[42]

When Bartels shortly thereafter informed his men that Governor Souchon wished to speak to their representative, Artelt commandeered a car, attached a huge red flag to it, and rushed off to station headquarters to attend a meeting that included Stoker Podolski of the *Grosser Kurfürst* and representatives of the two socialist parties. Without much ceremony the sailors presented a twofold list of demands that reflected their prime concern. First they demanded that Souchon free all Third Squadron prisoners, that he institute immediate court-martial proceedings to investigate the incident on the Karlstrasse and punish the guilty parties, and that he provide them with assurances that the navy's projected *Flottenvorstoss* against England would be abandoned. Then they asked that Souchon recognize their Sailors' Council and approve the list of demands it had drafted. Sensing, however, that these political demands were not within the governor's province, they agreed to a postponement until the expected arrival of the governmental representatives.

Indicative of the navy's and Souchon's impotence in the face of these demands was the governor's acquiescence to the enlisted men's threat that they would bombard the railroad station and the officer's section of town unless all troops were withdrawn from Kiel and that those who were on their way there be stopped in transit. Bowing once more to the superior numbers of the rebels, Souchon released an official proclamation announcing that the enlisted men's demands would be discussed that evening with the representatives of the government.[43]

If it had been Souchon's intention to merely buy time with these negotiations, his plan misfired the minute his proclamation was made public. Regarding it as a sign of their victory, the enlisted men of Kiel rose up in jubilation and took over the town. Ten thousand of them staged an impromptu parade in which they marched to the jails and freed all political prisoners. Not even the hospitals were immune; the patients, too, armed themselves and joined the celebration.[44]

More fatefully still, Souchon's proclamation was interpreted as an announcement of surrender by the officer corps of the garrison. As uncertainty spawned rumor after rumor, the officers came to the erroneous conclusion that the governor had ordered them to suspend all military resistance to the rebellion.[45] In the First Naval Division the officers labored under the misapprehension that the Berlin government had issued an order forbidding further bloodshed. In the absence of specific instructions from station headquarters all that day, the despondent commander disarmed the few loyal troops he still had and went home in disgust, relegating command over his unit to a junior officer.[46]

Thus far the naval rebellion in Kiel had not manifested any signs that it was a Bolshevik- or socialist-inspired conspiracy. True, the rebellious men had adopted the red flag of socialism as their emblem, but none of the programs or demands they made, not even those framed by such an avowed revolutionary as Artelt, revealed any connection with socialism. Even the communists, ever anxious to claim credit for the revolt, have been compelled to acknowledge that the events in Kiel constitute "almost exclusively a military revolt" rather than a socialist uprising, and that the demands of the men did not "exceed the dimensions of a very moderate democratic program." This, according to Artelt, was due to the fact that the men lacked "a revolutionary working-class party that might have imparted concrete goals and organizational strength" to their movement.[47]

Surprising as it may seem in the light of the charges of the right and the claims of the extreme left, once the men had gotten over their fear of being sent on a suicide mission and had recovered from the anger and shock of the Karlstrasse incident, their sense of humor returned and they came to look upon their revolt as a lark.

Korvettenkapitän Leistikow reports that while the rebels may have looked "like pirates," their behavior and bearing proved that they had still not become revolutionaries. Indeed, he was particularly impressed by the commander of the rebel watch in charge of his unit. Although armed with an officer's sword and two pistols, the young sailor "still maintained a straight military bearing." Depressed and demoralized as he was, Leistikow retained sufficient astuteness to note that the sailors' threats of violence were prompted not so much by revolutionary fervor as by hunger, none of the men having been fed since breakfast.[48]

Corroborating this impression is the testimony of Gustav Noske, who arrived in Kiel on the evening of November 4 as a representative of the government. Despatched to Kiel with Secretary of State Conrad Haussmann, on the navy's request that a socialist was needed to prevent the spread of an uprising throughout the fleet,[49] Noske, a burly former basket weaver and newspaper editor, conceived it his primary duty to restore order in that tumultuous town. "The bloodhound of the German Revolution," as he was subsequently to be called for suppressing a multitude of uprisings against the Weimar Republic, was puzzled when he was met at the railroad station by an immense throng of armed sailors who broke out in wild cheers over him. Noske's puzzlement grew when he was whisked off through town in a car that bore a sailor with a red flag who kept shouting in a hoarse voice, "Long live freedom! Long live freedom!"

On his way to be introduced to still another crowd at the Wilhelmsplatz, the Social Democrat deputy did not gain the impression that a great revolution had taken place in Kiel. He found the streets unusually crowded, but the people were in a jovial mood. There was much laughter; sailors flirted with the girls, and the only visible signs of revolution were the red insignia worn by many of the men. Noske was still more astonished when he delivered an impromptu speech calling for the immediate restoration of order and his words were received with much applause.[50]

Noske's mood quickly changed, however, when toward the end of his speech at the Wilhelmsplatz a number of shots rang out and scattered his audience in all directions. Turning to his escort, Noske demanded in outraged tones, "What kind of nonsense [Schweinerei] is this?" His impression of the situation did not improve when he was conducted before the Sailors' Council in the Trade Union Building and was apprised of its demands. He found everything dreadfully confused, chaotic, and disorderly.[51]

At a nine o'clock meeting between the rebels and the naval authorities at station headquarters, Noske's mood became even more somber as he witnessed the officers sitting "quite helplessly" while the sailors "with great joy but in correct form" made known their demands. With mounting confidence they called for the formation of a commission to release their jailed comrades, the abolition of all monarchies in Germany and of the Prussian House of Lords, as well as the introduction of universal franchise with proportional representation for all men and women. In addition, they requested an amnesty for all prisoners and the summoning of a prominent Independent Socialist to Kiel.

Although most of these demands clearly exceeded the competence of Souchon and Haussmann, Noske was dismayed when they were discussed at least three hours because, as he put it contemptuously, "the German revolution was inconceivable without endlessly long meetings and countless speeches." Finally promising that he and Haussmann would communicate the rebel views to Berlin and would recommend a "most liberal amnesty," Noske was able to close the meeting at about midnight.[52]

Rankled by the disorganized state of Kiel, the indecisiveness of the navy, the excessive demands of the mutineers, as well as by the sporadic rifle fire that disturbed his sleep that night,[53] Noske resolved the following morning to do what he could to prevent the situation from getting even more out of hand. This resolve must have been strengthened when he discovered that Governor Souchon had been held hostage for a good part of the night by the rebels, who felt that he had betrayed them by sending for additional troops.[54]

Everywhere the order-loving Noske turned on the morning of November 5, he saw nothing but revolutionary chaos. Some 20,-000 armed sailors were roaming through the town firing rifles and machine guns. A regular battle was raging in the suburb of Wik as the Torpedo Division fought with remnants of the Dock Division for control of the fortress.

Increasingly reckless, the enlisted men were beginning to tear off the epaulettes of officers they had captured and to subject them to a variety of indignities. Later on a meeting addressed by Noske at the Wilhelmsplatz was broken up at a cost of eight dead and twelve enlisted men wounded by officers who retaliated by firing at the assembly from surrounding houses.[55]

Determined that "Germany shall have order even during a revolution" and that it was necessary to know "with whom one was dealing," Noske looked around for the leaders of the revolt. Convinced that the revolt had somehow been triggered by the Independent Socialists, he was surprised to discover that the local leaders of that party received him with great sympathy and offered "almost no opposition" to his assumption of command.

In what constitutes the best refutation of the navy's conspiracy thesis, Noske describes the way that he was placed in charge of

Kiel. Upon inquiring "Where are the people who control things around here?" he received the vague answer that there was a Sailors' Council someplace. Only after a persistent search did Noske finally make contact with Artelt and trade-union leader Garbe, who "in a conversation held in the street" suggested that Noske assume the chairmanship of the Sailors' Council. Deciding that someone was needed to exercise control, Noske mounted the hood of a car parked at the Wilhelmsplatz and announced to the crowd that he was taking charge. The crowd cheered; the revolt had found its master.[56]

Even after he had taken a number of steps to stem the revolution, Noske did not encounter any trouble from the Independents, let alone the Bolsheviks. Thus when on November 8 Hugo Haase, the USPD leader for whom the radical sailors had been clamoring since the start of the rebellion, arrived in Kiel, no one made a move to depose Noske or to compel him to share power. Instead, Noske simply took Haase into his office, explained that he had the situation in hand, and convinced his potential rival that he should leave.[57]

Noske was elected chairman of the Sailors' Council because he was the only leader of any stature in Kiel and because the men were almost devoid of political knowledge. Even the communists are willing to concede as much in their more candid moments. Thus they complain that the enlisted men's movement, if one may even go so far as to call it that, was marked by "political weakness" and lack of organization. Only this can explain why in their view it failed "to force the imperialistic and militaristic forces to step off the stage." [58]

This weakness and the total lack of revolutionary ideology were all too evident in the program drafted by the Sailors' and Workers' Council during the night of November 4. Since the fourteen demands contained therein constitute the most widely adopted program in the navy and reflect the attitudes of the enlisted men, they deserve to be quoted in full.

The enlisted men of Kiel demanded:

1. The liberation of all the men under arrest and all political prisoners.
2. Complete freedom of speech and of the press.
3. Abolition of censorship of the mails.
4. Equitable treatment of crews by their superiors.
5. The return of all men to their ships and barracks without punishment.
6. Under no circumstances is the fleet to sail out.
7. Any steps that may lead to bloodshed are to be avoided.
8. Withdrawal of all troops not belonging to the garrison.
9. The Sailors' Council shall at once establish all measures to protect private property.
10. There are no more superiors outside of duty [hours].
11. The men are to enjoy unrestricted freedom from the [time] when they conclude their duties until the commencement of their next watch.
12. We welcome all officers who declare themselves in agreement with the Sailors' Council. All others are to terminate their [official] functions without being entitled to rations.
13. All members of the Sailors' Council are to be relieved of all duties.
14. All future measures are to be carried out only with the consent of the Sailors' Council.

These demands represent the orders of the Sailors' Council for all military personnel.[59]

Better than any other document, these demands—certainly no shining example of clarity[60]—illustrate that the enlisted men were "far too modest" and their thinking much too "confined to the military sphere" to launch a Bolshevik revolution.[61] Once the sailors had accomplished their immediate goal—the prevention of the navy's *Flottenvorstoss* and reprisals against their comrades—they lacked the ability and the desire to translate their military revolt into a socialist uprising.

This view is borne out by the jubilant proclamation of the Kiel Sailors' Council of November 5. This indicates that despite their joy over their victory over the navy the men were becoming increasingly concerned over the possible repercussions of their unorganized and unplanned rebellion. Their manifesto betrayed a strange ambivalence between revolutionary zeal and conservative caution.

> Comrades! [The events of] yesterday will forever occupy a memorable place in the history of Germany. For the first time sailors have succeeded in acquiring political power. There is no going back! Great tasks stand before us. We shall, however, need unity and solidarity to achieve this. You have elected a Sailors' Council which is working united in spirit with a Workers' Council. Obey its instructions and decisions. Take care to [restore] peace and order so that nothing will happen that can be used against us. Also take care to maintain order in the barracks. . . .[62]

Sensing that such rebel leadership as existed in the Sailors' Council wanted nothing more than a restoration of order while the Kiel naval command had lost all power, Noske, in order to prevent "stupidities," quickly swung into action. With characteristic forcefulness, he first held a meeting with Admirals Souchon and Küsel in which he demanded that he be given office space at naval headquarters and that all officers continue to perform their jobs.[63] Happy not to be swept away altogether by the enlisted men, Souchon complied with alacrity.

In a series of orders issued on November 5, Souchon first demanded that the officers who were still firing out of windows immediately suspend their resistance in "the interest of public safety" because "only cooperative understanding for the demands of the times can reestablish good order." Becoming even more cooperative, he next told his officers "to place their services at Noske's disposal." A little later Souchon went further by telling them to share their rations with the men, by keeping the officers' clubs closed and allowing the Sailors' Council the unobstructed right to search their quarters for weapons because that body was "in many respects conciliatory." Reaching the point of total capitulation that same day, Admiral Küsel instructed the officers to voluntarily surrender their weapons since this was the "unavoidable prerequisite for the creation of mutual trust." [64]

Coping with the enlisted men with the same speed and thoroughness, Noske, on the afternoon of November 5, appointed an executive committee of the Sailors' Council. By evening it had published a series of orders entitled "Decisions of the Soldatenrat" that brought about a virtual restoration of peace through the resumption of the regular distribution of rations and pay, and by providing for the unloading of supply trains. At the same time, Noske and his committee reinstituted naval patrols against enemy ships in the Baltic and prevented renewed outbreaks of violence in town through street patrols and the systematic disarming of the rebellious men.[65]

Equally successful was Noske's handling of the potentially explosive situation created by Prince Henry of Prussia's flight from Kiel. Perturbed by the invasion of his residence, the Kiel Schloss, by a band of sailors who openly insulted him,[66] the Kaiser's brother decided on November 5 to remove himself and his family from the center of the revolution. Prince Henry, his wife, and son, having left Kiel in a car equipped with a red banner, were headed North when they were stopped by some sailors clustered around a broken truck. Without recognizing him, two sailors jumped on the running-board of Prince Henry's car and drove off with him. Thereupon Prince Henry allegedly shot one sailor; the other one saved himself by jumping off in time. The remaining enlisted men retaliated by letting loose a volley of gunfire as the prince's car sped off in the distance.

When this story was made public in Kiel it generated tremendous excitement. Some of the enlisted men insisted that Henry be punished and wanted to set off in pursuit. One hysterical sailor kept yelling in Noske's presence, "Treason! Treason! We have been betrayed!" Noske, however, refused to become flustered or to allow any harm to befall a member of the royal family. He therefore procrastinated and delayed the men until it was too late for them to catch up with the prince.[67]

All in all, the speed and efficiency with which Noske managed to pacify the Kiel revolt was little short of miraculous. Although he could not altogether prevent the revolution from expanding its victory by assuming control over the municipal government—when it decreed on November 5 that Dr. Adler, a socialist councilman, be placed in charge of the mayor[68]—he did see to it, as the *Kieler Neueste Nachrichten* noted with evident satisfaction, that "the night from Tuesday to Wednesday [November 5–6] passed without disturbance. No shot was heard and after three days filled with excitement for the first time one could sleep without interruption. . . ." [69]

It was largely due to Noske that the great majority of burghers of Kiel could live through the days of the revolution very much as those of Berlin in 1806 by maintaining absolute quiet and unconcern. Acting on the historic precedent of King Frederick William IV that "quiet is the first obligation of the subject," the inhabitants of Kiel were encouraged by their newspapers to keep their windows shuttered and to mind their own business,[70] while the municipal council saw to it that they were advised to "practice and maintain peace and reasonableness" by avoiding all meetings, discounting all rumors, and once again maintaining peace.[71]

Because of Noske's influence the revolution returned to "quiet channels" by November 7, in the sense that the streetcars were running again, the banks had reopened so that the dockworkers received their pay checks, while the *Kieler Neueste Nachrichten* was able to keep up its uninterrupted serialization of *His Excellency's Daughter*, a cheap novel by Ernst Georgy.[72] This influence plus the undoubted conservatism of the revolutionary sailors was responsible for the fact that Kiel emerged virtually unscathed from the naval uprising. All told, the municipality suffered damages of only 7,817.70 marks, mainly broken windows, doors, furniture, and torn-up flags.[73] An even more telling commentary on the innate conservatism of the sailors and the nonrevolutionary nature of their revolt is the fact that the Sailors' Council accepted all responsibility for these damages by stating that it regarded it as "*selbstverständlich*" (self-evident) that proper compensation be paid.[74]

Having succeeded in putting a stop to the fighting, Noske managed in addition to conciliate Souchon into accepting the authority of the Sailors' Council while simultaneously keeping that body under complete control. On November 6 Souchon, having given up all hope of returning to power, instructed his officers to elect representatives to cooperate with the sailors in restoring order. Also he urged them to practice "extreme self-control and self-mastery" in avoiding all conflicts by regarding any insults to which they were subjected as the products of "momentary excitement and uncontrollable emotions." They must allow nothing to jeopardize their complete cooperation with the Sailors' Council, an organization which he regarded as "the only means to protect and further our common interest in the Fatherland." [75]

With Souchon having abdicated so completely, it was inevitable that Noske be urged to fill the power vacuum by assuming the post of governor of Kiel. On November 7 before a meeting of 300 sailors' delegates, the Social Democratic deputy was duly elected governor, having to compromise only to the extent that he granted parity to the independents by having Lothar Popp elected to the vacant position of chairman of the Sailors' Council. When Noske communicated this decision to the admiral, the latter vacated his office and retreated into the background.[76]

With Noske thus firmly entrenched in power, there was little opportunity for any latent bolshevism to assert itself within the rebellion. The order-loving socialist with a firm hand quickly maneuvered the Sailors' Council to sanction a return to a modified form of normalcy. On November 7 the new governor and the *Soldatenrat* reinstituted patrol duty at sea under the command of officers, prevailed upon the men to hoist the traditional battle flag instead of the revolutionary red banner on all ships, and prohibited the carrying of weapons to all but official patrols. As concessions to the triumphant revolt, they decreed that officers and men were to receive the same rations, that officers would enjoy a status superior to the men only while on duty, and would therefore no longer have to be addressed in the third person.[77]

Although the Kiel revolt reached its peak of success on November 7, its ultimate victory was by no means assured until then. When the town first came under the control of the rebellious enlisted men, there was ample cause for fear that the uprising would be squashed by the armed might of the state. Inexperienced and divided by the bewildering succession of events that flowed from its request for an armistice, the government of Prince Max von Baden still allowed the influence of the military to prevail over the more reasonable advice of its civilian representatives. Thus on November 5 it refused to endorse Noske's and Haussmann's request for an amnesty, but decided to heed the Secretary of the Navy's recommendation to "make an example" of Kiel by blockading the town by land and sea and subjecting the ringleaders of the rebellion to harsh punishment.[78]

By delaying the inevitable and allowing itself to be swayed by a navy that had not succeeded in learning the lesson that brute force alone could not bring its enlisted men back to their former obedience, the government became the unwitting dupe of the same officers who had concocted the plan for the suicide mission against England and who now wished to quell the rebellion they had unleashed with a bloodbath.

The most recalcitrant of these officers, Admiral von Levetzow, had as early as November 4 raised the idea of restoring "order and strict shore discipline" by placing the entire German coast under one command, as in Flanders. While he still endorsed the plan to isolate Kiel by means of a naval blockade,[79] he and Admiral Scheer, without so much as notifying Prince Max or Secretary von Mann, sought out the Kaiser on November 5 and persuaded him to set in motion a much more drastic scheme. On the strength of their advice, on November 5, a guileless Wilhelm II, without consulting either his Chief of Naval Cabinet or the Secretary of the Navy, issued an order to Admiral Ludwig von

Schroeder, the commander of the Naval Infantry Brigade in Flanders, to assume command over Kiel and to restore "peace and order with an iron hand." [80]

At 2 A.M. on November 6 Schroeder, the "lion of Flanders," received his orders and began at once to prepare a special train to leave for Kiel with a "battle-hardened naval shock battalion [equipped] with some [pieces] of artillery, a good machine gun company, and 20 excellent naval policemen." Thirteen hours later that same day, as he was about to depart for what he considered the merciless suppression of the Kiel uprising, he received orders rescinding his appointment. [81]

Fortunately for Schroeder, his thousand-man counterrevolutionary contingent, and the officer corps of Kiel who would doubtlessly have succumbed in a bloody battle to the finish with forty thousand armed sailors, [82] Secretary von Mann and Prince Max got wind of the plan and stopped it. Outraged at this latest "gross interference" on the part of the Seekriegsleitung, regarding it "as unheard of not to be consulted in such a highly political decision," both of these officials agreed that it would be "suicidal" to send an "aggressive type" like Schroeder to Kiel. Consequently, they prevailed upon the Kaiser to withdraw his appointment. [83] Thus the activists in the naval command lost what they considered their last chance to "suffocate the mutinies with blood and iron." [84]

Without realizing it, however, they lost much more than that. By deceiving the government about the real nature of the revolt and by delaying the issuance of an amnesty for nearly two days while they unsuccessfully sought to implement their plan, Levetzow and Scheer, and to a lesser extent von Mann, were directly responsible for the ultimate spread of the naval rebellion along the entire German coast to every naval installation, and from there to the rest of the country.

Although both Noske and Haussmann had since November 5 begged the cabinet to grant the rebels an amnesty, it was not until the evening of November 6 that Prince Max came out with the equivocal promise that the sailors' demands would be met only if they returned to their duties that very evening and handed in all the weapons they had acquired.[85]

Filled with mistrust for the government that had unjustly condemned their uprising against the rebellious officers, the enlisted men of Kiel felt they could not afford to accept this grudging offer. Their misgivings were not quieted in the least by Noske's behavior. The deputy took this opportunity to inform them that he "personally condemned the mutiny in sharpest terms," and counseled them to accept the government's offer and to beat a retreat.[86] Becoming increasingly belligerent with the recalcitrant sailors, Noske intimated that although their movement might have triumphed in Kiel, they were in an extremely vulnerable position because they stood alone and isolated.[87] This was undoubtedly true. Their situation was indeed a precarious one, so long as their rebellion was confined to Kiel. But a glimmer of hope was already rising over the horizon as their movement slowly, but at an ever accelerating pace, began to spread along the seaboard.

As early as November 4, individual sailors and groups of sailors had begun streaming out of Kiel by truck, train, and ship, fomenting revolution wherever they went.[88] Illustrative of this process are actions of the Third Squadron of the High Seas Fleet. On November 5 that unit, flying the red flag of revolution,[89] had anchored at Travemünde and landed five hundred men who marched off towards Lübeck. Without their firing a shot, the entire town with its garrison had surrendered and gone over to the revolution.[90]

In Hamburg, the mutineers were even more successful. On November 5, despite the blockade on Kiel, numerous sailors made their way across the peninsula and began to conduct an intensive propaganda campaign among the civilian population and the local garrison. Joining forces with the workers and dissident groups in the replacement companies during the night of November 5, they began disarming officers and removing their epaulettes. By morning they had gained control over the town and began to occupy the shipyards and the railroad station. According to the eye-witness account of Baurat Paech, this process took place with al-most ridiculous ease. All it required to stop all work at the gigan-tic Blohm and Voss Shipyard that employed twelve thousand workers was a group of ten to twelve sailors, while two or three armed sailors sufficed to gain control over the railroad station.[91]

Things went even smoother in Bremen on November 6. Ac-cording to a report of the *Weser Zeitung*, Colonel Lehmann, the commandant of the local garrison, simply handed over his power to the insurgent sailors upon their arrival in a "congenial fashion" that reflected the "spirit of the republican city-state." [92]

Lest it be imagined that civilian ports were alone in succumbing so easily to the revolutionary wave emanating from Kiel, it must be noted that Germany's naval installations were equally suscep-tible. In Cuxhaven, for instance, Admiral Engelhard and his staff were totally unprepared for the coming revolution and collapsed at the first sign of insurrection. On the evening of November 5, when the enlisted men of the naval base organized a demonstra-tion, Engelhard lost his nerve and capitulated without firing a shot. To Oberheizer Baier, the ostensible leader of the enlisted men, the admiral promised that he would take under advisement an eight-point program that bore a remarkable resemblance to the one drawn up in Kiel on November 4. That program demanded:

1. The immediate conclusion of peace
2. Granting an amnesty to all prisoners
3. Creation of a workers' and sailors' council
4. Better treatment for the enlisted men
5. Abolition of saluting
6. The establishment of equality between officers and men
7. Abolition of the officers' club
8. Lifting the state of siege.[93]

When, however, the men refused to bide their time and stormed the local jail that night, Engelhard became even more accommodating. On November 7 he instructed all his officers to suspend their resistance so that they might devote "all their energy to maintaining the functions" of the base. Increasingly intimidated by his rebellious enlisted men, the admiral on November 9 threatened that all officers who refused to subordinate themselves to the Sailors' Council would no longer be eligible to receive rations or pay, thus inducing all but two to sign an agreement not to oppose that revolutionary body "in word or in deed." [94]

It would, however, be unfair to single out this particular officer for behaving in a fashion that was widely emulated in the navy. On November 7 Admiral Karpf, the commander of the Fourth Reconnaissance Group of the High Seas Fleet, acted even more irresponsibly when, without consulting his superiors, he decommissioned the cruisers *Strassburg*, *Brummer*, and *Bremse* and allowed their crews to roam the countryside fomenting rebellion.[95] The commander of the naval air base outside Cuxhaven also did not cover himself with glory. Making no effort to protect his command from agitators from Cuxhaven, he allowed his men to follow them and was surprised when they returned that night carrying the red flag.[96]

Many less highly placed officers outdid their superiors. Panic-stricken by the speed with which the revolt seemed to spread, they abandoned their posts, fled from their garrisons, and made their way to Berlin and other urban centers. At least one officer, Kapitänleutnant Marquardt, commanding the *Sophie Charlotte* in Reval, is known to have gone over to the side of the revolution and shouted on November 9 before a crowd of enlisted men, "Long live the new Socialist Republic!" [97]

Even commanders who were forewarned and who expected trouble did not possess the knowledge or ability to stave off the floodtide of rebellion. Thus Admiral von Krosigk, the commander of Germany's largest naval base, at Wilhelmshaven, anticipated the impending revolt by several days. Having at his disposal only two hundred reliable men and fifteen machine guns,[98] he issued an urgent call to the Tenth Army Corps in Oldenburg for a battalion of infantry to be followed by a still larger number of troops. Aside from his pleas for outside help, Krosigk did virtually nothing to alert his officers to undertake defensive preparations. On November 5 Lammertz, a deck officer stationed in Wilhelmshaven, made it his business to inquire of a large number of officers what was being done to ward off an incipient rebellion. But he was told time and again not to worry; "the affair would be confined to Kiel." [99]

Von Krosigk's only positive step aided rather than impeded the onset of mutiny in his command. During the night of November 5 the admiral posted machine guns around a few of the public buildings in Wilhelmshaven. This so enraged the enlisted men on the following morning that they immediately began to organize a demonstration. No sooner did this become known on the ships in the harbor, than their crews, disregarding the pleas of their officers, streamed ashore to join in.[100] Waving makeshift flags of red blankets and sheets, they formed into a parade, complete with musical band, and proceeded on their march. Along the way they disarmed every patrol that accosted them.[101]

By noon the demonstrators numbered more than six thousand men. Abandoning all hope of relief and intimidated by the crowd that stood assembled before his headquarters, Admiral von Krosigk, whose main ambition it seems to have been to retire peacefully from the service, invited a delegation of five sailors to come in and negotiate. In quick order he acceded in principle to the creation of a negotiating body for the sailors, to remove all outside troops from the city, and to prevent others from disembarking. He suspended the requirement that enlisted men salute officers in town, agreed to free all prisoners, and established equality of rations between enlisted men and their superiors. Von Krosigk also granted the enlisted men's representatives unlimited access to all parts of the garrison and promised to abolish censorship of the mails. All these concessions were made with the proviso that the Berlin government would grant its approval.[102]

The incredible ease with which the enlisted men triumphed in

Wilhelmshaven naturally prompted the naval authorities to adopt a defensive pose. Thus Admiral Scheer, on the very day of the revolt, stated that the revolt was a "long carefully prepared and executed plan of the leaders of the revolutionary wing of the Social Democrats." [103] This accusation, however, cannot withstand close scrutiny. Seaman Stumpf, an eyewitness to that day's events, testified that he and his crewmates on the *Wittelsbach* joined the demonstration because it was the thing to do. Moreover, he found the mob was governed by mass hysteria rather than by any sort of leadership.[104] Even more convincing as a refutation of Scheer's charges are the actions of the Wilhelmshaven Sailors' Council.

Content with so small an achievement as Krosigk's tentative concessions, this council brought forth the most nonrevolutionary proclamation imaginable, one that indicated an overwhelming concern for the maintenance of order and no trace of revolutionary fervor. Praising Krosigk's "trustful cooperation," the council begged the sailors to "avoid useless bloodshed," to render all "agitators and provocateurs harmless," and to "preserve peace and quiet." In order to guarantee that peace and quiet, it immediately instituted official patrols and suspended the sale of alcoholic beverages.

Organizing itself formally that night, the Sailors' Council formed an executive committee, the so-called Council of Twenty-One. This was placed under the chairmanship of a Majority Socialist by the name of Bernhard Kuhnt, who immediately began to take steps to liquidate the revolution by instituting a strict pass control and an aeriel reconnaissance system against the enemy at sea.[105]

If the enlisted men in Wilhelmshaven proved to be even less revolutionary than those of Kiel, the naval authorities in that town also manifested considerably less courage and enterprise than their Baltic counterparts. Despite the presence of the High Seas Fleet in their port, they never offered any real resistance. On the contrary, Admiral Hipper and his ships' officers proved to be even less courageous than the shore units. At the outbreak of the rebellion Hipper collected all loyal officers and men on the *Baden*, his flagship, and made no move to come to Krosigk's rescue.

Abdicating all responsibility, the Chief of the High Seas Fleet was out of touch with the station command from noontime on November 6. Only at midnight did Hipper bestir himself to inform the *Seekriegsleitung* that he was without power since his men would no longer obey their officers. Therefore, he declared, "the means at my disposal for executing the command to forcibly suppress resistance no longer suffice." He and Krosigk had come to the conclusion that it would be best to attempt to influence the "reasonable elements" among the men to maintain order. The station commandant appeared equally resigned to his fate when he reported that the town was quiet, that the mutineers had not yet hoisted the red flag, but that his officers were without "any positive power." [106]

Rapidly becoming accustomed to his changed situation and the irreversible defeat that was signaled by a triumphal procession of ten thousand marchers on November 7,[107] Hipper declared that "in Wilhelmshaven everything is proceeding in the most exemplary [*mustergültige*] fashion" despite the fact that he could no longer guarantee the security of the German Bight against the enemy.[108]

That the final demise of the High Seas Fleet and the collapse of the navy's last stronghold on shore was caused much more by the paralytic state of the officers corps and its leaders than by the ardor or strength of the rebels is attested by two events on November 8. On that day Hipper's Chief of Staff, Admiral von Trotha, made an appearance at the Wilhelmshaven railroad station dressed in civilian clothes. Recognized by one of the mutineers, von Trotha was surprised when, instead of being subjected to insults or violence, he was treated with respect and deference when the mutineer shouted, "Our Chief of Staff! Make way!" [109] Equally revealing of the nature of the mutiny is the November 8 declaration of the Wilhelmshaven Sailors' Council. This enjoined the men to make even greater efforts to "maintain peace and order" and to obey the instructions of their officers, who were to be allowed to remain in possession of their weapons![110]

Having triumphed with ease in Kiel and Wilhelmshaven, it was only a matter of time before the enlisted men's rebellion spread to cities further inland, as the men fanned out in all directions in an effort to forget all about the war and to get home as quickly as possible. What is amazing, however, is the way in which "a handful of moderately well armed sailors" succeeded in removing the highest military authorities from power and toppling the governmental system of Frederick the Great and Bismarck.[111]

On November 7, for instance, a band of sailors waving red flags arrived by train in Cologne. Within a few hours they subverted a garrison of forty-five thousand men, opened all the jails, and assumed power through a Soldiers' Council. In Bielefeld a carload of ten sailors from Wilhelmshaven sufficed to take over the railroad station, to assume control over the garrison, and to seize power from the local army commander.[112]

More drastic were the events that transpired in Hanover, the seat of the powerful Tenth Army Command. On November 6 a contingent of prisoners from Kiel was brought in. Due to the overcrowded conditions of the local jail, the men were quartered in the barracks of the 73d Fusilier Regiment. When that same night a special train filled with "men on leave" from Kiel came into town, the prisoners began to mutiny. Joining up with their comrades, they took over the prisons, fraternized with the local troops, and then arrested the commanding general.[113]

The crumbling of the armed might of the Empire in Cologne, Hanover, Dresden, Frankfurt, and elsewhere was both a symptom and a cause of the total collapse of a system of government that had long ago outworn its viability. Just like the navy, the Empire was ruled by a small privileged minority that depended on the support and acquiescence of the great mass of the people. When that ruling class, like the ruling class of the navy, was discredited by the loss of the war, it was virtually inevitable that it be repudiated and overthrown. It was therefore something more than mere poetic justice that the navy, the pride of that Empire and the reflection of the outlook of its ruling groups, should precipitate—because of its *Kastengeist*, and its social and political rigidity—the revolution that swept the Empire away.

That the admirals' rebellion and the mutiny to which it gave rise was directly responsible for the German November Revolution is beyond dispute. Once the enlisted men's rebellion began striking inland, it was inevitable that the capital of the Empire also be affected. A chain reaction had been started; the final explosion could only occur in Berlin.

Fearful that an expected invasion by the rebellious sailors would cause an uprising, the military authorities of Berlin inadvertently accelerated the process they feared most. On November 6 General von Linsingen, the strong-willed military commander of the Berlin District, had machine guns erected at the main railroad station and thus succeeded in arresting a trainload of three hundred sailors before they could spread the revolt throughout the city. However, he simultaneously prohibited all socialist meetings, forbade the formation of workers' and soldiers' councils, and prohibited all newspaper coverage of the rebellion along the coast.

These measures forced the Majority Socialists, hard-pressed by the desertion of their supporters into the radical USPD, to present the government of Prince Max on November 7 with what proved to be an impossible ultimatum—the immediate relaxation of these restrictions and the abdication of the Kaiser by November 9. Unable to satisfy these demands in time, Prince Max von Baden's failure led to massive antigovernment demonstrations by the workers of Berlin. These in turn caused Philipp Scheidemann to step upon the balcony of the Reichstag and to proclaim the republic.[114] On November 9, 1918, the German Empire died an inglorious death—a death that was preceded and caused in part by the even more ignoble demise of its once-proud navy.

Notes

CHAPTER I

1. By and large, the literature treating Wilhelmine Germany has ignored the internal problems of the navy. See, for instance, Erich Eyck, *Das persönliche Regiment Wilhelms II* (Erlenbach-Zurich: Eugen Rentsch Verlag, 1948), *passim*; Golo Mann, *Deutsche Geschichte des neunzehnten und zwanzigsten Jahrhunderts* (Frankfurt: S. Fischer Verlag, 1953), *passim*; Johannes Ziekursch *Politische Geschichte des neuen deutschen Kaiserreiches*, 3 vols. (Frankfurt: Frankfurter Societäts Druckerei, 1925–30), Vol. III, *passim*; Arthur Rosenburg, *The Birth of the German Republic* New York: Russell & Russell, 1962), *passim*; William Harbutt Dawson, *The German Empire, 1867–1914*, 2 vols. (Hamden, Connecticut: Anchor Books, 1966), Vol. II, *passim*.

2. Jonathan Steinberg, *Yesterday's Deterrent. Tirpitz and the Birth of the German Battle Fleet* (London: Macdonald, 1965), p. 39.

3. Eckart Kehr, "Schachtflottenbau und Parteipolitik, 1894–1901," *Historische Studien*, No. 197 (Berlin: Ebering 1930). For a description of his alliance with the liberals and the use of "Ameri-

can" propaganda techniques, see Eyck, pp. 203–4, 260; Mann, p. 504.

4. Lothar Persius, *Menschen und Schiffe in der kaiserlichen Flotte* (Berlin: J. H. W. Dietz, 1925), p. 10.

5. Korvettenkapitän Hermann Lützow, *Die Seeoffizier-Laufbahn*, 2d ed. (Berlin: Verlag von R. Eisenschmidt, 1913), p. 2. This was a very stiff requirement by any standard. Young men whose fathers were farmers, artisans, or even retail merchants, let alone workers, were hardly ever enrolled in these regiments. See Gerhard Ritter, *Staatskunst und Kriegshandwerk. Das Problem des "Militarismus" in Deutschland*, 3 vols. (Munich: Verlag von R. Oldenbourg, 1958–64), Vol. II, pp. 128–29.

6. Korvettenkapitän G. Freiherr von Bülow, *Wie wird man Seeoffizier?* (Berlin: Ernst Siegfrieg Mittler und Sohn, 1912), pp. 7–8. See also Korvettenkapitän Karl Peter, "Seeoffizier-Anwärter-Ausbildung in Preussen/Deutschland, 1848–1945." (Manuscript: Militärgeschichtliches Forschungsamt, Freiburg im Breisgau, n.d. [1960]), p. 84, for the calculation that the cost was divided over a period of nine years and came closer to 8,000 marks. For still another estimate, consult Geheimer Rechnungsrat Bütow, *Die kaiserliche Deutsche Marine* (Berlin: Siefried Mittler und Sohn, 1880), p. 27.

7. Lützow, pp. 55–56.

8. Peter, p. 58.

9. Wahrhold Drascher, "Zur Soziologie des deutschen Seeoffiziers-korps," *Wehrwissenschaftliche Rundschau*, XII:10, 1962, pp. 559–60.

10. Max Klein (ed.), *Geschichte der Crew 1912* (Soest: Rocholsche Buchdruckerei W. Jahn, 1955), *passim*. For similar social breakdowns for other years, see Wilhelm Meisel, "Crew 1913," "Chronik Crew 1911," "Chronik Crew 1905," and "Crew Chronik 1906," all four of which are available in mimeograph form in the library of the Militärgeschichtliches Forschungsamt in Freiburg.

11. See Steinberg, p. 36, and p. 40, n. 29.

12. For this see Ritter, Vol. II, pp. 128–29. But for an apparent contradiction of his earlier position regarding the liberalism of the naval officers, see also Steinberg, p. 202: "These were the years

in which the commercial and industrial middle classes finally merged with the Prussian conservatives . . ."

13. For an excellent description of the feudalization of the German middle class, see Friedrich Meinecke, "Die geschichtlichen Ursachen der deutschen Revolution," *Deutsche Rundschau*, Vol. 45, 1919, pp. 183–84. For an analysis of this process in the army, see Gordon A. Craig, *The Politics of the Prussian Army, 1640–1945* (New York: Oxford University Press, 1964), pp. 219ff.

14. Drascher, p. 568.

15. Lothar Persius, *Der Seekrieg* (Charlottenburg: Verlag der Weltbühne, 1919), p. 66. For another description of this investigatory procedure, see Archibald Hurd and Henry Castle, *German Sea-Power. Its Rise, Progress and Economic Basis* (New York: Charles Scribner's Sons, 1913), p. 161.

16. *Das Werk des Untersuchungsausschusses der Verfassungsgebenden Deutschen Nationalversammlung und des Deutschen Reichstages 1919–1928. Vierte Reihe. Die Ursachen des Deutschen Zusammenbruches. Zweite Abteilung. Der Innere Zusammenbruch*, 12 vols., Vol. X/1, p. 80 (hereafter cited as: DWU).

17. *Ibid.*, pp. 80–84.

18. For the position of the deck officers, see Bund der Deckoffiziere, *Deckoffiziere der deutschen Marine. Ihre Geschichte 1848–1933* (Berlin: E. S. Mittler und Sohn, 1933), pp. 24, 98–99, 118. See also W. Lammertz, a former deck officer, *Die Marine von der Revolution bis zum Scapa Flow* (Duisburg: Johann Ewich Verlag, 1920), pp. 6–9, and the testimony of the founder and chairman of the Bund der Deckoffiziere, Emil Alboldt, in DWU, X/1, pp. 87–100.

19. Georg-Günther Freiherr von Forstner, *Die Marine Meuterei* (Berlin: Carl Curtius, 1919), p. 18; Korvettenkapitän Hintzmann, *Marine, Krieg und Umsturz. Der deutschen Flotte Werden, Wirken und Sterben. Ein Protest gegen Persius* (Berlin: Staatspolitischer Verlag, 1919), p. 20.

20. Adolf von Trotha, *Der Organismus der kaiserlichen Marine und der Weltkrieg* (Berlin: Reichswehrministerium, 1933), pp. 37–39.

21. Von Trotha to Admiral Scheer, *Kommando der Hochseestreitkräfte*, Fasc. 4055, PG 64724 (hereafter cited as KdH). Unless

otherwise noted, all documents cited are located at the Militärgeschichtliches Forschungsamt, Freiburg im Breisgau.

22. Kapitän Hugo von Waldeyer-Hartz, *Mannszucht bei Heer und Marine* (Berlin: Verlag von Georg Bath, 1920), p. 15.

23. KdH, Akten betreffend Gerichts-und-Disziplinar-Angelegenheiten, Bd. 5, Fasc. 862, PG 77936.

24. Lothar Persius, *Menschen und Schiffe in der kaiserlichen Flotte*, p. 59.

25. Reichs-Marine-Amt, *Denkschriften zum Immediatvortrage*, Fasc. 7165, PG 68834.

26. For this contention, see Drascher, p. 558.

27. A popular ditty commenting on this new state of affairs stated:

> Zwei Knaben zur Marine gehen,
> Sie wollten fremde Länder sehen,
> Da kamen sie zum Spotte
> Nur auf die Hochseeflotte.

> *Two boys joined the navy,*
> *To see strange lands,*
> *But to their chagrin,*
> *They merely entered the*
> *High Seas Fleet.*

Cited in Persius, *Menschen und Schiffe*, p. 124.

28. Walther Hubatsch, *Die Ära Tirpitz. Studien zur deutschen Marinepolitik 1890–1918* (Göttingen: Musterschmidt Verlag, 1955), pp. 26–27.

29. Persius, *Der Seekrieg*, pp. 14–15.

30. See Alfred von Tirpitz, *Erinnerungen* (Leipzig: Verlag von K. F. Koehler, 1919), pp. 124, 128, 130–31, for a description of the admiral's failure to prevent the intrusion into the navy of the "Prussian military spirit" and his inability to remove his officers from the evil influence of the "barracks and home coast." See also Arthur J. Marder, *From the Dreadnought to Scapa Flow: The Royal Navy in the Fisher Era, 1904–1914*, 3 vols. (London: Oxford University Press, 1961–66), Vol. I, p. 42, and Vol. II, p. 7.

31. See Hurd and Castle, p. 152, and Tirpitz, p. 127.

32. Anti-Nautikus (pseudonym for Richard Willi Sachse), *Deutschlands revolutionäre Matrosen* (Hamburg: Verlag Karl Schulzke, 1925), p. 8.
33. *Ibid.*, pp. 7–8.
34. For a discussion of the risk theory, see Steinberg, pp. 20–22 and *passim*; Kurt Assmann, *Deutsche Seestrategie in zwei Weltkriegen* (Heidelberg: Kurt Vowinkel Verlag, 1957), pp. 20–21; Hubatsch, pp. 7, 83; Eyck, 263 ff.
35. Assmann, p. 64; Marder, Vol. I, p. 431.
36. For this see Alexander Meurer, *Seekriegsgeschichte in Umrissen*, 3d edition (Leipzig: Verlag von Hase und Koehler, 1942), pp. 417–18; Assmann, pp. 23–24, 64.
37. Ritter, Vol. II, p. 201.
38. Admiral von Heeringen's statement in 1912, cited in Assmann, pp. 55–56.
39. Ritter, Vol. II, pp. 192, 202.
40. Assmann, p. 72; Hubatsch, p. 65.
41. Persius, *Der Seekrieg*, p. 24. The Kaiser's deep interest in naval affairs was not confined to merely such chance remarks. He frequently intervened personally by submitting designs of ships that were completely unseaworthy and impractical. See Tirpitz, pp. 133–34.
42. Meurer, p. 420; Tirpitz, p. 115; Hurd and Castle, p. 128; Persius, *Der Seekrieg*, pp. 16–17; Marder, Vol. I, p. 413–14.
43. See Persius, *Menschen und Schiffe*, pp. 99–100, for a description of the practice of inviting deputies on board the big ships and entertaining them lavishly in order to obtain their approval for the naval budget.
44. Ritter, Vol. II, pp. 174, 185.
45. Karl Galster, *England, deutsche Flotte und Weltkrieg* (Kiel: J. Scheible's Verlag, 1925), pp. 98ff., 104.
46. *Ibid.*, p. 124. See also Marder, Vol. III, pp. 202ff.
47. See Reinhard Scheer, *Vom Segelschiff zum U-Boot* (Leipzig: Quelle und Meyer, 1925), p. 318. Also cited in DWU, IX/1, p. 438.
48. See Galster, pp. 124, 126, 144–45. See also Ritter, Vol. III, p. 150, for the contention that the navy consistently exaggerated the number of its submarines. In 1916 the navy claimed that it had

203 submarines, while in reality only 54 were "ready for the front."
49. Galster, p. 155; Persius, *Der Seekrieg*, p. 51.
50. Hubatsch, *Die Ära*, pp. 115–16, citing Admiral Bachmann's response to a recommendation to go over to U-boat warfare.
51. For this surprising admission, see DWU, X/1, p. 128; Galster, p. 156; Lothar Persius, *Tirpitz, der Totengräber der deutschen Flotte* (Berlin: Verlag für Volksaufklärung, 1918), p. 9. See also Scheer, *Vom Segelschiff*, p. 343, for the admiral's statement, "What shall we do with so many submarines after the war?"
52. It ought to be noted that Capelle was no exception in this respect. In February 1917 Vice Admiral Kraft, the navy's Chief of Construction, went so far as to urge a cutback in submarine construction and to pressure the shipyards to eliminate fifteen submarines from Capelle's order for fifty. See DWU, X/1, p. 129.
53. Persius, *Der Seekrieg*, p. 79.
54. DWU, IX/2, pp. 258–59.
55. For this and a variation attributing Ingenohl's lack of enterprise to an English wife, see the testimony of Vice Admiral von Trotha and Seaman Richard Stumpf in DWU, IX/2, p. 86, and X/1, p. 45.
56. Anti-Nautikus, p. 10. Frequently labeled "coolies" by the civilian populace, the enlisted men were held in such low repute in Wilhelmshaven that children were wont to run after them pelting them with snow and manure. See Joachim Ringelnatz (pseudonym for Hans Bötticher), *Als Mariner im Weltkrieg* (Berlin: Karl H. Hennsel Verlag, 1955), p. 120.
57. See Bachmann to Captain von Levetzow, Levetzow Nachlass, Box 17, Bd. 3.
58. DWU, IX/2, pp. 82–86.
59. For a valuable memorandum complaining about the conduct of his officers and their rumormongering, see Admiral von Ingenohl, Überlegungen, Begründungen und Erläuterungen zum Verhalten der Hochseeflotte im ersten Kriegshalbjahr, II M 59/31, p, 31.
60. Dr. Ludwig Herz, a well-known jurist, went too far, however, when he labelled the unrest of the officers in 1915 as "the first naval mutiny." See his testimony in *Der Dolchstossprozess in München Oktober-November 1925. Eine Ehrenrettung des deut-*

schen Volkes (Munich: Verlag von G. Birk und Co., 1925), p. 308.

61. Cited in Lothar Persius, *Wie es kam dass der Anstoss zur Revolution von der Flotte ausging?* (Berlin: Arbeitsgemeinschaft für staatsbürgerliche und wirtschaftliche Bildung, n.d.), p. 14. Also cited in Ralph H. Lutz (ed.), *The Fall of the German Empire, 1914–1918*, 2 vols. (Stanford: Stanford University Press, 1932), pp. 669–70, and Tirpitz, p. 324.

62. Daniel Horn (ed.), *War, Mutiny and Revolution in the German Navy: The World War I Diary of Seaman Richard Stumpf.* (New Brunswick: Rutgers University Press, 1967), pp. 26–27, 29 (August 1914).

63. *Ibid.*, p. 50.

64. DWU, X/1, p. 4.

65. The schedule of the *Prinzregent Luitpold*, a battleship of the Third Squadron, for the week of June 18, 1917, is representative of the perpetual round of routines that by the summer of 1917 had succeeded in undermining the morale of the men.

June 18, 1917	Port of Kiel	7:00 A.M.	Cast off, ran out with squadron
	Kiel Fjord	9:47 P.M.	Anchored
June 19, 1917	Kiel Fjord	8:00 A.M.	Weighed anchor. Squadron maneuvers
		11:33 A.M.	Anchored
	Kiel Fjord	2:00 P.M.	Weighed anchor. Daylight artillery exercises
			Ran in to port
	Port of Kiel	8:12 P.M.	Tied up at Buoy 10
June 20, 1917	Kiel Fjord		Cast off. Antiaircraft firing
		11:50 A.M.	Anchored
		1:30 P.M.	Weighed anchor. Pulled targets for VIth Torpedo Boat Flotilla

		6:21 P.M.	Anchored
		11:10 P.M.	Raised anchor. Night artillery practice
June 21, 1917	Kiel Fjord	1:44 A.M.	Anchored
		9:45 A.M.	Raised anchor. Sailed out as target ship for Submarine School
		12:25 P.M.	Anchored
		1:27 P.M.	Raised anchor
		4:32 P.M.	Anchored
		10:45 P.M.	Raised anchor. Target ship for II Torpedo Half Flotilla
June 22, 1917	Kiel Fjord	12:02 A.M.	Anchored
		9:15 A.M.	Raised anchor for maneuvers in squadron formation. Ran in.
	Kiel Harbor	2:08 P.M.	Tied up at Buoy 10 Six hour alert
June 23, 1917 to June 24, 1917	Kiel Harbor		No entry

Admiralstab der Marine, Kriegstagebuch Prinzregent Luitpold. Kapitän zur See Hornhardt, Bd. 3, Fasc. 3910, PG 63351. See also a similar description for an entire squadron, Kriegstagebuch IV. Geschwader, Fasc. 3816, PG 62429.

66. Paul Behncke, *Unsere Marine im Weltkrieg und ihr Zusammenbruch* (Berlin: Karl Curtius Verlag, 1919), p. 45.
67. Werner Dette, *"Halbmast." Der deutschen Flotte Sterben. Der Geist des Offizierskorps und der Verhetzung der Mannschaft der Hochseeflotte* (Berlin: Eulenverlag, 1919), p. 9.
68. For the officers' point of view, see Hugo von Waldeyer-Hartz,

"Vom Geist der deutschen Kriegsmarine" in Friedrich Felger (ed.), *Was wir vom Weltkrieg nicht wissen* (Berlin: Wilhelm Andermann Verlag, 1929), p. 522; Marineoberpfarrer Albert Klein, "Der Zusammenbruch der Flotte von innen gesehen," in *Süddeutsche Monatshefte*, XVI:3, (March 1919), pp. 457–58.

69. Joachim Ringelnatz, p. 142.
70. Horn, pp. 82–83 (April 1915), and Stumpf's testimony in DWU, X/1, p. 44.
71. Horn, p. 75 (March 29, 1915).
72. *Ibid.*, p. 119 (August 1915).
73. Hans Kutscher, *Admiralsrebellion oder Matrosenrevolte. Der Flotteneinsatz in den letzten Tagen des Weltkrieges* (Stuttgart: Verlag von W. Kohlhammer, 1933), p. 35. Also Galster, p. 152, and Trotha in DWU, X/1, p. 22.
74. Dette, pp. 5–6; Behncke, pp. 55–56, Forstner, p. 17.
75. Horn, p. 75 (March 1915), and Stumpf's testimony in DWU, X/1, p. 45.
76. Interview with Herr Rudolf Krohne, a former naval lieutenant, in Munich, August 1965.
77. Trotha, *Der Organismus*, p. 54.
78. A. 1., Gg. XIa., Agitation der USP in der Flotte, Fasc. 3300.
79. See, for instance, the complaint by the captain of the *König Albert* that these officers "have little understanding for leadership and are too strict in certain cases while, on the other hand, fearful of reprimands, they allow many things to go unnoticed and without punishing the guilty parties." A. 1., Gg. XIa., Agitation der USP in der Flotte, Fasc. 3300.
80. For an interesting comparison of the German and English navies in this respect, see the memoirs of G. von Schoultz, *Mit der Grand Fleet im Weltkrieg* (Leipzig: K. F. Koehler Verlag, 1925), pp. 107, 360–61. Schoultz was attached to the British navy as a Russian observer.

For an account of the reform of the British navy and the extensive democratic measures introduced by Fisher and Churchill before the war, see Marder, Vol. I, pp. 28ff, 254, 267f.
81. Admiral von Trotha's testimony DWU, IX/2, p. 89.
82. Schoultz, pp. 360–62.

83. DWU, X/1, p. 108.
84. *Ibid.*, IX/2, p. 107. Stumpf claims that this did not occur until December 1915 on the *Helgoland*. See Horn, p. 148.
85. Peter, p. 93.
86. DWU, X/1, pp. 111–12.
87. See Waldeyer-Hartz, *Mannszucht*, p. 18, for the effect that being cooped up in these "iron barracks" had upon their morale.
88. See the August 7, 1917, report of Captain von Hornhardt of the *Prinzregent Luitpold*, A. 1., Gg. XIa., Agitation der USP in der Flotte, Fasc. 3300, pp. 52f.
89. See Trotha's testimony, DWU, IX/2, p. 128 for a statement of these regulations. However, see also Horn, p. 232, for Stumpf's feelings when he saw a ship run over a mine: "Why can't the *Helgoland* have such luck? Damn it, this bucket has barely left the dock and now she'll go right back. And then her crew will get leave again!"
90. Horn, p. 100 (June 1915). See also Ringelnatz, p. 119, for the reports that men could obtain an extra day of leave for every 100 gold marks they exchanged.
91. Korvettenkapitän Friedrich Forstmeier, "Zum Bild der Persönlichkeit des Admiral Reinhard Scheer (1863–1928)," *Marine Rundschau: Zeitschrift für Seewesen*, LVIII:2, (1961), p. 84.
92. Horn, p. 70 (March 1915).
93. *Ibid.*, p. 85 (April 1915).
94. Interview with Admiral Friedrich Rüge concerning his reminiscences as a young officer, Stuttgart, August 1965.
95. See Trotha, *Der Organismus*, p. 18. For a list of some of these rumors, see Alboldt's and Weber's testimony, DWU, X/1, pp. 65–68, and IX/2, pp. 295–96.
96. Erich Otto Volkmann, *Der Marxismus und das deutsche Heer im Weltkriege* (Berlin: Verlag Reimar Hobbing, 1925), p. 174.
97. Alboldt's testimony, DWU, X/1, pp. 71–72.
98. Lammertz, p. 10.
99. Anti-Nautikus, p. 9.
100. Tirpitz, *Erinnerungen*, p. 318.
101. Horn, p. 100 (June 1915).
102. *Ibid.*, p. 195 (June 1916).
103. Among the contemporary East German Communist historians

who have dealt with this subject is Hans Joachim Bernhard. See his chapter, "Die Enstehung einer revolutionären Friedensbewegung in der deutschen Hochseeflotte in Jahre 1917," in Albert Schreiner (ed.), *Revolutionäre Ereignisse und Probleme in Deutschland während der Periode der Grossen Sozialistischen Oktober-Revolutions 1917/1918* (East Berlin: Akademie Verlag, 1957).

104. Weber's testimony, DWU, IX/2, p. 303.

CHAPTER II

1. Galster, p. 121; Bernhard, p. 103.
2. Scheer, p. 318.
3. Hintzmann, p. 14.
4. Galster, pp. 33–37.
5. Horn, p. 237 (September–October 1916).
6. *Ibid.*, p. 176 (April 1916).
7. Persius, *Der Seekrieg*, p. 17.
8. Forstner, pp. 18–19.
9. Beckers' testimony in DWU, IX/2, pp. 404–5.
10. *Ibid.*, IX/1, pp. 13–14.
11. *Ibid.*, pp. 12–13, Calmus' testimony.
12. Reichs-Marine-Amt, Allerhöchste Kabinetts Ordres, Fasc. 7162, PG 68821.
13. *Ibid.* See also Reichs-Marine-Amt, Allerhöchste Kabinetts Ordres, Fasc. 7163, PG 68823, for the case of Leutnant Hapke, who was dismissed for a similar offense.
14. Reichs-Marine-Amt, Allerhöchste Kabinetts Ordres, Fasc. 7163, PG 68826.
15. Archiv der Marine: Kriegsakten, Revolution 1918 Kiel, Fasc. 1660.
16. See KdH, Akten betreffend Beschwerden, Bd. 3, Fasc. 867, PG 77956. For an attempted refutation, see DWU, IX/2, pp. 191, 192–97.
17. KdH, Akten betreffend Beschwerden, Bd. 3, Fasc. 867, PG 77956.
18. *Ibid.*
19. Ringelnatz, pp. 100–1.

20. See Admiral Scheer's secret order of October 1917, Gg 6025 B. I. in Befehlshaber der Ostseestreitkräfte, Propaganda, Fasc. 1139. Also cited in Kutscher, p. 124.

21. Ringelnatz, p. 124. But see Verein ehemaliger Matrosen der Kaiserlichen und der Reichsmarine, *War es die Marine?* (Berlin: August Scherl Verlag, 1926), p. 23, for the excuse that such things were natural and unavoidable.

22. Beckers' testimony, DWU, IX/2, p. 267.

23. Klein, p. 450.

24. Lammertz, pp. 6, 11.

25. See Lammertz, p. 10, for the embitterment of petty officers who could only rise in rank according to a rigid age schedule because of an alleged lack of funds, while the navy apparently had no trouble paying the salaries of eighty admirals.

26. Letters of Fritz Betz to Richard Stumpf, cited in DWU, IX/2, p. 168.

27. *Ibid.*, p. 259.

28. See my introduction, *War, Mutiny, and Revolution in the German Navy: The World War I Diary of Seaman Richard Stumpf.*

29. *Ibid.*, pp. 297–98.

30. See for instance the testimony of Captain Brüninghaus in DWU, IX/1, pp. 242–49, for the view that the food on the big ships was consistently good, but that it was difficult to find an "artist of a cook" who could please the tastes of a crew of 1,300 to 1,400 men.

31. KdH, Akta betreffend Verwaltungsangelegenheiten, Bd. 2, Fasc. 868, PG 77958.

32. See Nachlass Admiral Capelle, Fasc. 7635d.

33. Schramm to Capelle, *ibid.*

34. For an example of this, see Behncke, p. 46.

35. DWU, IX/1, p. 90.

36. *Ibid.*, X/1, p. 13.

37. Forstner, p. 20.

38. DWU, IX/1, p. 3; IX/2, p. 401.

39. Ringelnatz, p. 140.

40. Horn, p. 303 (March 1917).

41. Representative of this view are Adolf von Trotha, *Der Organismus*; Behncke, p. 48; Klein, p. 449. Several of these officers go so far as to claim that the stewards and lackeys often refused to eat

the food in the officers' mess because they found it much less filling than their own meals.

42. DWU, IX/2, p. 332.

43. For these figures, see von Trotha, *Der Organismus*, p. 43. Yet the admiral considered this a minimal difference. For a slightly different set of figures, see Kurt Zeisler, "Die revolutionäre Matrosenbewegung in Deutschland in Oktober/November 1918" in Albert Schreiner (ed.), *Revolutionäre Ereignisse und Probleme in Deutschland während der Periode der Grossen Sozialistischen Oktoberrevolution 1917/1918* ([East] Berlin: Akademie-Verlag, 1957), p. 189.

44. Ringelnatz, p. 147.

45. Zeisler, p. 189.

46. DWU, IX/1, p. 178. Approximately one third of the officers in in the navy stationed on small boats ate with their men.

47. Von Trotha, *Der Organismus*, p. 44.

48. DWU, IX/1, p. 14.

49. See KdH, Akta betreffend Beschwerden, Bd. 3, Fasc. 867, PG 77956 for a list of these charges as well as for Quaet Faslem's angry refutation of them as "irresponsible agitation of certain treasonable parties." Yet he admitted that he had received such provisions in his quarters, but stated that he relied on his cook's honesty to send him only his just dues. It is not altogether unreasonable to suppose that the cook, anxious to maintain his standing with the captain, did not measure too accurately and sent Faslem more than he really deserved.

50. Interview with Wilhelm Weber. Cited in Bernhard, p. 99.

51. Beckers' testimony in DWU, IX/2, p. 261.

52. *Ibid.*, p. 332.

53. Ringelnatz, pp. 296, 300–1, 304–5.

54. Scheer's order of October 7, 1917, Gg 6025 B.I. Cited in Kutscher, p. 120.

55. Cited in Heinrich Neu, *Die revolutionäre Bewegung auf der deutschen Flotte 1917–1918* (Stuttgart: Verlag von W. Kohlhammer, 1930), pp. 12–13. For a similar testimonial on the effect of boredom, see Seaman Geisteuer's statement in Verein ehemaliger Matrosen, p. 18.

56. Von Trotha's testimony, DWU, IX/1, pp. 178–79.

57. KdH, Akta betreffend Verwaltungsangelegenheiten, Bd. 2, Fasc. 868, PG 77958.
58. *Ibid.*, Scheer's order of July 29, 1917.
59. Kutscher, p. 122.
60. For Captain Hornhardt's report, see A. 1., Gg. XIa., Agitation der USP in der Flotte, Fasc. 3300.
61. *Ibid.*
62. See Brüninghaus in DWU, IX/1, p. 241.
63. Horn, p. 285.
64. KdH, Akta betreffend Beschwerden, Bd. 2, Fasc. 867, PG 77955.
65 *Ibid.*, Bd. 3, Fasc. 867, PG 77956. Even Captain Quaet Faslem concedes that this officer had an "unusually rough manner of expression."
66. Verein ehemaliger Matrosen, pp. 21–22.
67. *Ibid.*
68. KdH, Akta betreffend Beschwerden, Bd. 3, Fasc. 867, PG 77956.
69. Horn, p. 301 (March 1917).
70. For a comparison, see Schoultz, pp. 322–23, 454, and DWU, X/1, p. 76. In 1918 rations in the British navy consisted of 14 ounces of bread, 8 ounces of meat, 3 ounces of canned food, 1 ounce of butter or margarine, 2 ounces of sugar, 2 ounces of marmalade and one quarter ounce of tea per day.
71. Forstner, p. 20.
72. Behncke, p. 48.
73. Trotha, *Der Organismus*, p. 42. Instead of undertaking a thorough-going reform, the navy simply effected a slight raise in food allowances and left the old system intact.
74. See Beckers' testimony in DWU, IX/2, p. 332, for the contention that the officers began reading the Articles of War whenever the men protested.
75. *Ibid.*, IX/1, p. 421.
76. Horn, p. 262.
77. Paul von Hindenburg, *Aus meinem Leben* (Leipzig: Verlag S. Hirzel, 1920), p. 215.
78. Craig, pp. 311, 322f; Erich Ludendorff, *Meine Kriegserinnerungen, 1914–18* (Berlin: Mittler Verlag, 1919), p. 366.
79. Tirpitz, p. 286.
80. Of these remaining two thirds, one third had to be in port being

refitted while another third was on its way back to port. See Galster, pp. 144–45.

81. Fritz Fischer, *Griff nach der Weltmacht. Die Kriegszielpolitik des kaiserlichen Deutschland 1914/1918* (Düsseldorf: Droste Verlag, 1962), p. 360.

82. This result of this decision was catastrophic. It was only a question of time before it drove the United States of America into the war and unduly subordinated the civilian government of Germany to the military, thus paving the way for the establishment of the "dictatorship of Ludendorff." See Meinecke, p. 179.

83. For a good discussion of this, see Hans Gatzke, *Germany's Drive to the West. A Study of Germany's Western War Aims During the First World War* (Baltimore: Johns Hopkins Press, 1950), pp. 170–84.

84. Horn, p. 268 (November–December 1916).

85. For this see DWU, IX/1, p. 461, and Bernhard, p. 110. There is little evidence, however, to substantiate Bernhard's thesis that this contact had a revolutionary effect upon the men.

86. Stumpf's testimony, DWU, IX/1, p. 461.

87. Bernhard, p. 96, note 18.

88. Bernhard, pp. 109–110; Horn, p. 293 (February 1917). The latter found the navy's optimism "altogether outrageous."

89. For a communist viewpoint, Bernhard, pp. 101 ff., provides the best example. But see also Sachse's statement that the class-conscious German sailors and stokers knew all about the *Potemkin* Mutiny of 1905 in the Russian navy and that the outbreak of the March Revolution resulted in an upsurge of revolutionary organization and activity in the High Seas Fleet. DWU, IX/2, pp. 245, 253.

90. The military censors saw to it that the revolution did not receive undue publicity in the newspapers and that its details were not generally known. See Volkmann, *Der Marxismus*, pp. 286–87.

91. There is considerable evidence that many men, among them some of the leaders of the naval revolt of August 1917, knew very little about the actual course of the revolution and that they never regarded it as a model which they might emulate. See Weber's and Becker's testimony in DWU, IX/2, p. 334.

92. Ringelnatz, p. 194.

93. Horn, p. 324 (May 1917).
94. *Ibid.*, p. 325 (May 1917).
95. Neu, pp. 15–16.
96. Gatzke, p. 179.
97. Galster, p. 164.
98. This sort of protestation most frequently came from officers who were most active politically in clamoring for annexations and the continuation of the war. See, for example, Admiral von Trotha's testimony in DWU, IX/2, p. 126.
99. Drascher, p. 563.
100. Trotha, *Der Organismus*, p. 56.
101. Trotha's testimony, DWU, IX/2, p. 108.
102. Galster, p. 164. See also Horn, pp. 328–29 (May 1917), for Stumpf's statement that his superior had obtained the text of one of his speeches from the secretary of the highly conservative Agrarian League.
103. Cited in Gatzke, p. 217.
104. Ringelnatz, pp. 303–4.
105. Alboldt's testimony, DWU, X/1, p. 109. For a different description of the failure of this kind of instruction, see Volkmann, *Der Marxismus*, p. 171.
106. It it noteworthy that as late as 1956 Admiral Bauer, the chief of the German submarine fleet during World War I, should still rail against the July 1917 Peace Resolution. He called it "that infamous resolution" and insisted that if it had never been passed, Germany's submarines would have won the war within the prescribed six-month period. See Hermann Bauer, *Reichsleitung und U-Bootseinsatz 1914–1918* (Lipoldsberg: Klosterhaus Verlag, 1956), pp. 87, 89.
107. Albert Hopmann, *Das Kriegstagebuch eines deutschen Seeoffiziers* (Berlin: August Scherl Verlag, 1925), p. 239.
108. For a blatant admission nearly thirty years after the event, see Bauer, pp. 56–57, 81.
109. Gatzke, p. 218.
110. Stumpf's testimony in DWU, X/1, pp. 50–51. Stumpf states that he was exposed to much Pan-German propaganda, but that he did not object because he was "patriotic and anti-socialist."
111. Stumpf's testimony, *ibid.*, IX/2, p. 170.

112. Horn, p. 327.
113. *Ibid.*, pp. 329–30 (May 1917).
114. On the Vaterlandspartei, see Karl Wortmann, *Geschichte der deutschen Vaterlandspartei, 1917–1918* (Halle: Otto Hendel Druckerei, 1926).
115. Befehlshaber der Ostseestreitkräfte, Propaganda, Fasc. 1139. For excerpts, see DWU, IX/1, pp. 27f.
116. Befehlshaber der Ostseestreitkräfte, Propaganda, Fasc. 1139.
117. *Ibid.*
118. *Ibid.*
119. *Ibid.*, and DWU, IX/1, p. 29.
120. Befehlshaber der Ostseestreitkräfte, Propaganda, Fasc. 1139.
121. For this, see Dittman's statement in DWU, IX/1, p. 28.
122. *Ibid.*, X/I, p. 30; Gatzke, p. 215.
123. Kommando des Marinestation Ostsee, Sozialdemokratie, Bd. 3, Fasc. 1753, PG 91499.
124. Reichswehrministerium, Versammlungsrecht, Sozialdemokratische Propaganda, usw., Bd. 3, Fasc. 5423, Ef 928b, pp. 63–64. See also pp. 71–72 for the July 14, 1917, report of the Wilhelmshaven police chief to Admiral von Krosigk. This declared that the Majority Social Democrats in Wilhelmshaven gave no cause for concern because they kept the workers in line. On the other hand, the Independent Socialists were too weak and too few in number to stir up any trouble.
125. Admiral von Capelle was heartily disliked by the officer corps. He was regarded as a "desk man," a bureaucrat, and was called "the corporal" behind his back. See Persius, *Der Seekrieg*, p. 50.
126. DWU, IX/1, p. 30.
127. Bernhard, p. 112. Similarly, the banning of USPD newspapers by the Kiel naval station made them all the more attractive to the men. See DWU, IX/1, p. 211.
128. A. 1., Gg. XIa., Agitation der USP in der Flotte, Fasc. 3300.
129. Cited in *Illustrierte Geschichte der deutschen Revolution* (Berlin: Internationaler Arbeiter Verlag, 1928–29), p. 175. Also cited in Horn, p. 316 (April 1917).

CHAPTER III

1. Forstner, pp. 19–20.
2. See the scatching critique of these regulations in the very revealing "Excerpt from a Memorandum by Kapitän zur See [retired], Freiherr von Meerscheidt-Hüllessem," in Marinearchiv, 7741 III M 503/4.
3. Horn, p. 235 (September 1916).
4. See the testimony of Willi Sachse in KdH, Gerichtsangelegenheiten, Bd. 2, Fasc. 788, PG 77651, pp. 25ff., for the contention that this rivalry was so deep-rooted that the stokers on board the *Friedrich der Grosse* had to appoint a special liaison person to communicate with the sailors of that ship in so vital an area of common interest as the improvement of rations.
5. It is noteworthy that these were not the sentiments of some wild radical or socialist, but those of a conservative, nationalistic Catholic Centrist sailor, Richard Stumpf of the *Helgoland*. See Horn, pp. 298 (February 1917), 338 (June 1917).
6. Forstner, pp. 25–27.
7. For this, see Behncke, p. 52; Forstner, pp. 25–27; but also see Reichs-Marine-Amt, Allerhöchste Kabinetts Ordres, Fasc. 7163, PG 68824 for the text of Kaiser Wilhelm's amnesty of January 27, 1917.
8. Interview with Konteradmiral Günther Horstmann. However, also see Paul Schubert and Langhorne Gibson, *Death of a Fleet* (New York: Coward-McCann, 1932), p. 9.
9. See the report of Kapitänleutnant Herzbruch dated August 2, 1917, in A.1., Gg. XIa., Agitation der USP in der Flotte, Fasc. 3300.
10. It is noteworthy that the punishment rate for the fleet went down substantially early in 1918, when condition on the ships improved somewhat and the men at last saw action during the seizure of the Baltic islands of Dago, Moon, and Ösel from the Russians. Admiral von Trotha reports the following punishment rate for that period:

January 1918	3.5 percent
February 1918	3.9 percent

March 1918   4. percent

April 1918   2.7 percent

See DWU, IX/2, p. 128.

11. For admissions to this effect by Sachse, see his Anti-Nautikus, p. 11, and DWU, IX/2, p. 245.

12. Horn, p. 235 (September 1916).

13. KdH, Akta betreffend Verwaltungsangelegenheiten, Bd. 2, Fasc. 868, PG 77958.

14. Horn, p. 282 (January 1917).

15. For this and Sachse's unwarranted contention that this was the beginning of the revolutionary movement in the navy, see Anti-Nautikus, pp. 11–16. For an even more fanciful account, also by Sachse, according to which one of the stokers threatened an officer with a shovel, see his *Rost an Mann*, pp. 190ff.

16. Horn, p. 322 (May 1917).

17. For a listing of these expressions of antiwar sentiments, see DWU, IX/1, pp. 17–18.

18. Bernhard, pp. 108–9. See also, Beckers' testimony in DWU, IX/2, p. 274.

19. Sachse's testimony in DWU, IX/2, p. 245.

20. *Ibid.*, IX/1, p. 211; Bernhard, pp. 111–12.

21. Horn, p. 322 (May 1917).

22. KdH, Akten betreffend Beschwerden, Bd. 3, Fasc. 867, PG 77956.

23. KdH, Akten betreffend Mannschafts-Verpflegungsausschuss-Angelegenheiten, Bd. 1, Fasc. 871, PG 77970.

24. *Ibid.*, Capelle to Scheer, August 2, 1917.

25. *Ibid.* But see also DWU, IX/1, pp. 7–8.

26. KdH, Akten betreffend Mannschafts-Verpflegungsausschuss-Angelegenheiten, Bd. 1, Fasc. 871, PG 77970.

27. DWU, IX/1, p. 252.

28. KdH, Atken betreffend Mannschafts-Verpflegungsausschuss-Angeleheiten, Bd. 1, Fasc. 871, PG 77970.

29. See Bernhard, pp. 100, 102.

30. Although Sachse long maintained that a revolutionary movement had arisen in the fleet as early as 1915, he was eventually forced to admit before the Reichstag Investigating Committee that the movement lacked support until 1917, when the conditions in the

navy deteriorated. For his testimony see DWU, IX/2, p. 245, and his Anti-Nautikus, p. 11.

31. Testimony of Seaman Fritz Hoesch of *Friedrich der Grosse* in the investigation of the Zietz case on November 19, 1917, in KdH, Gerichtsangelegenheiten, Bd. 2, Fasc. 788, PG 77651, p. 156.

32. Admiral von Trotha's testimony in DWU, IX/1, p. 24, and Bernhard, pp. 97, 104.

33. Sachse reports that he and two other men began subscribing to the *Leipziger Volkszeitung* in March 1917; KdH, Gerichtsangelegenheiten, Bd. 2, Fasc. 788, PG 77651, p. 25. See also Bernhard, pp. 102–3, for the contention that these newspapers came on board the *Friedrich der Grosse* "by the bundle" in the spring of 1917.

34. KdH, Gerichtsangelegenheiten, Bd. 2, Fasc. 788, PG 77651, p. 25.

35. Bernhard, p. 105.

36. DWU, IX/1, p. 34; Anti-Nautikus, p. 32.

37. Bernhard, p. 104.

38. DWU, IX/2, p. 254.

39. *Ibid.*, p. 304.

40. Sachse's testimony in KdH, Gerichtsangelegenheiten, Bd. 2, Fasc. 788, PG 77651, pp. 25ff.

41. Reichswehrministerium: Marineleitung, Akten betreffend Flottenunruhen 1917, Fasc. 4078, PG 64923.

42. DWU, IX/1, p. 34.

43. KdH, Gerichtsangelegenheiten, Bd. 2, Fasc. 788, PG 77651, p. 18.

44. Reichswehrministerium: Marineleitung, Akten betreffend Flottenunruhen 1917, Fasc. 4078, PG 64923.

45. *Ibid.* See also DWU, IX/1, pp. 366–68, 446–47; IX/2, pp. 406–7; Emil Kloth, *Dittmanns Enthüllungsschwindel nach Eingeständnissen seiner Genossen* (Berlin: Brunnen Verlag-Karl Winkler, 1926), p. 25.

46. *Ibid.*; see also the testimony of Seaman Schneider in DWU, IX/2, p. 399.

47. See Sachse's testimony in the Zietz case; KdH, Gerichtsangelegenheiten, Bd. 2, Fasc. 788, PG 77651, pp. 25–27.

48. *Ibid.*

49. As an example, see the complaint dated July 23, 1917, which Seaman Conrad Lotter sent to his spiritual advisor, Domkapitular Leicht, who in turn forwarded it to Reichstag Deputy Dr.

Pfleger; A. 1., Gg. XIa., Agitation der USP in der Flotte, Fasc. 3300. Also cited in DWU, IX/2, pp. 38–40.

50. Horn, p. 189 (May 1916).

51. DWU, IX/1, p. 330. For a virtually identical estimation, see Behncke, pp. 56–57.

52. "Der Dolchstoss," p. 51.

53. Bauer, p. 88.

54. See Albert Röhr, *Handbuch der deutschen Marinegeschichte* (Oldenburg/Hamburg: Gerhard Stalling Verlag, 1963), pp. 101–2. For a similar opinion rendered a year earlier, see Erich Förste, "Zur Persönlichkeit von Admiral Scheer," *Marine Rundschau: Zeitschrift für Seewesen*, LIX:1, (1962), pp. 14–15.

55. Trotha, "Der Dolchstoss," p. 52.

56. See Reichpietsch's testimony in the case against Wilhelm Weber on August 10, 1917, in KdH, Gerichtsangelegenheiten, Bd. 1, Fasc. 788, PG 77650, pp. 31ff.

57. Richard Stumpf of the *Helgoland* was on leave at approximately the same time. He recorded the following impressions in his diary: "The people are so apathetic and without hope that it hurts my heart. It isn't so bad as long as the people still have the strength to vent their anger by cursing. Only when they have lost all hope and are totally depressed, do they appear as disconsolate and indifferent as they are nowadays." See Horn, p. 342 (July 1917).

58. Der Dolchstossprozess, p. 551. Testimony of Martin Gruber, the socialist editor of *Vorwärts*.

59. Kloth, p. 9.

60. For a description of this meeting, see Dittmann's testimony in DWU, IX/1, pp. 33–36, and in KdH, Gerichtsangelegenheiten, Bd. 2, Fasc. 788, PG 77651, p. 132. Consult also Reichpietsch's testimony in the case of Wilhelm Weber on August 10, 1917, for the unlikely contention that Dittmann and Zietz on that occasion informed him that the sailors were entitled to organize, to join the USPD, and that he received specific instructions to that effect from Frau Zietz. If Reichpietsch ever received such instructions, it is more likely that they were imparted to him at the second meeting he had a few days later; KdH, Gerichtsangelegenheiten, Bd. 1, Fasc. 788, PG 77650, pp. 31ff. Also of importance in this

connection is the testimony of Sachse in KdH, Gerichtsangelegen-heiten, Bd. 2, Fasc. 788, PG 77651, pp. 27f. where Sachse, too, commits the error of lumping Reichpietsch's two meetings into one.

61. Sachse's testimony in KdH, Gerichtsangelegenheiten, Bd. 1, Fasc. 788, PG 77650, pp. 15–17.

62. Reichpietsch told Sachse that she was present, but none of the other participants mention her presence; *ibid.*

63. *Ibid.*, Bd. 2, PG 77651, p. 17.

64. *Ibid.*, p. 22, Vogtherr's testimony of November 8, 1917, in the Zietz case.

65. *Ibid.*, pp. 17–19, Haase's testimony in the Zietz case.

66. For this part of the conversation, see Dittmann's testimony in DWU, IX/1, pp. 34–39. See also Dittmann's and Vogtherr's testi-mony in KdH, Gerichtsangelegenheiten, Bd. 2, Fasc. 788, PG 77651, pp. 137f., 21f.

67. DWU, IX/1, pp. 223–25.

68. *Ibid.*, p. 34.

69. Berlau, p. 147.

70. For a brilliant description of this controversy within the USPD, see Carl E. Schorske, *German Social Democracy, 1905–1917* (Cambridge: Harvard University Press, 1955), especially pp. 315–22. Also useful but dated is Eugen Prager, *Geschichte der USPD* (Berlin: Verlag "Freiheit," 1922).

71. For an example of this incorrect view, see Berlau, pp. 148–73. By failing to distinguish between the methods advocated by the mod-erates and the extreme left within that party, Berlau creates the impression that the entire party was bent on a revolutionary course.

72. See Dittmann's brilliant defense in DWU, IX/1, p. 40. He states that he and the party were opposed to all "revolutionary gym-nastic" and anything that might smack of "putsch or Komitatschi" tactics.

73. For a good but very Marxist interpretation along these lines, see Bernhard, pp. 115ff.

74. Weber's testimony in DWU, IX/2, p. 303.

75. Beckers' testimony, *ibid.*, p. 263.

76. Sachse's testimony in the Zietz case, KdH, Gerichtsangelegen-heiten, Bd. 2, Fasc. 788, PG 77651, p. 27.
77. Testimony of Seaman Kühnle in DWU, IX/1, p. 315.
78. *Ibid.*, IX/2, p. 387.
79. See Sachse's testimony in the Zietz case. KdH, Gerichtsangele-genheiten, Bd. 2, Fasc. 788, PG 77651, pp. 27–29.
80. See *ibid.*, p. 137, for Dittmann's vehement denial. But see also Reichpietsch's confession, in DWU, IX/1, pp. 302–3, for the curious admission that he could not remember if this phrase was actually used.
81. DWU, IX/1, pp. 299–300.
82. See the very judicious and balanced legal opinion of Dr. Zweigert, the Chief State Prosecutor of the Reich; cited in Reichswehr-ministerium; Marineleitung, Akten betreffend Flottenunruhen 1917, Fasc. 4078, PG 64923.

CHAPTER IV

1. Cited in DWU, IX/1, pp. 284–85. For the uncorroborated con-tention of Sachse that the men then passed a resolution in sup-port of the revolutionary sailors of Russia, see Anti-Nautikus, p. 17, Verein ehemaliger Matrosen, and *War es die Marine*, p. 75.
2. According to Herzbruch, it was von Reiche.
3. This account is drawn from Beckers' testimony in DWU, IX/2, pp. 275–80, and the official reports filed by Herzbruch on August 2 and Hornhardt on August 4 in A. 1., Gg. XIa., Agitation der USP in der Flotte, Fasc. 3300. See also Sachse's unsubstantiated claim that the *Prinzregent*'s crew refused to fire the boilers when so ordered. Anti-Nautikus, pp. 17–20.
4. DWU, IX/1, p. 2.
5. See, for example, Stumpf's revealing remark, "We are more workers than sailors." *Ibid.*, IX/2, p. 461.
6. *Ibid.*, IX/2, pp. 262–63, and IX/1, p. 4, Beckers' and Dittmann's testimony.
7. Bernhard, p. 107.
8. See, nevertheless, Wolfgang Breithaupt, *Volksvergiftung 1914–1918. Dokumente der Vorbereitung des 9. November 1918* (Ber-lin and Leipzig: K. F. Koehler Verlag, 1925), p. 92, for the claim

that this event constituted the first political success of the USPD's propaganda campaign.

9. Beckers' testimony in DWU, IX/2, 268–70.
10. The precise dates of Reichpietsch's leave have never been determined. *Oberreichsanwalt* Zweigert, the state prosecutor, states that Reichpietsch was away from June 12 to 21, 1917. Dittmann maintains the sailor was on leave between June 6 and 21, while the courtmartial sentence stipulates that his leave commenced on June 21. See DWU, XI/1, pp. 32, 211, and X/1, p. 324.
11. Beckers states that he found out about the *Menagekommission* from a Wilhelmshaven newspaper, that he had heard the name before but never realized that the men could influence it in any way. He believes that someone wrote a letter to Berlin inquiring about it. This may be his garbled way of referring to Reichpietsch's visit with the USPD. See DWU, IX/2, pp. 263–64.
12. Beckers' testimony, *Ibid.*, IX/2, p. 266.
13. *Ibid.*, p. 262.
14. For these particulars, see KdH, Akten betreffend Gerichtsangelegenheiten, Bd. 1, Fasc. 788, PG 77650, pp. 1–2, 41; DWU, IX/2, pp. 257, 356.
15. See Beckers' pretrial interrogation in KdH, Akten betreffend Gerichtsangelegenheiten, Bd. 1, Fasc. 788, PG 77650, pp. 1–2, 204–205.
16. *Ibid.*, pp. 204f.; DWU, IX/1, p. 323.
17. A. 1., Gg. XIa., Agitation der USP in der Flotte, Fasc. 3300, p. 223.
18. *Ibid.* See also Sachse's testimony in DWU, IX/2, p. 225.
19. DWU, IX/2, pp. 269–71; Neu, p. 17.
20. DWU, IX/2, pp. 4, 401; Bernhard, p. 130.
21. DWU, IX/1, p. 8; Bernhard, p. 130.
22. See, for instance, Bernhard, p. 130, n. 210.
23. Sachse's leave is generally regarded to have begun either on June 21 or 23, and it is agreed that he visited Dittmann in the Reichstag on approximately July 2. *Ibid.*, p. 120.
24. For these details about Weber, see KdH, Akten betreffend Gerichtsangelegenheiten, Bd. 1, Fasc. 788, PG 77650, pp. 104–5; DWU, IX/2, p. 297.

25. Beckers' testimony in DWU, IX/2, pp. 261–62; Bernhard, p. 135.
26. Beckers' testimony in DWU, IX/2, pp. 263–65.
27. Only on the *Posen* did the crew's strike attempt fail. Perhaps this was due to the fact that the strike, a refusal to pick up a meal of spoiled turnips, was confined to the engine room crew and lacked support of the sailors. The chief engineer of the *Posen* replied to one of the stokers, "You *Schweinehund!* You ought to be glad that you get anything at all to eat." Nevertheless, the men were apparently not punished. See DWU, IX/1, p. 5.
28. Horn, pp. 340–42 (July 1917).
29. DWU, IX/1, p. 5; IX/2, p. 266.
30. KdH, Akten betreffend Gerichtsangelegenheiten, Bd. 1, Fasc. 788, PG 77658, pp. 217–23; DWU, IX/1, p. 5; IX/2, p. 276.
31. For an expression of this view, see Admiral Scheer's report on the mutinies of October 7, 1917, Befehlshaber der Ostseestreitkräfte, Akten betreffend Propaganda, Fasc. 1139, Order Gg. 6025 B.I. The Commander of the High Seas Fleet explained that his officers failed to deal adequately with the first signs of unrest among the men which took the form of hunger strikes because they felt that these were merely the fault of the food shortage and war-weariness.
32. DWU, IX/1, p. 121.
33. See Drascher, pp. 561, 564.
34. For Lotter's letter to Domkapitular Leicht, see A. 1., Gg. XIa., Agitation der USP in der Flotte, Fasc. 330. It is also cited in DWU, IX/2, pp. 38–40.
35. DWU, IX/1, p. 120.
36. *Ibid.*, p. 16; *Der Dolchstossprozess*, p. 51; Ewald Beckmann, *Der Dolchstossprozess in München vom 19. Oktober bis 20. November 1925* (München Süddeutsche Monatshefte Verlag, 1925), p. 37.
37. For Hornhardt's report of August 7, 1917, see A. 1., Gg. XIa., Agitation der USP in der Flotte, Fasc. 330, pp. 52–53.
38. Philipp Schneidemann, *Der Zusammenbruch* (Berlin: Verlag für Sozialwissenschaft, 1921), p. 115.
39. See Dittmann's testimony in DWU, IX/1, pp. 24–25, 205.
40. See, for instance, Reichpietsch's testimony of August 10, 1917, in the case against Weber. On that occasion he stated that he regarded it as his mission to recruit supporters for the USPD in the

navy but admitted that he did not recall that Dittmann of Frau Zietz had ever "in so many words" urged him to compile such lists. KdH, Akten betreffend Gerichtsangelegenheiten, Bd. 1, Fasc. 788, PG. 77650.

See also the testimony of Obermatrose Georg Schmidt of the *Friedrich der Grosse* for the statement that Reichpietsch made no mention of these lists right after his return but that he came up with this idea later and that it was never entirely clear whether this was his own idea or that of the deputies. DWU, X/1, p. 308.

On the other hand, Weber and Sachse were under the impression that Reichpietsch had received instructions to draw up membership lists. See Weber's testimony, *ibid.*, p. 312.

As usual, Sachse's testimony is contradictory. He stated on November 17, 1917, that he had implicit faith in the accuracy of Reichpietsch's description of his conversation with the deputies, while on November 11 he maintained that he felt that Reichpietsch had not discussed these lists in Berlin. See KdH, Akten betreffend Gerichtsangelegenheiten, Bd. 2, Fasc. 788, PG 77651, pp. 102 ff., and 29.

Oberheizer Louis Bräuner tells still another story. According to him the initiative came from Reichpietsch. Reichpietsch told him that he had convinced the deputies that the enlisted men should stage a general strike at the end of the Stockholm conference. At first, the deputies did not want to "bite" at this for they considered it too dangerous, but he had managed to persuade them to give him a "wink" upon which the men would "throw down everything."

41. For the Peace Resolution, its origins and effects, see Arthur Rosenberg, *The Birth of the German Republic* (New York: Russell and Russell, Inc., 1962), pp. 153ff., and Ralph H. Lutz, "The July, 1917 Crisis in Germany," *Proceedings of the Pacific Coast Branch of the American Historical Association*, Vol. V (1930), pp. 87–98.

42. It was not realized at that time that Michaelis had qualified his acceptance of that Peace Resolution by his phrase, "as I interpret it," and that this was to undermine the entire resolution.

43. Paradoxically, the Independent Socialists, because they mistrusted all bourgeois politicians and governments, had not voted in favor

of the Peace Resolution. However, it was well known that they strongly supported any sincere effort to obtain an early peace.

44. DWU, IX/1, p. 25.
45. *Ibid.*, pp. 23–24.
46. *Ibid.*
47. For an expression of this view by Dittmann, see *ibid.*, pp. 31–32, and IX/2, p. 366.
48. Neu, p. 26.
49. *Ibid.*, p. 23.
50. See DWU, IX/1, pp. 303f. and 204 f., for Reichpietsch's secret correspondence. For the various ruses employed by him and his like-minded comrades, see pp. 146, 226ff., 299, 304f. However, see also Dr. Zweigert's legal opinion refuting Neu's charges of treason, *ibid.*, pp. 226–27.
51. With the exception of some minor variation in detail, Sachse's and Dittmann's versions of the meeting coincide. See KdH, Akten betreffend Gerichtsangelegenheiten, Bd. 1, Fasc. 788, PG 77650, pp. 5–7, and DWU, IX/1, pp. 34–35, 206; IX/2, pp. 236–38.
52. DWU, IX/2, p. 273; Bernhard, pp. 121–22.
53. See Sachse's testimony in KdH, Akten betreffend Gerichtsangelegenheiten, Bd. 2, Fasc. 788, PG 77651, pp. 29–30.
54. Bernhard, p. 125.
55. Sachse's testimony, KdH, Akten betreffend Gerichtsangelegenheiten, Bd. 2, Fasc. 788, PG 77651, pp. 29–30.
56. For this see the testimony of Sachse and Sens, *ibid.*, pp. 102ff. It should, however, be noted that Sens testified that he could not recollect this conversation and admitted only that he had received a letter from Dittmann stating that he trusted Reichpietsch and that he was to be supplied with propaganda material.
57. KdH, Akten betreffend Gerichtsangelegenheiten, Bd. 1, Fasc. 788, PG 77650, pp. 31ff.
58. See KdH, Akten betreffend Gerichtsangelegenheiten, Bd. 2, Fasc. 788, PG 77651, p. 103; Bernhard, p. 131.
59. *Ibid.*, Vol. II, p. 32, and Vol. I, pp. 26–30. See also DWU, IX/1, pp. 243, 245, 305–6.
60. See Reichsbund Deutscher Seegeltung, *War es die Marine?* (Berlin: Montanus und Weuster Verlag, 1940), p. 24, for the estimate that a maximum of eight percent of the enlisted men belonged

to the movement. See also Verein ehemaliger Matrosen, *War es die Marine?* p. 14, for the contention that the movement numbered 5,000 men out of a total of 65,000, thus amounting to a mere seven percent.

61. See the police report of Oberwachmeister Labohm, dated August 7, 1917, in KdH, Akten betreffend Gerichtsangelegenheiten, Bd. 1, Fasc. 788, PG 77650, p. 4.
62. Reichswehrministerium; Marineleitung, Akten betreffend Flottenunruhen 1917, Fasc. 4078, PG 64923. See also DWU, IX/1, p. 9, for an admission by naval counsellor Dr. Loesch that this was true but that Bieber was nevertheless sentenced to prison.
63. DWU, IX/2, p. 402.
64. KdH, Akten betreffend Gerichtsangelegenheiten, Bd. 1, Fasc. 788, PG 77650, pp. 39–40.
65. *Ibid.*, pp. 21–22.
66. See for instance Sachse's contemptuous observation to this effect in DWU, IX/2, p. 225.
67. For Beckers' testimony see *ibid.*, pp. 271–72.
68. *Ibid.*, pp. 272–73.
69. Adolf von Trotha, "Der Dolchstoss auf der Flotte," *Süddeutsche Monatshefte*, XXI:7, (April 1924), p. 52.
70. Volkmann, *Der Marxismus*, p. 180.
71. For a good compedium of this speech, see Neu, pp. 22–23.
72. See Weber's testimony in DWU, IX/2, pp. 291–92 and 328–29.
73. See Sachse's testimony on November 11, 1917, in KdH, Akten betreffend Gerichtsangelegenheiten, Bd. 2, Fasc. 788, PG 77651, p. 29.
74. See Reichswehrministerium, Marineleitung, Akten betreffend Flottenunruhen 1917, Fasc. 4078, PG 64923.
75. DWU, IX/2, pp. 270–71.
76. Sachse's testimony in KdH, Akten betreffend Gerichtsangelegenheiten, Bd. 2, Fasc. 788, PG 77651, pp. 30ff.
77. DWU, IX/1, p. 286; Neu, p. 25.
78. KdH, Akten betreffend Gerichtsangelegenheiten, Bd. 1, Fasc. 788, PG 77650.
79. *Ibid.*
80. See, for instance, the anonyomus *Illustrierte Geschichte der deutschen Revolution*, especially p. 158.

81. See his testimony in DWU, IX/2, pp. 246–48. For a complete refutation of such claims, see the testimony of Beckers and Beckers in DWU, IX/2, pp. 304, 335.

82. See for instance Bernhard, p. 110, who bases his entire argument to this effect on a single interview with a former dockworker by the name of Karl Krake.

83. Neu, p. 31.

84. Seaman Richard Stumpf of the *Helgoland*, who had no connection with either the movement or the USPD, provides an extremely valuable and an almost clinical description of the state of mind prevailing in the navy that drove the men into the opposition. In his diary he wrote: "High state of excitement caused by a total lack of confidence in the officers. Persistence of the fixed notion that the war is conducted and prolonged solely in the interests of the officers. Manifestation of bitter anger due to the fact that the enlisted men are starving and suffering while the officers carouse and roll in money." See Horn, p. 346 (July–August 1917).

85. For descriptions of the events on *Prinzregent Luitpold* from July 31 to August 1, see Beckers' testimony in DWU, IX/2, pp. 275–80, and Captain von Hornhardt's report in A. 1., Gg. IXa., Agitation der USP in der Flotte, Fasc. 3300.

86. For a detailed description, see in this book, p. 149.

87. Alboldt's testimony. DWU, X/1, p. 135.

88. *Ibid.*, p. 136.

89. *Ibid.* See also p. 52 for Stumpf's testimony. The sailor states that the officers would have been content if the strikers had been punished with fourteen days' imprisonment and that they "were stunned upon hearing of the injustice [*Unheil*] that the naval counsellors had wrought."

90. See the testimony of a prominent legal witness, Dr. Ludwig Herz, in *Der Dolchstoss-Prozess*, pp. 308–9, 312.

91. A. 1., Gg. XIa., Agitation der USP in der Flotte, Fasc. 3300.

92. KdH, Akten betreffend Gerichtsangelegenheiten, Bd. 1, Fasc. 788, PG 77650, pp. 1–2.

CHAPTER V

1. Beckers' testimony. DWU, IX/2, p. 280.
2. See Befehlshaber der Ostseestreitkräfte, Propaganda, Fasc. 1139.
3. S.M.S. *Ostfriesland*, Politisches, Fasc. 1685, PG 92141.
4. Befehlshaber der Ostseestreitkräfte, Propaganda, Fasc. 1139.
5. See Kommando des IV. Geschwader to Kommandatur Wilhelmshaven: Reichswehrministerium, Versammlungsrecht, Sozialistische Propaganda usw. Bd. 3, Fasc. 5423, Ef 928b, p. 94.
6. See Kriegstagebuch S.M.S. *Deutschland*, Fasc. 1668, PG 91933.
7. See Beckers' testimony in DWU, IX/2, pp. 281–82. Beckers also insists that he was interrogated in this manner, not once as Dobring and his transcript would seem to indicate, but six or seven times. This unnerved him to such an extent that he could no longer sleep.
8. For the text of Beckers' interrogation, see KdH, Akten betreffend Gerichtsangelegenheiten, Bd. 1, Fasc. 788, PG 77650, pp. 1ff.
9. Sache's testimony in DWU, IX/2, p. 252.
10. For this and Sachse's statement that the prisoners were allowed to communicate with each other and even managed to maintain contact with the outside world through guards who acted as messengers, see Anti-Nautikus, p. 22.
11. See Sachse's confession of August 8, 1917, in KdH, Akten betreffend Gerichtsangelegenheiten, Bd. 1, Fasc. 788, PG 77650, pp. 24–26. See also DWU, IX/2, p. 249, for allusions to the plan to blow up the ship and to commit other "acts of terror and sabotage."
12. Stenographer Steinmeier's testimony in DWU, IX/1, p. 287.
13. Dobring's testimony, *ibid.*, IX/2, p. 345.
14. Stenographer Steinmeier's testimony, *ibid.*, IX/1, p. 552.
15. For Sachse's confession of August 9 and this version of the program, see KdH, Akten betreffend Gerichtsangelegenheiten, Bd. 1, Fasc. 788, PG 77650, pp. 26–30. See also Beckers' testimony in DWU, IX/2, p. 284.
16. DWU, IX/2, pp. 223–24.
17. KdH, Akten betreffend Gerichtsangelegenheiten, Bd. I, Fasc. 788, PG 77650, pp. 26ff.

18. DWU, IX/1, p. 491.
19. See *ibid.*, IX/2, pp. 368–70, for the debate between Dittmann and Dobring on this disputed point.
20. *Ibid.*, IX/1, p. 553.
21. *Ibid.* But see also the transcript of Reichpietsch's interrogation on August 13, which records the appearance of Sachse. KdH, Akten betreffend Gerichtsangelegenheiten, Bd. 1, Fasc. 788, PG 77650, pp. 5ff.
22. For a detailed description of Calmus's confession and its repercussions, see pp. 176–82, this book.
23. See Reichsanwalt Doctor Zweigert's legal opinion, DWU, IX/1, pp. 217–19.
24. For Becker's confession of August 16, see KdH, Akten betreffend Gerichtsangelegenheiten, Bd. 1, Fasc. 788, PG 77650, pp. 41–46.
25. *Ibid.*, pp. 51ff.; DWU, X/1, p. 301.
26. Beckers' testimony, DWU, IX/2, p. 405.
27. *Ibid.*, pp. 293f., 299ff.
28. Undated letter of Linke to Stumpf, *ibid.*, p. 468. Linke also maintained that Dr. Loesch regarded the investigation as a wonderful opportunity to add the Iron Cross to the Bavarian Order he already held.
29. John Ulrich Schroeder, *Im Morgenlichte der deutschen Revolution* (Hamburg: Konrad Hanf-Verlag, 1921), p. 8.
30. See Rebe's interrogation and confession in KdH, Akten betreffend Gerichtsangelegenheiten, Bd. 1, Fasc. 788, PG 77650, pp. 493–94, 499–500, 503–4. See also DWU, IX/1, p. 49.
31. For Rebe's appeal of October 19, 1917, and corroboration by a number of witnesses that he had spoken out only about the deplorable condition of Moltke's stokers, who were "dropping like flies from malnutrition," see KdH, Akten betreffend Gerichtsangelegenheiten, Bd. 1, Fasc. 788, PG 77650, pp. 508 ff.
32. Cited in DWU, IX/1, p. 50.
33. For the denials of Dobring and the interrogation stenographers, see *ibid.*, IX/2, pp. 343–44, and IX/1, 529–61. The stenographers' statements plainly indicate, however, that they completely identified with the officer corps and must therefore be regarded as prejudiced witnesses. Dittmann, for instance, was able to prove

that Stenographer Nöckel, who had participated in the Rebe case, testified on Dobring's behalf before the Reichstag Investigating Committee because the latter had promised to help him find a position in civilian life. *Ibid.*, IX/2, pp. 377–78.

34. *Ibid.*, p. 554.

35. Weber's testimony, *ibid.*, pp. 360–61.

36. Beckers' testimony, *ibid.*, p. 335.

37. Thus at one meeting one of their leaders proposed that all complaints be forwarded to the *Prinzregent Luitpold*, that the men try to gain control over their rations, and that they ought to strive to make the saluting of officers voluntary.

38. Cited in the October 20, 1917, arraignment against the *Westfalen* crew. KdH, Akten betreffend Gerichtsangelegenheiten, Bd. 1, Fasc. 788, PG 77650, pp. 271–95.

39. See the statements of Captain Brüninghaus in DWU, IX/2, pp. 268–70. See also the admission of Oberleutnant Beyer in the court-martial proceedings against the *Westfalen* crew. KdH, Akten betreffend Gerichtsangelegenheiten, Bd. 1, Fasc. 788, PG 77650, pp. 376f.

40. See Haase's testimony at his court martial, *ibid.*, p. 350.

41. *Ibid.*, pp. 353, 366.

42. Dittmann's statement in DWU, IX/2, pp. 55–56.

43. In addition to Adams, at least four other spies and agents were employed on the *Westfalen*. These were the enlisted men Pretsch, Paillart, Gross, and Zapp. KdH, Akten betreffend Gerichtsangelegenheiten, Bd. 1, Fasc. 788, Pg. 77650, pp. 156–58, 306, 332–33, 387.

44. *Ibid.*, pp. 306ff.

45. For testimony to this effect by Oberleutnant Beyer and Detective Hager of the criminal police, see *ibid.*, pp. 128 and 107. Also see Befehlshaber der Ostseestreitkräfte, Propaganda, Fasc. 1139. For a brief account of Adams' involvement with his officers and the police, consult DWU, IX/2, pp. 54–55.

46. For the text of Scheer's order, Gg. 6025 B.I., see Befehlshaber der Ostseestreitkräfte, Propaganda, Fasc. 1139. Also cited in Kutscher, pp. 119–26.

47. Befehlshaber der Ostseestreitkräfte, Propaganda, Fasc. 1139.

48. KdH, Akten betreffrend Gerichtsangelegenheiten, Bd. 1, Fasc. 788, Pg. 77650, p. 197.
49. *Ibid.*, p. 203, and S.M.S. *Ostfriesland* Politisches, Fasc. 1685, PG 924141.
50. Anti-Nautikus, p. 28.
51. DWU, IX/2, p. 286.
52. Logically these records should be included in the Naval Archive at the Militärgeschichtliches Forschungsamt at Freiburg im Breisgau under the provenance KdH, Akten betreffend Gerichtsangelegenheiten, Bd. 1 or Bd. 2. However, the court-martial records of Reichpietsch, Sachse, Weber, Beckers, and Köbis are not to be found there. Nor are they to be located at the Bundesarchiv-Zentralnachweisstelle Kornelimünster or at the Staatsanwaltschaft bei dem Landgericht in Flensburg. Drs. Deist and Sandhofer, *Archivräte* at Freiburg, believe that this material was probably removed from the files by either the navy or the National Socialist regime. The archivist at Kornelimünster expressed the view that they may have been destroyed during the course of World War II.
53. For the proceedings in this case, see KdH, Akten betreffend Gerichtsangelegenheiten, Bd. 1, Fasc. 788, PG 77650, pp. 210–16.
54. DWU, IX/2, p. 51.
55. KdH, Akten betreffend Gerichtsangelegenheiten, Bd. 1, Fasc. 788, PG 77650, pp. 332–37. It is significant to note that two other men, Driesen and Fritz, took the opportunity at this trial to join the chorus of complaints about their interrogation. Both claimed that they were so confused and nervous that they did not know what they said. *Ibid.*, pp. 339, 375.
56. *Ibid.*, p. 337.
57. For the court-martial proceedings of February 21, 1918, see Reichswehrministerium: Marineleitung, Akten betreffend Flottenunruhen 1917, Fasc. 4078, PG 64923.
58. *Ibid.*
59. For this as well as for most of the other legal issues raised by the court-martial, consult the very valuable article by Ludwig Herz, "Die Marinemeuterei von 1917: Eine juristische Betrachtung," *Die Justiz*, Bd. 1, Heft 6, pp. 600ff.

60. For Sachse's letter and Dr. Zweigert's legal opinion that it raised very "considerable doubt" about his credibility, see DWU, IX/1. pp. 369, 217.
61. Herz, p. 600.
62. *Neue Zeitung*, November 3, 1925; cited in Herz, p. 600.
63. *Ibid.*, p. 601.
64. For Dittmann's statement, see DWU, IX/2, p. 458.
65. See *ibid.*, IX/1, p. 102, for the comment of Dr. Holthöfer of the Reich Ministry of Justice, who stated, "I believe that even the naval justice officials who conducted the investigation had no precise knowledge of the official program of the USPD."
66. *Ibid.*, pp. 86–88.
67. Herz, p. 613.
68. See Dobring's testimony in *Der Dolchstoss-Prozess*, p. 64. For a similar excuse, see Verein ehemaliger Matrosen, p. 95.
69. Herz, pp. 602–3.
70. *Ibid.*
71. Schroeder, p. 7.
72. Reichswehrministerium: Marineleitung, Akten betreffend Flottenunruhen 1917, Fasc. 4078, PG 64923.
73. *Ibid.* Also cited in DWU, IX/1, p. 82.
74. For an analysis by Dr. Felisch that makes the same point, see DWU, IX/7, 82–83.
75. For this, see the text of the sentence handed down on August 28, 1917. KdH, Akten betreffend Gerichtsangelegenheiten, Bd. 1, Fasc. 788, PG 77650, p. 208.
76. Dr. Felisch wrote: "On the basis of the facts that have been established to date, the court cannot rule that the prerequisites of these two articles have been met since an 'actual rebellion' has not broken out. Therefore it may only consider a penalty for attempt." DWU, IX/1, p. 71, and Herz, pp. 607–8.
77. Cited in Herz, p. 607. For a similar opinion, see Schroeder, p. 6.
78. Schroeder, p. 7.
79. Cited in two slightly different versions in DWU, IX/1, pp. 72–73, 317–19.
80. Forstmeier, pp. 83, 91.
81. For the expression regarding death sentences, see Georg Alexander von Müller, *Regierte der Kaiser?* (Göttingen: Musterschmidt-

Verlag, 1959), p. 313. See also Scheer, *Vom Segelschiff*, pp. 348–49.

82. DWU, IX/2, p. 336.

83. See Weber's plea for mercy, dated August 28, 1917. Reichswehr-ministerium: Marineleitung, Akten betreffend Flottenunruhen 1917, Fasc. 4078, PG 64923.

84. *Ibid.*

85. *Ibid.* Also DWU, IX/1, p. 82.

86. Herz, pp. 608, 610.

87. Forstmeier, p. 84.

88. For this see Herz, pp. 611, 613.

89. DWU, IX/1, pp. 77–78.

90. For Breil's and Meurer's excuses, see KdH, Akten betreffend Gerichtsangelegenheiten, Bd. 2, Fasc. 788, PG 77651, pp. 47–50.

91. Reichswehrministerium: Marineleitung, Akten betreffend Flottenunruhen 1917, Fasc. 4078, PG 64923.

92. DWU, IX/1, p. 76. See also *Illustrierte Geschichte*, p. 159, for the not very plausible contention that the navy could not find any firing squad closer to Wilhelmshaven than Cologne that was willing to carry out this execution.

93. See Capelle's memorandum of November 25, 1917, attempting to answer these charges. Reichswehrministerium: Marineleitung, Akten betreffend Flottenunruhen 1917, Fasc. 4078, PG 64923.

94. *Ibid.*

CHAPTER VI

1. DWU, IX/1, p. 85.

2. Von Müller, p. 313.

3. Scheer, *Vom Segelschiff*, p. 348.

4. See Reichbund Deutscher Seegeltung, *War es die Marine?*, p. 23.

5. DWU, IX/1, p. 86.

6. *Ibid.*, p. 80.

7. For an analysis of Michaelis' political position, see Rosenberg, *The Birth of the German Republic*, pp. 198–99; Gatzke, pp. 214f., 235f.; Von Müller, p. 324.

8. Leo Stern (ed.), *Archivalische Forschungen zur Geschichte der deutschen Arbeiterbegung. Die Auswirkungen der Grossen Sozial-*

istischen Oktoberrevolution, 4 vols. (Berlin: Institut für Geschichte der deutschen Akademie der Wissenschaft zu Berlin, Rütten und Loening, 1959), Vol. II, pp. 646–50. Hereafter cited as *Archivalische Forschungen*. See also DWU, IX/1, pp. 89–90.

9. See the letter of complaint by Haase to Michaelis on August 20 in which the deputy objected to the government's discriminatory practices against the USPD and to the illegality of the raid. Reichswehrministerium: Marineleitung, Akten betreffend Flottenunruhen 1917, Fasc. 4078, PG 64923, pp. 86–87.

10. A. 1., Gg. XIa., Agitation der USP in der Flotte, Fasc. 3300, p. 142.

11. Reichswehrministerium: Marineleitung, Akten betreffend Versammlungsrecht, Sozialistische Propaganda, usw, Fasc. 5423, Ef928b, pp. 142–44.

12. For the minutes of this meeting held at the Chancellery, see Reichswehrministerium: Marineleitung, Akten betreffend Flottenunruhen 1917, Fasc. 4078, PG 64923, pp. 2–7. For a briefer version, see DWU, IX/1, p. 88.

13. For the minutes of this meeting as well as a meeting with Deputies Noske and Pfleger on August 26 in which Capelle denied the existence of any abuses in the fleet, see Reichswehrministerium; Marineleitung. Akten betreffend Flottenunruhen 1917, Fasc. 4078, PG 64923, pp. 14–23, 43–45.

14. *Ibid.*, pp. 25–39. See also DWU, IX/1, p. 89.

15. Waldeyer-Hartz, *Vom Geist*, p. 523.

16. See DWU, IX/1, pp. 90, 93–94.

17. *Ibid.*, p. 86; *Archivalische Forschungen*, 4/II, p. 697.

18. Capelle to Prince Henry on September 10, 1917. Befehlshaber der Ostseestreitkräfte, Akten betreffend Propaganda, Fasc. 1139.

19. See interpolation of Antrick *et al.*, *Verhandlungen des Reichstages*, XIII. Legislaturperiode, II. Session, Bd. CCCX, *Stenographische Berichte*, pp. 3713ff. Hereafter cited as *Stenographische Berichte*.

20. For a good description, see Karl Helfferich, *Der Weltkrieg*, 3 vols. (Berlin: Ullstein Verlag, 1919), Vol. III, pp. 187ff.

21. Neu, pp. 43–44.

22. DWU, IX/1, p. 78.

23. *Stenographische Berichte*, CCCX, pp. 3769–70.

24. KdH, Akten betreffend Gerichtsangelegenheiten, Bd. 1, Fasc. 788, PG 77650, p. 254.

25. Testimony of Obermaat Feuersänger of *Rheinland* in DWU, IX/1, p. 534.

26. According to Seaman Stumpf's diary, Sachse's strategem of confessing what the navy wanted to hear was widely known in the fleet. See Horn, pp. 362–63.

27. For this "confession," see the court-martial transcript as well as a shorter summary version taken by Fregattenkapitän Graudecker in KdH, Akten betreffend Gerichtsangelegenheiten, Bd. 1, Fasc. 788, PG 77650, pp. 453–57, 258ff.

28. See Geier's affidavit in DWU, IX/1, p. 536.

29. *Ibid.*, p. 540.

30. *Ibid.*, p. 498.

31. Reichswehrministerium: Marineleitung, Akten betreffend Flottenunruhen 1917, Fasc. 4078, PG 64923.

32. See, for instance, the absurd ease with which Dittmann refuted the charges against him during the investigation of the Zietz case; KdH, Akten betreffend Gerichtsangelegenheiten, Bd. 2, Fasc. 788, PG 77651, p. 136.

33. KdH, Akten betreffend Gerichtsangelegenheiten, Bd. 1, Fasc. 788, PG 77650, pp. 461–62.

34. See Brüninghaus' testimony in DWU, IX/1, pp. 262–63.

35. *Stenographische Berichte*, CCCX, pp. 3770–71.

36. Helfferich, Michaelis' Vice Chancellor, states that he had not been informed of the change in plans and was greatly surprised by the chancellor's deviation from his original speech. See Helfferich, Vol. III, p. 197.

37. For an attempt to protect Capelle from this charge of incompetent haste, see Captain Brüninghaus' testimony in DWU, IX/1, pp. 262–63. The captain denies that his superior was influenced in any way by the Calmus confession or the fear of incurring the displeasure of the officer corps and the Kaiser. He asserts that Capelle acted only on the basis of a "most serious concern" for the maintenance of the fighting effectiveness of the fleet. If this were true, Capelle would hardly have acted so precipitously. In

all probability he would have attempted to refute Dittmann in the secrecy of the Reichstag's Main Committee, or if he insisted on publicly discrediting the Independents, he would most certainly have obtained the prior sanction of the Reichstag leaders instead of subjecting them to this painful surprise.

For a similar effort, see also Neu, p. 48. The rightist historian argues that Capelle could not have been influenced by the confession, otherwise he would surely have drawn attention to Ledebour as well as Dittman in his Reichstag speech. Neu fails to realize, however, that it would have been folly for Capelle to disclose the uncorroborated and laconic telegram by Loesch. It simply did not supply enough information to level such specific charges. Consequently, Capelle probably hoped to keep it in reserve for later use and to help him substantiate the general charges he was about to make.

38. *Stenographische Berichte*, CCCX, p. 3773; Georg Michaelis, *Für Staat und Volk* (Berlin: Furche-Verlag, 1922), p. 363.
39. *Stenographische Berichte*, CCCX, pp. 3774–75. According to the later excuse of the chancellor, Capelle had not really intended to imply active participation on the part of the deputies, but merely their moral guilt. See Michaelis, pp. 363–64.

Captain Boy-Ed of the navy press department, however, saw the situation differently. Writing to Prince Henry on October 12, he maintained that Capelle had committed his blunder because he had been "hypnotized by the documents." This was, of course, correct. But then Boy-Ed could not know that the document in question was not Reichpietsch's or Sachse's confession, but rather Loesch's telegram regarding the Calmus "movie novel." See Befehlshaber der Ostseestreitkräfte, Akten betreffend Politisches, Fasc. 1139.

40. *Stenographische Berichte*, CCCV, pp. 3775–76.
41. *Ibid.*, pp. 3785–88.
42. *Ibid.*, pp. 3789–95.
43. *Ibid.*, p. 3794.
44. *Ibid.*, pp. 3799, 3804.
45. Helfferich, Vol. III, pp. 196–97.
46. Michaelis, pp. 363–65.

47. Befehlshaber der Ostseestreitkräfte, Akten betreffend Propaganda, Fasc. 1139.
48. Von Müller, p. 326.
49. DWU, IX/1, p. 101.
50. *Ibid.*, IX/2, pp. 371–72.
51. Neu, p. 51. Paradoxically, the major reason why none of the charges against Frau Zietz could be substantiated, in the words of Dr. Zweigert, was that "the principal witness in the case, Seaman Reichpietsch, is dead." See Reichswehrministerium: Marineleitung, Akten betreffend Flottenunruhen 1917, Fasc. 4078, PG 64923.
52. See Persius, *Der Seekrieg*, pp. 52–53.
53. One example is a black-bordered card inscribed as follows: "Comrades! / Remember our brothers who were shot by a court-martial in Stepember, / Remember the Sailors Reichpietsch and Sachse. / They died for our freedom, their blood cries for revenge. / Remember Liebknecht! / Down with the War! / Down with the government!"

    Writing from Switzerland, Karl Radek immortalized "the martyrdom of Seaman Reichnitz [*sic*]" in the *Züricher Volksrecht* of October 17, 1917, when he labeled him the victim "of the flunkies of German imperialism," called him "a fighting pioneer of the German Revolution," and gave him an honored place among the ranks of "the holy martyrs of the Russian working class."

    In January 1918 an illegal Spartacist pamphlet entitled "Follow Their Example" called upon the German workers to emulate the deeds of "sailors Reichpietsch and Cöbes" (*sic*) and called them "the true heroes of the German proletariat."

    See Reichswehrministerium: Marineleitung, Akten betreffend Flottenunruhen 1917, Fasc. 4078, PG 64923. Also Ernst Drahn and Susanne Leonhard, *Unterirdische Literatur im revolutionären Deutschland während des Weltkrieges* (Berlin: Verlag Gesellschaft und Erziehung, 1920), pp. 95–96.
54. Kloth, p. 49, and Dobring's testimony in Beckmann, p. 62.
55. Waldeyer-Hartz, p. 524.
56. See Eberhard von Mantey, *Unsere Kriegsmarine: Vom Grossen*

Kurfürsten bis zur Gegenwart (Berlin: "Offene Worte," 1934), p. 309, for an expression of this view.

57. See his testimony in DWU, IX/2, pp. 122–23, 146/47; Beckmann, pp. 39, 98. For an endorsement by Captain Brüninghaus, see DWU, IX/2, p. 135.
58. Förste, pp. 15–16.
59. A. 1., Gg. XIa., Agitation der USP in der Flotte, Fasc. 3300, p. 76.
60. KdH, Akten betreffend Mannschafts-Verpflegungsausschuss-Angelegenheiten, Bd. 1, Fasc. 871, PG 77970.
61. A. 1., Gg. XIa., Agitation der USP in der Flotte, Fasc. 3300, p. 162.
62. *Ibid.*, p. 160.
63. For these as well as very similar reports from the First and the Third Squadrons, see KdH, Akten betreffend Gerichts-und-Disziplinarangelegenheiten, Bd. 5, Fasc. 862, PG 77936.
64. *Ibid.* But see also a more pessimistic and realistic appraisal by the Admiralty declaring "that individual attempts at incitement" were likely to continue and that the widespread dissatisfaction in the enlisted ranks plus the prospect of inactivity would make it impossible for the rebellious mood to vanish all at once. Admiralstab der Marine, Akten betreffend Immediatvorträge, Bd. 30, Fasc. 2022, PG 65983, pp. 120–21.
65. For the text of the order, see Befehlshaber der Ostseestreitkräfte, Akten betreffend Propaganda, Fasc. 1139, or S.M.S. *Ostfriesland*, Akten betreffend Politisches, Fasc. 1685, PG 92141. Also cited in full in Kutscher, pp. 119–26.
66. See, for instance, Forstner, pp. 24–25.
67. Horn, p. 354.
68. Ringelnatz, p. 340; Horn, p. 351.
69. On August 31, 1917, Admiral von Capelle indicated that plentiful rations would now become available and declared that he had the "highest expectation that the current difficulties will be surmounted by the navy." KdH, Akta betreffend Verwaltungs-Angelegenheiten, Bd. 2, Fasc. 868, PG 77598.
70. Horn, pp. 351, 355. Also DWU, X/1, p. 53.
71. See his testimony in DWU, X/1, pp. 51–52.

72. Levetzow Nachlass, Box 4, Bd. 10.
73. Kutscher, p. 40.
74. S.M.S. *Ostfriesland*, Akten betreffend Politisches, Fasc. 1685, PG 92141.
75. See A. 1., Gg. XIa., Agitation der USP in der Flotte, Fasc. 3300, p. 353.
76. *Ibid.*, p. 390.
77. S.M.S. *Ostfriesland*, Akten betreffend Politisches, Fasc. 1685, PG 92141.
78. A. 1., Gg. XIa., Agitation der USP in der Flotte, Fasc. 3300, p. 422.
79. For an order of November 7, 1917, to this effect, see S.M.S. *Ostfriesland* Akten betreffend Politisches, Fasc. 1685, PG 92141.
80. *Ibid.*, order Gg. 8462 dated November 27, 1917. See also A. 1., Gg. XIa., Agitation der USP in der Flotte, Fasc. 3300, p. 269.
81. A. 1., Gg. XIa., Agitation der USP in der Flotte, Fasc. 3300, p. 200; Befehlshaber der Ostseestreitkrafte, Akten betreffend Propaganda, Fasc. 1139.
82. A. 1., Gg. XIa., Agitation der USP in der Flotte, Fasc. 3300, p. 201.
83. S.M.S. *Ostfriesland*, Akten betreffend Politisches, Fasc. 1685, PG 92141. So persistent were these rumors that the story of the death of the *Seydlitz's* captain is still heard in naval circles today.
84. These were the *Volkszeitung* of Düsseldorf; *Tribune* of Erfurt; *Reusschische Tribüne* of Gera; *Generalanzeiger für Gotha*, *Volksblatt für Halle, Leipziger Volkszeitung, Norhäuser Volkszeitung, Bergische Arbeiterstimme* of Soligen; *The Volksbote* of Zeitz; *Volkszeitung für Muldenthal*, the *Mitteilungsblatt* of Berlin; *Pirnaer Volkszeitung, Remscheider Arbeiterzeitung, Reusschische Volkszeitung*, and *Der Sozialdemokrat* of Stuttgart. See Kutscher, pp. 40–41.
85. See this book pp. 59–64.
86. See Scheer's order of November 12, 1917, in Reichswehrministerium, Akten betreffend Versammlungsrecht, Sozialdemokratische Propaganda, Flugschriften, Plakate, Staatsfeindliche Organizationed, Streiks, Bd. 3, Fasc. 5473, Ef 928b, p. 169.
87. Kommando der Marinestation Ostsee, Akten betreffend Sozialdemokratie, Bd. 3, Fasc. 1573, PG 91499.

88. See Reichswehrministerium, Akten betreffend Versammlungs-recht, Sozialdemokratische Propaganda, usw., Bd. 3, Fasc. 5423, Ef 928b, p. 321.

89. Kommanda der Marinestation der Ostsee, Akten betreffend Sozialdemokratie, Bd. 3, Fasc. 1573, PG 91499.

90. Reichswehrministerium, Akten betreffend Versammlungsrecht, Sozialdemokratische Propaganda, usw., Bd. 2, Fasc. 5473, Ef 928a, p. 338.

91. Ringelnatz, p. 344.

92. DWU, X/1, pp. 333–34. For a similar tract, see also Drahn and Leonhard, pp. 87–88.

93. Reichswehrministerium, Akten betreffend Versammlungsrecht, Sozialdemokratische Propaganda, usw., Bd. 2, Fasc. 5473, Ef 928a, p. 41.

94. Not even naval officers were exempt from the suspicion of harboring revolutionary designs. In June 1918 Leutnant Blinne was accused of advocating the conclusion of a "Bolshevik piece" by means of a revolution and a general strike. See Reichs-Marine-Amt, Allerhöchste Kabinetts Ordres, Fasc. 7164, PG 68829.

95. Reichswehrministerium, Akten betreffend Versammlungsrecht, Sozialdemokratische Propaganda, usw., Bd. 3, Fasc. 5423, Ef 928b, p. 220.

96. See Reichswehrministerium, Akten betreffend Sabotage, Fasc. 5473, Ef 929.

97. See Archiv der Marine: Kriegsakten, Revolution 1918 Kiel, Fasc. 1660.

98. KdH, Akten betreffend Beschwerden, Bd. 3, Fasc. 867, PG 77956. See also Kurt Zeisler, "Die revolutionäre Matrosenbewegung in Deutschland im Oktober/November 1918" in Revolutionäre Ereignisse und Probleme in Deutschland während der Periode der Grossen Oktoberrevolution 1917/1918. Ed. by Albert Schreiner (Berlin: Akademie Verlag, 1957), p. 790.

99. For the "egg episode," see the reports of January 29, 1918, and February 1 and 4, 1918, in KdH, Akten betreffend Gerichtsangelegenheiten, Bd. 2, Fasc. 788, PG 77651, pp. 114, 115, 119.

100. Ibid., pp. 163–69.

101. DWU, IX/1, p. 415.

102. See Alboldt's testimony in DWU, X/1, pp. 158–60.

103. See Deputy Struve's memorandum of November 4, 1918, in Conrad Haussmann Nachlass, Württembergisches Staatsarchiv, Stuttgart, Bd. 21.

104. See Küsel's report of April 16, 1918, in Archiv der Marine: Kriegsakten, Revolution 1918 Kiel, Fasc. 1660.

105. See Struve's November 4, 1918, report in Conrad Haussmann Nachlass, Bd. 21.

106. DWU, X/1, p. 166.

107. *Ibid.*, pp. 185–86. For a similar case against Kapitänleutnant Schultz of the *Cöln*, who was accused of deserting his post, being drunk while on duty, leaving his ship to pick up a woman of ill repute who entertained him and several friends on board the ship, see KdH, Akten betreffend Gerichts-und-Disziplinarangelegenheiten, Bd. 6, Fasc. 863, PG 77937.

108. See Struve's November 4, 1918, memorandum in Conrad Haussmann Nachlass, Bd. 21.

109. There is no reliable numerical estimate of communist or Spartacist infiltration in the navy. Without a doubt the General Staff estimate of April 14, 1918—that one third of the enlisted men supported these groups—and that of the East German historian Kurt Zeisler were vastly exaggerated. Until the very end, the crews lacked concrete political orientation. However, see *Archivalische Forschungen*, 4/III, p. 1291; Zeisler, p. 188.

110. As early as April 1918 Admiral Küsel had reported that the enlisted men unanimously agreed with the current ditty, "*Gleiche Löhnung, gleiches Essen, und der Krieg wär längst vergessen!*" (Equal pay and equal rations and the war would long be over.) See Küsel's report in Archiv der Marine: Kriegsakten, Revolution 1918 Kiel, Fasc. 1660. The ditty is also cited in Drahn and Leonhard, p. 109.

CHAPTER VII

1. Scholars owe a debt of gratitude to Wilhelm Dittmann for his pioneering work and for being the first to charge the navy with having staged an admirals' rebellion in October 1918. See his six-hour speech before the Reichstag Investigating Committee, DWU, IX/1, pp. 2–124, or his *Die Marine-Justiz-Morde von 1917*

und die Admiralsrebellion von 1918 (Berlin: J. H. W. Dietz, 1926).

For attempts to repudiate Dittmann's thesis, Neu and Kutscher are still the best. Paradoxically, the communists have never shown much interest in this problem, largely because they have taken it for granted that the officers were responsible. For example, see Zeisler, p. 193 and *passim*; *Illustrierte Geschichte, passim*.

2. To date the contents of the former naval archive in respect to this problem have been studied only by Dr. Wilhelm Deist, of the Militärgeschichtliches Forschungsamt in Freiburg im Breisgau, and me. During the summer of 1965 we arrived simultaneously at the conclusions set forth below. See Wilhelm Deist, "Die Politik der Seekriegsleitung und die Rebellion der Flotte Ende Oktober 1918," in *Vierteljahrshefte für Zeitgeschichte*, XIV:4, (October 1966), pp. 341–68.

   As its title implies, Deist's work is principally an examination of the policies of the *Seekriegsleitung*, while my objective is to describe the causes of this revolt in terms of the culminating effect of a variety of social and political forces that had been at work in the navy since the outbreak of the war.

3. Von Müller, p. 399; Deist, pp. 344–45.

4. See Levetzow to Scheer, July 7, 1918, Levetzow Nachlass, Box 17, Bd. 3.

5. The analogy is Levetzow's. See Von Müller, p. 412.

6. *Ibid.*, p. 437.

7. Levetzow to Göring, December 1, 1931, Levetzow Nachlass, Box 16, Bd. 3.

8. Levetzow to Class on February 4, 1926, and May 22, 1926. *Ibid.*, Box 6, Bd. 21, 22.

9. In 1924 Erich Kuttner, one of the editors of the socialist *Vorwärts*, published an article entitled "The Death Ride of the German Fleet," charging the navy with having planned a suicide mission at the end of the war. The *Süddeutsche Monatshefte*, an extreme right-wing periodical, turned to Levetzow to publish a rebuttal. See *Süddeutsche Monatshefte* to Levetzow, June 25, 1924, Levetzow Nachlass, Box 5, Bd. 16. He had come to the magazine's attention when he wrote his defamatory article, "Der letzte Akt," which he wanted published before the elections so as to

conduct "a truly great and energetic propaganda campaign" against the democratic parties. See Levetzow to *Süddeutsche Monatshefte*, March 31, 1924, Levetzow Nachlass, Box 5, Bd. 15. From that point on, the magazine and Levetzow conducted a joint campaign that saw to it that the proponents of the Stab-in-the-Back Legend did not contradict each other. "We do not want to create disunity about the Dolchstoss," wrote *Süddeutsche* to Levetzow on May 2, 1924; Levetzow Nachlass, Box 5, Bd. 16. Levetzow marshaled the forces of the right and bore a large responsibility for the conduct of the navy's case in Munich. See, for example, Trotha to Levetzow, September 22, 1925, and Levetzow to Deck Officers Schrecke and Friedrich on October 23 and 25, 1925; Levetzow Nachlass, Box 5, Bd. 19.

10. See *Der Dolchstoss-Prozess*, pp. 71–73.
11. See his testimony in DWU, X/1, pp. 25–26.
12. Kutscher, pp. 13–14.
13. The *Seekriegsleitung* had admitted as much to the Kaiser on September 22. See Levetzow Nachlass, Box 21, Bd. 1.
14. Deist, pp. 346–47.
15. Kriegstagebruch der Seekriegsleitung, Stichworte zu den stattgehabten Besprechungen des Chefs des Admiralstabes, Fasc. 4055, PG 64726. See also Magnus von Levetzow, "Der letzte Akt," in *Süddeutsche Monatshefte*, XXI:7, (April 1924), p. 54.
16. For these developments see Kriegstagebuch der Seekriegsleitung, Stichworte zu den stattgehabten Besprechungen des Chefs des Admiralstabes, Fasc. 4055, PG 64726; Levetzow, "Der letzte Akt," pp. 60–66; Prinz Max von Baden, *Erinnerungen und Dokumente* (Berlin: Deutsche Verlags-Anstalt, 1928), pp. 438–39, 459, 464–69; Kutscher, pp. 18–24.

For the governmental and political meetings that discussed this issue, see Erich Matthias and Rudolf Morsey (eds.), *Quellen des Parlamentarismus und der politischen Parteien*. Erste Reihe, Bd. 2, *Die Regierung des Prinzen Max von Baden* (Düsseldorf: Droste Verlag, 1962), pp. 220ff.

17. Prinz Max, pp. 471–72, 499–504.
18. Deist, p. 351.
19. *Ibid.*, p. 352.
20. See Levetzow Nachlass, Box 4, Bd. 9. See also Michaelis' letter

of March 10, 1926, to Professor Hans Delbrück stating that he felt that Germany could have won because the British could not have declined to give battle and because the submarines would have given Germany a decisive edge over the enemy. Bernhard Schwertfeger Nachlass, Bundesarchiv Koblenz, Nr. 124, pp. 1–3.

21. Levetzow Nachlass, Box 4, Bd. 9, and Box 17, Bd. 3. Also cited in Deist, pp. 352–53.

22. Deist, p. 354.

23. Levetzow Nachlass, Box 18, Bd. 1.

24. Levetzow to Trotha, August 18, 1924, *ibid.*, Box 6, Bd. 17.

25. See Kriegstagebuch der Seekriegsleitung, Stichworte zu stattgehabten Besprechungen des Chefs des Admiralstabes, Fasc. 4055, PG 64726. Also Levetzow Nachlass, Box 21, Bd. 3.

26. Kriegstagebuch der Seekriegsleitung, Stichworte zu stattgehabten Besprechungen des Chefs des Admiralstabes, Fasc. 4055, PG 64726. Levetzow, "Der letzte Akt," pp. 59–60; Deist, p. 355.

27. Not being a mind reader, Wilhelm II raised no objections to this inoccuous proposal, thus giving Scheer what he considered a general approval. See Kriegstagebuch der Seekriegsleitung, Stichworte zu stattgehabten Besprechungen des Chefs des Admiralstabes, Fasc. 4055, PG. 64726. See also Scheer, *Vom Segelschiff*, p. 355.

28. Kriegstagebuch der Seekriegsleitung, Stichworte zu stattgehabten Besprechungen des Chefs des Admiralstabes, Fasc. 4055, PG 64726; Levetzow Nachlass, Box 22, Bd. 2; Scheer, *Vom Segelschiff*, p. 356.

29. Levetzow Nachlass, Box 6, Bd. 27. But see also Erich Eyck, *A History of the Weimar Republic*, 2 vols. (Cambridge, Massachusetts: Harvard University Press, 1962), Vol. I, p. 41, for the view that this argument is completely "unconvincing" and "spurious."

30. See Reinhard Scheer, "Das Märchen von der Admiralsrebellion" in *Allgemeine Thüringische Landeszeitung*, May 22, 1926, included in Levetzow Nachlass, Box 25, Bd. 2. Scheer asserted that if Prince Max was of the opinion that a naval mission would disrupt his diplomatic efforts for an armistice he should have notified the *Seekriegsleitung* to that effect. "On his own volition the

chancellor could and should have made the demand that the fleet was to refrain from any major undertaking if he deemed that necessary for any political reason. He was informed that it would remain active and would not disgrace its freedom of movement by lying idly in port."

For supporting echoes of this illogical view, see Aldolf von Trotha, "Zum Flottenvorstoss 1918," in *Preussische Jahrbücher*, CCIX (1927), pp. 108–9; Captain Brüninghaus' testimony in DWU, IX/1, pp. 196, 346–347; Kloth, p. 52; Kutcher, p. 81.

31. It was certainly no accident that the only person in whom Scheer confided was General Ludendorff who, at this point, was also bent on preserving the honor of the army at whatever cost to the state. This occurred on October 22, when Scheer told the general that "before the fleet became an object of trade in a dishonorable peace it would be necessary to throw it into battle." Ludendorff promptly gave his approval. See Levetzow Nachlass, Box 22, Bd. 2.

32. In his memoirs, however, Prince Max indicates that he might have approved even a "suicide mission" if it had been staged at the proper moment, when the confidence of the German people in President Wilson had been shattered by his "impossible armistice terms." See Prinz Max, pp. 574–75.

33. Forstmeier, pp. 89–90.

34. Kriegstagebuch der Seekriegsleitung, Stichworte zu stattgehabten Besprechungen des Chefs des Admiralstabes, Fasc. 4055, PG 64726; Levetzow Nachlass, Box 21, Bd. 3.

35. See Levetzow Nachlass, Box 22, Bd. 2.

36. Levetzow Nachlass, Box 22, Bd. 1; Levetzow, "Der letzte Akt," p. 69.

37. Scheer, *Vom Segelschiff*, p. 387.

38. See his "Das Märchen von der Admiralsrebellion," in *Allgemeine Thüringische Landeszeitung*, May 22, 1926, Levetzow Nachlass, Box 25, Bd. 2. For a similar argument, see Joachim Lehment, *Kriegsmarine und politische Führung* (Berlin: Junker und Dünnhaupt, 1937), p. 79.

39. Strangely enough, Rosenberg, usually so astute and perceptive, falls into Scheer's trap and argues that the *Seekriegsleitung* was

not bound by these changes of the constitution. This can only be explained by the fact that Rosenberg had no knowledge of the background and real motivation for the *Flottenvorstoss*. See Arthur Rosenberg, *The Birth of the German Republic*, p. 265. For a more recent version of the same argument, see A. J. Ryder, *The German Revolution of 1918* (Cambridge: Cambridge University Press, 1967), p. 140.

40. See his testimony in DWU, pp. 197–98.

41. Upon giving Scheer his reluctant consent to form the *Seekriegsleitung* on August 11, 1918, Wilhelm II had made it a special point to caution the admiral, "However, do not imagine that you are now completely in charge [*dass Sie nun alles zu regieren haben*], I am still here." See Levetzow to Trotha on August 16, 1918. Levetzow Nachlass, Box 18, Bd. 11.

42. For this vitally important order, see Akten des Kaiserlichen Marinekabinets, betreffend allgemeine Erwägungen, Bd. 3, Fasc. 3580, PG 68124.

43. See Dittmann in DWU, IX/1, p. 435.

44. See *ibid.*, IX/1, pp. 109–10, for Dittmann's statement: "This was rebellion, open mutiny; it was treason against the constitutional government and at the same time treason against the state." For an identical view, see Erich Kuttner's charge in *Der Dolchstoss-Prozess*, p. 114.

45. The report by Captain Gladisch that he visited Prince Max on November 1 and informed him of the *Flottenvorstoss* without engendering any outraged response by the chancellor, who was at that time in bed with the grippe, does not make much sense. Max would have had to be delirious not to have reacted strongly when he heard of the navy's deception. See Gladisch's affidavit in DWU, Vol. IV, pp. 342–44. See also Prinz Max, p. 574, for the denial: ". . . Even after Hipper had abandoned the attack I was not informed. I first learned the truth and extent of the planned naval action long after the revolution." See also Deist, p. 357, for the statement that Gladisch's report is probably apocryphal.

46. See Levetzow Nachlass, Box 21, Bd. 4; also Deist, p. 367.

47. See Prinz Max, p. 572.

48. *Ibid.*, pp. 573–74. See also Kutscher, pp. 106–7, for the assertion

that this did not constitute deception, but something much more harmless, a *Verschleierung* (concealment).

49. Cited in Prinz Max, pp. 572–73; DWU, IX/1, p. 439.

50. See for this, Erich Kuttner, "Von Kiel bis Berlin" in *Handbuch der Politik. Der Weltkrieg*, edited by Gerhard Anschütz et al. (Berlin and Leipzig: Dr. Walter Rothschild, 1920), p. 262. See also Kuttner's testimony in *Der Dolstoss-Prozess*, p. 57, and in DWU, IX/1, p. 470. For a similar account by the chief editor of *Vorwärts*, see Friedrich Stampfer, *Der 9. November. Gedenkblätter zu seiner Wiederkehr* (Berlin: Buchhandlung Vorwärts, 1919), p. 20.

51. For the view that the *Flottenvorstoss* had aimed at relieving the Western Front, see Trotha, DWU, X/1, p. 6; Behncke, p. 58; Forstner, p. 5; Rosenberg, *The Birth of the German Republic*, p. 264; S. William Halperin, *Germany Tried Democracy* (New York: W. W. Norton, 1965), pp. 84–85.

For the opinion that Kuhl's assertion was "ridiculous," see Dr. Bergstraesser in DWU, IX/1, pp. 194–95, and 476–77.

52. For this see Prinz Max, p. 574; Friedrich von Payer to Dr. Ludwig Herz on January 13, 1926, in DWU, VI, p. 245; Hans Delbrück's and Gustav Noske's testimony in *Der Dolchstoss-Prozess*, pp. 287, 117.

53. Nottweg to Levetzow, February 5, 1925, Levetzow Nachlass, Box 5, Bd. 18.

54. For these optimistic views, see Scheer, *Vom Segelschiff*, p. 357; Brüninghaus' testimony in DWU, IX/1, p. 345; Trotha's and Fregattenkapitän Hintzmann's testimony in Beckmann, pp. 41–42, 64. For a summation of all these views, see Kutscher, pp. 95–101.

55. Delbrück's testimony in *Der Dolchstoss-Prozess*, p. 284.

56. See Vice Admiral Galster, "Das Einsetzen der Hochseeflotte im Oktober 1918," in DWU, X/1, pp. 357–68, and Viktor Bredt, Schlusswort zu den Ausführungen des Vizeadmirals a.D. von Trotha," in *Preussische Jahrbücher*, CCIX (1927), pp. 110–12.

57. See Alboldt in DWU, X/1, pp. 188–89; Zeisler, p. 192.

58. See Levetzow Nachlass, Box 4, Bd. 9; also cited in Deist, pp. 347–48.

59. Deist, p. 348.

60. See Scheer's order Gg. 2654 B.I. in S.M.S. *Ostfriesland*, Akten betreffend Politisches, Fasc. 1685, PG 92141.
61. *Ibid.*
62. See the report by Dr. Sturker, the Police President of Hamburg, in Reichswehrministerium, Akten betreffend Versammlungsrecht, Sozialdemokratische Propaganda, usw., Bd. 3, Fasc. 5473, Ef 928.
63. *Ibid.*
64. See S.M.S. *Ostfriesland*, Akten betreffend Politisches, Fasc. 1685, PG 92141.
65. *Ibid.*, Order Gg. 1187 A.III of October 12, 1918.
66. *Ibid.* Even after the first disturbances had already broken out on the ships at Wilhelmshaven Roads, reports of a probable uprising continued to come in. On October 30 Dr. Dobring informed the Naval Secretary that an uprising was scheduled to take place in Wilhelmshaven at 10 P.M. on November 5. See Reichswehrministerium, Akten betreffend Versammlungsrecht, Sozialdemokratische Propaganda, usw., Bd. 3, Fasc. 5473, Ef. 928.
67. "Admiral von Trotha answers the question with an unqualified affirmative and presents his operational plan." Levetzow Nachlass, Box 21, Bd. 3.

   Trotha was not alone in misrepresenting the mood of the fleet. Sometime in October 1918 Captain Brüninghaus blithely told a Reichstag Committee that the morale of the crews was "still the same as during the Battle of Jutland." See DWU, IX/1, p. 182.
68. Trotha, "Zum Flottenvorstoss," p. 109.
69. Deist, pp. 360–61.
70. *Ibid.*, p. 361.
71. See Struve's November 4, 1918, report in Haussmann Nachlass, Bd. 21.
72. See Meinecke, p. 181; Alboldt's testimony in DWU, X/1, pp. 195–96.
73. Prinz Max, pp. 492–94, 509; Rosenberg, *The Birth of the German Republic*, pp. 262–63.
74. *Der Dolchstoss-Prozess*, p. 70; Beckmann, p. 91.
75. Stumpf's diary entry of October 5, 1918, in Horn, p. 410.
76. *Ibid.*
77. See Noske's testimony in *Der Dolchstoss-Prozess*, p. 176.
78. See Trotha in DWU, IX/1, p. 186; Max Foss, *Enthüllungen*

über der Zummenbruch (Halle: Richard Müllman Verlagsbuchhandlung, 1919), pp. 28–29; Kutscher, p. 75.

79. See the testimony of Rear Admiral Heinrich in Beckmann, p. 62,
and *Der Dolchstoss-Prozess*, p. 69.

80. Albrecht von Thaer, *Generalstabsdienst an der Front und in der
OHL* (Göttingen: Vandenhoek und Rupprecht, 1958), pp. 271–
72.

81. For admissions to this effect, see Neu, p. 58; Volkmann, *Der
Marxismus*, pp. 216–17.

82. See Admiral Meurer's entry of October 26 in the squadron log-
book. Admiralstab der Marine, Kriegstagebuch des IV. Geschwader, Bd. 2a, Fasc. 3816, PG 62428.

83. Zeisler, p. 183.

84. Deist, p. 361.

85. See Stumpf's and Alboldt's testimony in DWU, X/1, p. 55, 197.
Also Dette, p. 4.

86. Even Karl Artelt, who was soon to rise to prominence as leader
of the revolutionary forces in Kiel, maintains that he got wind of
the mission through rumors "that the fleet was to fight a battle
of desperation from which in all probability no one would return." See his affidavit in DWU, IX/2, pp. 579–81, as well as his
"Mit der roten Fahne zum Vizeadmiral Souchon," in Institut für
Marxismus-Leninismus beim Zentralkomitee der Sozialistischen
Einheitspartei Deutschlands, *Vorwärts und nichts Vergessen.
Erlebnisberichte aktiver Teilnehmer der Novemberrevolution
1918/1919* (Berlin: Dietz Verlag, 1958), p. 91.

87. DWU, IX/1, p. 113.

88. *Ibid.*, pp. 112–13.

89. Testimony of Seaman Raumschüssel and John, *ibid.*, pp. 114, 117.

90. Kutscher, p. 74.

91. Cited in Kuttner, *Von Kiel bis Berlin*, p. 12, and *Illustrierte Geschichte*, p. 185. However, see also Forstner, pp. 6–7, for admission that while it was true that some of the younger officers
may have spoken this way, the men should have disregarded them
because they spoke without authorization.

92. See, for instance, Behncke, pp. 59–60, for the assertion that the
crews acted in the belief that "they had to protect the government from the Pan-German *Machenschaften* of the officers."

93. Korvettenkapitän Otto Weddigen, *Erlebnisse der Kreuzers "Strassburg" vom 27. Oktober bis 27. November 1918* (Stettin: Stettiner Druckerei, 1918), p. 5.

94. Zeisler, pp. 194–95.

95. Kutscher, pp. 54–55.

96. *Ibid.*, pp. 56–58; Zeisler, p. 195. For a very brief description of events at Wilhelmshaven, see David Woodward, "Mutiny at Wilhelmshaven, 1918" in *History Today* XVIII:11 (November 1968), pp. 779–85.

97. See the report of Korvettenkapitän Yorck of November 1 to the *Seekriegsleitung*; Levetzow Nachlass, Box 21, Bd. 4.

98. *Ibid.*

99. Kutscher, pp. 63–65.

100. See Korvettenkapitän Yorck's report, Levetzow Nachlass, Box 21, Bd. 4.

101. *Ibid.* See also Kutscher, pp. 66–67; Neu, 60–61; Zeisler, 195.

102. Trotha's testimony in DWU, IX/1, pp. 485–86. This same Admiral Kraft in 1917 had proven himself a failure as Chief of the Submarine Construction Department.

103. Korvettenkapitän Yorck's report, Levetzow Nachlass, Box 21, Bd. 4.

104. Kutscher, p. 68.

105. See IM 44/2 Militärgeschichtliches Forschungsamt, Kriegstagebuch der VII. Torpedobootsdivision 16.2.17–31.10.18, for the order to lay alongside the *Thüringen* and *Helgoland*.

106. For this, in addition to Korvettenkapitän Yorck's report in Levetzow Nachlass, Box 21, Bd. 4, see Kutscher, pp. 68–70; Volkmann, *Revolution über Deutschland* (Oldenburg: Gerhard Stalling, 1930), pp. 16–17; Zeisler, p. 196; Fikentscher, p. 28. See also A. A. Hoehling, *The Great War at Sea: A History of Naval Action 1914–1918* (New York: Thomas Y. Crowell, 1965), pp. 268–69, for an account based on the reminiscences of Admiral Friedrich Ruge, then a young lieutenant.

107. Zeisler, p. 197.

108. Trotha's testimony in DWU, IX/2, p. 163; Neu, p. 61; Kutscher, pp. 65–66.

109. Johannes Spiess, *Sechs Jahre U-Bootfahrten* (Berlin: E. Steiniger, 1925), pp. 200–1.

110. See Levetzow Nachlass, Box 21, Bd. 4.
111. Albert Röhr, Handbuch der deutschen Marinegeschichte (Oldenburg/Hamburg: Gerhard Stalling Verlag, 1963), p. 104.
112. Hipper to Scheer, November 2, 1918; Levetzow Nachlass, Box 21, Bd. 4.
113. For an account of this entire series of meetings, see Levetzow Nachlass, Box 21, Bd. 4.
114. Trotha's testimony in Beckmann, p. 43.
115. See Oberpfarrer Albert Klein, pp. 452–53.
116. Levetzow to Admiral Eberhardt Schmidt, May 16, 1928; Levetzow Nachlass, Box 6, Bd. 30.
117. See A. 1., Gg. XIa., Agitation der USP in der Flotte, Fasc. 3300, pp. 493–95. Also cited in DWU, X/1, pp. 206–10.
118. For a small sample of this view, see Scheer, *Vom Segelschiff*, pp. 357–58; Scheer, "Warum der Krieg verloren ging," p. 419; Mantey, p. 339; Forstner, p. 7; Behncke, p. 60; Hintzmann, pp. 23–24; Lammertz, p. 16; Waldeyer-Hartz, *Vom Geist*, p. 527; Röhr, p. 104.
119. Reichs-Marine-Amt, Akten betreffend Streike, Aufruhrbewegungen, Sozialpolitik. Heft 2, "Bericht über die Verhandlungen des Reichsmarineamts mit den Vertrauensleuten des III. Geschwaders am Donnerstag, den 7. November, nachmittag 3 Uhr.
120. Fikentscher, p. 23; Rosenberg, *The Birth of the German Republic*, p. 266.
121. See the testimony of Seaman Käppel in DWU, IX/1, pp. 116–17.
122. Reichs-Marine-Amt, Akten betreffend Streike, Aufruhrbewegungen, Sozialpolitik. Heft 2, Bericht über die Verhandlungen des Reichsmarineamts mit den Vertrauensleuten des III. Geschwaders.
123. *Ibid.*
124. For an excellent example of this tactic, see Zeisler, pp. 196–98 and *passim.*
125. *Illustrierte Geschichte*, p. 185; Zeisler, pp. 192, 198.
126. Arthur Rosenberg, *A History of the German Republic* (London, Methuen and Company, 1936), p. 8; Eyck, *A History of the Weimar Republic*, Vol. I, p. 42.

CHAPTER VIII

1. Scheer, *Vom Segelschiff*, p. 358.
2. For a list of these accusations and documentation for the attempt on the part of young naval officers to refute them in order to obtain employment with patriotic firms that refused to hire them, see "Aufruf zu Beiträgen zur Geschichte der 'Revolution in der Marine!" I M 15, p. 2, Militärgeschichtliches Forschungsamt in Freiburg dated March 15, 1919.
3. Reichs-Marine-Amt, Akten betreffend Streike, Aufruhrbewegungen, Sozialpolitik, Heft 2; Trotha's testimony in DWU, IX/1, p. 486; Neu, pp. 62–63; Zeisler, p. 199.
4. Unfortunately there is no good study of Souchon. The biography by Mäkelä is much too apologetic and is virtually useless for this crucial stage of the admiral's career. See Matti E. Mäkelä, *Souchon der Göbenadmiral greift in die Weltgeschichte ein*. (Braunschweig: Friedrich Vieweg, 1936), p. 188. See also Müller, p. 396.
5. See Lammertz, p. 17; Ludwig, p. 59; Halperin, p. 86; Persius, *Der Seekrieg*, p. 71; Neu, p. 62; as well as *Kieler Neueste Nachrichten*, October 31, 1918, for a joyous announcement of Souchon's appointment.
6. See Souchon to *Seekriegsleitung*, November 3, 1918, in Akten des Kaiserlichen-Marine-Kabinetts betreffend Kriegsgerichten, Bd. 24, Fasc. 3579, PG 68131. Also Lothar Popp and Karl Artelt, *Ursprung und Entwicklung der November-Revolution 1918* (Kiel: Verlag Hermann Behrens, 1918), p. 10; Artelt, p. 91; Rausch, 12; Zeisler, pp. 199–200; Neu, 63.
7. See *Schleswig-Holsteinische Volkszeitung*: November 4, 1918.
8. Ludwig, p. 60.
9. See the reports of November 16 and November 24, 1917, in Kommando der Marinestation Ostsee, Akten betreffend Sozialdemokratie, Bd. 3, Fasc. 1573, PG 91499.
10. Popp and Artelt, p. 11; Artelt, p. 89.
11. See pp. 193–94 this book, and Zeisler, p. 200.
12. For a description of these events, see Souchon to *Seekriegsleitung* on November 3, 1918. Akten des Kaiserlichen-Marine-Kabinetts, betreffend Kriegsgerichte, Bd. 24, Fasc. 3579, PG 68121; Popp and

Artelt, p. 11; Artelt, 91; Rausch, p. 12; Breithaupt, p. 135; Volkmann, *Revolution*, pp. 21–23.

13. For this see Popp and Artelt, pp. 11–12; Rausch, pp. 12–13. But see also Souchon's report to the *Seekriegsleitung* on November 3, in which he concealed these signs of solidarity by explaining that he had been unable to apprehend the demonstrators because they had evaded his patrols in the dark. Akten des Kaiserlichen-Marine-Kabinetts, betreffend Kriegsgerichten, Bd. 24, Fasc. 3579, PG 68121.

14. See Akten des Kaiserlichen-Marine-Kabinetts, betreffend Kriegsgerichten, Bd. 24, Fasc. 3579, PG 68121.

15. For a description of this meeting, see the January 8, 1919, report of Fregattenkapitän von Waldeyer-Hartz, the commander of the schoolship *Schlesien*, in Archiv der Marine: Kriegsakten, Revolution 1918 Kiel, Fasc. 1660. For a similar but less outspokenly critical account, see Waldeyer-Hartz's *An Bord des Kriegsschiffs "Schlesien" bei Ausbruch der Revolution* (Berlin: Verlagsbuchhandlung Fr. Zillessen, 1919), pp. 7–8, and his *Vom Geist*, p. 528.

16. Rausch, p. 13; Popp and Artelt, p. 12; Zeisler, p. 201.

17. Zeisler, pp. 200–1.

18. For reports to this effect, see Waldeyer-Hartz and Korvettenkapitän Hollmann, the Deputy Commander of the First Dock Division. Archiv der Marine: Kriegsakten, Revolution 1918 Kiel, Fasc. 1660. Also Weddigen, p. 6.

19. *Schleswig-Holsteinische Volkszeitung*: November 4, 1918.

20. For descriptions of the meeting, see Souchon to *Seekriegsleitung*, November 3, 1918, Akten des Kaiserlichen-Marine-Kabinetts, betreffend Kriegsgerichten, Bd. 24, Fasc. 3579, PG 68121; Artelt, pp. 92–93; Popp and Artelt, pp. 12–13; Rausch, p. 14; Neu, p. 65.

   For the route of march and timing, see *Kieler Zeitung*: November 4, 1918, and *Kieler Neueste Nachrichten*: November 5, 1918.

21. The description of the fight at the Karlstrasse is a composite drawn from the following sources: *Kieler Neueste Nachrichten*: November 5, 1918; *Schleswig Holsteinische Volkszeitung*: November 4, 1917; *Kieler Zeitung*: November 4, 1918; Artelt, p. 83; Popp and Artelt, pp. 14–15; Rausch, p. 14.

For new archival material, see Korvettenkapitän Oskar Leisti-kow, "Wie ich die Revolution in Kiel vom 3–5 November 1918 erlebte" in Militärgeschichtliches Forschungsamt im Freiburg, II M (A) 3, p. 2. For the role of the Kiel fire department, see the letter of the fire chief to the Oberbürgermeister of November 4, 1918, complaining that Kapitän zur See Heine had illegally used his equipment and men. Akten des Magistrats zu Kiel, Staatsum-wältzung November 1918. Organe zur Durchführung der Revolu-tion. Bd. 1.

See also the telegram by Souchon to Seekriegsleitung, Novem-ber 4, 1918, in Akten des Kaiserlichen-Marine-Kabinettes, betref-fend Kriegsgerichten, Bd. 24, Fasc. 3579, PG 68121, for the esti-mate that four to six people had been killed and thirty wounded.

22. Volkmann, *Der Marxismus*, pp. 218–19.
23. Leistikow, II M (A) 3, p. 2. See also Halperin, p. 86.
24. Popp and Artelt, p. 15; Artelt, pp. 93–94.
25. Zeisler, p. 202.
26. Souchon to Seekriegsleitung, November 4, 1918. Akten des Kaiserlichen-Marine-Kabinetts, betreffend Kriegsgerichten, Bd. 24, Fasc. 3579, PG 68121.
27. Artelt, pp. 94–95; Popp and Artelt, p. 16; DWU, IX/2, pp. 579–81.
28. See the January 25, 1919, report of Admiral Küsel in Archiv der Marine: Kriegsakten, Revolution 1918 Kiel, Fasc. 1660.
29. *Ibid.*
30. *Ibid.*
31. See *ibid.* for Admiral Küsel's and Korvettenkapitän Hollmann's reports on these events. For the text of Souchon's proclamation, see *Kieler Neueste Nachrichten*: November 5, 1918.
32. Some of the more obvious examples of this kind of condemnation are Neu, p. 67; Foss, pp. 30–31; Volkmann, *Der Marximus*, p. 220; Bund der Deckoffiziere, p. 121.
33. Admiral Küsel's report, Archiv der Marine: Kriegsakten, Revolu-tion 1918 Kiel, Fasc. 1660.
34. Rausch, p. 16.
35. See Küsel's report, Archiv der Marine: Kriegsakten, Revolution 1918, Kiel, Fasc. 1660.
36. Waldeyer-Hartz's report, *ibid.*

37. For the text of that proclamation and an assessment of its impact upon the men, see p. 213, this book.

38. See Noske's testimony in *Der Dolchstoss-Prozess*, pp. 178–79.

39. Weniger, although hit five times, survived, while his two officers died immediately.

    See Lammertz, p. 18; Forstner, pp. 12–13; Behncke, p. 68; Ludwig, p. 64; Popp and Artelt, p. 24. Also *Kieler Zeitung*: 5 November 1918; *Kieler Neueste Nachrichten*: 6 November 1918.

40. Noske, *Von Kiel*, pp. 18–19; Rausch, p. 21; *Kieler Neueste Nachrichten*: 6 November 1918.

41. For an example of idle promises of help, see Reichs-Marine-Amt to Souchon on November 4, stating that the army had declared itself prepared to send twelve companies from the Second Army Corps in addition to those already promised. Kaiserliches Kommando der Marinestation der Ostsee, MS Spezial Akten, Fasc. 1660, PG 91844.

    However, see also the transcript of a telephone conversation between Fregattenkapitän Erich Raeder and Levetzow during the afternoon of November 4, in which the former stated that army reinforcements had been ordered to Kiel, but that it was doubtful that they could arrive in time. Levetzow Nachlass, Box 21, Bd. 4.

42. Popp and Artelt, p. 16; Artelt, p. 95; DWU, IX/2, pp. 579–81.

43. See Kaiserliches Kommando der Marinestation der Ostsee, MS Spezial Akten betreffend Umsturz November 1918 Unruhen, Bd. 1, PG 91844; Popp and Artelt, pp. 17–20, Artelt, 96; Rausch, pp. 16–17.

44. Rausch, p. 17; Popp and Artelt, p. 20; Artelt, p. 98; Zeisler, pp. 205–6.

45. See, for example, the report of Korvettenkapitän Hollmann, Archiv der Marine: Kriegsakten, Revolution 1918 Kiel, Fasc. 1660.

46. See Leistikow, II M (A) 3, p. 5.

47. See for these admissions, *Illustrierte Geschichte*, p. 191; Zeisler, pp. 203–4; Artelt, p. 97. Cf. Joos, p. 687.

48. Leistikow, II M (A) 3, p. 5.

49. For the background of Noske's and Haussmann's mission, see Matthias and Morsey, *Die Regierung des Prinzen Max*, pp. 491–97; Haussmann to Scheidemann, October 8, 1919, in Hauss-

mann Nachlass, Bd. 117 as well as Bd. 21; Scheidemann, *Der Zusammenbruch*, pp. 190–91; Gustav Noske, *Erlebtes aus Aufstieg und Niedergang einer Demokratie* (Offenbach-Main: Bollwerk Verlag, 1947), pp. 69–70; Noske, *Von Kiel*, p. 8.

50. For these impressions, see Noske, *Von Kiel*, pp. 10–11, Conrad Haussmann, *Schlaglichter, Reichstagsbriefe und Aufzeichnungen* (Frankfurt: Frankfurter Societäts-Drückerei, 1924), p. 265; Rausch, p. 18.

51. Noske, *Von Kiel*, pp. 11–12.

52. For this meeting, see Kaiserliches Kommando der Marinestation der Ostsee, MS-Spezial Akten betreffend Umsturz November 1918 Unruhen, Bd. 1, PG 91844; Report of November 6, 1918, in Kriegstagebuch der Seekriegsleitung, Stichworte zu stattgehabten Besprechungen des Chefs des Admiralstabes, Fasc. 4055, PG 64726; Conrad Haussmann's November 5 report to the Cabinet in Haussmann Nachlass, Bd. 21; Noske, *Von Kiel*, pp. 13–14; Popp and Artelt, pp. 20–22; Haussmann, *Schlaglichter*, p. 265.

53. Noske, *Von Kiel*, p. 14; Haussmann, *Schlaglichter*, p. 265.

54. Although there is considerable contradiction on this point, it is clear that the men did not trust Souchon's promises and that some sort of fighting went on at the railroad station that night. See November 7 report of the *Seekriegsleitung* stating that the arrival of a Jäger regiment resulted in a fight that produced twelve dead and twenty-six wounded. Kriegstagebuch der Seekriegsleitung, Stichworte zu stattgehabten Besprechungen des Chefs des Admiralstabes, Fasc. 4055, PG 64726.

For a slightly different version involving the expected arrival of a unit of Wandsbecker Hussaren, see Souchon's report of November 5 in Kaiserliches Kommando der Marinestation der Ostsee, MS-Spezial Akten betreffend Umsturz November 1918 Unruhen, Bd. 1, PG 91844. See also Popp and Artelt, pp. 23–24; Rausch, p. 18.

55. See Noske, *Von Kiel*, pp. 15–17; Haussmann Nachlass Bd. 21; Forstner, p. 14; Popp and Artelt, p. 15; Rausch, pp. 22–23; *Kieler Zeitung*: November 5 and 6, 1918.

56. See Noske, *Von Kiel*, pp 15–18; DWU, IX/2, pp. 71–73; Artelt, p. 99; Rausch, p. 25.

57. Popp and Artelt, p. 27; Noske, *Von Kiel*, pp. 26–27; Noske's

testimony in DWU, IX/2, pp. 74–75; Scheidemann, p. 197; Neu, p. 72; Ryder, p. 142.

58. See Zeisler, p. 209; Artelt, p. 100. Actually, however, some of the more rabid revolutionaries such as Barth of the Revolutionary Shop Stewards in Berlin, deplored the outbreak of the revolution in Kiel because it spoiled their own plans. For this see Rosenberg, *A History of the German Republic*, p. 28; Ryder, p. 142.

59. Cited in Popp and Artelt, pp. 21–22. Also cited in Eberhard Buchner (ed.), *Revolutionsdokumente. Die deutsche Revolution in der Darstellung der zeitgenössigen Presse* (Berlin: Deutsche Verlagsgesellschaft für Politik und Geschichte, 1921), an excellent press summary of the German Revolution, pp. 41–42.

60. Popp and Artelt, pp. 22–23.

61. For a startling admission of this, see Zeisler, pp. 206–7. However, see also Rosenberg, *A History of the German Republic*, p. 9, for the view that the sailors felt compelled to pretend that they were socialists in order to create some ideological justification for their revolt.

62. See Archiv der Marine: Kriegsakten, Revolution 1918 Kiel, Fasc. 1660; Rausch, p. 19; *Kieler Zeitung*: November 5, 1918.

63. Noske, *Von Kiel*, p. 18.

64. See Kaiserliches Kommando der Marinestation der Ostsee, MS-Spezial Akten betreffend Umsturz November 1918 Unruhen Bd. 1, PG 91844; for the first of these proclamations, see also Kiel Stadtarchiv.

65. For this order, signed by Noske and Artelt, see Kiel Stadtarchiv, Poster Collection. For a reproduction, see *Kieler Neueste Nachrichten*: November 7, 1918; also, Noske, *Von Kiel*, pp. 19, 22.

66. For a description, see the November 4 report by Oberstückmeister Winkelmann, Archiv der Marine: Kriegsakten, Revolution 1918 Kiel, Fasc. 1660. The Prince made the mistake of asking a sailor if he thought that the prince ate better than the men, whereupon he received the reply, "Yes. You have more to eat [*fressen*]! You carouse just like the Silesian lords!"

67. For descriptions of this incident, see Noske, *Von Kiel*, pp. 20–21; Popp and Artelt, pp. 25–26; Matthias and Morsey, *Die Regierung*, p. 547; *Schleswig-Holsteinische Volkszeitung*: November 6, 1918; *Kieler Zeitung*: November 7, 1918.

68. See Akten des Magistrats zu Kiel, Staatsumwälzung November 1918. Organe zur Durchfuhrung der Revolution. Bd. 1.
69. *Kieler Neueste Nachrichten*: November 7, 1918.
70. *Ibid.*, November 6, 1918. For a similar admonition, see *Kieler Zeitung*: November 5, 6, 1918.
71. See the *Flugblatt* of November 6, 1918, in Akten des Magistrats zu Kiel.
72. *Kieler Neueste Nachrichten*: November 7, 1918.
73. See the December 6, 1918, report of the Municipal Building Department; Akten des Magistrats zu Kiel, betreffend die bei von Unruhen Anfang November 1918 an städtischem Eigentum entstandenen Schäden, Bd. 1.
74. *Kieler Zeitung*: November 9, 1918.
75. See Kaiserliches Kommando der Marinestation der Ostsee, MS-Spezial Akten betreffend Umsturz November 1918 Unruhen, Bd. 1, PG 91844.
76. See Noske, *Von Kiel*, p. 25; Popp and Artelt, p. 27; Rausch, pp. 25–26. Despite Popp's new position, he and the Independent Socialists remained without influence over the Kiel revolution. Popp was never very popular with the sailors, who after a while simply disregarded him. See Noske's testimony in DWU, IX/2, p. 74.
77. See Kriegstagebuch der Seekriegsleitung, Stichworte zu stattgehabten Besprechungen des Chefs des Admiralstabes, Fasc. 4055, PG 64726; Popp and Artelt, pp. 28–29; Noske, *Von Kiel*, pp. 27–28.
78. For descriptions of the government's deliberations and the way it arrived at the decision to place Kiel under blockade, see Matthias and Morsey, *Die Regierung*, pp. 536–44; *Archivalische Forschungen*, 4/IV, pp. 1736–37; Prinz Max, pp. 585–87; Haussmann, *Schlaglichter*, p. 266; Scheidemann, pp. 192–4; Neu, pp. 71–72.
79. See Levetzow Nachlass, Box 21, Bd. 4; Kriegstagebuch der Seekriegsleitung, Stichworte zu stattgehabten Besprechungen des Chefs des Admiralstabes, Fasc. 4055, PG 64726, entry of November 6, 1918.
80. See Levetzow to Justizrat Class, November 25, 1925. Levetzow Nachlass, Box 15, Bd. 1; see also Kapitän zur See Restorff to Ritter von Mann, November 5, 1918, Reichs-Marine-Amt, Akten

betreffend Streike-und-Aufruhrbewegungen, Heft 2, Fasc. 3202.

81. See the newspaper article by Schroeder of June 8, 1928, in *Deutsche Zeitung* in Levetzow Nachlass, Box 5, Bd. 2.

82. For a warning to the government to this effect by Noske on November 5, see Matthias and Morsey, *Die Regierung*, pp. 547–48.

83. See von Müller, diary entry of November 6, 1918, p. 445. See also Levetzow's transcript of a telephone conversation with the office of the Naval Secretary on Novemebr 6 in Levetzow Nachlass, Box 21, Bd. 4.

84. Levetzow to Justizrat Class, November 25, 1925. Levetzow Nachlass, Box 15, Bd. 1. For a similar view, see Trotha's testimony, DWU, IX/2, p. 156.

85. Matthias and Morsey, *Die Regierung*, pp. 553–54, 563; Scheidemann, pp. 193–97; Neu, pp. 72–73.

86. Noske, *Von Kiel*, pp. 23–24; Ludwig, p. 65.

87. Popp and Artelt, p. 26.

88. *Illustrierte Geschichte*, p. 192; Kuttner, *Im Weltkrieg*, p. 263; Kuttner, *Von Kiel bis Berlin*; Noske's testimony, *Der Dolchstoss Prozess*, p. 187.

89. On November 6 the *Seekriegsleitung* responded by ordering all loyal vessels to regard all ships flying the red flag as enemy vessels that were to be fired upon. See Levetzow Nachlass, Box 21, Bd. 4; Kriegstagebuch der Seekriegsleitung, Stichworte zu stattgehabten Besprechungen des Chefs des Admiralstabes, Fasc. 4055, PG 64726.

90. Volkmann, *Der Marxismus*, pp. 224–25.

91. See the November 6 report of Baurat Paech. Archiv der Marine: Kriegsakten, Revolution 1918 Kiel, Fasc. 1660. See also Volkmann, *Der Marxismus*, pp. 225–26; Neu, pp. 75–76; Ryder, pp. 142–43.

92. See *Weser Zeitung*: November 7, 1918. Cited in Buchner, pp. 78–79. For more detailed descriptions, see Paul Müller and Wilhelm Breves, *Bremen in der deutschen Revolution* (Bremen: Verlag Franz Leuwer, 1919), pp. 9–17; Forstner, p. 15; Zeisler, pp. 217–19.

93. For these events and the Cuxhaven program, see "Die Vorgänge in Cuxhaven vom 5. November 1918," Reichs-Marine-Amt, Akten betreffend Streike, Aufruhrbewegungen, Sozialpolitik, Heft 2.

328 Notes to Pages 261 to 262

94. *Ibid.* For an even more scathing account of Engelhard's capitulation without making an effort to stem the rebellion and leaving his officers without instructions, see Ringelnatz, pp. 424, 427.

95. See Trotha to Levetzow, November 7, 1918, for a condemnation and a simultaneous order by the *Seekriegsleitung* relieving Karpf of his command; Levetzow Nachlass, Box 21, Bd. 4. See also the report of Dr. Schrecker, "Kleiner Kreuzer 'Bremse.' Bericht über Revolution 1918 und englische Internierungszeit," I M (A) 1 Militärgeschichtliches Forschungsamt Freiburg im Breisgau, for confirmation of Admiral Karpf's act and the statement that most of the crew members returned after several days because they could find neither food nor transportation ashore.

It must also be noted, however, that a highly respected officer like Fregattenkapitän Waldeyer-Hartz committed the very same error when, on November 7, he, too, liberated a large part of his crew by giving it the option of staying aboard the *Schlesien* or joining the rebels ashore; see Waldeyer-Hartz, *Am Bord des Kriegsschiffs "Schlesien,"* p. 27.

96. Interview with Rear Admiral Günther Horstmann in August 1965.

97. For the flight of officers, see the November 7 report by Levetzow in Kriegstagebuch der Seekriegsleitung, Stichworte zu stattgehabten Besprechungen des Chefs des Admiralstabes, Fasc. 4055, PG 64726, as well as *Schleswig-Holsteinische Volkszeitung*: November 7, 1918.

For the actions of Marquardt and the revolution in Reval, see the November 27, 1918, report of Oberleutnant der Reserve Cramer in Kaiserliches Kommando der Marinestation der Ostsee, MS-Spezial Akten betreffend Umsturz November 1918 Unruhen, Bd. 1, Fasc. 1660, PG 91844.

98. See *Seekriegsleitung* to Secretary of the Navy, November 4, 1918, for an estimate of Wilhelmshaven's strength and for Scheer's immediate order to double the number of machine guns, to bring in a thousand reliable troops, and to transfer all prisoners; Levetzow Nachlass, Box 21, Bd. 4.

99. Lammertz, p. 19. For confirmation that the onset of rebellion was common knowledge, see Kliche, p. 7. However, see also *Weser Zeitung*: November 6, 1918, cited in Buchner, p. 42, for the com-

placent expression of the view that Kiel was "a special case" and that the tradition of Wilhelmshaven for quiet and understanding would make "such an upheaval impossible."

100. Kliche, pp. 9–10; Horn, p. 420.
101. Horn, pp. 420–22.
102. Kliche, pp. 12–13; Lammertz, p. 22.
103. See the November 6 report in Kriegstagebuch der Seekriegsleitung, Stichworte zu stattgehabten Besprechungen des Chefs des Admiralstabes, Fasc. 4055, PG 64726.
104. Horn, pp. 420–21.
105. Kliche, p. 13; Lammertz, p. 22.
106. Levetzow Nachlass, Box 21, Bd. 4, Kriegstagebuch der Seekriegsleitung, Stichworte zu stattgehabten Besprechungen des Chefs des Admiralstabes, Fasc. 4055, PG 64726, entry of November 7, 1918.
107. Kliche, p. 13; Horn, p. 424.
108. See the November 8, 1918, entry in Kriegstagebuch des Seekriegsleitung, Stichworte zu stattgehabten Besprechungen des Chefs des Admiralstabes, Fasc. 4055, PG 64726.
109. See Trotha's testimony in Beckmann, p. 84; *Der Dolchstoss-Prozess*, p. 120.
110. See Kliche, p. 14; also Zeisler, pp. 220–21.
111. Volkmann, *Der Marxismus*, p. 227.
112. See the November 9, 1918, report by the Prussian Interior Ministry in Reichs-Marine-Amt, Akten betreffend Arbeiter und Soldatenrat, Heft 1, Fasc. 4086. See also Volkmann, *Der Marxismus*, p. 228; Zeisler, pp. 223–24.
113. See the November 8 report of the Tenth Gendarmerie Brigade, Hannover, *Archivalische Forschungen*, 4/IV, pp. 1786–87; also Volkmann *Der Marxismus*, pp. 226–27; Zeisler, p. 223.
114. See Prinz Max, pp. 592, 606–7; Scheidemann, pp. 193–97, 204–8. For new documentary evidence, see Matthias and Morsey, *Die Regierung*, pp. 548ff., especially pp. 620–28, for the November 16, 1918, report by General von Linsingen.

Bibliography

ARCHIVAL SOURCES:

Militärgeschichtliches Forschungsamt in Freiburg im Breisgau:
Various documentary collections assembled under the title of I M,
  II M, III M Series
Admiralstab der Marine; Abteilungen A, B, C, N
Seekriegsleitung im Grossen Hauptquartier
Admiralstab im Grossen Hauptquartier
Schiffsakten
Kommando der Hochseeflotte
Akten verschiedener Kommandos
Oberbefehlshaber der Ostseestreitkräfte
Station Ostsee
Station Nordsee
Reichs-Marine Amt
Reichs-Marine-Amt-Nachrichtenbüro
Reichs-Marine-Amt-Zentralabteilung
Reichswehrministerium
Marinekabinett

Kriegsnachrichten des Chefs des Admiralstabes
Kriegstagebücher
Kriegstagebücher-Kommando der Hochseestreitkräfte
Nachlässe:
Kapitän zur See Groos
Admiral von Levetzow
Admiral Capelle
Admiral Scheer I M 40/1–4
Bundesarchiv Koblenz:
Schwertfeger Nachlass
Gothein Nachlass
Württembergisches Staatsarchiv:
Haussmann Nachlass
Stadtsarchiv Kiel:
Revolution 1918

PRINTED DOCUMENTARY SOURCES:

Beckmann, Ewald. *Der Dolchstossprozess in München vom 19. October bis 20. November 1925.* München: Süddeutsche Monatshefte Verlag, 1925.

Buchner, Eberhard, ed. *Revolutionsdokumente. Die deutsche Revolution in der Darstellung der zeitgenössigen Presse.* Berlin: Deutsche Verlagsgesellschaft für Politik und Geschichte, 1921.

Das Werk des Untersuchungsausschusses der Verfassungsgebenden Deutschen Nationalversammunlung und des Deutschen Reichstages 1919–1928. Vierte Reihe. *Die Ursachen des Deutschen Zusammenbruches.* Zweite Abteilung. *Der Innere Zusammenbruch.* 12 vols. Vols. IV–X/2. Berlin: Deutsche Verlagsgesellschaft für Politik und Geschichte, 1919–28.

Der Dolchstoss-Prozess in München Oktober-November 1925, Eine Ehrenrettung des deutschen Volkes. Munich: Verlag von G. Birk und Co., 1925.

Drahn, Ernst, and Leonhard, Susanne. *Unterirdische Literatur im revolutionären Deutschland während des Weltkrieges.* Berlin: Verlag Gesellschaft und Erziehung, 1920.

Lutz, Ralph H., ed. *The Fall of the German Empire, 1914–1918.* 2 vols. Stanford: Stanford University Press, 1932.

Matthias, Erich, and Morsey, Rudolf. *Quellen zur Geschichte des*

Parlamentarismus und der Politischen Parteien. Erste Reihe. Von der konstitutionellen Monarchie zur Parlamentarischen Republik. Der Interfraktionelle Ausschuss 1917–1918. 2 vols. Düsseldorf: Droste Verlag, 1959.

———. *Die Regierung von Max von Baden.* Düsseldorf: Droste Verlag, 1963.

Stern, Leo, ed. *Archivalische Forschungen zur Geschichte der Deutschen Arbeiterbewegung. Die Auswirkungen der Grossen Sozialistischen Oktoberrevolution auf Deutschland.* 4 vols. Berlin: Institut für Geschichte der deutschen Akademie der Wissenschaft zu Berlin, Rütten und Loening, 1959.

Verhandlungen des Reichstags. XIII. Legislaturperiode. II. Session, Vol. CCCX, *Stenographische Berichte.*

NEWSPAPERS:

Kieler Neueste Nachrichten
Kieler Zeitung
Schleswig-Holsteinische Volkszeitung

MEMOIRS, CONTEMPORARY ACCOUNTS, AND PAMPHLETS:

Admiralstab. *Stellungnahme zu den Angriffen des Kapitäns zur See a.D. Persius.* Berlin: Admiralstabsdruckerei, 1918.

Alboldt, Emil. *Die Tragödie der alten deutschen Marine.* Berlin: Deutsche Verlagsgesellschaft für Politik und Geschichte, 1928. (Material originally presented in Das Werk des Untersuchungsausschusses, X/1.)

Anti-Nautikus [Sachse, Richard Willi]. *Deutschlands revolutionäre Matrosen.* Hamburg: Verlag Karl Schulzke, 1925.

Baden, Prinz Max von. *Erinnerungen und Dokumente.* Berlin and Leipzig: Deutsche Verlags-Anstalt, 1928.

Bauer, Hermann. *Reichsleitung und U-Bootseinsatz, 1914–1918.* Lipoldsberg: Klosterhaus Verlag, 1956.

Behncke, Paul. *Unsere Marine im Weltkrieg und ihr Zusammenbruch.* Berlin: Karl Curtius Verlag, 1919.

Brüninghaus, Wilhelm. *Die politische Zersetzung und die Tragödie der deutschen Flotte.* Berlin: J. H. W. Dietz, 1926. (Material originally presented in Das Werk des Untersuchungsausschusses, IX/2.)

Bülow, G. Freiherr von. *Wie wird man Seeoffizier?* Berlin: Ernst Siegfried Mittler und Sohn, 1912.

Bütow, Geheimer Rechnungsrat. *Die kaiserliche deutsche Marine.* Berlin: Seigfried Mittler und Sohn, 1880.

Dette, Werner. *"Halbmast." Der deutschen Flotte Sterben. Der Geist des Offizierskorps und der Verhetzung der Mannschaft der Hochseeflotte.* Berlin: Eulenverlag, 1919.

Dittmann, Wilhelm. *Die Marine-Justiz-Morde von 9117 und die Admirals-Rebellion von 1918.* Berlin: J. H. W. Dietz, 1926. (Material originally presented in Das Werk des Untersuchungsausschusses, IX/1, pp. 2–124.)

Forstner, Georg-Günther, Freiherr von. *Die Marine Meuterei.* Berlin: Carl Curtius, 1919.

Haussmann, Conrad. *Schlaglichter, Reichstagsbriefe und Aufzeichnungen.* Frankfurt: Frankfurter Societäts-Drückerei, 1924.

Helfferich, Karl. *Der Weltkrieg*, Vol. III, *Vom Eingreifen Amerikas bis zum Zusammenbruch.* Berlin: Ullstein Verlag, 1919.

Hindenburg, Paul von. *Aus meinem Leben.* Leipzig: Verlag S. Hirzel, 1920.

Hintzmann, Korvettenkapitän. *Marine, Krieg und Umsturz. Der deutschen Flotte Werden, Wirken und Sterben. Ein Protest gegen Persius.* 2 Aufl. Berlin: Staatspolitischer Verlag, 1919.

Hopmann, Albert. *Das Kriegstagebuch eines deutschen Seeoffiziers.* Berlin: August Scherl, 1925.

Horn, D. *Warum liess Gott unsere Niederlage zu? Predigt am Busstage 20, November 1918.* Hamburg: Agentur des Rauhen Hauses, 1918.

Horn, Daniel, ed. and transl. *War, Mutiny and Revolution in the German Navy: The World War I Diary of Seaman Richard Stumpf.* New Brunswick: Rutgers University Press, 1967.

Klein, Max, ed., *Geschichte der Crew, 1912.* Soest: Rocholsche Buchdruckerei, 1955.

Kliche, Josef. *Vier Monate Revolution in Wilhelmshaven.* Rüstringen: Verlag von Paul Hug und Co., 1919.

Kuttner, Erich. *Von Kiel bis Berlin; der Siegeszug der deutschen Revolution.* Berlin: Verlag für Sozialwissenschaft, 1918.

Lammertz, W. *Die Marine von der Revolution bis zum Flottengrab bei Scapa Flow.* Duisburg: Johann Ewich Verlag, 1920.

Ludendorff, Erich. *Meine Kriegserinnerungen, 1914–1918.* Berlin: Mittler Verlag, 1919.

Ludwig, Emil. *An die Lanterne! Bilder aus der Revolution.* Charlottenburg: Felix Lehmann Verlag, 1919.

Lützow, Hermann. *Die Seeoffizier-Laufbahn.* 2. Aufl. Berlin: Verlag von R. Eisenschmidt, 1913.

Michaelis, Georg. *Für Staat und Volk.* Berlin: Furche-Verlag, 1922.

Müller, Georg Alexander von. *Regierte der Kaiser? Kriegstagebücher, Aufzeichnungen und Briefe des Chefs des Marine-Kabinetts Admiral Georg Alexander von Müller.* Edited by Walter Görlitz. Göttingen: Musterschmidt-Verlag, 1959.

Noske, Gustav. *Erlebtes aus Aufstieg und Niedergang einer Demokratie.* Offenbach-Main: Bollwerk Verlag, 1947.

———. *Von Kiel bis Kapp.* Berlin: Verlag für Politik und Wirtschaft, 1920.

Persius, Lothar. *Menschen und Schiffe in der kaiserlichen Flotte.* Berlin: J. H. W. Dietz, 1925.

———. *Der Seekrieg.* Charlottenburg: Verlag der Weltbühne, 1919.

———. *Tirpitz, der Totengräber der deutschen Flotte.* Berlin: Verlag für Volksaufklärung, 1918.

———. *Wie es kam dass der Anstoss zur Revolution von der Flotte ausging?* Berlin: Arbeitsgemeinschaft für staatsbürgerliche und wirtschaftliches Bildung.

Popp, Lothar, and Artelt, Karl. *Ursprung und Entwicklung der November-Revolution, 1918.* Kiel: Verlag Hermann Behrens, 1918.

Rausch, Bernhard. *Am Springquell der Revolution: Die Kieler Matrosenerhebung.* Verlag von Chr. Haase & Co. (Schleswig-Holsteinische Volkszeitung), 1918.

Ringelnatz, Joachim [Hans Bötticher]. *Als Mariner im Weltkrieg.* Berlin: Karl H. Hennsel Verlag, 1955.

Sachse, Willi Richard. *Rost an Mann und Schiff. Ein Bekenntnisroman um Skagerrak.* Berlin: Traditions-Verlag Kolk, 1934.

Scheer, Reinhard. *Deutschlands Hochseeflotte im Weltkrieg.* Berlin: Verlag von August Scherl, 1919.

———. *Vom Segelschiff zum U-Boot.* Leipzig: Quelle und Meyer, 1925.

Scheidemann, Philipp. *Der Zusammenbruch.* Berlin: Verlag für Sozialwissenschaft, 1921.

Schoultz, G. von. *Mit der Grand Fleet im Weltkrieg.* Leipzig: K. F. Koehler, 1925.

Schroeder, John Ulrich. *Im Morgenlichte der deutschen Revolution.* Hamburg: Konrad Hanf Verlag, 1921.

Stampfer, Friedrich. *Der 9. November. Gedenkblätter zu seiner Weiderkehr.* Berlin: Buchandlung Vorwärts, 1919.

Stumpf, Richard. *Warum die Flotte zerbrach? Kriegstagebuch eines christlichen Arbeiters.* Mit einem Vorwort von Wilhelm Dittmann M.d.R. Berlin: J. H. W. Dietz Verlag, 1927.

Thaer, Albrecht von. *Generalstabsdienst an der Front und der OHL.* Göttingen: Vandenhoek und Rupprecht, 1958.

Tirpitz, Alfred von. *Erinnerungen.* Leipzig: Verlag von K. F. Koehler, 1919.

Trotha, Adolf von. *Der Organismus der kaiserlichen Marine und der Weltkrieg.* Berlin: Reichswehrministerium, 1933.

Verein ehemaliger Matrosen der Kaiserlichen und der Reichsmarine. *War es die Marine?* Berlin: August Scherl, 1926.

Waldeyer-Hartz, Hugo von. *An Bord des Kriegsschiffs "Schlesien" bei Ausbruch der Revolution.* Berlin: Verlagsbuchandlung Fr. Ziltessen, 1919.

————. *Mannszucht bei Heer und Marine.* Berlin: Verlag von Georg Bath, 1920.

Weddigen, Otto. *Erlebnisse des Kreuzers "Strassburg" vom 27. Oktober bis 27. November 1918.* Stettin: Stettiner Druckerei, 1918.

SECONDARY SOURCES:

Anonymous. *Illustrierte Geschichte der deutschen Revolution.* Berlin: Internationaler Arbeiter Verlag, 1928–29.

Assmann, Kurt. *Deutsche Seestrategie in zwei Weltkriegen.* Heidelberg: Kurt Vowinkel Verlag, 1957.

Berlau, A. Joseph. *The German Social Democratic Party, 1914–1921.* New York: Columbia University Press, 1949.

Breithaupt, Wolfgang. *Volksvergiftung, 1914–1918, Dokumente der Vorbereitung des 9. November 1918.* Berlin and Leipzig: K. F. Koehler, 1925.

Bund der Deckoffiziere. *Deckoffiziere der deutschen Marine. Ihre Geschichte 1848–1933.* Berlin: E. S. Mittler und Sohn, 1933.

Coper, Rudolf. *Failure of a Revolution*. Cambridge: Cambridge University Press, 1955.

Craig, Gordon A. *The Politics of the Prussian Army, 1640–1945*. New York: Oxford University Press, 1964.

Dawson, William Harbutt. *The German Empire, 1867–1914*. 2 vols., 2d ed. Hamden, Connecticut: Anchor Books, 1966.

Eyck, Erich. *Das persönliche Regiment Wilhelms II*. Erlenbach-Zürich: Eugen Rentsch Verlag, 1948.

———. *A History of the Weimar Republic*. 2 vols. Cambridge, Massachusetts: Harvard University Press, 1962.

Fischer, Fritz. *Griff nach der Weltmacht. Die Kriegszielpolitik des kaiserlichen Deutschland, 1914–1918*. Düsseldorf: Droste Verlag, 1962.

Foss, Max. *Enthüllungen über den Zusammenbruch. Eine Betrachtung über die Ursachen, dass es so gekommen ist*. Halle (Saale): Richard Mühlmann Verlagsbuchhandlung, 1919.

Freiwald, Ludwig. *Die verratene Flotte. Aus den letzten Tagen der deutschen Kriegsmarine*. 2d. Aufl. Munich: J. F. Lehmanns Verlag, 1937.

Galster, Karl. *England, deutsche Flotte und Weltkrieg*. Kiel: J. Scheible's Verlag, 1925.

Gatzke, Hans. *Germany's Drive to the West. A Study of German War Aims During the First World War*. Baltimore: Johns Hopkins Press, 1950.

Groos, Otto. *Seekriegslehren im Lichte des Weltkrieges*. Berlin: E. S. Mittler, 1929.

Halperin, S. William. *Germany Tried Democracy*. New York: W. W. Norton and Company, 1965.

Herzfeld, Hans. *Die deutsche Sozialdemokratie und die Auflösung der nationalen Einheitsfront im Weltkriege*. Leipzig: Quelle und Meyer, 1928.

Hoehling, A. A. *The Great War at Sea. A History of Naval Action, 1914–18*. New York: Thomas Y. Crowell Company, 1965.

Hubatsch, Walter. *Der Admiralstab und die obersten Marinebehörden in Deutschland 1848–1945*. Frankfurt am Main: Verlag für Wehrwesen Bernard und Graefe, 1958.

———. *Die Ära Tirpitz, Studien zur deutschen Marinepolitik, 1890–1918*. Göttingen: Musterschmidt Verlag, 1955.

Hurd, Archibald, and Castle, Henry. *German Sea-Power. Its Rise, Progress and Economic Basis*. New York: Charles Scribner's Sons, 1913.

Icarus (pseudonym). *The Wilhelmshaven Revolt: A Chapter of the Revolutionary Movement in the German Navy, 1918–1919*. London: Freedom Press, 1944.

Kloth, Emil. *Dittmanns Enthüllungsschwindel nach Eingeständnissen seiner Genossen*. Berlin: Brunnen Verlag-Karl Winkler, 1926.

Kutscher, Hans. *Admiralsrebellion oder Matrosenrevolte? Der Flotteneinsatz in den letzten Tagen des Weltkriegs*. Stuttgart: Verlag von W. Kohlhammer, 1933.

Lehment, Joachim. *Kriegsmarine und politische Führung*. Berlin: Junker und Dünnhaupt, 1937.

Mäkelä, Matti E. *Souchon der Goebenadmiral greift in die Weltgeschichte ein*. Braunschweig: Friedrich Vieweg, 1936.

Mann, Golo. *Deutsche Geschichte des neunzehnten und zwanzigsten Jahrhunderts*. Frankfurt am Main: S. Fischer Verlag, 1958.

Mantey, Eberhard von. *Unsere Kriegsmarine: Vom Grossen Kurfürsten bis zur Gegenwart*. Berlin: "Offene Worte," 1934.

Marder, Arthur J. *From the Dreadnought to Scapa Flow: The Royal Navy in the Fisher Era, 1904–1919*. 3 vols. London: Oxford University Press, 1961–66.

Müller, Paul, and Breves, Wilhelm. *Bremen in der deutschen Revolution*. Bremen: Verlag Franz Leuwer, 1919.

Neu, Heinrich. *Die revolutionäre Bewegung auf der deutschen Flotte, 1917–1918*. Stuttgart: Verlag von W. Kohlhammer, 1930.

Peter, Karl. "Seeoffizier-Anwärter-Ausbildung in Preussen/Deutschland, 1848–1945." (Manuscript: Militärgeschichtliches Forschungsamt, Freiburg im Breisgau, ca. 1960)

Prager, Eugen. *Geschichte der USPD*. Berlin: Verlag "Freiheit," 1922.

Reichsbund Deutscher Seegeltung. *War es die Marine?* Berlin: Montanus und Weuster, 1940.

Reventlow, Graf Ernst zu. *Der Einfluss der Seemacht im Grossen Kriege*. Berlin: E. S. Mittler, 1918.

Ritter, Gerhard. *Staatskunst und Kriegshandwerk. Das Problem des "Militarismus" in Deutschland*. 3 vols. Munich: Verlag R. Oldenbourg, 1958–64.

Röhr, Albert. *Handbuch der deutschen Marinegeschichte.* Oldenburg/ Hamburg: Gerhard Stolling Verlag, 1963.

Rosenberg, Arthur. *The Birth of the German Republic.* New York: Russell & Russell, 1962.

———. *A History of the Weimar Republic.* London: Methuen and Co., 1936.

Ryder, A. J. *The German Revolution of 1918. A Study of German Socialism in War and Revolt.* Cambridge: Cambridge University Press, 1967.

Schorske, Carl E. *German Social Democracy, 1905–1917.* Cambridge, Massachusetts: Harvard University Press, 1955.

Schubert, Paul, and Gibson, Langhorne. *Death of a Fleet, 1917–1919.* New York: Coward-McCann, Inc., 1932.

Spiess, Johannes. *Sechs Jahre U-Bootfahrten.* Berlin: E. Steiniger, 1925.

Steinberg, Jonathan. *Yesterday's Deterrent. Tirpitz and the Birth of the German Battle Fleet.* London: Macdonald, 1965.

Vidil, Charles. *Les mutinieries de la marine allemande, 1917–1919.* Paris: Payot, 1931.

Volkmann, Erich Otto. *Der Marxismus und das deutsche Heer im Weltkriege.* Berlin: Verlag Reimar Hobbing, 1925.

———. *Revolution über Deutschland.* Oldenburg: Gerhard Stalling Verlag, 1930.

Wortmann, Karl. *Geschichte der deutschen Vaterlandspartei, 1918–1919.* Hale: Otto Hendel Druckerei, 1926.

Zeisler, Kurt. "Die Revolutionare Matrosenbewegung in Deutschland im Oktober/November 1918" in *Revolutionäre Ereignisse und Probleme in Deutschland während der Periode der Grossen Sozialistischen Oktober-Revolutions 1917/1918.* Ed. by Albert Schreiner. Deutsche Akademie der Wissenschaft zu Berlin. Berlin: Akademie-Verlag, 1957.

Ziekursch, Johannes. *Politische Geschichte des Neuen Deutschen Kaiserreiches.* 3 vols. Frankfurt am Main: Frankfurter Societäts Druckerei, 1925–30.

PERIODICALS AND ARTICLES:

Artelt, Karl. "Mit der roten Fahne zum Vizeadmiral Souchon," Institut für Marxismus-Leninismus beim Zentralkomitee der Sozialistischen Einheitspartei Deutschlands, *Vorwärts und Nichts Vergessen. Erlebnisberichte aktiver Teilnehmer der November-revolution, 1918/1919.* Berlin: Dietz Verlag, 1958, pp. 80–100.

Bernhard, Hans Joachim. "Unveröffentlichte Dokumente zum Aufstand in der deutschen Hochseeflotte im Sommer 1917," *Zeitschrift für Geschichtswissenschaft*, V:5, 1957, pp. 1053–69.

Bredt, Viktor. "*Schlusswort zu den Ausführungen des Vizeadmirals* a.D. von Trotha," *Preussiche Jahrbücher*, CCIX, 1927, pp. 110–12.

Deist, Wilhelm. "Die Politik der Seekriegsleitung und die Rebellion der Flotte Ende Oktober 1918," *Vierteljahrshefte für Zeitgeschichte*, XIV:4, October 1966, pp. 341–68.

Drascher, Wahrhold. "Zur Soziologie des deutschen Seeoffizierskorps," *Wehrwissenschaftliche Rundschau*, XII:10, 1962, pp. 555–69. (Same article in *Marine-Offizier-Hilfe-Nachrichten*, XII:3, 1 March 1963, pp. 43–46, and XII:4, 1 April 1963, pp. 67–69.

Förste, Erich. "Zur Persönlichkeit von Admiral Scheer," *Marine Rundschau: Zeitschrift für Seewesen*, LIX:1, 1962, pp. 10–18.

Forstmeier, Friedrich. "Zum Bild der Persönlichkeit des Admirals Reinhard Scheer (1863–1928)," *Marine-Rundschau: Zeitschrift für Seewesen*, LVIII:2, 1961, pp. 73–93.

Herz, Ludwig. "Die Marinemeuterei von 1917: Eine juristische Betrachtung," *Die Justiz*, I:6, 1924, pp. 598–613.

Joos, Joseph. "Die Vorgänge in der Marine, 1917/1918," in Dr. Georg Schreiber, *Politisches Jahrbuch, 1927/1928.* München-Gladbach: Volksverein-Verlag, 1928, pp. 682–88.

Kehr, Eckart. "Schlachtflottenbau und Parteipolitik, 1894–1901," *Historische Studien*, Nr. 197, Berlin: Ebering, 1930.

Klein, Albert. "Der Zusammenbruch der Flotte von innen gesehen," *Süddeutsche Monatshefte*, XVI:3, March 1919, pp. 446–54.

Kuttner, Erich. "Von Kiel bis Berlin," in Gerhard Anschütz *et al.*, *Handbuch der Politik. Der Weltkrieg*, Berlin and Leipzig, Dr. Walter Rothschild, 1920, pp. 260–66.

Levetzow, Magnus von. "Der letzte Akt," *Süddeutsche Monatshefte*, XXI:7, April 1924, pp. 55–71.

Lutz, Ralph H., "The July 1917 Crisis in Germany," *Proceedings of the Pacific Coast Branch of the American Historical Association*, Vol. V, 1930, pp. 87–98.

Meinecke, Friedrich. "Die geschichtlichen Ursachen der deutschen Revolution," *Deutsche Rundschau*, XXXXV, 1919, pp. 177–94.

Scheer, Reinhard. "Warum der Krieg verloren ging," *Süddeutsche Monatshefte*, XVI:3, March 1919, pp. 410–19.

Trotha, Adolf von. "Der Dolchstoss auf der Flotte," *Süddeutsche Monatshefte*, XXI:7, April 1924, pp. 49–54.

———. "Zum Flottenvorstoss 1918," *Preussische Jahrbücher*, CCIX, 1927, pp. 107–9.

Waldeyer Hartz, Hugo von. "Vom Geist der deutschen Kriegsmarine," in Friedrich Felger, ed., *Was wir vom Weltkrieg nicht wissen*. Berlin and Leipzig: Wilhelm Andermann Verlag, 1929, pp. 517–30.

Woodward, David. "Mutiny at Wilhelmshaven, 1918," in *History Today*, XVIII:11 (November 1968), pp. 779–85.

Index

ABOUT THE AUTHOR

Daniel Horn graduated from Brooklyn College and obtained his master's degree and doctorate from Columbia University. Now associate professor of history at Douglass College of Rutgers University, The State University of New Jersey, he has also taught at the College of the City of New York and Temple University.

His interest in the history of World War I may not be unrelated to the fact that he was born in Vienna. When the German naval archives became available for inspection at the end of World War II, Dr. Horn began a survey of the underlying causes of the mutinies, the collapse of the German navy, and the end of the German Empire which has resulted in this book and in his previous work—*War, Mutiny and Revolution in the German Navy: The World War I Diary of Seaman Richard Stumpf.*